Countdown to Chaos

The answer to the question of "can the United States elections be compromised?" is fully answered in this body of work. When reading Countdown to Chaos these are some of the questions you should be considering when you ingest this research:

- Did Barack Obama deliver on his October 30, 2008, promise to "fundamentally transform the United States of America"?
- Do we have a decentralized election system which is fully controlled by the States as prescribed by law?
- Have elections in the United States become silently "Federalized"?
- Has the advent of Public-Private Information Sharing Platforms compromised the integrity of United States elections?
- Could our elections become overlorded and monitored in a silent and invisible way?
- Has what that had been initially created for good become used for bad in the American elections?
- Is the true and authentic voice of the American voter heard through its election systems?
- Is the United State Constitution, including the 10th Amendment, still the unfettered law of the land regarding elections?
- Is the American voting system both sound and secure?
- Has "what we don't know" hurt American Voters?
- Are our elections run by a federal agency of some sort?
- Are our elections run by a nationwide quasigovernmental authority?
- Did "multi-directional information sharing" destroy American voting systems and elections?
- What role do Fusion Centers really play in American elections?
- Did "Flow Records" compromise American elections?
- Did the Homeland Security Act of 2002 compromise American elections?
- Did the Deep State hide directives programs and toolboxes in the fine print of government documents?
- Did the United States, in order to create deniability, create programs and systems to operate constitutionally outside its jurisdictions?
- Did the United States government literally release the blueprint to compromise all American elections?
- Is there remote access to our election systems?
- Did commercially available intrusion detection abilities compromise American elections?
- Does the United States government deploy specific lawfare strategy to prevent investigations into election fraud?
- Did the United States provide "no cost" cyber services in exchange for data structural access?
- Are there "outside the firewall" network connections which have compromised our American elections?
- Is there a reason that all logs and data do not remain on certain systems within the jurisdiction of state or local agencies?
- Did the United States provide vulnerable systems and programs to each state under the guise of "cyber security"?
- Are American elected officials now selected not elected?
- Are the American voting systems forever damaged?
- Can we ever have a safe and secure American election ever again?

	Introduction	p. 1
	Prologue	p. 5
Chapter 1	Decentralized Election History and Security	p. 11
Chapter 2	A Brief History of ISACs	p. 15
Chapter 3	The Evolution of the DHS Cyber Programs (EINSTEIN) (2000 – 2004)	p. 23
Chapter 4	MS-ISAC, IT-SCC, and US-CERT (2004 – 2006)	p. 29
Chapter 5	US-CERT, EINSTEIN 2, and EINSTEIN 3 Pilot (2006 – 2010)	p. 35
Chapter 6	TIME OUT TO FOCUS ON: The Albert Sensor (Albert Monitoring Services - 2011)	p. 45
Chapter 7	EINSTEIN 3A, The CIA, IT-ISAC, CrowdStrike, the Birth of Election Related Executive Orders, and the Cybersecurity Act of 2015 (2013-2015)	p. 67
Chapter 8	EINSTEIN 3, Albert Monitoring, AIS, CrowdStrike, and the Presidential Election (2016)	p. 81
Chapter 9	Crossfire Hurricane, Critical Infrastructure, SolarWinds, and the GCC (2016 – 2017)	p. 119
Chapter 10	EI-SCC, EI-ISAC, IT-ISAC, Executive Order 13848, Help America Vote Act, CISA Cybersecurity Summit, SolarWinds (2018-2019)	p. 151
Chapter 11	EDR Monitoring Beyond Albert, RABET-V Pilot System, The 2020 Presidential Election, SolarWinds (2020)	p. 177
Chapter 12	TIME OUT TO FOCUS ON: National Fusion Centers (2001 - present)	p. 205
Chapter 13	SolarWinds (Post Election 2020 - 2021)	p. 241
Chapter 14	The Arizona Audit, EI-ISAC Appointments, Eric Coomer Deposition (2021)	p. 255
Chapter 15	DHS Terror Warning, John Durham Filings, Neustar, Inc., Rodney Joffe, Hillary Clinton and "Spygate", DHS Disinformation Governance Board, Sussman Trial, The FBI (2022)	p. 269
Chapter 16	Discussion	p. 343
Chapter 17	Solution and Conclusion	p. 369
	Consolidated Timeline	p. 385
	Epilogue	p. 405
	Bibliography	p. 433
	Index	p. 499

INTRODUCTION

Introduction

As I finish up this introduction, I just finished re-watching the CNN Town Hall featuring President Trump. Like many of you, the surprise came when there were actual conservatives in the audience. It was refreshing. One part of me thought "Ok, CNN is going to try to redeem themselves and do an actual fair, but tough, interview of President Trump." After all, town halls are for the people to learn and get their questions asked. Boy was I wrong!

As soon as the "moderator" began asking President Trump questions it became clear the broadcast was going to evolve into an attempt at a hit job on President Trump. The moderator was Kaitlan Collins, and it was billed as President Donald Trump taking questions from Republican and undeclared New Hampshire voters. In other words, for the voters by the voters.

It was anything but. It was a broadcast of elite CNN views and questions which gave no never-mind to the thoughts, real life questions and concerns of the American voters. In other words, mainstream media as usual.

Now, as I complete the introduction to "Countdown To Chaos" I am sitting at Trump National Doral, Miami pounding the rest of this introduction out. Here to speak at an event with General Flynn, Eric Trump and others, the American voters still want answers about what really happened in the 2020 election.

CNN played off any questions or talk of election fraud, nefarious acts or malfeasance in the Town Hall as flat out lies. I could not help but think to myself "How would they even know? They actually did not investigate the election for fraud, nefarious acts or maladministration. All they did was take the "system's word" that "this was the safest and most secure election ever" - we all choked on that one.

Even our nation's top intelligence and law enforcement agencies have confirmed that there is no evidence of significant voter fraud in American elections and that the 2020 election was secure. It is my contention that more than half of America calls bullshit on this statement.

Countdown to Chaos

The Brennan Center for Justice reports the following:

Federal Bureau of Investigation (FBI)

"We have not seen, historically, any kind of coordinated national voter fraud effort in a major election, whether it's by mail or otherwise." – Christopher Wray, FBI Director, September 24, 2020, hearing before the U.S. Senate Committee on Homeland Security and Government Affairs. (Director Wray was appointed by President Trump in 2017.)

Department of Homeland Security – Cybersecurity and Infrastructure Security Agency (CISA)

"The November 3rd election was the most secure in American history . . . There is no evidence that any voting system deleted or lost votes, changed votes, or was in any way compromised . . . While we know there are many unfounded claims and opportunities for misinformation about the process of our elections . . . we have the utmost confidence in the security and integrity of our elections, and you should too." – Joint Statement by CISA, the Election Infrastructure Government Coordinating Council (GCC), and the Election Infrastructure Sector Coordinating Council (SCC), November 12, 2020.

"[Election] Day was quiet. There was no indication or evidence that there was any evidence of hacking or compromise of election systems on, before, or after November 3 . . . . We did a good job. I would do it one thousand times over." – Chris Krebs, Former Director of CISA, November 29, 2020.

Department of Justice (DOJ)

"To date, [DOJ investigators] have not seen fraud on a scale that could have effected a different outcome in the election." – Attorney General William Barr, December 1, 2020, announcement.

Those statements were primarily issued when votes were still being counted in 2020. Even the most logical of individuals would know "if votes are still being counted, how could anyone ever make those statements and represent them as absolute facts?"

INTRODUCTION

The point is, they could not. It was all a cover story. I can say this since in my work both creating and conducting the full forensic audit of the Maricopa County, Arizona Election we discovered that 138,000 plus votes were counted and run into the systems in Maricopa on December 8th and 9th, 2020.

Yep, you got it! More than one month after the 2020 General Election and after the so-called experts released their findings which were quoted above - here we are.

It's May 2023 and the CNN Town Hall began its broadcast stating election fraud in 2020 was a big lie. Most logical people know something went horribly wrong. Many know something went wrong, but they cannot seem to put their finger on what exactly went wrong.

This book comes at the issue of "could our elections be hacked or compromised" from a different perspective. We approached the problem just like conducting the full forensic audit in Maricopa County, Arizona for the 2020 election. We went into the deep forensic research with no preconceived ideas and only measured the findings against what the so-called election officials issued as statements and official reports and canvasses. We simply took what the Board of Supervisors in Arizona said happened and claimed the results were and measured their own words against our actual full forensic audit findings.

As you may already know (but the media, Deep State and Uniparty has suppressed), in every single category the Maricopa County Board of Supervisors failed. Not one fact they presented as fact about the 2020 election could be confirmed. Not only not absolutely confirmed, but even giving them a wide margin of leniency they even failed.

The final account of the votes cast in the 2020 Maricopa County Election was akin to an Olympic Gymnast's leotard after doing an impressive routine on the balance beam. How is that? After pulling off an impressive stunt, the leotard still has to be pulled out of the ass of the gymnasts once they have landed. Same as the results of the 2020 election in Maricopa County, Arizona - pulled right out of the ass of the Maricopa County Board of Supervisors.

Countdown to Chaos

The vote total of 2,089,517 in Maricopa County, Arizona was made up - totally made up to look like a tight race.

But nonetheless, here we sit in May 2023 and talk of proof of election fraud is still forbidden and taboo, plus the media leads the charge in continuing to gaslight the American public.

President Trump handled the topic of election fraud very "presidentially" when asked in the Town Hall. As a result of it even being talked about on the air during the town hall the left has gone nuts. The left is now calling for a boycott of CNN (as if its ratings can get any lower) and they are even demanding the firing of CNN CEO Chris Licht for allowing President Trump on their airway. They will go to any length to suppress the truth, will they not?

That is just how "tolerant" the left is. The left and the Deep State are in lock step in making sure the public does not question elections in America, but also does not allow any real truth to be allowed out regarding the inner goings on of American elections.

This is why this book had to be handled the exact same way we handled the Full Forensic Audit of the 2020 Election in Maricopa County, Arizona.

We took one simple baseline question "Could the elections in America be compromised in any manner by anyone?" Then with that simple question we dug into the actions, words, policies, laws and edicts of our "so-called election officials", agencies, lawmakers and the entire voting apparatus in the United States of America. In doing a deep forensic dive into the actions and words of the very officials we are supposed to trust with our elections, could we find a real answer to "Could the elections in America be compromised in any manner by anyone?"

If you read this entire book and absorb what "they told us and implemented" you will find your answer. WORD OF WARNING - if you do not want the truth - the absolute truth - put this book down right now!

Jovan Hutton Pulitzer

Thursday, May 11, 2023

Trump Doral, Miami

Prologue

The research that encompasses the information in the pages to follow began with an innocent investigation into people and situations documented surrounding the 2020 Presidential Election. The act of pulling that proverbial thread led to information, while nearly entirely available in the public domain, is scattered and well hidden from the American people.

Knee deep into the research the clichés "ever in history has anything that was created for good ever been used for bad?" and, "what you don't know can't hurt you," became an absolute driver for getting to the bottom of questions that continued emerging. The litany of questions never relented, and to this day, continues to yield further inquiries that need answering, causing this report to continue growing. The questions that began this research were few and quite innocent. The list of questions that conclude this report became long and complicated. The questions this report began with were:

- Are the American people still, without question, one hundred percent unequivocally having their voices heard fairly at the ballot box?
- Is the American election system truly sound?
- Is the Constitution, including the 10th Amendment, still the unfettered law of the land regarding elections?
- Could Americans recognize a federalized election system? Would today's Americans care?

The thread pulling began with simple information about an individual named in the aftermath of the 2020 Presidential Election, who, in addition to being connected to allegations of fraud and election manipulation, also held an important position in both a significant company on the election stage, and within an

Countdown to Chaos

association directly connected with the events of the election. This association and its members were featured in an election integrity conference presented by the Cybersecurity and Infrastructure Security Agency (CISA) in 2019. The presentation the author of this report was seeking and all other content of the conference from that day appears to literally have been scrubbed from the internet. This is information that was owned and presented by the federal government in a fully public forum, is now completely gone, as if it never even happened. The relentless search for that publicly presented information led to the discovery of associations that are interwoven throughout the public and private domains of business and government. The emerging public-private relationships at their conception were created with caveats about the potential dangers of private information sharing among companies and agencies, but the partnerships were nevertheless created, and created in various areas with various scopes of function. As the research matured, evidence strongly emerged that portions of the powers obfuscated by the federal government were used minimally in a biased way, and perhaps to an extreme extent, in a blatantly unconstitutional manner with potential criminal actions involved, displaying for every American and the world, why local, decentralized control of elections is critical to maintaining the foundational republic of the United States.

A lesson learned by America as well as the author and researcher of the information presented within this report happened in January of 2019 when Covington Catholic student, Nicholas Sandman, was destroyed by the mainstream media and in social media for a viral video involving Mr. Sandman and career activist Nathan Philips.[1] The narrative changed dramatically, however, when a news agency built a second-by-second timeline of exactly what transpired that day with literally every snippet of video found

---

[1] https://www.statesman.com/news/20190131/commentary-greatest-news-media-fail-of-all-time---nick-sandmann-case

PROLOGUE

on the internet entered into their research record. The result was the clear, unfettered truth, that resulted in multiple court case losses costing mainstream media multiple hundreds of millions of dollars, and a seriously embarrassing need for corporate agencies and false narrative peddling individuals to apologize to Mr. Sandman, his parents, and the world. The timeline was the key to seeing the truth.

As information began to emerge while researching this topic, a precise timeline was also meticulously built. The sources entered into the timeline were strictly scrutinized public records. When an event from another topic outside of the scope of the original subject had material bearing on the initial timeline, a new layer was added to the originating timeline. The result became a stark view of events of the past nearly twenty-five years, with the events accelerating and coming to a head after the 2016 election of President Donald Trump. This report walks through the research findings as an individual walking through time, with two pauses to focus on two key findings, and a consolidated timeline is presented at the end of the discussion. What emerged from this exercise was an absolute shocking revelation regarding the quiet, behind-the-scenes inner workings of our federal government. This is information every American needs to read, digest, and fully comprehend. This report exposes what ends up being a complete "end around" of the United States Constitution undertaken by mostly unelected officials within our extensive government bureaucracy. There are elected legislators and presidents, including, likely without knowing his part, President Donald Trump, that materially contributed to the result of two decades of quiet workings of the government machine. The hope is that this report opens the eyes of every American, of every political party, ideology, race, creed, gender, and economic status to find the inner patriots within Americans willing to stand and fight for the Constitution to return this country to standards of freedom and liberty intended

Countdown to Chaos

by the Founders when they penned the Constitution of the United States.

The birth of everything within this report came from Presidential Decision Directive-63, May 22, 1998, signed and enacted by Bill Clinton. This directive acknowledged the vulnerability of cyber systems in America stating, "Many of the nation's critical infrastructures have historically been physically and logically separate systems that had little interdependence."[2] The directive further laid out the plans to establish public-private information sharing among agencies and companies identified to be critical infrastructure with cyber-based information systems. One intent of the directive was "to the extent feasible, seek to avoid outcomes that increase government regulation or expand unfunded government mandates to the private sector."[3] Seemingly understanding the inherent safety in segregated and unconnected systems, the directive states, "Every department and agency of the Federal Government shall be responsible for protecting its own critical infrastructure, especially its cyber-based systems." As a result of this mandate, over time, infrastructure sectors were declared in areas that included aviation, transportation, utilities, emergency management, banking, healthcare, media, and national defense.[4]

As the information sharing platforms began to become viable, further organization and management was pursued. This report will expose the birth and evolution of these information sharing platforms, will document the early warnings from many well-known individuals within different layers of government with regard to the significant intrusion these structures could have on Constitutional privacy rights, and will highlight how information

---

[2] https://irp.fas.org/offdocs/pdd/pdd-63.pdf
[3] https://irp.fas.org/offdocs/pdd/pdd-63.pdf
[4] https://www.nationalisacs.org/member-isacs-3

PROLOGUE

sharing has grown into an interwoven part of the federal government that in as much as it provides for the common good, can and has now potentially already rewritten the Constitution with regard to elections, voting rights, and ultimately equal protection.

On October 30, 2008, when then presidential candidate Barack Obama proclaimed, "We are five days away from fundamentally transforming the United States of America," he may have been far more correct in that prediction and may be far more deserving of hanging a banner that declared "Mission Accomplished" in a follow up to that statement than President George W. Bush was in making the now infamous claim about the Iraq War. This report will expose silent and invisible actions made within the federal government, mainly within the Executive Branch, that collected nearly full control of the United States election system to itself. Citizens of the United States, lovers of the Constitution, and individuals treasuring the very basis of freedom need to understand this report shines a white-hot light on the previously invisible actions and proclaims, as loudly as any report can, information that should pierce the silence in which this potentially unconstitutional action was perpetrated.

Countdown to Chaos

Chapter 1
Decentralized Election History and Security

The framers of the Constitution at the founding of the United States of America, wisely recognized that centralized power was a detriment to a free society. Their construction of a government of separate but equal powers, each branch being a check upon the other, was and remains a brilliant mode to keep a tyrannical faction of any party or government from overthrowing the power of the people. The framers well knew that throughout history, unfettered power placed upon either government in its entirety or people in an absolutely pure democracy, had failed spectacularly. Understanding the fragility of freedom, the fight that was necessary to achieve it at that point in world history, and the monolithic task they had upon them to preserve it, the Constitution was written establishing a representative republic, always placing power closest to the populace in the most critical areas of the structure.

The greatest power manifested and preserved to the individual by the Constitution is the right to vote. The founders realized that, while a representative republic was necessary to preserve a free society for all, both a majority and minority, it was always the choice of people that would determine matters of the direction of the country. As such, all elections, not just local BUT ALSO FEDERAL elections, were conducted, monitored, and certified by the people in the states. States' constitutions further determine the manner of elections, delegating their operations to counties and further to precincts.

Prior to the drafting of the U.S. Constitution, Alexander Hamilton opined in *Federalist Paper 61* that decentralized elections were beneficial for the enfranchisement of remote voters. Great concern was given to remote rural voters, who were not likely to

Countdown to Chaos

travel any great distance to vote. To preserve their voice and their livelihoods, Hamilton found it necessary to keep elections for all offices local and accessible. In addition, in *Federalist 61*, Hamilton expresses concern that **centralized voting locations would result in an undesirable consolidation of power and influence** in populous centers, using Albany, New York, as an example. For the benefit of all voters at the inception of the unification of the new United States of America, **centralized power was a threat to the individual's right to vote.**[5]

The Constitution of the United States eventually affirmed Hamilton, in Articles I and II, known as "The Elections Clause"[6] outlay that the time, place, and manner for which representatives for the federal offices in the House chamber, and the U.S. Senate would be provided by the state legislatures.[7] This power has never changed since the adoption of the Constitution on June 21, 1788, and from that time forward, American elections have been held in small precincts in counties drawn to enfranchise citizens, and the process being regulated by the state legislatures. The adoption of the Tenth Amendment has also affirmed and protected the election process from federalization, stating implicitly **"The powers not delegated to the United States by the Constitution, nor prohibited by it to the States, are reserved to the States respectively, or to the people."**[8]

Certainly, decentralization in many things lends itself to security by its very nature. Alexander Hamilton saw it in a very simple but important context penning that centralization focuses power, and power in the hands of one entity can be perverted. Today we see

---

[5] https://guides.loc.gov/federalist-papers/text-61-70
[6] https://constitutioncenter.org/interactive-constitution/interpretation/article-i/clauses/750
[7] https://www.eac.gov/sites/default/files/eac_assets/1/1/U.S.%20Constitutional%20Provisions%20on%20Elections.pdf
[8] https://constitution.congress.gov/constitution/amendment-10/

CHAPTER 1

it in the context of technology. Computer systems and networks are always vulnerable, however, a network that is not interconnected would not be subjected to a focused attack. A decentralized election system, in and of itself, is more secure if it is not connected or networked in ANY way.

In a Cato Institute post on December 3, 2020, author Walter Olson notes with regard to the importance of decentralized elections, "...it prevents a power from being centralized that would be dangerously tempting to demagogues and authoritarians."[9] Further quoted in this *Cato Institute* blog post is economist Steve Landsburg from his opinion piece published in *The Wall Street Journal*:

> "Imagine a future presidential election in which the incumbent refuses to concede and enlists the full power of the federal government to overturn the apparent democratic outcome. **Now imagine that the election in question is actually run by a federal agency or by some nationwide quasigovernmental authority** charged with collecting and aggregating the results from all 50 states. I don't know about you, but I might worry a bit about the pressure that could be brought to bear on that single authority."[10] [11]

Steven Landburg's commentary is critically important to consider and understand at this particular time in history when data is collected, transmitted, and compiled digitally at nearly every point in the election process in the United States. The control and chain of custody is critically important even in cyberspace, where the

---

[9] https://www.cato.org/blog/framers-wisely-left-election-practice-decentralized
[10] https://www.cato.org/blog/framers-wisely-left-election-practice-decentralized
[11] https://www.wsj.com/articles/want-a-coup-abolish-the-electoral-college-11605134162

Countdown to Chaos

visual evidence of the physical vote literally becomes invisible. The question of who is in control of the "invisible" tallied vote from a visible ballot is likely going to have to be addressed in court, and at the highest level. Do states lose their jurisdiction over their local elections at some point in modern day federal elections when digital information is transferred?

This report will delve very deeply into a place this country has never been in before with regard to the digitization, management, and oversight of the physical vote. In addition, never has there been a time at any other point in the history of the United States of America, that the country has been under the thumb of the number of public-private partnerships and quasigovernmental agencies than it is today. As such, problems of legislation, jurisdiction, and local management or control of elections are becoming more frequently created and with discovery shared within this report, will be exposed. Truly, the lines between local, state, and federal government management are becoming fuzzier and delineated every single election cycle. This report unrepentantly reports these issues as they desperately need to be documented, understood, and potentially adjudicated to the Supreme Court in order to preserve the integrity of the individuals' rights to and the equal protection of their vote. These actions must also be undertaken to preserve the enduring integrity of the Constitution as the Founders wrote it and intended it to be applied.

Chapter 2
A Brief History of ISACs

The Presidential Directive-63 of May 22, 1998 is the entity that gave birth to employing the concept of information sharing across public and private entities and the private companies or governing bodies that include ISAOs (Information Sharing Analysis Organizations) and ISACs (Information Sharing Analysis Centers). The first established entity, the Center for Internet Security (CIS) was established on August 22, 2000, by founders Frank Reeder and Allen Paller. The IT-ISAC (Information Technology - Information Sharing Analysis Center) was subsequently formed in December of 2000 by additional leaders of the information technology sector.[12] As of the writing of this report, the members of the original board of directors of the IT-ISAC cannot be found. The mission of the IT-ISAC is published on its website is:

> "...the mission of the Information Technology-Information Sharing and Analysis Center (IT-ISAC) is to grow a diverse community of companies that leverage information technology and have in common a commitment to cybersecurity, and serve as a force-multiplier **that enables collaboration and sharing of relevant, actionable cyber threat information,** effective security policies, and practices for the benefit of all. The IT-ISAC augments member companies' internal capabilities by providing them access to curated cyber threat analysis, an intelligence management platform, and a trusted forum to engage with senior analysts from peer companies. The IT-ISAC global membership base consists of leading companies from three critical infrastructure sectors---IT, food and agriculture, and

---

[12] https://www.it-isac.org/20th-anniversary

Countdown to Chaos

elections. The IT-ISAC is recognized by the Department of Homeland Security and the IT Sector Coordinating Council as the IT sector's designated information-sharing forum, and has helped industry and government respond to the world's most significant cyberattacks over the past two decades."[13]

The IT-ISAC website highlights an important characteristic of ISACS which is "multi-directional information sharing." This mode of sharing is achieved through: Technical Committee and Special Interest Group Listservs, directly with our Operations Team, TruSTAR, a secure chat platform, or through our Technical Committee Meeting and Special Interest Group meetings.[14]

While the tech committees meet on a weekly basis, an important sector to take special note of is the special interest group organizations under the IT-ISAC. Within that structure is the EI-SIG (Election Infrastructure Special Interest Group) which "meet bi-weekly and provide an opportunity for companies to collaborate on issues affecting their specific group's topic of expertise...The Elections Industry SIG supports voting technology providers by giving them an industry-only forum to share information about threats to their enterprises and systems, and to collaborate on election security challenges..."[15] This organizational entity and its structure will be addressed later in this report.

While information sharing can yield many positive outcomes, too often throughout history things that are created for good become a platform for bad or nefarious activities. The presidential directive

---

[13] https://www.it-isac.org/about
[14] https://130760d6-684a-52ca-5172-0ea1f4aeebc3.filesusr.com/ugd/b8fa6c_181a8bf980554d6aad98607495f3448b.pdf
[15] https://130760d6-684a-52ca-5172-0ea1f4aeebc3.filesusr.com/ugd/b8fa6c_181a8bf980554d6aad98607495f3448b.pdf

CHAPTER 2

creating these ISAC platforms clearly states that such entities create a public-private partnership. The short history of public-private partnerships has now drawn Constitutionalists to criticize them for being an "end around" of the U.S. Constitution. Clearly when powers of the federal and state governments enumerated in their constitutions are delegated by the governing legislatures to private organizations or institutions, an appropriate oversight of the private sector participating in a "P3" (Public Private Partnership) deal becomes not only problematic to appropriately engage in, but legally complicated as well. Such structures are challenging to say the least to preserve the rights of the governed under our constitutions, as Freedom of Information Act searches and Sunshine Laws become clouded in their application which creates potential space for impropriety to abound out of the sight of the general public.

On September 11, 2001, America became the victim of a well-organized terror attack plotted by Islamist terrorists and based from operations in Afghanistan and Pakistan. The details and intelligence behind this attack continue to grow and gain specificity as the historical record continues to be built around the events of that day and beyond. Questions continue to be asked and answered, while many questions asked, remain ignored and unanswered. As life moves on, history continues to be written about this event, however, the immediate governmental repercussions of this event become a part of this report.

As a result of the attack of September 11th, the government of the United States of America passed the Homeland Security Act of 2002 establishing the Department of Homeland Security - a new cabinet level addition to the Executive Branch of the U.S. government. This reorganization is now considered the largest reorganization of U.S. government since the National Security Act of 1947.[16] The Act was

---

[16] https://www.nap.edu/read/10968/chapter/24

Countdown to Chaos

signed into law by President George W. Bush on November 19, 2002.[17] Interestingly, both President Bush and Vice-President Cheney were initially very concerned that action taken by the House and Senate at the time was a government overreach and it was destined to curb individual Constitutional rights of even average Americans. "When we look at the emerging Department of Homeland Security, we see that it incorporates 22 government agencies and some 179,000 people into a single organization. We also see an organization with a proposed budget for FY 2004 of $36.2 billion—roughly one-tenth the size of the nation's military defense budget…" as well as "an intelligence analysis and infrastructure protection mission, a science and technology mission, and coordination functions involving the federal government, state and local governments, foreign governments, and the private sector."[18]

Under the Homeland Security Act of 2002, the new Department of Homeland Security took the newly developed ISAC structure, and the mission of the IT-ISAC and turned it into a multi-billion-dollar government organized and managed super structure. The DHS "formally began operating on January 24, 2003, and by March 1 had absorbed representatives from most of its component parts."[19] Full maturity of the department would take years.

On June 1, 2003, another layer of the public-private partnership was added to the ISAC structure when the National Council of ISACs (NCI) was formed, growing into an organization of 26 separate sector specific ISACs over time. To date, the membership includes the Elections Infrastructure ISAC (EI-ISAC), Communications ISAC, Information Technology ISAC (IT-ISAC), Multi-State ISAC (MS-ISAC), and the National Defense ISAC (ND-ISAC). The NCI website states

---

[17] https://www.congress.gov/bill/107th-congress/house-bill/5005
[18] https://www.nap.edu/read/10968/chapter/24#177
[19] https://www.nap.edu/read/10968/chapter/24#178

CHAPTER 2

the following with regard to its mission and scope on the NCI website:

> "The NCI is a true cross-sector partnership, providing a forum for sharing cyber and physical threats and mitigation strategies among ISACs and with government and private sector partners during both steady-state conditions and incidents requiring cross-sector response. **Sharing and coordination is accomplished through daily and weekly calls between ISAC operations centers, daily reports, requests-for-information, monthly meetings, exercises, and other activities as situations require.** The NCI also organizes its own drills and exercises and participates in national exercises.
>
> **The Council and individual members collaborate with agencies of the federal government, fusion centers, the State and Local Tribal Territorial Government Coordinating Council (SLTTGCC),** the Regional Consortium Coordinating Council (RCCC), **the Partnership for Critical Infrastructure Security (PCIS)** – the Cross-Sector Council, and international partners."[20]

An interesting ISAC member-organization of the NCI is the National Defense ISAC (ND-ISAC). Its website lists partners of the organization as the DHS, the FBI Cyber Division and the Department of Defense. The site outlines:

> "ND-ISAC is recognized nationally within the US as the ISAC for the nation's defense industry critical infrastructure sector by the Defense Industrial Base Sector Coordinating Council (DIB SCC), the US Department of Homeland Security (DHS), the FBI, and

---

[20] https://www.nationalisacs.org/about-nci

Countdown to Chaos

the National Council of ISACs. **The National Council of ISACs provides framework for cross sector interaction among ISACs as well as private and public sector security entities."**[21]

Research into this entity has yielded some curious discoveries – one being the membership of Ernie Magnotti, whose name was in and out of behind-the-scenes reporting after the 2020 Presidential Election. Mr. Mangotti's LinkedIn profile reads:

> "Ernie Magnotti, Chief Information Security Officer (CISO) for Leonardo DRS. He is a Cybersecurity Leader who executes the enterprise-wide strategic direction to align with business and IT objectives that directly impact security compliance. An IT visionary with excellent analytical skills complement an extensive knowledge of Information Security Frameworks, including ITIL, NIST, and ISO. Driven by integrity with the ability to articulate highly technical information across all levels in a dynamic environment, welcomes challenges, and completes projects with industry-leading outcomes."[22]

The information about Mr. Magnotti is only mentioned as fact-based evidence for the reader to consider and contemplate if doing further independent research on the 2020 election. At a later point in this report the topic of the creation of the Homeland Security Information Network and subsequent situation rooms will appear in the timeline at the beginning of 2018. The emergence of Mr. Magnotti's name within other research surrounding the 2020 election should be observed through the prism of the ISAC infrastructure.

---

[21] https://ndisac.org/partners/
[22] https://www.linkedin.com/in/erniemagnotti/

CHAPTER 2

In order to get a clear picture of the impact these public-private partnerships have on the Constitution and the individual American, it is important to walk through the evolution of each piece of the structure, their charters, boards of directors, scope, and reach. And while there are considerably important reasons for these structures to exist, certainly there is evidence that some of the structures should not wield the power they have been handed as these powers are in direct conflict with the Constitution of the United States and the rights of the individual.

Countdown to Chaos

CHAPTER 3

Chapter 3

The Evolution of the DHS Cyber Programs (EINSTEIN) (2000 – 2004)

After the ISAC structure was initiated from 2000 through about 2003, specifics of management and scope of the sectors became an important issue to be addressed. Early in the function of the Department of Homeland Security, the US-CERT (United States Computer Emergency Readiness Team) was formed. US-CERT was established by the DHS in 2003 as its operational arm of the National Cyber Security Division of the DHS. Purposed "to protect the nation's Internet infrastructure, US-CERT coordinates defense against and responses to cyber-attacks across the nation." However, history now shows that the main reason for the organization of US-CERT was to develop and implement the government's EINSTEIN program alongside the NSA (National Security Agency). "Under the Federal Information Security Management Act of 2002 (FISMA) (44 U.S.C. § 3541 et seq.), all federal departments and agencies must adhere to information security best practices."[23]

"Launched in 2004, EINSTEIN was meant to build and enhance national cyber related situational awareness, identify and respond to cyber threats and attacks, improve network security, increase the resiliency of critical, electronically delivered government services, and enhance the survivability of the Internet. EINSTEIN was also developed to satisfy security mandates created by the Homeland Security Act and the Homeland Security Presidential Directive 7, and was intended to satisfy the Congressional requirements for information security outlined in the Federal

---

[23] https://www.dhs.gov/sites/default/files/publications/privacy-pia-nppd-einstein2-june2013-3-year-review_0.pdf

Countdown to Chaos

Information Security Management Act (U.S. Department of Homeland Security, 2004)"[24]

To be clear, DHS Presidential Directive 7 enacted by President Barack Obama, superseded the 1998 Clinton Presidential Directive-63 and began to intensify the expectations of public-private partnerships in the cyber realm. In point twenty-five of the text, the directive specifies:

> "In accordance with applicable laws or regulations, the Department and the Sector-Specific Agencies will collaborate with appropriate private sector entities and continue **to encourage the development of information sharing and analysis mechanisms.** Additionally, the Department and Sector-Specific Agencies shall collaborate with the private sector and continue to support sector-coordinating mechanisms:
>
> a. to identify, prioritize, and coordinate the protection of critical infrastructure and key resources; and
>
> b. to facilitate sharing of information about physical and cyber threats, vulnerabilities, incidents, potential protective measures, and best practices."[25]

Further at point twenty-seven of the directive, additional specifications regarding sharing of information, including the structure of state and local government cyber architecture is described:

---

[24] https://calhoun.nps.edu/bitstream/handle/10945/32877/13Mar_Oree_William.pdf?sequence=1
[25] https://www.cisa.gov/homeland-security-presidential-directive-7

CHAPTER 3

"Consistent with the Homeland Security Act of 2002, the Secretary shall produce a comprehensive, integrated National Plan for Critical Infrastructure and Key Resources Protection to outline national goals, objectives, milestones, and key initiatives within 1 year from the issuance of this directive. The Plan shall include, in addition to other Homeland Security-related elements as the Secretary deems appropriate, the following elements:

a. a strategy to identify, prioritize, and coordinate the protection of critical infrastructure and key resources, including how the Department intends to work with Federal departments and agencies, State and local governments, the private sector, and foreign countries and international organizations;

b. a summary of activities to be undertaken in order to: define and prioritize, reduce the vulnerability of, and coordinate the protection of critical infrastructure and key resources;

c. a summary of initiatives for sharing critical infrastructure and key resources information and for providing critical infrastructure and key resources threat warning data to State and local governments and the private sector; and

d. coordination and integration, as appropriate, with other Federal emergency management and preparedness activities including the National Response Plan and applicable national preparedness goals."[26]

---

[26] https://www.cisa.gov/homeland-security-presidential-directive-7

Countdown to Chaos

In addition, the directive states: "In developing a national indications and warnings architecture, the Department will work with Federal, State, local, and non-governmental entities to develop an integrated view of physical and cyber infrastructure and key resources."[27]

The Department of Homeland Security described the Einstein 1 program, upon the rollout of Einstein 2 as:

> "EINSTEIN 1, developed in 2003, provides an automated process for collecting, correlating, and analyzing computer network security information from voluntary participating federal executive agencies. It works by collecting network flow records. "Flow records" are records of connections made to a federal executive agency's IT systems... Using network flow records, the US-CERT can detect certain types of malicious activity and coordinate with the appropriate federal executive agencies to mitigate those threats and vulnerabilities. **The US-CERT shares this analysis, along with additional computer network security information, with both the public and private sectors**, via its web site."[28]

To the average American, busy at home with their job and family, too involved in the daily grind of life to worry about government work, this structure likely sounds like a positive step in securing America's cyber infrastructure. However, integration of such standards under the umbrellas of public-private partnerships leaves the mode or toolbox utilized to achieve the directive hiding in fine print, FOIA protected paperwork, and out of mind of most or all people for whom this has the potential of affecting. The historical timeline of what has been implemented under these

---

[27] https://www.cisa.gov/homeland-security-presidential-directive-7
[28] https://www.dhs.gov/sites/default/files/publications/privacy-pia-nppd-einstein2-june2013-3-year-review_0.pdf

CHAPTER 3

structures, who has managed the implementation, and the apparent limitless scope of reach the underwritten cyber platforms utilized with be revealed in the next several chapters of this report.

Countdown to Chaos

CHAPTER 4

Chapter 4

MS-ISAC, IT-SCC, and US-CERT (2004 – 2006)

After the deployment of the federal government's cyber monitoring tool, EINSTEIN, the Department of Homeland Security may have found an urgent need to better organize state, local, tribal, and territorial governments (SLTTs), which are Constitutionally outside of their jurisdiction. Any federal government intrusion into state and local policy has historically been met with resistance and aversion by those governing them. The era of the cyber information age has additionally created a few generations quite wary of the concept of "1984 Big Brother".

Perhaps to assuage these aversions, the Department of Homeland Security built on the quick and early success of the ISAC programs up to this point, and in 2004 organized the MS-ISAC (Multi-State Information Sharing Analysis Center), and began providing funding for the organization in September 2004.[29] **The MS-ISAC is currently made up of members from all fifty states and over 4,000 entities**, but this level of participation only came after the Department of Homeland Security, in 2009, approached the Center for Internet Security (CIS) and proposed the CIS "absorb" the MS-ISAC.[30]

The services provided to SLTTs by the MS-ISAC include:

- Real time network monitoring and threat analysis
- Incident response and remediation
- Training sessions and webinars
- Development and distribution of strategic, tactical, and operational intelligence to provide timely, actionable information

---

[29] https://homeland.house.gov/imo/media/doc/Testimony%20-%20Gilligan.pdf
[30] https://www.cisecurity.org/blog/20-years-of-creating-confidence-in-the-connected-world/ (at 4:13)

Countdown to Chaos

- Cyber security resources

After the absorption of the MS-ISAC into the CIS as requested by DHS, **these services were provided for free in exchange for specific information provided by the entity receiving services.** The information to be exchanged by an SLTT entity includes:

- …work collaboratively with all entities within their organization…
- Agree to share appropriate information between and among peer MS-ISAC Members to the greatest extent possible.
- Agree to collaborate and share across the critical sectors…
- Agree to recognize the sensitivity and protect the confidentiality of the information shared and received in the MS-ISAC, taking all necessary steps and at least the same or similar precautions to protect information from others as is taken to protect your own sensitive information.
- Agree to transmit sensitive data to other Members[31]

Further the MS-ISAC statement of Terms and Conditions also lays out the following:

- MS-ISAC and Member both acknowledge that the protection of shared Data is essential to the security of both Member and the mission of the MS-ISAC. The intent of the Data protection terms are to: (a) enable Member to **make disclosures of Data** to MS-ISAC while still maintaining rights in, and control over, the Data; and (b) set common information sharing protocol that will determine the extent to which Data can be shared with others.
- … **all Data provided by Members may be shared** with MS-ISAC's federal partners (including, without limitation, the

---

[31] https://www.cisecurity.org/ms-isac/ms-isac-charter/

CHAPTER 4

U.S. Department of Homeland Security), and may be shared with other MS-ISAC members...

Finally, an official MS-ISAC Services Guide denotes the following technical information that will be shared by the MS-ISAC members:

- Server type and version (IIS, Apache, nginx, etc.)
- Web programming language and version (PHP, Python, Perl)
- Content Management System and version (WordPress, Drupal, etc.)
- Other web server software and version (OpenSSL)
- Software type and version (OpenSSH, Cisco, IIS, etc.) Publicly available hardware (ICS and SCADA devices, printers, cameras, routers, switches, etc.)
- **Ports**[32]

While the MS-ISAC's charter lists it as a division of the Center for Internet Security, Inc., this structure did not happen until 2009 as reported earlier. The MS-ISAC is governed currently, and was likely governed upon organization, by an Executive Committee elected by MS-ISAC primary members. The chair of the MS-ISAC Executive Committee, among several responsibilities will "Guide the Executive Committee in providing strategic guidance regarding the MS-ISAC and SLTT community to the senior executive leadership of CIS, DHS/CISA, and other key partners as necessary."[33]

The important takeaways from the framework of the MS-ISAC are that all member entities of the states (SLTTs) are interconnected through this organization, and clearly, all entities are digitally networked via remote connectivity to the MS-ISAC via the CIS location in East Greenbush, NY. Secondly, the management of the

---

[32] https://www.marc.org/Government/Cybersecurity/assets/MS-ISAC_ServicesGuide_8-5x11_Print_v2.aspx
[33] https://www.cisecurity.org/ms-isac/ms-isac-charter/

Countdown to Chaos

data from SLTTs is no longer solely directly that of the SLTT entity. This report will clearly later show that this shared data includes ALL election management infrastructure and election related data. Thirdly, as the agreement entered into by SLTTs constitutes a public-private partnership, access by the public to the association between the SLTT entity and the MS-ISAC and CIS is limited by a unique legal code governing such associations.[34]

On January 27, 2006, the IT-SCC (Information Technology Sector Coordinating Council) was formed. Formed as a 501(c)3, according to its bylaws, the IT-SCC was "established for the purpose of working collaboratively with the Department of Homeland Security, other government agencies and officials and other critical infrastructure SCC's in fostering and facilitating the coordination of activities, initiatives and policies designed to improve the security and resilience of the nation's information technology infrastructure."[35]

The IT-SCC is another public-private partnership structure governed by an executive committee. Again, the Department of Homeland Security is the public/government arena for the information sharing from this council. The importance of the creation of this public-private partnership for this report is first that the IT-SCC recognizes the IT-ISAC, (outlined in Chapter 2 of this report) for its official information sharing mechanism, and secondly, the membership of this council includes:

- Amazon Web Services (AWS)
- Center for Internet Security (CIS)
- CrowdStrike
- VOSTROM
- Neustar, Inc.

---

[34] https://sgp.fas.org/crs/intel/R43941.pdf
[35] https://www.it-scc.org/uploads/4/7/2/3/47232717/it_scc_bylaws_update_final_030817.pdf

CHAPTER 4

- Cyber Threat Alliance
- Dell
- Information Technology – Information Sharing Analysis Center (IT-ISAC)
- McAfee
- Microsoft
- SafeNet Government Solutions
- Splunk
- Unisys Corporation[36]

These members of the IT-SCC have a role to play in the structure and organization of elections in the United States. Most of these companies will be mentioned within other areas of this report. Three members will prove to be of high significance in information presented in chapter fifteen of this report. It is important to note again that this organization is directly connected to the Department of Homeland Security.

---

[36] https://www.it-scc.org/current-members.html

Countdown to Chaos

CHAPTER 5

Chapter 5
US-CERT, EINSTEIN 2, and EINSTEIN 3 Pilot (2006 – 2010)

A September 2004 report summed up the way the cyber program began under the umbrella of the DHS:

> "Within DHS, the National Cyber Security Division (NCSD) serves as the Federal government's cornerstone for cyber security coordination and preparedness. The operational arm of the NCSD is the United States Computer Emergency Readiness Team (US-CERT), a partnership between NCSD and the public and private sectors that has the responsibility to:
>
> - Compile and analyze information security incident information;
> - Inform agencies about information security threats and vulnerabilities; and
> - **Consult with national security agencies and operators** of national security systems to promote cyber security best practices and preparedness."[37]

This was the birthplace of the federal government's EINSTEIN program which was rolled out in 2003 as this report explains in Chapter 3. A benignly conceived idea, EINSTEIN became the backbone from which the DHS and multiple ISACs would build monitoring and intrusion detection systems, which will be outlined later in this report, and establish wide connectivity of both information and network structure. Further, 6 U.S. Code § 485 – "Information Sharing"[38] set forth the definitions and structure for an information sharing complex to be built throughout the federal government. The Homeland Information Sharing Network

---
[37] https://www.dhs.gov/xlibrary/assets/privacy/privacy_pia_eisntein.pdf
[38] https://www.law.cornell.edu/uscode/text/6/485

Countdown to Chaos

becomes an important piece of the federal government cyber network superstructure. (The HSIN will take the stage for the scope of this report again in 2018.)

On November 20, 2007, an Office of Management and Budget (OMB) Memorandum: M-08-05, required that all federal executive agencies use EINSTEIN 2 sensors.[39] This deployment would exempt both the Department of Defense and the Intelligence Community. Very soon after that, on January 8, 2008, the Comprehensive National Cybersecurity Initiative, directed the DHS to deploy intrusion detection and prevention sensors, a.k.a. EINSTEIN 2, across federal civilian agencies.[40]

A Privacy Impact Statement released by the Department of Homeland Security on May 19, 2008, describes the specific operations of EINSTEIN and the EINSTEIN 2 systems:

> "EINSTEIN 1 analyzes network flow information from participating federal executive government agencies and provides a high-level perspective from which to observe potential malicious activity in computer network traffic of participating agencies' computer networks.
>
> The updated version, EINSTEIN 2, will incorporate network intrusion detection technology capable of alerting the United States Computer Emergency Readiness Team (US-CERT) to the presence of malicious or potentially harmful computer network activity in federal executive agencies' network traffic. EINSTEIN 2 principally relies on commercially available intrusion

---

[39] https://www.cisa.gov/sites/default/files/publications/PIA%20NPPD%20E3A%2020130419%20FINAL%20signed-%20508%20compliant.pdf

[40] https://www.cisa.gov/sites/default/files/publications/PIA%20NPPD%20E3A%2020130419%20FINAL%20signed-%20508%20compliant.pdf

detection capabilities to increase the situational awareness of the US-CERT."[41]

Two interesting pieces of historical intelligence appear at this moment in the comprehensive timeline of the growth of these monitoring systems. One is a paper leaked to WikiLeaks from, at the time, the former CIA Executive Director, John Brennan. The paper appears to have been written within the period between his departure from his position of Executive Director at the CIA, his position as President and CEO of the private civilian company, The Analysis Corporation, located three miles away from the CIA in McLean, Virginia, and his simultaneous position on the Board of Directors at The Intelligence and National Security Alliance (INSA), another ten-mile drive from the CIA. The second interesting data point, is that on March 1, 2018, CNN would report that John Brennan, in his capacity as CEO of the Analysis Corporation, was involved in spying on presidential candidates John McCain, Hillary Clinton, and Barack Obama.[42]

While The Analysis Corporation was a private, for-profit private intelligence agency, INSA is "a not-for-profit professional association of public and private sector leaders of the intelligence and national security communities." INSA's mission states that it "provides a nonpartisan forum for collaboration among the public, private, and academic sectors of the intelligence and national security communities..."[43] The John Brennan authored draft of intelligence sharing paper found in the WikiLeaks cache, dated July 2007, details a need for "a 'national' security architecture that knits together the capabilities and requirements of all levels of

---

[41] https://www.dhs.gov/sites/default/files/publications/privacy-pia-nppd-einstein2-june2013-3-year-review_0.pdf
[42] https://www.cnn.com/2008/POLITICS/03/22/passport.files/
[43] https://www.insaonline.org/about/

Countdown to Chaos

government as well as those of the private sector... these communities can interoperate with one another..."[44]

While John Brennan was serving at the board of the INSA, the second white paper published by it as an organization was titled "Critical Issues for Cyber Assurance Policy Reform – An Industry Assessment". The paper was written and published with a date of October 19, 2008, in response to a Presidential commission asking for "a comprehensive cyber assurance study in order to identify public and private sectors that have a stake in cyber assurance... The Intelligence and National Security Alliance (INSA), which represents the defense, intelligence, national security, and telecommunications industries, formed a task force to address several of these questions." [45] Key points and conclusions included in this paper directed at key policy makers were:

- "In order to deter, enforce, and defend, the government and private sector need to work together to fund technologic innovation in the ability to do **advanced, real time analytics and processing** to achieve attribution. For success in "driving analytics" to achieve attribution, **improved information sharing and data access are essential.** Additionally, **the government and private sector must eliminate or resolve legal and policy impediments to accessing and sharing data.** The government should build and promote multiple virtual communities of interest around cyber issues. Such **network-connected communities are now firmly established as responsive and efficient structures for innovation and collaboration** by analysts. While there will always be a need for classification

---

[44] https://wikileaks.org/cia-emails/Draft-Intel-Position-Paper/Draft-Intel-Position-Paper.pdf
[45] https://www.insaonline.org/wp-content/uploads/2017/04/INSA_CritialIssuesCyber_WP-1.pdf

and compartmented information, the U.S. should strive to maximize the connectivity."
- "The importance of a public/private partnership to address the many technical and policy issues facing our nation in this critical area cannot be understated."[46]

On Inauguration Day, January 20, 2009, John O. Brennan became the Deputy National Security Advisor for Homeland Security and Counterterrorism under newly elected President Barack Obama. Additionally on January 20, 2009, DHS, IT-ISAC and Communications ISAC collaborated to form the National Cybersecurity and Communications Integration Center (NCCIC) - a single combined operations center.[47] Only six months into the Obama Administration, the White House issued a paper titled "Cyberspace Policy Review -Assuring a Trusted and Resilient Information and Communications Infrastructure." This policy review Executive Summary states:

> "The United States needs a comprehensive framework to ensure a coordinated response by the Federal, State, local, and tribal governments, the private sector, and international allies to significant incidents. Implementation of this framework will require developing reporting thresholds, adaptable response and recovery plans, and the necessary coordination, information sharing, and incident reporting mechanisms needed for those plans to succeed. The government, working with key stakeholders, should design an effective mechanism to achieve a true common operating picture that integrates information from the government and the private sector and serves as the

---

[46] https://www.insaonline.org/wp-content/uploads/2017/04/INSA_CritialIssuesCyber_WP-1.pdf
[47] https://www.it-isac.org/post/isacs-beyond-information-sharing

basis for informed and prioritized vulnerability mitigation efforts and incident response decisions."[48]

As the transfer of power was taking place from the Bush Administration to the Obama Administration, a number of standard reviews of the previous administration took place which have been reported to be about a ninety-day process. Former member of the National Security Council during those years, Col. John Mills (Ret.), also a Senior Dept. of Defense representative for the Comprehensive National Cybersecurity Initiative (CNCI) recounted the Obama administrative review during that time, particularly that of the exponentially growing CNCI:

> "The Obama Administration reviewed that [CNCI cyber], and their assessment was not only did they like it, **they LOVED it, and they wanted more of it, and they wanted to pour gasoline on it because it provided breathtaking and magical capabilities**..."

> "There [were] capabilities developed... back during the 2005 – 2008 before Obama was onboard called remote access capabilities, which allowed user to have access and do anything they wanted to."

> "...With the ramp up of these cyber capabilities which provided an intoxicating exponential increase year per year in the ability to collect...if you were able to stand on the watch floors of these major centers, and watch and see the simultaneous capabilities, it was breathtaking..."

> "It really matured in 2012 under Gen. Keith Alexander...we also created Cyber Command in addition to NSA... the simultaneous capability to collect data of all

---

[48] https://web.archive.org/web/20110424173823/http://www.whitehouse.gov/assets/documents/Cyberspace_Policy_Review_final.pdf

CHAPTER 5

kinds ... monitor, collect, integrate... was an incredible capability."

"...once this magic is unleashed, and policy makers appointed, elected, or careerist start to see the capabilities, **it becomes intoxicating,** and it's no longer CAN we, the question a reasonable person who took an oath to the Constitution should be raising is, 'SHOULD we?,' and 'Do we have the proper control mechanisms?,' and 'Are people doing this for the correct and right purposes?'"[49]

In September of 2009, the charter for the Multi-State Information Sharing Analysis Center (MS-ISAC) was updated. Shortly thereafter, the MS-ISAC was "absorbed" into the Center for Internet Security (CIS).[50] As this report outlined previously in Chapter 4, one **purpose of this structural change was to offer SLTTs (State, Local, Tribal and Territorial governments), cyber services at no cost in exchange for data and other structural access and information**, in effect, beginning to build and fortify the national "comprehensive framework" detailed in the 2009 White House paper on cyber infrastructure and cyber security.

Six short months later, on March 18, 2010, the Department of Homeland Security presented a Privacy Impact Assessment (PIA) for the approval of the deployment of a pilot program for the next generation of the EINSTEIN program, into which the federal government was heavily invested. Logically coined "EINSTEIN 3", while the project added to the existing EINSTEIN technology deployed throughout most federal agencies, this upgraded platform included "DHS test deployment of technology developed by the National Security Agency (NSA) that includes an intrusion

---

[49] https://centerforsecuritypolicy.org/author/john-mills/
[50] https://www.cisecurity.org/blog/20-years-of-creating-confidence-in-the-connected-world/ (minute 4:13)

Countdown to Chaos

prevention capability."[51] The important new features of EINSTEIN 3 included:

- "...the ability of an existing Internet Service Provider that is a designated as a Trusted Internet Connection Access Provider (TICAP) to select and redirect Internet traffic from a single participating government agency through the Exercise technology [EINSTEIN 3], for US-CERT to apply intrusion detection and prevention measures to that traffic and for US-CERT to generate automated alerts about selected cyber threats."
- "...technology that will include intrusion detection and add intrusion prevention."
- "...will enable DHS to respond appropriately to counter known or suspected cyber threats identified within the participating agency's network traffic..."
- "...draw on commercial technology and specialized government technology to conduct real-time full packet inspection and threat-based decision-making on network traffic entering or leaving these executive branch networks..."
- "...automatically detect and respond appropriately to cyber threats..."
- "...support enhanced information sharing by US-CERT with federal departments..."
- "...giving DHS the ability to automate alerting of detected network intrusion attempts and, when deemed necessary by DHS..."
- "The ability of US-CERT, utilizing the Exercise technology, to analyze redirected agency-specific traffic to detect cyber threats, and to respond appropriately to those threats."

---

[51] https://www.dhs.gov/sites/default/files/publications/privacy_pia_nppd_initiative3.pdf

CHAPTER 5

- "The ability of a TICAP to deliver the traffic back to the particular participating agency in a timely and efficient fashion."
- The ability of the TICAP to "Direct the participating agency's traffic back on its original path to or from the participating agency's network once it has passed through the Exercise technology."[52]

This pilot program was reported in the privacy impact assessment (PIA) document to encompass no longer than a twelve-month period. With completion of this phase of the EINSTEIN program, the United States of America was about to transition into a critical era of public-private partnerships, information sharing, reinforcement and expansion of multi-state network superstructures, unprecedented information monitoring, and real-time automated systems alteration. Control of elections in the United States of America would become clouded and fully debatable beginning in 2011, with the DHS deployment of the ALBERT IDS monitoring systems and the CIS Security Operations Center (SOC).

---

[52] https://www.dhs.gov/sites/default/files/publications/privacy_pia_nppd_initiative3.pdf

Countdown to Chaos

CHAPTER 6

Chapter 6

TIME OUT TO FOCUS ON:

The Albert Sensor (Albert Monitoring Services - 2011)

The Albert Sensor (aka Albert Monitoring Services) is an intrusion detection system (IDS) that "has its origin in the U.S. Department of Homeland Security's Einstein program, which does network intrusion detection for federal agencies."[53] It is provided and implemented by the Center for Internet Security (CIS), which is self-described as a "community-driven nonprofit, responsible for the CIS Controls® and CIS Benchmarks™, globally recognized best

THE ALBERT SENSOR

- Intrusion Detection System (IDS)
- Deployed on a network perimeter
- Both hardware and software based
    - 1U Server
    - Span port off a router or switch
- Constantly monitored
- Utilizes Advanced Persistent Threat (APT) indicators vis CIS
- Utilizes a passive sensor
    - Collects data
    - Encrypts data
    - Transmits data to the CIS Security Operations Center (SOC)
- Enabled for use with voting systems, ePoll books, voter registration systems and ballot marking devices
- Can potentially be updated via Johns Hopkins SOAR platform IACD

---

[53] https://statetechmagazine.com/article/2019/11/states-can-get-election-security-assist-albert-sensors

Countdown to Chaos

practices for securing IT systems and data,"[54] while "under the sponsorship of the U.S. Department of Homeland Security."[55] According to the CIS Terms and Conditions agreement posted for its customers, CIS "has been recognized by the United States Department of Homeland Security as the governmental ISAC and as a key Albert Monitoring resource for all fifty states, local governments, tribal nations and United States territories ("SLTTs")."[56]

The Albert Sensor and monitoring system is both hardware and software based, deployed on a system or network, and is monitored constantly.[57] The Albert monitoring system "uses open-source software combined with the expertise of the CIS 24x7 Security Operations Center (SOC) to provide enhanced monitoring capabilities and notifications of malicious activity. Albert leverages a high-performance IDS engine for the identification and reporting of malicious events. It also monitors raw network packets and converts data into a net flow format for efficient storage and analysis of historical data. "[58] Typically configured on the perimeter of a network, outside the firewall, "the Albert Sensor uses IDS signatures and behavior-based detection to identify malicious or potentially harmful network activity."[59]

In addition to active monitoring Albert further runs a passive sensor. "The passive sensor sits on the network and collects data, which is then **encrypted and transmitted around the clock to the CIS center for analysis**. When an alert is verified as actionable, CIS

---

[54] https://www.cisecurity.org/about-us/
[55] https://www.cisecurity.org/wp-content/uploads/2018/02/CIS-Elections-eBook-15-Feb.pdf (P 68)
[56] https://www.cisecurity.org/terms-and-conditions-table-of-contents/cis-albert-network-monitoring-services/
[57] https://cityofjerseycity.civicweb.net/document/27088
[58] https://www.cisecurity.org/services/albert-network-monitoring/
[59] https://www.nass.org/sites/default/files/2020-01/white-paper-bandura-cyber-nass-winter20.pdf

CHAPTER 6

sends an event notification to the organization."[60] **All logs and data DO NOT REMAIN on the sensor within the jurisdiction of the state or localities.** "All data collected is compressed, encrypted, and sent to the CIS SOC every few minutes for analysis...Monitoring, as well as full management of the sensor, is handled by the CIS SOC. "[61]

Beyond these measures, CIS also reports it "may utilize the CIS API service to programmatically ingest event notifications and associated logs..." Additionally, a white paper published by Bandura Cyber reports "the use of open application programming interfaces (APIs) and the use of open standards like STIX/TAXII to connect and exchange threat intelligence among systems. Security Orchestration & Automated Response (SOAR) solutions are being used by progressive, well-resourced security organizations to enable the automated integration and exchange of threat intelligence between multiple security controls."[62]

The CIS website reports the basic specifications of the Albert system: "The Albert service utilizes commodity hardware to help provide a robust offering at a low cost. Typically, this can be run on a 1U server (or a VM for smaller installations). We recommend supplying an Albert sensor with network traffic by way of a network tap or data aggregator (such as a gigamon) if your infrastructure already supports these options. For smaller <1Gb networks, a span port off a router or switch will work well."[63]

---

[60] https://statetechmagazine.com/article/2019/11/states-can-get-election-security-assist-albert-sensors
[61] https://www.cisecurity.org/services/albert-network-monitoring/
[62] https://www.nass.org/sites/default/files/2020-01/white-paper-bandura-cyber-nass-winter20.pdf
[63] https://www.cisecurity.org/services/albert-network-monitoring/

Countdown to Chaos

In addition to hardware provided to CIS for the Albert Monitoring Services, state, local, tribunal nations and territories (SLTTs) also agree to provide the following internal governmental information:

- Current network diagrams and any changes to networks at future dates within the contracts
- Public and Private IP address ranges including a list of servers being monitored including the type, operating system and configuration information, as well as a list of IP ranges and addresses that are not in use by Customer (DarkNet space);[64]
- Assessments and plans that relate specifically and uniquely to the vulnerability of Customer's information systems[65]
- ..."information otherwise marked as confidential by Customer..."[66]

Importantly, the CIS Terms and Conditions for its customers published on its website reveal evidence that the Albert Sensor technology, while it is described as "both hardware and software based,"[67] is primarily a software-based solution as created by the source code writer, and hardware based as purchased and deployed by the customer in accordance with the requirements of the Albert Sensor system. The terms and conditions state: "Customer shall provide the sensor(s)/server(s) to be used for Albert Monitoring Services, using the specifications provided by CIS..."[68]

---

[64] https://www.cisecurity.org/terms-and-conditions-table-of-contents/cis-albert-network-monitoring-services/
[65] https://www.cisecurity.org/terms-and-conditions-table-of-contents/cis-albert-network-monitoring-services/
[66] https://www.cisecurity.org/terms-and-conditions-table-of-contents/cis-albert-network-monitoring-services/
[67] https://cityofjerseycity.civicweb.net/document/27088
[68] https://www.cisecurity.org/terms-and-conditions-table-of-contents/cis-albert-network-monitoring-services/

CHAPTER 6

At the outset of this report, the specific author of the pilot version of the Albert Monitoring system software (and/or Einstein, Einstein 1 & 2, and Einstein A3, aka Ea3 and E^3A Systems from which it emanates) was unclear. The developers credited in public citations are the US-CERT (United States Computer Emergency Readiness Team) in partnership with the NSA (National Security Agency), and private industry[69]. "US-CERT is the operational arm of the National Cyber Security Division (NCSD) at the Department of Homeland Security (DHS)."[70] In testimony to the House Appropriations Committee, April 16, 2010, Deputy Undersecretary of the NPPD (National Protection and Programs Directorate), Philip Reitinger reported the "US-CERT funds also support the development, acquisition, deployment, and personnel required to implement the National Cybersecurity Protection System (NCPS), operationally known as EINSTEIN." While companies that specifically partner with the DHS regarding intrusion detection are not found enumerated in public information, they all are members of DHS information sharing and analysis centers (ISACs) and/or the National Cybersecurity Center of Excellence (NCCoE). There are very few leading private IT companies that do not partner with the federal government, however as of 2010, the approximate year the EINSTEIN 3 system was in development, Mark Kagan in an article at Govtech.com found that "Only Cisco, McAfee and Symantec have ventured into the realm of selling software as a service."[71] However, further discovery on this topic has yielded new knowledge regarding the creator of the Albert monitoring software specifically and is updated and provided at the end of this chapter.

---

[69]
https://calhoun.nps.edu/bitstream/handle/10945/32877/13Mar_Oree_William.pdf?sequence=1

[70] https://web.archive.org/web/20080525134358/http://www.us-cert.gov/aboutus.html#events

[71] https://www.govtech.com/pcio/top-ten-government-it-security-vendors.html

Countdown to Chaos

On January 16, 2013, the Department of Homeland Security filed a Privacy Impact Assessment (PIA) for the addition of Enhanced Cybersecurity Services (ECS) to the underlayment of its EINSTEIN monitoring systems deployed throughout both critical infrastructure points and other department systems.[72] A month later, President Barack Obama signed Executive Order 13636 to facilitate the rollout of the program.[73] On November 30, 2015, the DHS filed another PIA regarding the ECS systems to add NetFlow Analysis to the network environments (this service was to be provided by Cisco Sytems).[74] Just months prior to this expansion, a vulnerability in the Cisco NetFlow Traffic Analyzer 4.1 platform was reported to the Exploit Database.[75] The vulnerability was described as "...a couple SQL injection vulnerabilities in the core Orion service used in most of the Solarwinds products (SAM, IPAM, NPM, NCM, etc...)." The significance of this discovery will be further explained in Chapter 12, however, the DHS pressed on with deployment and integration of NetFlow Analysis in the Albert systems. The platform is a prominent feature of services presented by CIS on the Albert Monitoring webpage.[76]

The timing of an update to a platform as critical as NetFlow Analysis to contain such a significant vulnerability is noteworthy in the opinion of the author of this report. Certainly, companies such as Cisco Systems take into account the deployment points of their tech throughout the world and must take extreme care with each update rolled out for use by all areas of government and

---

[72] https://web.archive.org/web/20161018125245/https://www.dhs.gov/sites/default/files/publications/privacy_pia_28_nppd_ecs_jan2013.pdf

[73] https://www.federalregister.gov/documents/2013/02/19/2013-03915/improving-critical-infrastructure-cybersecurity

[74] https://web.archive.org/web/20161018125255/https://www.dhs.gov/sites/default/files/publications/privacy-pia-28-a-nppd-ecs-november2015.pdf

[75] https://www.exploit-db.com/exploits/36262

[76] https://www.cisecurity.org/services/albert-network-monitoring/

CHAPTER 6

commerce. Considering the vulnerability involved SQL injection capabilities, the level of risk NetFlow Traffic Analyzer 4.1 posed to the systems it was installed upon was, according to the FBI, a vulnerability utilized by nation-state actors. [77] This version of NetFlow Analysis was integrated into networks used by the government monitoring systems during the 2016 election.

Fewer than 25 states utilized the Albert monitoring system prior to 2017. Reuters reported that during the November 8, 2016 Presidential Election of Trump vs. Clinton, only 14 Albert election monitoring systems were in use.[78] On January 6, 2017, the Department of Homeland Security (DHS) Secretary Jeh Johnson declared elections part of the nation's critical infrastructure.[79] (This critical event will be discussed in complete detail later in the timeline of this report.) Because of the multi-levels of collaboration between state and federal agencies, and private companies, the EI-ISAC was formed (Election Infrastructure Information Sharing and Analysis Center) in 2018. "This was at the request of federal government as well as the state and local elections community, who asked CIS to oversee EI-ISAC in order to develop focused products and services for the election community. EI-ISAC offers a forum for election officials, associations, technology vendors, federal partners and cybersecurity experts to share threat landscape information, create educational opportunities and implement technical security controls to help ensure the security and integrity of elections."[80] The aforementioned Bandura Cyber white paper further states, "The Albert Sensor is powered by threat

---

[77] https://www.wired.com/2016/08/hack-brief-fbi-warns-election-sites-got-hacked-eyes-russia/
[78] https://www.reuters.com/article/us-usa-election-cyber/more-u-s-states-deploy-technology-to-track-election-hacking-attempts-idUSKBN1L11VD
[79] https://www.eac.gov/sites/default/files/eac_assets/1/6/starting_point_us_election_systems_as_Critical_Infrastructure.pdf
[80] https://statetechmagazine.com/article/2019/11/states-can-get-election-security-assist-albert-sensors

Countdown to Chaos

intelligence from DHS and CIS, which operates the Multi-State Information Sharing & Analysis Center (MS-ISAC) and the Elections Infrastructure ISAC (EI-ISAC). The Albert sensor also has historical analysis capabilities, with the ability to correlate threat data against historical logs. The threat intelligence that powers Albert is tailored to protect SLTT environments and includes threat intelligence from DHS, MS-ISAC, and election-specific threat intelligence from EI-ISAC."[81]

In 2018, election information was monitored from 135 Albert sensors which were deployed for the midterm primaries and elections. The sensors were active within the voter registration infrastructure as well as election night reporting. In testimony to United States Senate Permanent Subcommittee on Investigations Homeland Security & Government Affairs, CIS CEO John Gilligan provided the following details regarding Albert sensor utilization and deployment for the record: "Moreover, CIS was processing data from 135 Albert sensors monitoring the networks, which supported on-line elections functions such as voter registration and election night reporting. The Albert sensors processed 10 petabytes of data during 2018, resulting in over three thousand actionable notifications to elections offices."[82] Election night monitoring is facilitated through the MS-ISAC Security Operations Center (SOC).

In a 2019 directive by the Ohio Secretary of State, the state reported its contract details with CIS to employ the Albert system into the election system. The 2019 Ohio directive reads: "the Secretary of State's Office will **provide Albert intrusion detection devices to the voting system, epollbook, voter registration system, and remote marking ballot device vendors that are**

---

[81] https://www.nass.org/sites/default/files/2020-01/white-paper-bandura-cyber-nass-winter20.pdf
[82] https://www.hsgac.senate.gov/imo/media/doc/Gilligan%20Testimony.pdf

CHAPTER 6

operational in Ohio."[83] This statement published by the Ohio Secretary of State yields evidence the Albert System has capability to reach inside the firewall into the state and local election environment.

By 2020, all states were using the DHS/CIS Albert Monitoring Services. The CIS Year In Review report for 2020 reported that by the end of the year, 751 total Albert sensors were deployed and monitored in the SLTTs.[84] Many states found funding through federal funds such as HAVA (Help America Vote Act) and the Albert Monitoring Services became integrated directly into state election systems. In the Senate Select Committee on Intelligence Report on "Russian Active Measures Campaigns and Interference" the investigation reported that "As of mid-2018, DHS's ALBERT sensors covered up to 98% of voting infrastructure nationwide, according to Undersecretary Krebs."[85]

With regard to the breadth of the program, in 2018 via PRNewswire, Election Systems and Software (ES&S) announced "...deeper partnerships with the Department of Homeland Security (DHS) and Information Sharing and Analysis Centers (ISAC), plus the installation of advanced threat monitoring, to further security in the U.S. voting environment. First, ES&S will soon begin the installation of **Albert network security sensors in its voter registration environments**. Albert is a unique network security monitoring solution that provides continuous remote monitoring and delivery of automated alerts on both traditional and advanced network threats for state and local jurisdictions, allowing election

---

[83] https://www.ohiosos.gov/globalassets/elections/directives/2019/dir2019-08.pdf?_cf_chl_jschl_tk_=pmd_Bv28nbkvmVJdVHKOHhdxJw00Q6yErlYNQow5yvPV5jI-1629397494-0-gqNtZGzNAlCjcnBszQil

[84] https://learn.cisecurity.org/CIS-YIR-2020

[85] https://www.intelligence.senate.gov/sites/default/files/documents/Report_Volume1.pdf

Countdown to Chaos

jurisdictions and ES&S to respond quickly when data may be at risk. Combined with an in-depth review conducted by expert analysts through the Center for Internet Security's (CIS) 24/7 Security Operations Center, Albert is a fully monitored and managed service which will complement ES&S' existing, robust suite of cybersecurity controls."[86]

In July 2020 Johns Hopkins University, in coordination with the Department of Homeland Security (DHS) and the National Security Agency (NSA)[87], rolled out a pilot SOAR platform called the Integrated Adaptive Cyber Defense framework (IACD) that among other mitigation protocols, includes automated responses.[88] The program was piloted in the states of Arizona, Louisiana, Massachusetts and Texas, in addition to and specifically being deployed in Maricopa County, AZ. [89] Greg Temm, CIRO of FS-ISAC, specifies that part of this program includes, ..."**IDS sensors can be updated with a new signature....through automation.**"[90] As Albert is an IDS Sensor, and as IACD is deployed for use in real time and to act automatically, changes to the election security infrastructure happen immediately and invisibly.

While the CIS and Albert Monitoring System are sold as a high-performance security tool, the CIS Terms of Service expressly state with regard to the user's membership: "You acknowledge and agree that: (1) **no network, system, device, hardware, software, or component can be made fully secure;** (2) **You have the sole responsibility to evaluate the risks** and benefits of the Non-

---

[86] https://www.prnewswire.com/news-releases/ess-establishes-top-level-partnerships-albert-installation-to-further-security-300701631.html
[87] https://thenewstack.io/phantom-coordinates-security-software-playbook-operations/
[88] https://www.cisecurity.org/press-release/johns-hopkins-apl-enlist-states-for-cyber-defense-technology-pilot-program/
[89] https://www.cisecurity.org/media-mention/four-states-join-soar-cybersecurity-automation-pilot/
[90] https://youtu.be/gQ29k-lq_l0?t=243

Member Products to your particular circumstances and requirements; and (3) **CIS is not assuming any of the liabilities associated with your use** of any or all of the Non-Member CIS Products."[91] And further also clearly states with regard to the Albert Sensor: **"CIS does not assume any responsibility or liability for any act or omission or other performance related to the provision of ALBERT MONITORING SERVICES** or for the accuracy of the information provided as part of the services. The services are provided on and "AS-IS" basis, without warranty of any kind, either express or implied."[92]

A further examination of the integration of the Albert Sensor (Albert Monitoring Services), which is closely overseen and indirectly managed by the Department of Homeland Security and the National Security Agency, and a thorough examination of the private information sharing across both public and private lines (EI-ISACs, MS-ISACs, ND-ISACS, EI-SIGs, etc), is critical. Certainly, the fact that the Albert Monitoring Services require a high level of internal and confidential structural and data information be disclosed by the customer as terms of use of the system, when election infrastructure is implicated in the service, a question of management of elections becomes valid and pressing. The Constitution of the United States of America clearly outlines and stipulates that elections are specifically under the purview of state and local governments. The integration of tools and services funded, created, written, and very closely managed by the highest federal government agencies is blurring, if not eliminating the line of jurisdiction regarding elections between federal, state, and local governments.

---

[91] https://www.cisecurity.org/cis-securesuite/cis-securesuite-membership-terms-of-use/
[92] https://www.cisecurity.org/terms-and-conditions-table-of-contents/cis-albert-network-monitoring-services/

Countdown to Chaos

In October 2019, in an interview with ABC News Karen Travers, CISA Director Chris Krebs admitted that the Albert Monitoring System was not protective against attack. In the lead-up to the 2020 Presidential Election Krebs stated, "So earlier this year [2019] we got our fiftieth state up and running on our Albert Sensor, which is our intrusion detection system. It's not going to stop any attacks..." In the same interview Krebs makes another curious comment saying, "We've taken a number of voting machines from the various vendors and taken it to one of our labs and done open ended vulnerability testing."[93] These statements again draw into question the purpose of the Albert Monitoring System as it is not protective in any way. To be sure, all evidence suggests its main value appears to be to the federal government, specifically the DHS, which created the system as a massive nationwide election cybernetwork. Furthermore, testing of voting systems by the federal government leaves the results and the mitigation in the hands of the federal government. Mitigation of election security by the federal government would appear to fit the definition of "election management." Certainly it would be very important to know if state officials were or are ever provided specific details of vulnerabilities found in the election voting machines tested by CISA as described by Krebs in the 2019 interview, or if such results are the intellectual property of simply the federal government and its vendors (i.e. Dominion Voting Systems, Hart Intercivic, etc.).

Notable in the evolution of the federal government's intrusion detection, and network infrastructure building programs is the knowledge that the Albert monitoring system is operated by CrowdStrike's Falcon software. This information was discovered in a Memorandum of Agreement between the Center for Internet Security and a county in Nebraska (the county will remain unnamed at this point to preserve the source of the documentation). The MOA specifies CrowdStrike Falcon runs the system and provides a

---

[93] https://youtu.be/e-DhumE2gal

CHAPTER 6

link to every component that makes up the system.[94] A search of the open-source software that comprises the CrowdStrike Falcon platform in the Vulnerability Database (https://vuldb.com) yielded a number of components with critical unresolved vulnerabilities, including NDK classified as "critical."

Research into this program and the specifications of the CrowdStrike Falcon software for the context of this report uncovered further information that will remain unpublished here pending its verification. The information was hidden in an invisible blogsite file structure on an unassuming location on the web. With great specificity, the post laid out instructions for hacking CrowdStrike Falcon, and discussed it directly in terms of the 2020 Presidential Election. This information, pending verification and further investigation, may be released at a later date.

The initial date of CrowdStrike's deployment into the Albert monitoring system is unclear, however, circumstantial evidence becomes available during testimony given by Shawn Henry in an executive session of the House of Representative's Permanent Select Committee on Intelligence with regard to his part in the events included in the FBI's Crossfire Hurricane investigation. It is within this testimony that Mr. Henry, retained by the Democratic National Committee, acknowledged that his company deployed the CrowdStrike Falcon monitoring system onto the DNC network, stating for the record, "…we deployed technology into the environment 'into the network', software called Falcon that essentially looks at the processes that are running on different computers in the environment."[95] As other testimony by Shawn Henry on the same day mentions monitoring programs in classified terms, there is reason to believe the monitoring system deployed on the DNC system was a version of the Albert network monitor,

---

[94] https://falcon.CrowdStrike.com/login/open-source
[95] https://intelligence.house.gov/uploadedfiles/sh21.pdf

Countdown to Chaos

indicating CrowdStrike likely serviced this system since its inception.

As an update to the information in this chapter since its origin, and to help understand the cybersecurity picture within the United States government at the time of the deployment of the Albert monitoring system in 2011, a few significant events must be reported. In October of 2010, Shawn Henry, a career FBI agent and executive became the Executive Assistant Director (EAD) of the FBI.[96] He was promoted from his previous position as Deputy Assistant Director of the FBI Cyber Division. In his new position as EAC, the FBI Cyber division would fall directly under Shawn Henry's administration and oversight. Appointed to EAD by then FBI Director Robert Mueller, Shawn Henry would remain in the FBI EAD position for about eighteen months, resigning from that position in March of 2012. The day after Henry retired, he took a position at CrowdStrike Services as President.[97] Further, critical, firsthand insight into other circumstances involving Mr. Henry appear in Chapter 8 of this report.

The capabilities of the IDS system referred to as ALBERT were now widely deployed throughout much of the federal government, were being integrated into the networks of SLTTs all over the United States, sat WITHIN the network environment of any system on which it was deployed, and with other complex software platforms being developed, would be **able to automatically respond and update any system within the network environment, remotely and in real-time.**

In a confidential whitepaper that surfaced after the 2020 Presidential Election, more information about Albert came to light which must be considered and interpreted in the scope of this report. A review of the IDS system known as "Albert" by a high-

---

[96] https://intelligence.house.gov/uploadedfiles/sh21.pdf
[97] https://intelligence.house.gov/uploadedfiles/sh21.pdf

CHAPTER 6

level IT analyst yielded information that the hardware embodying the Albert Monitoring System is misplaced in the election environment. The review speculates the placement may be intentional. It states:

> "...the DHS "Albert" sensor is placed above what cyber investigators have already discovered in various locations, i.e. open ports (port 1433 and port 80) where the current threat is possibly accessing real time information on vote totals ... [data] can then be directly injected into the database through port 1433 and 80 without detection or audit trail... The "Albert" sensor is higher up in the operating system and is not seeing the activity below the operating system where threat actors are entering the electronic pollbooks. This seemingly intentional, misplacement of the Albert Sensor is willful, bad, incompetent or all of the above. CISA can say they are watching the networks, while the real game is going on below where the sensor is placed. In other words, DHS/CISA has a camera watching the front door of the warehouse, but the action is taking place at the open, unsecure back door of the warehouse where anyone can walk into the warehouse...
>
> ... These sensors are meant to be installed into every election count facility nationwide and is relayed to an unknown DHS SOC for monitoring of intrusions. A similar system exists within Dominion and their internal network is heavily fortified with SIEM systems."[98]

According to this whitepaper, the DHS, CISA, and CIS's main tool and capability in what they sell as cybersecurity is NOT monitoring open ports. According to the cited review, the IDS is misplaced, and not guarding the right point of the network. The mention of

---

[98] https://spectrumgrp.com/john-mills/

Countdown to Chaos

Dominion within this resource is also a curious and troubling notation. While many individuals in the past year have been publicly criticized and even sued by Dominion Voting Systems over questions and findings about their systems, this report pulls that company back into the technical discussion. This must be addressed thoroughly, particularly finding the reference to a "DHS SOC" which in this scope of this report, appears to be connected to CIS via the EI-ISAC. Further thorough independent investigations must follow this report.

What may prove to be an important topic within the whitepaper quoted above is the mention of Ms. Jen Easterly. The subject matter for which she is discussed in the paper steps just beyond the scope of this report, however, the whitepaper declares that her cyber background, being at the highest levels of military and government, was such that placement of the Albert Sensor was certainly something she should have known everything about. For the record here, Jen Easterly, later named Director of CISA in 2021, had served in other military capacities throughout her career. Her career resume includes:

- Member of the National Security Council as Special Assistant to President Obama and Senior Director for Counterterrorism
- Deputy for Counterterrorism at the National Security Agency
- Executive Assistant to National Security Advisor Condoleezza Rice
- As Lieutenant Colonel, Easterly accepted command of the ANWB (Army Network Warfare Battalion)
- Held command and staff assignments in intelligence and cyber operations, as well as tours of duty in Haiti, the Balkans, Iraq, and Afghanistan.

CHAPTER 6

- Responsible for standing up the Army's first cyber battalion, Easterly was also instrumental in the creation of United States Cyber Command
- Director's fellow for the director of the National Security Agency[99] [100]

The vulnerabilities to the election system via the Albert Monitoring System divulged within the findings of the above cited white paper, if proven to be true, are monumental, as the electronic pollbooks are a part of the election system that sits on an open port. Furthermore, as this report highlighted earlier in this chapter, the potential technical error of placement of the Albert IDS when layered with other high level critical vulnerabilities such as the SQL injection vulnerability discovered in the NetFlow Analysis platform and the critical vulnerabilities reported in the CrowdStrike Falcon software, demonstrates the Albert Monitoring System has incredible problems beyond the Constitutional question of management of elections. The Albert Monitoring System may actually pose more harm to the American election system than it offers as security.

Outside of the extremely important technical problems and vulnerabilities herein reported, the Albert Monitoring System created then and still creates a serious question as to the true management of state and local elections. Harri Hursti, Finnish technologist, founding partner of Nordic Innovation Labs, and featured technology expert in the documentary film *Kill Chain*, stated that the Albert Monitoring System was deployed into the election system prior to the 2016 election with the intention of keeping the system hidden from public knowledge. As Hursti stated in a recent interview, "Elections are all about transparency, and

---

[99] https://www.army.mil/article/10569/army_activates_network_warfare_unit
[100] https://www.newamerica.org/our-people/jen-easterly/

Countdown to Chaos

trust, and evidence, and proof and you have to give that proof..."[101] This federally managed IDS system in and of itself, without regard for the layers of federally engineered agencies protecting this network that will be explained in the next chapters of this report, is an overstep by the federal government into state and local elections, taking far too much of the management of elections away from the people and veiling it in an invisible cyber web.

In the spring and summer of 2022, the first strike against the Albert Monitoring System took place in Washington State. On February 14, 2022, the Ferry County Commission in Northeastern Washington state made the decision to remove the Albert Monitoring System from its election environment. The news organization, NPR, reported the system in these terms:

> "More than 900 Albert sensors have been deployed across the country, primarily to states and counties, and they have been a key component of the federal government's cybersecurity response following Russian election interference around the 2016 election."[102]

The decision by officials in Ferry County, Washington began what led to another county removing the system and a third refusing to implement it. The CISA official charged with spearheading cybersecurity issues leading up to the 2020 Presidential Election, Matt Masterson, stated:

> "There was zero information-sharing going on in the elections realm with relation to cybersecurity until 2016...The less participation, the less broad deployment of Albert sensors — or frankly, to take it out one step

---

[101] https://www.jordanharbinger.com/harri-hursti-the-cyber-war-on-americas-elections/ (16:29)
[102] https://www.npr.org/2022/08/28/1119692541/washington-state-albert-sensor-cybersecurity-election-security

CHAPTER 6

further, the less information being shared broadly across the community, the less secure our elections are..."[103]

The NPR story also stated that Masterson admitted that the need for the Albert Monitoring System was to allow "national visibility." The article further corroborated the Krebs statement made in 2019 as the article stated, "CIS said that while Albert sensors can detect ransomware attacks, they're not foolproof because the program only recognizes known hostile addresses in a rapidly shifting threat landscape," once again validating the function of the Albert Sensor is far more one of national networking and visibility than of security.[104]

Most importantly, the system, in official state documentation and contracts, clearly outlines the fact that the Albert system has the ability to reach every component within the election environment. The federal government by way of the Department of Homeland Security certainly understood this was a very sensitive topic in government and layered multiple quasi-governmental agencies and governing bodies upon each other to make the legal argument exceptionally complex. This report will carefully outline the history, structure, governance, and personnel of the multiple agencies that buffer the Department of Homeland Security from the State legislatures' Constitutional plenary power to administer elections. It is necessary for the citizens of the United States to fully understand the system that has been implemented to oversee perhaps the most important right of each of us - the right to vote, and the right to know that the process was free, fair, and fully transparent.

---

[103] https://www.npr.org/2022/08/28/1119692541/washington-state-albert-sensor-cybersecurity-election-security
[104] https://www.npr.org/2022/08/28/1119692541/washington-state-albert-sensor-cybersecurity-election-security

Countdown to Chaos

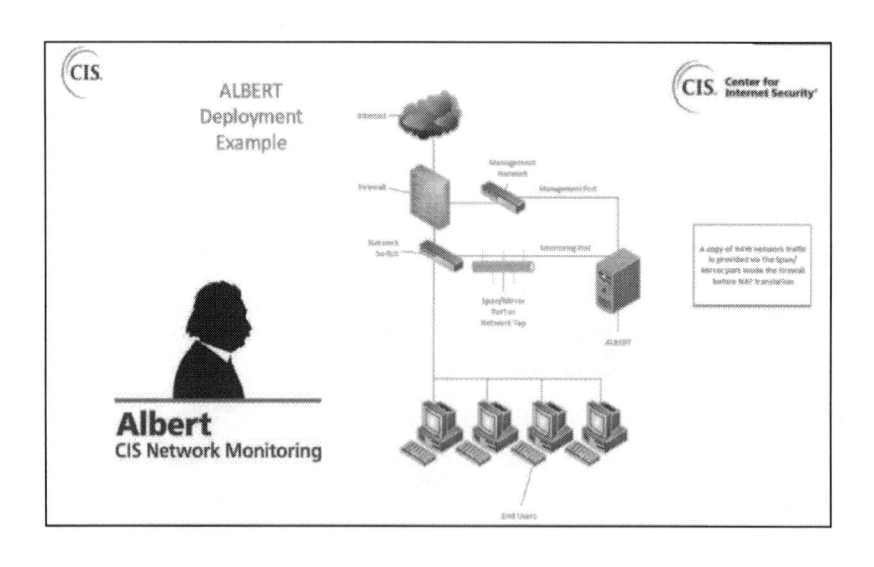

Breadth of Collaboration — The rate of adoption for IACD tenets

ALBERT Deployment Example

Albert
CIS Network Monitoring

CHAPTER 6

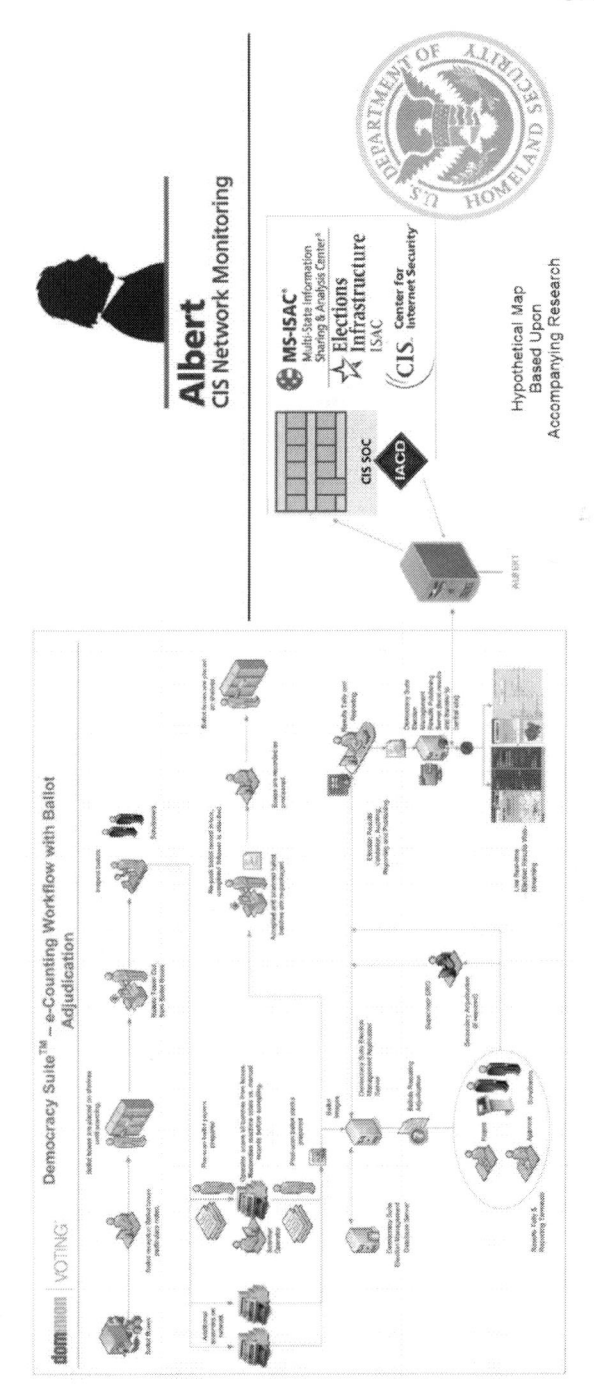

Countdown to Chaos

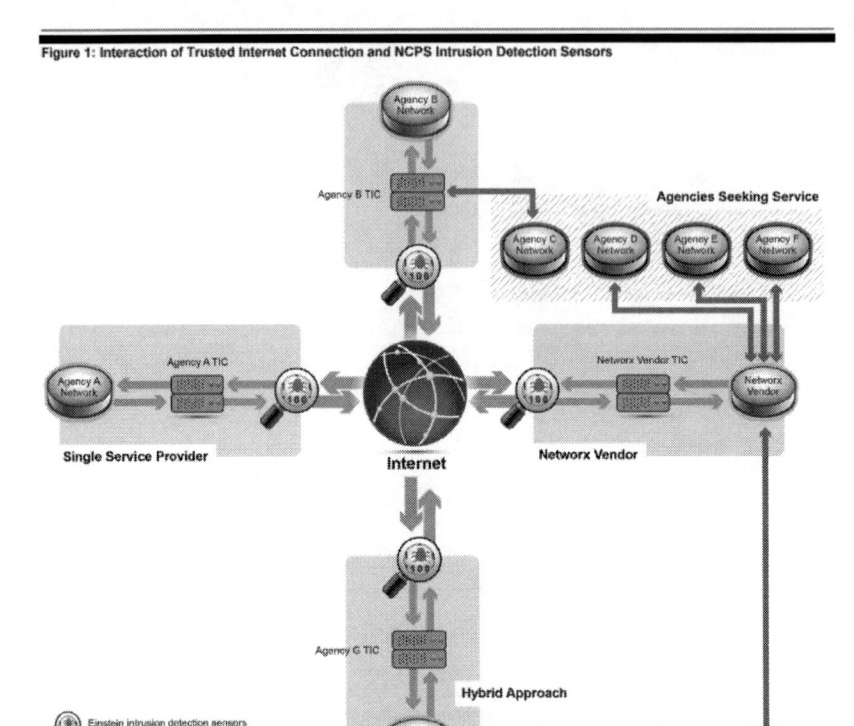

Figure 1: Interaction of Trusted Internet Connection and NCPS Intrusion Detection Sensors

[105]

---

[105] https://www.gao.gov/assets/gao-16-294.pdf

CHAPTER 7

Chapter 7

EINSTEIN 3A, The CIA, IT-ISAC, CrowdStrike, the Birth of Election Related Executive Orders, and the Cybersecurity Act of 2015

(2013-2015)

Upon reflection of the ten years preceding the controversial 2020 election cycle, most if not all citizens would not identify the years from 2013 to 2016 as being anything other than standard, rather common years. The country and the world were in a very slow, practically flatline recovery from the 2008 housing crash and banking implosion overseen by President Barack Obama. However, in context of the timeline built within this report concerning cyber intelligence and network infrastructure, these years begin an escalation of events that allow the result of the 2020 election to be seen through a clearer lens. Each and every historic piece of the cyber intelligence and infrastructure puzzle becomes critically timed and critically placed. A remarkable series of events also began to unfold in this time period with strategically authored and timed executive orders that, when chained from beginning to end, were greatly responsible for making one of the biggest impacts upon the American election system ever in the country's 240-year history.

This period begins on January 16, 2013 with a Privacy Impact Assessment filed by the Department of Homeland Security to act as an underlayment or foundation for the EINSTEIN systems and other systems deployed and monitored by the DHS within the country's critical infrastructure that the DHS has primary management of throughout the country. The PIA states:

> "ECS consists of the operational processes and security oversight required to share unclassified and classified

Countdown to Chaos

> cyber threat indicators with companies that provide internet, network, and communication services to enable those companies to enhance their services to protect U.S. Critical Infrastructure entities. ECS is intended to support U.S. Critical Infrastructure, however, pending deployment of EINSTEIN intrusion prevention capabilities, ECS may also be used to provide equivalent protection to participating Federal civilian Executive Branch agencies….ECS is the latest evolution of the government's efforts to enhance the cybersecurity of critical infrastructure and other private sector networks."[106]

The main focus of the deployment of ECS was on critical infrastructure. To that end, less than a month later, on February 12, 2013, President Barack Obama would sign Executive Order 13636 titled "Improving Critical Infrastructure Cybersecurity" which was the vehicle to direct the ECS program into place throughout the cyber infrastructure. The order reads:

> "The cyber threat to critical infrastructure continues to grow and represents one of the most serious national security challenges we must confront. The national and economic security of the United States depends on the reliable functioning of the Nation's critical infrastructure in the face of such threats. It is the policy of the United States to enhance the security and resilience of the Nation's critical infrastructure and to maintain a cyber environment that encourages efficiency, innovation, and economic prosperity while promoting safety, security, business confidentiality, privacy, and civil liberties. **We can achieve these goals through a partnership with the**

---

[106] https://web.archive.org/web/20161018125245/https://www.dhs.gov/sites/default/files/publications/privacy_pia_28_nppd_ecs_jan2013.pdf

CHAPTER 7

owners and operators of critical infrastructure to improve cybersecurity information sharing and collaboratively develop and implement risk-based standards."[107]

The importance of this executive order will become clear within the perspective of the 2016 Presidential Election. This order and its foundation, apart from being the signature ideology of John Brennan, would become the first in a pivotal string of executive orders that, as mentioned, changed the entire system of American elections.

March 8, 2013, began in this timeline with John O. Brennan being sworn in as the CIA director within the Obama Administration. The nomination and eventual confirmation were not without controversy, however, as Brennan was opposed in a bipartisan manner over his part in Obama White House secretive and controversial policies.[108] The information detailed earlier in Chapter 5 of this report provides a good point of reference with regard to the ideology of the new CIA Director, John O. Brennan. The reader might quickly review that information (including information provided in the citations) prior to reading further in this report. In addition, the later chapter twelve about fusion centers will clarify the depth of John Brennan's influence on the American voting system from 2017 and forward.

A second startling event opening this timeframe is marked by the admission of the leak by the young American intelligence officer, Edward Snowden. In 2009 Snowden moved from the CIA to a position at the NSA. On June 9, 2013, Snowden revealed to the world that the National Security Agency (NSA) was spying on

---

[107] https://www.federalregister.gov/documents/2013/02/19/2013-03915/improving-critical-infrastructure-cybersecurity
[108] https://www.cbsnews.com/news/brennan-confirmed-as-cia-director-but-not-without-drama/

Countdown to Chaos

average Americans and collecting their data every single day.[109] While a startling revelation at the time, in context with the cyber superstructure being created and expanded by the federal government, the revelation of harvesting of private information of ordinary citizens could have very easily been a byproduct of an overarching expansive monitoring program being implemented in all critical sectors of infrastructure and private networks nationwide. While an interesting point of speculation, the Snowden information is simply presented here for context as to the state of the U.S. Intelligence Community in light of the historical timeline being detailed here.

On July 24, 2013, the Department of Homeland Security armed the first federal agency with the new Einstein 3A intrusion detection and mitigation system.[110] The Office of Inspector General of the Department of Homeland Security released an audit report in March of 2014 detailing the upgrades the EINSTEIN 3A (a.k.a. E^{3}A) made to the preceding EINSTEIN 1 and 2 versions. The capabilities of EINSTEIN 3A include:

- "blocking a detected threat by terminating the network connection or restricting access to the target;
- detecting evasion techniques and duplicating a target's processing;
- removing or replacing malicious code within an attack to make it inoperable;
- disrupting an ongoing attack by implementing security controls and **modifying configuration settings in real-time**; and
- collecting more detailed information for a specific session after malicious activity has been detected."[111]

---

[109] https://www.britannica.com/biography/Edward-Snowden
[110] https://www.oig.dhs.gov/assets/Mgmt/2014/OIG_14-52_Mar14.pdf
[111] https://www.oig.dhs.gov/assets/Mgmt/2014/OIG_14-52_Mar14.pdf

CHAPTER 7

Additionally, the report outlines the three components that construct the EINSTEIN 3A system. They are:

- The Intrusion Prevention Security Service
- The Nest
- The Top Secret Mission Operating Environment

The functionality of these components is further described in the DHS report by the Inspector General:

> "...ISPs will deploy the Intrusion Prevention Security Service at Nests, which are Top Secret/Sensitive Compartmented Information facilities located at each ISP. Participating Federal agencies enter into a Memorandum of Agreement with NPPD to authorize the deployment of E3A on their networks. Under the direction of NPPD, ISPs administer threat-based decision making on traffic entering and leaving participating Federal networks. The Top Secret Mission Operating Environment is a Top Secret/Sensitive Compartmented Information network that will be used by US-CERT analysts to conduct day-to-day E3A operations, such as receiving, creating, validating, and refining classified and unclassified indicators."[112]

The report provides the following diagram of the system:

---

[112] https://www.oig.dhs.gov/assets/Mgmt/2014/OIG_14-52_Mar14.pdf

Countdown to Chaos

Top Secret Mission Operating Environment

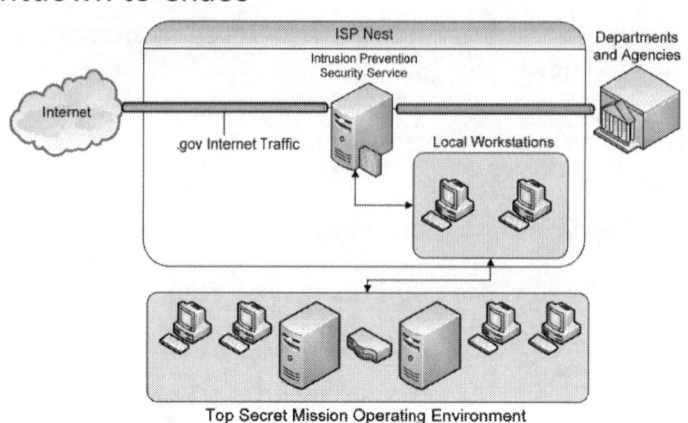

The network diagram the DHS includes with this report clearly shows the "Top Secret Mission Operating Environment" is a portion of the system independently monitored outside the purview and management of the department or agency entity which the system purports to protect. Information flows both into and out of the "Top Secret Mission Operating Environment" and the evolution of EINSTEIN 3A now allows for mitigation and other "changes" to be directed into the network of the agency or department, in real time.

Until this point, there were no audits or inspections of the cyber intrusion program Congress was investing billions of dollars in. The interesting findings of the 2014 DHS Office of the Inspector General audit report of the Einstein 3 Accelerated system would be the first documented inspection of the growing system. The Inspector General released a twenty-seven page report, and the findings included:

- "NPPD needs to address two minor vulnerabilities and out-of-compliance United States Government Configuration Baseline configuration settings.
- ...unmitigated vulnerabilities may expose the system and the data it processes and stores to potential exploits.

CHAPTER 7

- We identified two vulnerabilities that may create opportunities for exploitation of the system... We determined that the vulnerabilities identified could be attributed to the improper configuration of software when the system was initially built and incompatibilities among different software products.
- Mitigation of the vulnerabilities we identified will reduce the risk that sensitive information could be compromised. Additionally, failure to accept risk and account for known out-of-compliance configuration settings in the system Risk Management Matrix could deny the Designated Accrediting Authority updated information to make credible, risk-based decisions regarding E3A."[113]

Clearly, for as bold as the scope of the EINSTEIN 3A program was, the system was clearly found to be vulnerable according to the audit findings. In consideration that the greatest portion of this system was run within an environment titled "Top Secret Mission Operating Environment" the findings take on another level of critical nature.

About one year after the deployment of the EINSTEIN 3A program, an interesting allegation was launched by California Senator Diane Feinstein. On March 11, 2014, the Democrat Senator "said the CIA had searched -- without her knowledge or consent -- a stand-alone computer network established for the committee in its investigation of allegations of CIA abuse..." and "At issue is whether the CIA violated an agreement made with the Senate Intelligence Committee about monitoring the panel's use of CIA computers."[114] CIA Director John Brennan flatly denied any such actions had been undertaken by the agency, however, four months later on July 31,

---

[113] https://www.oig.dhs.gov/assets/Mgmt/2014/OIG_14-52_Mar14.pdf
[114] https://www.washingtonexaminer.com/dianne-feinstein-cia-spied-on-senate-intelligence-committee

Countdown to Chaos

2014, Brennan issued a private apology admitting that the agency did, in fact, spy on the computers of the staff of Senator Feinstein.[115] This incident is mentioned in context with this report as first, the CIA demonstrated in this incident that it had the capability to monitor computers within this system in real time as identified in the *Washington Examiner* article. Secondly, such activity was not outside of the ideology of the director of the agency at the time, John Brennan, who historically not only supported such mass government cyber infrastructure, but wrote and approved papers advocating for similar actions in the realm of information sharing across most any government agency line. Seeing the CIA agency utilizing the abilities of the system is intriguing historical evidence.

Early the next year, on February 12, 2015, President Obama signed an Executive Order promoting private sector cybersecurity information sharing which "encourages the development of information sharing and analysis organizations (ISAOs) to serve as focal points for cybersecurity information sharing and collaboration within the private sector and between the private sector and government. Information Sharing and Analysis Centers (ISACs) are already essential drivers of effective cybersecurity collaboration and could constitute ISAOs under this new framework."[116] This EO enhances and reinforces the policy direction presented by the 2009 Obama Administration White House white paper titled "Cyberspace Policy Review - Assuring a Trusted and Resilient Information and Communications Infrastructure"[117] issued while John Brennan was Deputy National

---

[115] https://www.nbcnews.com/news/us-news/cia-director-brennan-apologizes-senate-leaders-computer-hack-n169706
[116] https://obamawhitehouse.archives.gov/the-press-office/2015/02/12/fact-sheet-executive-order-promoting-private-sector-cybersecurity-inform
[117] https://web.archive.org/web/20110424173823/http://www.whitehouse.gov/assets/documents/Cyberspace_Policy_Review_final.pdf

CHAPTER 7

Security Advisor for Homeland Security within the White House. This EO will also prove to be the predecessor and harbinger of Presidential Executive Orders yet to come that will directly dictate terms and conditions of the cyber security of elections and other protocols. Such actions must be strictly scrutinized in light of Articles I and II of the U.S. Constitution that clearly state, the time, place, and manner of all elections is to be determined by state legislatures. When these executive orders are closely examined in context with the cyber network superstructure that was built by the federal government since 2000, the impending chain of executive orders would build and link the structure together during the Obama years, creating intentional new federal control over elections in the United States through the Executive Branch of the government. The question certainly must be asked and answered whether such orders are, in fact, constitutional. If deemed as such, the American citizen still has the ability to circumvent this incredible federal overreach and power grab. This report will outline this fully as the events continue to unfold.

On March 2, 2015, a vulnerability/exploit of SolarWinds Orion platform was discovered that reported SQL Injection vulnerabilities including to NetFlow Traffic Analyzer 4.1.[118] This information was presented in Chapter 6 regarding the Albert Monitoring Systems, however its significance will loom large in just another year from this point in time. Yet with this discovery documented and shared, the Department of Homeland Security decided in November 2015 to continue to deploy NetFlow Analysis to all of its Enhanced Cybersecurity Services filing a Privacy Impact Assessment (PIA) prior to the rollout.[119] The Department of Homeland Security announced the deployment with a public statement on January 26,

---

[118] https://www.exploit-db.com/exploits/36262
[119] https://fcw.com/articles/2016/01/27/dhs-netflow-analysis.aspx

Countdown to Chaos

2016.[120] **The timing of both the discovery of the vulnerability and the deployment of the system are very curious in light of the 2016 Presidential Election.** An SQL injection vulnerability, according to the FBI, leaves servers and other systems in a network environment, including specifically election environments, susceptible to nation-state attacks.[121] If the exploit was unknown to the DHS, and the agency rolled out the change to the ECS system with this issue present, this would have been a display gross mismanagement and incompetence. However, if the issue was in fact known, then the question must be asked whether the federal government was able to manage the patching and upgrades necessary of every single system in its nationwide infrastructure, to mitigate this serious vulnerability. This technical fact will carry additional significance after the 2020 election cycle and the federal management of the election will become an event that would go under a serious postmortem analysis which continues to the present day. This report will explain the seriousness of these details further in chapters eleven through fourteen.

Additional notable cyber related events at this moment in time include an entry in the month of September 2015, the IT-ISAC (Information Technology – Information Sharing Analysis Center) deployed its automated information capability.[122] About that same time, "on September 16, 2015, the Global Cyber Alliance was formed."[123] In the next month of October of 2015, Shawn Henry, former career FBI agent upper executive, and current President of CrowdStrike Services, joined the Board of Directors of the Global

---

[120] https://web.archive.org/web/20160812172519/https://www.dhs.gov/blog/2016/01/26/dhs%E2%80%99s-enhanced-cybersecurity-services-program-unveils-new-%E2%80%9Cnetflow%E2%80%9D-service-offering

[121] https://www.wired.com/2016/08/hack-brief-fbi-warns-election-sites-got-hacked-eyes-russia/

[122] https://www.it-isac.org/20th-anniversary

[123] https://www.globalcyberalliance.org/our-history/

CHAPTER 7

Cyber Alliance. **Part of the mission of the Global Cyber Alliance, (GCA) was/is the design and support of the Cybersecurity Toolkit for Elections for CIS (launched in 2019).** "The toolkit was designed to augment the security programs of election offices with free operational tools and guidance that have been selected and curated to implement the recommendations in the CIS Handbook for Elections Infrastructure Security." (In 2016, the GCA named Phillip Reitinger, former director of the National Cyber Security Center within the Department of Homeland Security, president of the organization.[124])

The last entry to the U.S. cyber timeline for 2015 is the Congressional Cybersecurity Act of 2015. Referred to as CISA 2015, this act is codified at 6 U.S.C. §§ 1501–1510.[125] CISA outlines the program on its website:

> "Automated Indicator Sharing (AIS), a Cybersecurity and Infrastructure Security Agency (CISA) capability, **enables the real-time exchange of machine-readable cyber threat indicators** and defensive measures to help protect participants of the AIS community and ultimately reduce the prevalence of cyberattacks. The AIS community includes private sector entities; federal departments and agencies; state, local, tribal, and territorial (SLTT) governments; information sharing and analysis centers (ISACs) and information sharing and analysis organizations (ISAOs); and foreign partners and companies. AIS is offered at no cost to participants as part of CISA's mission to work with our public and private sector partners to identify and help mitigate cyber threats through information sharing and provide

---

[124] https://www.globalcyberalliance.org/our-history/
[125] https://www.cisa.gov/sites/default/files/publications/Non-Federal%20Entity%20Sharing%20Guidance%20under%20the%20Cybersecurity%20Information%20Sharing%20Act%20of%202015_1.pdf

technical assistance, upon request, that helps prevent, detect, and respond to incidents."[126]

The Cybersecurity Act of 2015 tasked CISA with providing two-way information sharing and live update capabilities to all participants within the federal and non-federal cyber infrastructure. The participation became free and simple through ISACs and the CIS. The mode of information sharing was set using STIX and TAXII for data transmission and is part of framework of the Albert Monitoring Sytem described in Chapter 6.

The AIS program's "Procedures and Guidance" outlines receipt and sharing of participant data. The access to participant networks (automatically and remotely) is provided for procedurally with somewhat wide-ranging language. In guidance provided non-federal government entities in an official document written by the Department of Homeland Security and the Department of Justice titled "Guidance to Assist Non-Federal Entities to Share Cyber Threat Indicators and Defensive Measures with Federal Entities under the Cybersecurity Information Sharing Act of 2015," entities are told:

> "Similar to cyber threat indicators, defensive measures are composed of an "action, device, procedure, signature, technique, or other measure" that is commonly associated with cybersecurity activities. Some examples of defensive measures include but are not limited to:
>
> • **A computer program** that identifies a pattern of malicious activity in web traffic flowing into an organization.

---

[126] https://www.cisa.gov/ais

CHAPTER 7

- **A signature that could be loaded into a company's intrusion detection system** in order to detect a spear phishing campaign with particular characteristics.

- **A firewall rule** that disallows a type of malicious traffic from entering a network.

- **An algorithm that can search through a cache of network traffic** to discover anomalous patterns that may indicate malicious activity.

- A technique for quickly matching, in an automated manner, the content of an organization's incoming Simple Mail Transfer Protocol (SMTP, a protocol commonly used for email) traffic against a set of content known to be associated with a specific cybersecurity threat without unacceptably degrading the speed of email delivery to end users."[127]

There is no doubt the AIS program not only monitors network traffic as was standard throughout the entire development of the EINSTEIN program, the AIS program set up remote access capabilities to allow providers to access and CHANGE the participant's network environment on demand.

CISA 2015, to encourage non-federal SLTT participation, set up numerous limits to liability with regard to the outlined information sharing structure. These limits to liability include:

- "Exemption from anti-trust laws;

- Exemption from federal, state, tribal, and local disclosure laws;

---

[127] https://www.cisa.gov/sites/default/files/publications/Non-Federal%20Entity%20Sharing%20Guidance%20under%20the%20Cybersecurity%20Information%20Sharing%20Act%20of%202015_1.pdf

Countdown to Chaos

- Exemption from certain state and federal regulatory uses;

- No waiver of privilege for shared material;

- Treated as commercial, financial, and proprietary information when so designated; and

- Not subject to any executive branch rules or judicial doctrine regarding ex parte communications with a decision-making official."[128]

Finally, in context with the timeline of information sharing structures, agencies, and laws, one event in the timeline during the year 2015 is of immense significance and yields evidence that it became an accelerated driver for events that follow it (perhaps including the Cybersecurity Act of 2015). The event that began a tidal wave of maneuvers throughout various areas within the United States government arena happened on June 16, 2015 when Donald J. Trump descended the infamous golden escalator in Trump Tower, New York, and announced his candidacy for President of the United States. Within months a self-described CIA whistleblower would be interviewed for three hours on December 21, 2015 in the Washington D.C. FBI office by FBI agents Walter Giardina and William Bennett.[129] The topic presented by the whistleblower included allegations that the federal agencies had begun spying on candidate for the Presidency, Donald J. Trump.

---

[128] "Participant Protections": https://www.cisa.gov/ais
[129] https://regmedia.co.uk/2017/06/08/01-main.pdf

CHAPTER 8

Chapter 8

EINSTEIN 3, Albert Monitoring, AIS, CrowdStrike, and the Presidential Election (2016)

History will prove the year 2016 and following to be tumultuous in the context of many aspects of American socioeconomic and political life. The country was divided and continuing to become further split apart by many factors. The addition of presidential primaries for both parties added a particularly contentious air among American citizens, and as in nearly every single election, the election of 2016 was being coined the "most important election of our lifetimes". The primaries themselves were peppered with incivility and controversies of their own. While Republicans were split over the candidacy of Donald Trump and questions surrounding his ability to unify the party in leadership of the country, the Democrats were pointing fingers of blame surrounding allegations of election fraud and vote system tampering. Accusations surrounding election impropriety mainly involved the Bernie Sanders campaign charging the Hillary Clinton campaign throughout the primary season.[130] These accusations would crescendo with the final straw that broke the Sanders campaign in California.[131]

Beyond the campaign, Washington bureaucracies and agencies continued their infrastructure work behind the scenes. The timeline in 2016 of this report starts in January, 2016 when The United States Government Accountability Office (GAO) published a report to Congressional Committees titled "INFORMATION SECURITY - DHS Needs to Enhance Capabilities, Improve Planning,

---

[130] https://lawandcrime.com/high-profile/what-actually-happened-in-iowa-caucus-alleged-voter-fraud-video/
[131] https://observer.com/2016/07/california-calls-fraud-demands-dnc-investigation/

Countdown to Chaos

and Support Greater Adoption of Its National Cybersecurity Protection System."[132] The shorthand version of the sixty-one page report simply looks at the entirety of the federal cyber program in light of the billions of dollars invested in it, and the findings reported the system was ineffective and incomplete. In a scathing article about the audit on CSOonline.com the author wrote a headline that shouted the newest government failure loud and clear: "DHS EINSTEIN Firewall Fails to Detect 94% of Threats, Doesn't Monitor Web Traffic - GAO Issued a Harsh Report Following an Audit of Homeland Security's $6 Billion Dollar EINSTEIN Intrusion Detection System."[133]

The opening of the audit findings publishes this immediate statement:

> "The Department of Homeland Security's (DHS) National Cybersecurity Protection System (NCPS) is partially, but not fully, meeting its stated system objectives:
>
> • **INTRUSION DETECTION**: NCPS provides DHS with a **limited ability to detect potentially malicious activity** entering and exiting computer networks at federal agencies. Specifically, NCPS compares network traffic to known patterns of malicious data, or "signatures," but does not detect deviations from predefined baselines of normal network behavior. In addition, **NCPS does not monitor several types of network traffic** and its "signatures" do not address threats that exploit many common security vulnerabilities and thus may be less effective.

---

[132] https://www.gao.gov/assets/gao-16-294.pdf
[133] https://www.csoonline.com/article/3030028/dhs-einstein-firewall-fails-to-detect-94-of-threats-doesnt-monitor-web-traffic.html

CHAPTER 8

- **INTRUSION PREVENTION:** The capability of NCPS to prevent intrusions (e.g., blocking an e-mail determined to be malicious) is limited to the types of network traffic that it monitors. For example, the intrusion prevention function monitors and blocks e-mail. However, it does not address malicious content within web traffic, although **DHS plans to deliver this capability in 2016**.

- **ANALYTICS**: NCPS supports a variety of data analytical tools, including a centralized platform for aggregating data and a capability for analyzing the characteristics of malicious code. In addition, DHS has further enhancements to this capability planned through 2018.

- **INFORMATION SHARING: DHS has yet to develop most of the planned functionality** for NCPS's information-sharing capability, and requirements were only recently approved. Moreover, agencies and DHS did not always agree about whether notifications of potentially malicious activity had been sent or received, and agencies had mixed views about the usefulness of these notifications. Further, DHS did not always solicit—and agencies did not always provide—feedback on them."[134]

A closer in-depth review of the GAO audit reveals the following:

- "...while DHS has developed metrics for measuring the performance of NCPS, they **do not gauge the quality, accuracy, or effectiveness of the system's intrusion detection and prevention capabilities**. As a result, DHS is unable to describe the value provided by NCPS."

- "...current information sharing efforts are manual and largely ad hoc..."

---

[134] https://www.gao.gov/assets/gao-16-294.pdf

Countdown to Chaos

- "Until NCPS's intended capabilities are more fully developed, **DHS will be hampered in its abilities to provide effective cybersecurity**-related support to federal agencies."
- "According to DHS documentation and NSD officials, NCPS was always intended to be a signature-based intrusion detection system, and thus it **does not have the ability to employ multiple intrusion detection methodologies**."
- "...stated **that it is the responsibility of each agency to ensure their networks and information systems are secure**..."
- "By employing only signature-based intrusion detection, NCPS is unable to detect intrusions for which it does not have a valid or active signature deployed. **This limits the overall effectiveness of the program**."
- "NCPS is **not currently evaluating all types of network traffic**."
- "The NCPS intrusion detection signatures provided some degree of coverage for approximately **6 percent of the total vulnerabilities** selected for review (i.e., 29 of 489)."
- "...the current tool DHS uses to manage and track the status of intrusion detection signatures deployed within NCPS **does not have the ability to capture CVE information** [Common Vulnerabilities and Exposures]."
- "US-CERT officials agreed with the results of our analysis of client vulnerabilities, but reiterated that **the goal of NCPS was not to protect against all vulnerabilities**."
- "...officials from one customer agency stated that DHS has no way of determining which of its analysts were responsible for transmitting a particular notification."
- "US-CERT officials stated that **standard operating procedures and a quality control procedure... were not developed**..."

CHAPTER 8

- "Without verifying the receipt of intrusion detection notifications and soliciting feedback on their usefulness, DHS may be hindered in assessing the effectiveness of NCPS's current information-sharing capabilities."
- "…while the Executive Road Map indicates that NCPS will detect malware on customer agency internal networks using log data from DHS's Continuous Diagnostics and Mitigation program, it is unclear how DHS plans to accomplish this."
- **"NCPS is limited in its ability to identify potential threats."**
- "DHS may not be providing the ability to detect attacks that exploit known vulnerabilities."[135]

This GAO report would be the second audit that exposed the EINSTEIN program as deficient at the least and completely ineffective and a waste of federal funds at worst. Yet, with these incredible failures completely exposed, the Department of Homeland Security would continue to march forward with the ALBERT MONITORING program (see Chapter 6 of this report). And while the end users were being sold a system that was a cutting edge, tested intrusion protection system, the facts bore a harshly different story. State and local agencies that would participate in the Albert Monitoring System, in exchange for complete access to their systems and data, were receiving in return, nothing more than a federally built and managed cyber network super structure. These monitors would be deployed throughout SLTTs all over the country, within multiple different government agencies, including, with minimal limitation, election network environments.

In March 2016, the IT-ISAC joined the Department of Homeland Security's Automated Indicator Sharing program (AIS).[136] Other ISACs (including MS-ISAC) added AIS to their security platforms as

---

[135] https://www.gao.gov/assets/gao-16-294.pdf
[136] https://www.it-isac.org/20th-anniversary

Countdown to Chaos

well. These associations further provided SLTT agencies with federal cyber products outlined in this report in the name of "information security" despite audit reports outlining counter-factual information.

In April 2016, in an interesting arena, the CIS and U.S. information sharing policy received an endorsement in a white paper published by the World Economic Forum,[137] an international NGO (non-governmental organization) founded in 1971 by Klaus Schwab. Included as key takeaways within the paper, titled "Global Agenda Council on Cybersecurity" include:

- "Effective collaboration between the public and private sectors requires that they recognize and address the obstacles and limitations to collaboration, including their lack of trust, and difficulties in lawmaking and enforcement, and obstacles to research and information sharing."
- "The public and private sectors, when collaborating in standard-setting, lawmaking and legal enforcement, must find the right balance between government interventions and innovation, and between deliberative legal processes and the need for quick resolutions."
- "It is necessary to experiment with new paradigms for distributed and collaborative governance that will enable cybersecurity challenges to be addressed jointly by the public and private sectors." [138]

Troubling language within this report includes "COMPELLED PARTICIPATION" and "BLENDED GOVERNANCE." Perhaps a more

---

[137] https://www3.weforum.org/docs/GAC16_Cybersecurity_WhitePaper_.pdf
[138] https://www3.weforum.org/docs/GAC16_Cybersecurity_WhitePaper_.pdf

CHAPTER 8

deeply troubling factor beyond the timing of the emergence of this globalist white paper, was that a number of the members of the Global Agenda Council on Cyber Security of the World Economic Forum responsible for drafting the contents of the report and for its publishing ARE AMERICANS. They included:

> **Jane Holl Lute** - President and Chief Executive Officer - Council on CyberSecurity, USA
>
> **Cheri McGuire** - Vice-President, Global Government Affairs and Cyber Security Policy - Symantec Corporation, USA
>
> **Jeffrey Moss** - President - DEF CON, USA
>
> **Catherine Lotrionte** - Assistant Professor of Government and Foreign Service -Georgetown University, USA
>
> **James Stavridis** - Dean, Fletcher School of Law and Diplomacy - Tufts University, USA
>
> **Herbert Lin** - Senior Research Scholar for Cyber Policy and Security - Stanford University, USA
>
> **John Villasenor** - Senior Fellow - Brookings Institution, USA
>
> **Dave DeWalt** - Chief Executive Officer and Chairman of the Board – FireEye, USA[139]

Two Chinese participants made up the Global Agenda Council on Cyber Security as well. They were:

> **John Suffolk** - President and Global Cyber Security and Privacy Officer - Huawei Technologies People's, Republic of China

---

[139] https://www3.weforum.org/docs/GAC16_Cybersecurity_WhitePaper_.pdf

Countdown to Chaos

>**Lee Xiaodong** - President and Chief Executive Officer - China Internet Network Information Center, People's Republic of China[140]

This document is the first piece of evidence in the research of this report that uncovered a true global nature to the "blended governance" of public-private partnerships, and the power structure that was being built and flexed with information sharing. This structure will begin to exponentially expand as the months move forward from this point in time.

A multi-faceted event that began to wildly unfold in April of 2016 found strangely curious connections to the information presented to this point within this report. The event or combination of connected events involved an alleged hack of the Democrat National Committee server which was reported to have happened early in 2016. Additionally connected events came to light years later and have significance having alleged to have happened at this point in the timeline of this report. In addition to a purported hack of the DNC server was the accusation and later verification of simultaneous surveillance of communications of presidential candidate Donald J. Trump. Of critical consequence was the revelation in a Durham federal court filing on April 15, 2022[141] which exposed the Michael Sussman client referred to in all Durham federal filings as "Tech Executive-1." This individual presented Michael Sussman with technical evidence from surveillance he has been alleged to have collected from a phone and server claimed to be in the possession of Donald Trump and/or his team or campaign. The data, that was shared with the FBI by Michael Sussman and further described in CIA notes also filed in the Durham report of April 2022, was reported to have been

---

[140] https://www3.weforum.org/docs/GAC16_Cybersecurity_WhitePaper_.pdf
[141] https://www.scribd.com/document/570091923/70-Memorandum-in-Opposition-Re-Sussmann-Motion-in-Limine-by-USA

CHAPTER 8

collected as early as April 2016. The importance of this date in the timeline will be presented later in this report at the chronological place in time of the Durham filing. The more significant point of this revelation will prove to be the thread of personal and professional relationships interwoven through the individuals and agencies involved in these allegations and their further connections to topics of this report.

As the summer of 2016 forged ahead, its waning days were marked with an important meeting mentioned above. On September 19, 2016, multiple sources including and perhaps primarily the John Durham indictment of Michael Sussman[142] divulge that parallel to Sussman's professional work as counsel to the Clinton campaign along with his role surrounding the alleged Russian hack of the DNC server, Mr. Sussman met with FBI general counsel James Baker. During this meeting Sussman turned over data and evidence to the bureau about surveillance work just referenced above that he had in his possession, keeping the source of the information concealed.

Details of the Sussman/FBI meeting that were released as attachments to the federal filing by U.S. Attorney John Durham included emails and notes from the CIA taken about events that happened in early April 2016 and following through the summer of that year. The information included in the case against Michael Sussman includes the following statement:

> "...while the FBI did not reach an ultimate conclusion regarding the data's accuracy or whether it might have been in whole or in part genuine, spoofed, altered, or fabricated, Agency-2 concluded in early 2017 that the Russian Bank-1 data and Russian Phone Provider-1 data was not "technically plausible," did not "withstand technical scrutiny," "contained gaps," "conflicted with

---

[142] https://www.scribd.com/document/570091923/70-Memorandum-in-Opposition-Re-Sussmann-Motion-in-Limine-by-USA

Countdown to Chaos

[itself]," and was "user created and not machine/tool generated."[143]

With this information revealed by Attorney John Durham about the technical status of data collected by "Tech Executive-1", a seriously troubling picture begins to emerge in the timeline of events of 2016 and moving forward. **According to both caches of evidence presented by John Durham, not only did the parties within the agencies know the information they collected and were using against Donald Trump was false, much, most, or all of it may have been created by those divulging and/or using it.** The facts presented in federal criminal case number 21-582, United States v. Michael Sussman, displayed undisputed evidence of fabricated information that was actively used by individuals within agencies closely connected to the cyber security infrastructure that had become the basis for American election security. Further details of other related actions of John Brennan (CIA), James Comey (FBI), and others in the federal government within the Executive Branch including President Barack Obama and the Department of Homeland Security, that dramatically effected and changed the management of elections in the United States of America will be provided in Chapter 9 of this report. Extensive details involving the John Durham filing's significance to the topics discussed in this report are further discussed in depth in Chapter 15. However, the actions of these key players are important to fully understand moving ahead with information to be further presented within this report.

In response to the cyber intrusion reported by the DNC, Perkins Coie attorney, Michael Sussman, retained CrowdStrike Services President, Shawn Henry, on behalf of the DNC to investigate the

---

[143] https://www.scribd.com/document/570091923/70-Memorandum-in-Opposition-Re-Sussmann-Motion-in-Limine-by-USA

CHAPTER 8

incident.[144] Pertinent information for this report includes a number of statements made by Shawn Henry on December 5, 2017, in sworn testimony to the House Select Committee regarding events of the May and June 2016 examination of the DNC server by CrowdStrike Services. Exchanges of note include the following:

> "MR. [ERIC] SWALWELL: A point of order. My understanding is this interview was unclassified. Is that right? Can we just clarify if the witness had classified -- my sense is that there's some sensitivities around classified information, and this setting is part of the issue.

> MR. STEWART OF UTAH: Okay. Did they indicate to you at any time who they suspected or who they feared, any inference at all about who might have been responsible for this hack, or these hacks?
>
> MR. HENRY: I don't recall when we came in. There had been some I mentioned notification to the DNC in the months prior to the phone call that I received from Sussmann. When Michael Sussmann provided me with information that the FBI had contacted the DNC, he said that they had told him-they used a term that I know is related to the Russian Government.
>
> MR. STEWART OF UTAH: And that was I'm sorry, that was when, at what point in this relationship or this work?
>
> MR. HENRY: I found that out from Sussmann the first day or two after he made notification, so April 30th or May

---

[144] https://intelligence.house.gov/uploadedfiles/sh21.pdf

1st of 2016, but that that notification had been made to the DNC months prior.

MR. STEWART OF UTAH: Okay. So the DNC is notified by the FBI that they've been hacked and that they believe the hack occurred by a foreign government, in this case Russia.

MR. STEWART OF UTAH: And would you just conclude with what you discovered and how you discovered it and what you did with that information?

MR. HENRY: So we did - we did some forensic analysis in the environment. We deployed technology into the environment, into the network, software called Falcon that essentially looks at the processes that are running on different computers in the environment. We also looked historically at the environment, using a different piece of software to look backwards at what was happening in the environment. And we saw activity that we believed was consistent with activity we'd seen previously and had associated with the Russian Government.

MR. STEWART OF UTAH: And can you identify that as being -- with a fair degree of confidence that it's associated with the Russian Government?

MR. HENRY: We said that we had a high degree of confidence it was the Russian Government. And our analysts that looked at it that had looked at these types of attacks before, many different types of attacks similar to this in different environments, certain tools that were used, certain methods by which they were moving in the

CHAPTER 8

environment, and looking at the types of data that was being targeted, that it was consistent with a nation-state adversary and associated with Russian intelligence.

MR. STEWART OF UTAH: Okay. Are there other nation-states that could have -- based on this evidence, that could have been the perpetrator?

MR. HENRY: There are other nation-states that collect this type of intelligence for sure, but the -- what we would call the tactics and techniques were consistent with what we'd seen associated with the Russian state.

MR. CONAWAY: The guys that are doing the cyber forensics, what do they look like?
MR. HENRY: Former U.S. Government, a couple of them.

MR. CONAWAY: FBI?

MR. HENRY: No. DOD, military.

MR. CONAWAY: NSA?

MR. HENRY: NSA. And former contractors or employees of defense contractors. Extensive experience in this area, in computer forensics and in working in this type of an environment.

MR. CONAWAY: Okay. And so the body of stuff that was prepped to be stolen, you can't unequivocally say it was or was not exfiltrated out of DNC, from what you know of?

MR. HENRY: I can't say based on that. But I think I said earlier that there was some - and I want to make sure I'm correct here -- that there were some hash values, which are algorithms essentially, that were provided by the FBI that were consistent with files that were on the DNC. I think that that is accurate.

MR. CONAWAY: So how did the FBI get those if they didn't get them from you?

MR. HENRY: I don't know.

[Discussion off the record.]

MR. HENRY: They had gotten them from documents that had been dumped, and then they created the hash value, the algorithm.

MR.CONAWAY: Oh, it was dumped into the public arena?

MR. HENRY: Yes, sir.

ERIC SWALWELL: One of the questions we're supposed to answer for the public is the sufficiency of the government response to the attack, meaning once the FBI learned about the attack, once the Obama administration learned about the attack, and then actions that were taken. And just in your expertise as a former FBI agent with cyber expertise and working on the private sector, are there any recommendations you would make to the committee, based on your public knowledge and intimate knowledge, having worked partially in this investigation, as to what the government response could have been to have been more effective to stop this intrusion?

SHAWN HENRY: I'd be happy to have that conversation. I don't know – I want to focus on the DNC here, if that's all right.

CHAPTER 8

ERIC SWALWELL: Sure.

SHAWN HENRY: And I would be happy to have that conversation.

ERIC SWALWELL: "And is that, in part, because it would involve conveying to us classified information?

SHAWN HENRY: Yes.

MR. STEWART OF UTAH: Alright. So I think that's one of the more interesting things that we've learned from you today, again, that there is no evidence it was actually exfiltrated. Is it -- it seems unlikely to me that in the real time that they're watching these emails that they'd be able to collect the hundreds or thousands that they had but with screenshots or whatever.

MR. HENRY: So there is circumstantial evidence that it was taken.

MR. STEWART OF UTAH: And circumstantial is less sure than the other evidence you've indicated. Circumstantial evidence is less sure than definitive.

MR. HENRY: So, to go back, because I think it's important to characterize this. We didn't have a network sensor in place that saw data leave. We said that the data left based on the circumstantial evidence. That was a conclusion that we made. when I answered that question, I was trying to be as factually accurate. I want to provide the facts. So I said that we didn't have direct evidence. But we made a conclusion that the data left the network.

MR. STEWART OF UTAH: Okay. That's fair. But it gives us, kind of, context. Some things are more sure than others.

Page 95

> And we appreciate that. Any evidence that any entity other than Russia had access to the DNC servers?
>
> MR. HENRY: We have no evidence of that." [145]

The first point of note was Henry's testimony on page eight of the official transcript where Henry informed the committee that it was the FBI that first informed the DNC about the hack of their system. Further, according to Henry, someone at the FBI notified the DNC, prior to the forensic investigation undertaken by CrowdStrike, that the Russians were identified as the perpetrators of the hack. And while on its own this is not an earth shattering fact that the FBI was involved in the alleged crime prior to the involvement of CrowdStrike Services as this order of events does happen "periodically" according to Henry's testimony, but this point *with the addition* that the FBI informed Sussman and the DNC that the Russians were responsible will prove a curious admission with further facts added to the record by Attorney John Durham in the Spring of 2022.

Another fascinating admission by Henry is that CrowdStrike deployed monitoring software on the DNC network for analysis. He states on the record, **"...we deployed technology into the environment into the network software called Falcon that essentially looks at the processes that are running on different computers in the environment**. We also looked historically at the environment, using a different piece of software to look backwards at what was happening in the environment."[146] This exchange provides important insight into the CrowdStrike Falcon platform. Here it is important to note that Henry stated on the record under oath that **the function of the Falcon technology was to <u>monitor live processes</u> of a various computers within a network environment**. With what is known and has been presented in this

---

[145] https://intelligence.house.gov/uploadedfiles/sh21.pdf
[146] https://intelligence.house.gov/uploadedfiles/sh21.pdf

CHAPTER 8

report about the Albert Monitoring System installed within American election system network environments also being a classified system and proven in later documentation to also run the CrowdStrike Falcon software, a question arises as to whether CrowdStrike may have employed the same identical technology used and networked throughout all government systems within the DNC network environment. If the technology in fact was the same, was any of the information collected, stored, analyzed, and/or reviewed by anyone with any further access to the information sharing framework of the government cyber structure? More information needed to answer this question becomes available in the timeline, appearing in early 2022 with the second John Durham indictment covered in chapter fifteen.

In an exchange between Mr. Conaway and Henry, the topic of the FBI being in possession of "hash values...essentially algorithms" as stated by Henry that the FBI "provided" from the DNC server initiated a sidebar discussion between Henry and his counsel. The question by Mr. Conaway that prompted Henry's off the record discussion with counsel was, "So how did the FBI get those [hash values] if they didn't get them from you?" Henry's answer to the question pointed that the FBI fielded the evidence from public document dumps.

For further understanding, the tech firm Trend Micro defines and explains hash values in this way on their website:

> "Hash values can be thought of as fingerprints for files. The contents of a file are processed through a cryptographic algorithm, and a unique numerical value – the hash value - is produced that identifies the contents of the file. If the contents are modified in any way, the value of the hash will also change significantly. Two

algorithms are currently widely used to produce hash values: the MD5 and SHA1 algorithms."[147]

Understanding both CrowdStrike and the FBI had access to the DNC server environment from the very beginning of the investigation, this question and answer create a bit of a conundrum for both the FBI and Henry. For as CrowdStrike was investigating a hack that was reported to have resulted in the exposure of the stolen data dumped into a public domain (i.e. Wikileaks and DCLeaks.com), the files CrowdStrike was investigating should perfectly match those in the possession of the FBI as well as those published on such sites. Any change of hash values would indicate the information was potentially tampered with between having been stolen and having been published, or between being accessed first by the FBI and then later by CrowdStrike. In essence, this testimony suggests the FBI was providing CrowdStrike forensic information, hash values, that CrowdStrike should have already been in the possession of. Future evidence will draw this exchange into much sharper focus and should leave the reader and American voters questioning each and every bit and byte of data in the chain of custody of all things digital in the American election process.

Another point of interest in the testimony of this day inside the walls of the House Committee came within exchanges between Shawn Henry and California Rep. Eric Swalwell. From very early in the record Swalwell is obsessed with identifying classified topics and steering clear of them. Swalwell's point of order early in the hearing about classified information did not appear to surround his concern about details regarding the action of hacking the DNC, nor any of the information openly being shared about identifying Russian infiltration, purported Russian hackers, or leaked information alleged to have been from the DNC server. Rather, the context of Swalwell's focus on classification of information

---

[147] https://www.trendmicro.com/vinfo/us/security/definition/hash-values

CHAPTER 8

apparently curiously surrounded the remediation solution, CrowdStrike Falcon.

Finally, Henry reveals in testimony that a number of employees within the CrowdStrike Services cyber forensic division are former government employees. These employees moved to CrowdStrike from the Department of Defense, the NSA, and the military according to Henry, himself a former high-ranking FBI official.

In order to see this incident from another angle, the testimony of Yared Tamene was also reviewed. Mr. Tamene was a contracted employee for the DNC, officially employed by Management Information Systems, Inc., and was tasked with managing and maintaining the IT network and security infrastructure of the Democratic National Committee. Mr. Tamene testified to the House of Representatives in an Executive Session of the Permanent Committee on House Intelligence. This testimony was given four months prior to the testimony of CrowdStrike Services President, Shawn Henry, and took place on August 30, 2017. The testimony of Mr. Tamene confirmed that it was the FBI that initiated the alert regarding the purported hacking of the DNC network. Within just days the FBI had attributed the hack to Russian hackers, later naming a hacking team from the Russian government. The testimony yielded a curious pattern in which the FBI appeared to lead Mr. Tamene to specific incidences of intrusion. Additionally, Mr. Tamene's testimony revealed that not only was the FBI working on the case, but other agencies in the wider Intelligence Community were also involved very early in identifying the reported hack. Mr. Tamene's testimony recorded in the congressional record included these points of interest:

- **"We found nothing on our networks to suggest that what the FBI agent was suspecting were actually true**...
- ... found nothing to corroborate what the FBI had said...

Countdown to Chaos

- ...**the [FBI] agent was speaking with other Intelligence Community agencies**, and they were providing him [FBI agent] information that was about 3 weeks or a month or so old...
- ... I would say that **the information that the FBI was providing honestly was frustrating in how redacted it was...**
- ... if I remember correctly, the first time the FBI agent mentioned Russia I think was in a phone call I had with him in November of 2015...
- ...one of the things that he [FBI agent] did was provide us with four or five sheets of paper that were cut, you know, a regular 8-and-a-half-by-11 sheet of paper that was cut into pieces, so four or five strips stapled together. And there were one line, one or two lines per page that were timestamps of the kind of activity that he had mentioned in September, the [REDACTED]. **Now, the IP address and the actual web address was redacted**. The only thing that was present was the [REDACTED] and the timestamp... And so what we did was looked at the logs that we had, looked at timestamps. We expanded the timestamp. These were, if I remember correctly, December 2015 timestamps. So we looked in November through January to see if just in case time zones and whatever were different. **And we didn't find anything to corroborate what those strips of paper had mentioned...**
- ... one of the things that the agent did was send to me an email listing personnel, DNC personnel email addresses, stating that these email addresses were sent phishing attacks by the same adversaries that he's interested in, right. And so can I confirm that these mailboxes exist and if they were -- they got an email with subject lines and so on and so on, timestamp so-and-so, and, you know, anything you can tell us about that...I'm sorry, but let's say

CHAPTER 8

three or four at least of the email addresses that the FBI had listed were valid email addresses. And we did confirm that the subject line, email, and timestamp were valid, and emails were sent to those mailboxes on those dates with the subject lines that matched what the FBI had said. The only problem is that they didn't actually make it to the mailboxes themselves, because **our spam filter had caught them all as phishing attacks and blocked them from being delivered. We confirmed that they didn't actually make it. We sent him evidence to confirm that back in email form to the FBI...** With specific emails being sent to specific email addresses and us looking at it. And I think of all of them, one email had been delivered to a mailbox that was a phishing attempt that we confirmed using our spam filter logs and exchange logs, but we confirmed that that was not actually opened. It was immediately deleted...

- ...Then came the next question from the FBI, which was I want to say early April of 2016, where **the FBI asked us to provide them logs, which is, in effect, metadata about emails, from our exchange servers...**

- ... On the 28th. So we saw sort of very loud activity, if you will, on one of our Window servers that couldn't have been done by one of us... It had nothing to do with anything that the FBI had said up to that point...I want to also say that the actors that we noticed, it turns out, on the 28th of April were different actors than the FBI had been looking at.. What we found was another one called Fancy Bear or APT-28 on April 28th, right, unfortunately...

- ...**we stopped looking for what-ifs as soon as we had CrowdStrike in place**, because they're experts in the field, and they had toolsets that were able to get the full scope and nature of what was going on relatively quickly, within, I don't know, a few days of us engaging with them...

Countdown to Chaos

- ...And so, thankfully, **one of the people on the phone was, I had mentioned before, Michael Sussmann, who knows a lot about this space and knew Shawn Henry from CrowdStrike** as well. And so we got on the phone with Shawn Henry, who's, you know, a former FBI employee, served as executive assistant director investigating cybercrimes, which is the kind of expertise that we needed. And so we got on the phone with Shawn Henry and another gentleman named Chris Scott, who worked for CrowdStrike...
- ...the FBI had already identified APT-29, Cozy Bear, as having been on the DNC network... **They hadn't given us concrete evidence to say that this was actually happening...**
- ...They had given them the name Cozy Bear for APT-29 and Fancy Bear for APT-28. And CrowdStrike uses terms like "bear" to refer to Russians, Russian Government-sponsored agents or adversaries... So, **from that moment on [first Monday in May 2016], the FBI's requests for information were being handled directly from CrowdStrike...**
- Q: At some point, did the FBI reach, independently, conclusions consistent with CrowdStrike's, do you know? MR. TAMENE: Well, I don't know if it was independent or influenced or -- I don't know. But I do know of reports that were published, statements and reports that were published by the FBI, the Department of Homeland Security, by the Office of Director of National Intelligence that came in the fall, in October, in December, and then in January of 2017, that had statements that were concurrent or confirmed the conclusions that CrowdStrike had reached from their analysis and their forensic analysis and their investigation of web traffic, systems logs, any unusual behavior within the DNC systems...

CHAPTER 8

- Q: ...you said CrowdStrike made the decisions over which servers to mirror, copy, slash –
A: [TAMENE] Correct. Clone.
Q: ...so they didn't copy all the servers that the DNC has, right?
A: [TAMENE] Correct...I want to say 38 systems. Some of those systems were laptops, for instance, right? And, you know, I think one or two of them were interesting enough for us to clone them to see if they had any forensic value...
Q: -- but whatever servers and systems were copied, mirrored, cloned, that material was given over to the FBI.
A: [TAMENE] My understanding is yes. **I don't know if all of it was given** -- ... I mean, CrowdStrike didn't do any copying and mirroring. We did... provided those to CrowdStrike. And **CrowdStrike may not have given all the things to the FBI...**"

- Q: So CrowdStrike was brought in on or about [Sunday] May 1st, 2016, for everything we're talking about here.
A: [TAMENE] Correct.
Q: When was the DNC's first contact with the FBI in regards to what we're discussing here?
A: [TAMENE] September 2015 is the first phone call that I received.
MR. ELIAS: I think he means in May, right?
[REDACTED QUESTIONER]: Yeah, just so we're clear, you engaged CrowdStrike after you discovered -
MR. TAMENE: Evidence
[REDACTED QUESTIONER]: - evidence -
MR. TAMENE: Right. Correct.
[REDACTED QUESTIONER]: - not because of the FBI contacting them
MR. TAMENE: ...so May 3rd or 4th [Tuesday or Wednesday] is when **[FBI] Agent [REDACTED] confirmed that he had reached out to Robert Johnson**

Countdown to Chaos

> **[CrowdStrike], they had spoken.** And Robert Johnson confirmed that, as well, on the phone. I mean, I had a 9:00 a.m. phone call with Robert Johnson everyday for, oh, I don't know, 2 months.
>
> - ...One thing in addition to that that **he [FBI Agent] did is send a script to run on our systems** to see if we could find some activity. And that was **in April, I think, of 2016. And we ran that script or a modified version of that script in May...**"[148]

Of the comments from the testimony of Mr. Yared Tamene in the congressional record, a few interesting points surfaced while other questions arose. Important points of fact as presented for the record include that the FBI not only informed the DNC of a purported hack with apparently no visible evidence from the DNC server itself, but the FBI attributed the activity to Russia almost immediately. For months, with time and date stamps provided to Mr. Tamene by the FBI, none of the activity the FBI was reporting as a Russian hack was discovered and corroborated on any of the DNC servers or client machines. Also of interest, and worthy of not glossing over, was Mr. Tamene's statement to the committee that from the very beginning, the FBI "was speaking with other Intelligence Community agencies, and they were providing him [FBI agent] information."

Other facts found in Mr. Tamene's testimony include the curious apparent exchange of information between the FBI and CrowdStrike before anyone at the DNC had any personnel from CrowdStrike on the premises to examine the server environment and the ongoing situation. The timing of this FBI-CrowdStrike exchange seems unusual, as does the apparent need for the revelation of that information by Yared Tamene to the House

---

[148] https://www.dni.gov/files/HPSCI_Transcripts/Yareda_Tamene-MTR_Redacted.pdf

CHAPTER 8

Committee to be interrupted by Attorney Mark Elias. A questioner in that exchange was curiously redacted as well.

Another curiosity from the hours of testimony was Mr. Tamene's divulgence of the fact that while no hacking activity was found in the DNC system, the FBI also never presented any other concrete evidence to the DNC of any such hack. The first time any unusual activity appeared was April 28, 2016, long after the FBI alerted the DNC of a hack in 2015. CrowdStrike took over the entirety of the remediation efforts just one or two days after the first activity was discovered. Mr. Tamene testified that he and his team yielded all investigative activities to CrowdStrike from that point forward.

Another point of interest within the witness statements of Yared Tamene was the FBI's knowledge of a purported phishing email sent to the DNC. Interestingly, the FBI had knowledge of the sender, a list of the recipients, the subject of the email, and may have had some knowledge of the body of the email as the FBI labeled it as "phishing." The email was finally discovered, but with all but one in a spam filter. The single email making it to a recipient, Mr. Tamene testified was confirmed unopened. Mr. Tamene immediately sent that evidence to the FBI. The level of knowledge of the details of this email by the FBI, its status confirmed by Mr. Tamene as "isolated" and "unopened," as well as the request by the FBI for internal metadata from the email exchange server is curious and worthy of facing further scrutiny. Clearly the request for the metadata required a multi-level administrative and legal review and approval process. This approval process ended up including attorney Michael Sussman.

Further information of note in the testimony of Yared Tamene was that the FBI ran a script of some type on the server on two separate occasions. One script was received in late April, and another in May. As this situation was being described as a sensitive hacking attempt, why would anyone change the environment of what

Countdown to Chaos

should be a forensic investigation with something that can change multiple system settings such as a script?

This inquiry segways into other questions this testimony raises: First, if the FBI was truly watching the nation-state of Russia, specifically who the agency believed was the Russian government hacking the DNC servers, why didn't they take immediate action to block those IP addresses or activity? Why, when trying to lead the DNC IT security team to the purported evidence of a foreign hack, did the FBI redact very important key information to find the access and the damage, such as the alleged infiltrating IP addresses? Furthermore, considering the information known about the alleged phishing email, how was the FBI able to intercept such an email sent to a private company? If the FBI's intercept of this email was legitimate, why wasn't the email isolated and remediated immediately if it was truly being sent from a threatening nation state hacker? Why didn't the FBI present the phishing email in an isolated environment, not allowing it to actually reach its destination? Was the phishing email the source of what the FBI felt was a server hack? If the FBI believed the phishing email was the back door into the DNC server, how does one explain the evidence presented by the DNC IT security team led by Yared Tamene that all but one email was isolated in a spam filter, and the last one reaching its destination was confirmed unopened? What was the script the FBI asked the DNC to run on their system and why did they ask for the DNC to run such a script/program? Did the DNC know specifically what the script did versus just trusting what someone told them it would do? Was the script fully vetted before installation? Did the script in any way pervert the forensic integrity of the system being monitored?

The points to follow summarize the facts yielded in both the Yared Tamene testimony to the House of Representatives on August 30, 2017, and the Shawn Henry testimony to the House of Representatives on December 5, 2017:

CHAPTER 8

- The FBI was the first organization to notify the DNC that they were hacked, as early as November 2015.
- The FBI told the DNC prior to CrowdStrike's involvement in the investigation that the Russian government was responsible for the hack.
- All information given to the DNC IT security to lead them to the purported hacker entry point was heavily redacted. The FBI only included time and date stamps for identification of the breach. The IP addresses of the origin of the hack were not provided.
- The DNC IT security team headed by Yared Tamene was unable to confirm any breach with the information the FBI presented to them.
- After CrowdStrike stepped into the investigation, the DNC IT security team yielded the investigation to them.
- Michael Sussman and Shawn Henry had a known professional relationship.
- **CrowdStrike Falcon software technology runs within an environment to monitor live processes**.
- The use of CrowdStrike Falcon by the government happens in a classified manner.
- The FBI was in possession of forensic data, namely hash values, that were either not in the possession of or different from data in the possession of CrowdStrike Services.
- CrowdStrike has a forensic team that is partly populated by former federal government employees. Shawn Henry is also a former employee of the FBI.
- The evidence regarding Russian hackers' purported access to the DNC server was considered circumstantial.
- Yared Tamene, the IT Security professional contracted by the DNC, stated in his testimony that the FBI never provided any concrete proof that a hack had actually occurred.

Countdown to Chaos

- CrowdStrike could not confirm if data was in fact exfiltrated from the DNC server.
- Shawn Henry stated on the record that there was *no doubt* that Russian hackers infiltrated the DNC server.

With these facts enumerated, the questions worthy of further investigation are: Why did the FBI have forensic evidence that CrowdStrike did not initially possess according to the testimony of Shawn Henry, when CrowdStrike was the firm hired to assess and confirm the forensic footprints of an alleged hack? As the FBI was the first to notify the DNC of the alleged hack of its server, and to assign responsibility to the Russian government, was the recommendation to retain CrowdStrike Services also provided to the DNC by the FBI? Was the choice to retain CrowdStrike Services at all based upon the CrowdStrike Services President Shawn Henry's previous position at the FBI as Executive Assistant Director of Cyber Security? Was the choice to retain CrowdStrike Services at all based upon the number of former federal agents and contractors employed by their cyber forensics division? All of these points will be worthy of review after the reader of this report has consumed the remainder in its entirety as there are some very interesting points in the timeline here that cannot be ignored.

The classified nature of the use of CrowdStrike Falcon technology by the government alluded to in the testimony lends itself to details of ongoing sensitive government operations later unsealed in the Durham indictment. The Sussman indictment and later trial alleged that information that was being collected and analyzed under the direction of a government agency as reported in the Sussman indictment was allegedly about Donald Trump and was originating from the framework of a classified government project. According to the indictment this information WAS shared by some mode or method from within the government collection project to the Clinton campaign. The new questions that need asking are, what type of information being monitored by a government monitoring

CHAPTER 8

system would have been of interest to the Clinton campaign and was the system used for purposes beyond its assigned scope? What role, if any, did CrowdStrike Falcon technology play in the monitoring and collection of the data within the government operation described in the Durham case? Who or what was the mode of sharing the information? The findings in the case USA vs. Sussman further reinforce the questions posed above as well as those just asked originating from the testimony given to the House Select Committee by CrowdStrike's Shawn Henry.

Some hints to answers to some of these questions become addressed in John Durham's second filing in February of 2022 and discussed chronologically in chapter fifteen of this report. However, of important note at this precise moment in time, on September 27, 2016, members of the Department of Justice exchanged emails with Michael Sussman asking for key digital evidence needed to corroborate the allegations being made regarding Russian hacking attempts.[149] A similar, more in depth request was further made by the FBI as shown in an email exchange between Sussman and FBI agent Adrian Hawkins dated September 30, 2016. The digital evidence the FBI sought included hard drive images, system, Netflow, and firewall logs, in addition to an *unredacted* security report compiled by CrowdStrike Services.[150]

Additional pertinent evidence which later appeared in Volume 1 of the Senate report on Russian interference in elections from the United States Senate Select Committee on Intelligence completed many months after the alleged DNC hack and Trump surveillance events occurred, detailed a coordinated effort during the summer of 2016 by the DHS and the FBI to reach out to states on the topic of cyber security. The committee reported:

---

[149] https://www.documentcloud.org/documents/22046130-dx-147_redacted
[150] https://www.documentcloud.org/documents/22046130-dx-147_redacted

Countdown to Chaos

> "For DHS and other agencies and departments tasked with intelligence collection or formulating policy options through the interagency process, **the full scope of the threat began to emerge in the summer of 2016.** Secretary Johnson told the Committee that "**I know I had significant concerns by [summer of 2016]** about doing all we could to ensure the cybersecurity of our election systems. Mr. Daniel said in his interview that by the end of July, **the interagency was focused on better protecting electoral infrastructure as part of a 'DHS and FBI-led domestic effort.'**"[151]

The actions detailed about Secretary Jeh Johnson will take on further significance after the 2016 Presidential Election. It is important to note here however, that already in 2016, while Shawn Henry was working closely with the FBI and Michael Sussman was meeting with FBI general counsel James Baker, both being the result of the alleged DNC server hack, Jeh Johnson and the DHS were simultaneously hard at work with the FBI reaching out to individual states on the topic of elections in the name of cybersecurity. In testimony further reported in the Senate report, DHS officials admitted the resulting phone calls to state officials did not go well. Details given in the report were:

> "States also reported that the call did not go well...DHS also did not anticipate a certain level of suspicion from the states toward the federal government. As a State 17 official told the Committee, 'when someone says 'we're

---

[151]

https://www.intelligence.senate.gov/sites/default/files/documents/Report_Volume1.pdf

CHAPTER 8

from the government and we're here to help,' it's generally not a good thing.'"[152]

Additional details about these calls and actions will be reported in the chapter to follow; however, within this context, this report pivots back to an interesting and troubling incident just weeks later in early October 2016 involving CrowdStrike's Shawn Henry. The incident was documented in an interview by former member of the National Security Council at the White House, and senior Department of Defense representative for the Comprehensive National Cybersecurity Initiative (CNCI), Col. John Mills (Ret.). While Henry is not mentioned by name, the full description of the incident leaves little doubt the individual recounted in the event was Henry. On October 6, 2016, Col. John Mills detailed attending a dinner in London, England, while he was in the country for meetings regarding information sharing. Mills described the dinner as one attended by globalist dignitaries, many from the intelligence community. He recalls the typical format of these evenings consisted of attendees introducing themselves as they stood up to address the group. When the microphone passed to who this report can identify as Shawn Henry, Mills described the incident in the following terms:

> "[In] this serendipitous but incredibly important meeting, on a plane, going to London in early October of 2016, which, where I met, a very senior former FBI official who then... retired and worked and still works for a cybersecurity company. He was unclear, and really wouldn't share why he was there. I would also even more serendipitously, if there's such an expression, had a dinner with him, that I didn't even know even after

---

[152]

https://www.intelligence.senate.gov/sites/default/files/documents/Report_Volume1.pdf

being on the plane with him. And [at the dinner] he had a meltdown – because we would all go around the room and tell people what our passions were – and he said, "We are going to show and prove Trump is a Russian asset." You've got to remember, this is early October 2016. This is a dinner party essentially filled with people you would call globalists and elites. I was not one, but I was invited because I knew several of the people. I was a Trump supporter…probably one of the few, but when this former senior FBI official, who I'd trusted and known for years, been at many meetings with, helped provide security for me when I was on a sensitive overseas trip, most people had no idea what he was talking about in October '16 because one, everybody felt Hillary was going to beat Trump, and two, the Russia story was really not a known thing at that time. So [it was] very curious."[153]

This incident in London in the context of Henry's other activities during the summer of 2016 create huge red flags. Again, the reader might find it beneficial to earmark these facts and reread this information after consuming the rest of this report.

Back in America at this point in time, **as the FBI and DOJ were still waiting for digital forensic evidence to be sent to agencies from CrowdStrike,** the Russian hack and interference narratives were being hotly distributed. On October 7, 2016, Barack Obama gave approval for the Intelligence Community (USIC) to make an official statement regarding Russian hacking of the DNC (specifically naming an identity "Guccifer 2.0") and potential hacking of the American election system. In that statement the USIC implicitly states:

---

[153] https://frankspeech.com/video/ret-col-john-mills-recaps-how-false-narrative-linking-president-trump-russia-was-created-and

CHAPTER 8

"The U.S. Intelligence Community (USIC) is confident that the Russian Government directed the recent compromises of e-mails from US persons and institutions, including from US political organizations. The recent disclosures of alleged hacked e-mails on sites like DCLeaks.com and WikiLeaks and by the Guccifer 2.0 online persona are consistent with the methods and motivations of Russian-directed efforts. **These thefts and disclosures are intended to interfere with the US election process.** Such activity is not new to Moscow—the Russians have used similar tactics and techniques across Europe and Eurasia, for example, to influence public opinion there. We believe, based on the scope and sensitivity of these efforts, that only Russia's senior-most officials could have authorized these activities.

Some states have also recently seen scanning and probing of their election-related systems, which in most cases originated from servers operated by a Russian company...

Nevertheless, **DHS continues to urge state and local election officials to be vigilant and seek cybersecurity assistance from DHS.** A number of states have already done so. **DHS is providing several services to state and local election officials to assist in their cybersecurity.** These services include cyber "hygiene" scans of Internet-facing systems, risk and vulnerability assessments, information sharing about cyber incidents, and best practices for securing voter registration databases and addressing potential cyber threats."[154]

---

[154] https://www.dhs.gov/news/2016/10/07/joint-statement-department-homeland-security-and-office-director-national

Countdown to Chaos

On October, 13, 2016, six days *after* the Obama-authorized USIC statement blaming Russia for the DNC hack was made, another email exchange between Michael Sussman, a member of CrowdStrike, and the FBI demonstrated **the federal bureau was still not yet in possession of the forensic digital image evidence they had requested necessary to corroborate the allegations** and official statement being made that the Russians were the perpetrators of the alleged hacking activity reported by Sussman.[155] Of further interest in the Obama-approved October 7, 2016 statement is the attribution of the DNC hack to the Russian Government, outing of the specific identity of the hacker as "Guccifer 2.0" who the U.S. Intelligence Community attempted to connect to a previous Russian entity known as "GRU".[156] With the information presented in court proceedings by Robert Mueller and the Department of Justice, independent investigators including IT investigator Adam Carter, did a multi-years-long review of the data and found minimally the information presented by the United States Government "fails to conclusively demonstrate that the GRU were responsible for that which has been attributed to them." By the end of the independent investigation, after years of digging through all data and metadata, the group found:

> "...some of Guccifer 2.0's Russian breadcrumbs were created through deliberate processes and some of the evidence providing Russian signals seems contrived.
>
> We have found that, when digging beyond the Russian breadcrumbs scattered on the surface, there are conflicts that point to other locales (within the US).
>
> Regarding time zone indicia, we have found more unique types of time zone indication that point to US time zones

---

[155] https://www.documentcloud.org/documents/22046125-dx-152_redacted
[156] https://www.justice.gov/file/1080281/download

CHAPTER 8

than Russian for which we haven't seen a coherent explanation.

There are numerous inconsistencies in the evidence relied upon by those attributing Guccifer 2.0 to the GRU and a significant volume of evidence exists that, especially for time zone indicators, almost uniformly suggests a different origin for Guccifer 2.0.

We don't need conspiracy theories.

The available evidence, considered in aggregate, clearly provides ample justification for skepticism of the GRU attribution."[157]

With the fully documented review of the Guccifer 2.0 attribution provided by this independent investigative team of Mr. Adam Carter, serious questions arise regarding the validity of the government's October 6, 2016 statement. The timing of the emails between Michael Sussman, CrowdStrike, and FBI coupled with the details in the announcement raise many more questions about the motives behind the USIC statement. Clearly, **the statement included certain language directing states' election officials toward the federally instituted DHS election security data management solution.**

As the facts surrounding events now referred to as Crossfire Hurricane unfolded during the summer of 2016, the London dinner incident coupled with the other information presented in this report regarding Shawn Henry, the company CrowdStrike, the Albert Monitoring System, Michael Sussman, John Brennan, the FBI, DHS movements, the USIC statement, and the federal cybernetwork superstructure, all raise very serious issues both legally for the participants' actions and Constitutionally for the voters regarding every part of the election systems governed by the

---

[157] http://g-2.space/guccifer2-evidence-versus-gru-attribution/#s24

Countdown to Chaos

Department of Homeland Security. The storm of actions that took place from this point in time through Inauguration Day 2017 was an incredible display of minimally flagrant abuses of power and perhaps maximally illegal criminal behavior, the repercussions of which may prove to be difficult to diffuse and remediate.

To wrap up the tumultuous year of 2016, it was also during October 2016, as documents and intelligence later declassified by acting Director of National Intelligence, Ric Grenell, detailed regarding this time period, CIA Director John Brennan and FBI Director Jim Comey continued moving forward with intelligence their respective agencies were reviewing regarding Russian interference in the 2016 election and the Trump campaign, **even though they knew the intelligence was false**.[158] Brennan and Comey would continue to move the machinery of the federal government in an offensive attack using this information they knew was false up to and past Inauguration Day, 2017.

A month later, in November 2016, just prior to the election, according to the indictment unsealed in the John Durham investigation (USA v. Sussmann Criminal Case No. 21-582, unsealed in Sept. 2021), the government case described evidence of a contract having been signed between an unnamed government agency and a university to enable researchers who worked under the "Agency-I Contract" to "protect U.S. networks from cyberattacks." Identities in this indictment and case will be revealed later in this timeline. Of interest at this point is that some information provided in this indictment was considered classified. Researchers working on the classified project also provided data harvested within the scope of the project to Clinton campaign.[159] Based upon what has been revealed in this report to this point, one

---

[158] https://www.hsgac.senate.gov/imo/media/doc/2020-04-16%20RHJ-CEG%20to%20FBI%20(Crossfire%20Hurricane%20Intel%20Memos).pdf
[159] https://www.justice.gov/sco/press-release/file/1433511/download

CHAPTER 8

must wonder, was the government agency work revealed in the Sussman indictment to "protect U.S. networks from cyberattacks" in any way connected to government work rooted in EINSTEIN 1, 2, 3, 3A, or ALBERT?

This report opened with a few questions that need answering, but the revelations within the investigation have clearly made the entire picture far more complex due to the nature and scope of the information this report presents within it. All Americans need to consider the list of questions developed during this investigation that appear near the end of the report. The depth of information here presented has exposed that the state and local election systems now belong to a complex federal cyber network infrastructure governed by private quasi-government entities. Who is now truly running American elections? Who is responsible for the data and network information on either side of the federal cyber structure? Who can see SLTT data and when is it shared? How secure is that data? How true and accurate is the data? When is the non-federal data available to other information sharing entities? Is the portion of the election network system that is considered "classified" transparent to appropriate state and local election officials and ultimately to the American people for whom the Constitution guarantees the right to free and fair elections?

The questions arising from all these issues begin to shine a light on what murky waters become created by the complex structure of network and information sharing created by the layers of quasi-governmental groups that are run just outside the umbrella of the federal government. These operations, while agents/agencies know they are running, are invisible to the user, the general public, and other oversight committees or individuals. In addition, most of these operations are kept outside of the reach of Freedom of Information Act (FOIA) requests. Certainly, the intermingling of both public and private information on systems that can be questioned as to whether their simple existence is either public or

Countdown to Chaos

private at different points in their network architecture, is a serious problem the public should demand clarification about in light of the ever-expanding use of such technology, particularly when it comes to its parallel use in election environments. Additionally, when transparency is lost under the veil of "classified" operations, participants in the process such as Henry, Sussman, Brennan, Comey, Obama, and others yet to appear in this report, are practically free to operate in various roles hidden within this environment and in about any way they desire.

In what will prove to be a pivotal time in American history, on November 8, 2016, Donald J. Trump was elected President of the United States. **Fourteen Albert Sensors were deployed for that election.**[160] Events following this critical moment in time moved furiously and evidence began to hemorrhage from multiple points within the government system.

---

[160] https://www.reuters.com/article/us-usa-election-cyber/more-u-s-states-deploy-technology-to-track-election-hacking-attempts-idUSKBN1L11VD

Chapter 9
Crossfire Hurricane, Critical Infrastructure, SolarWinds, and the GCC (2016 – 2017)

The election of Donald Trump was a surprise to many in 2016, but perhaps none more than career members of what is now commonly termed "The Deep State".[161] Whether one prescribes to the idea of the Deep State or not, the fact is that the federal Intelligence Community (IC) is the entity that is most often assigned the moniker. In December 2016, just a couple days before and after the Electors were to meet and be seated in their respective states, a flurry of activity began within the intelligence community. From entries in the Senate document titled "Timeline of Key Events Related to Crossfire Hurricane Investigation" we find the following activities:

- **Dec. 2, 2016**: Samantha Power and DNI James Clapper ask to unmask the identity of a U.S. person in intelligence reporting that turns out to be [Gen. Michael] Flynn.
- **Dec. 7, 2016**:
    - Samantha Power asks to unmask a U.S. person in intelligence reporting that turns out to be Flynn.
    - *Associated Press* article, "Why Donald Trump's NSA Pick Is Scaring Some National Security Experts."[162]
- **Dec. 14, 2016**: Samantha Power, John Brennan, Treasury Secretary Jacob Lew, and five other Treasury Department officials ask to unmask a U.S. person in intelligence reporting that turns out to be Flynn.

---

[161] https://www.huffpost.com/entry/the-deep-state_b_58c94a64e4b01d0d473bcfa3
[162] https://fortune.com/2016/12/07/donal-trump-michael-flynn-national-security-advisor/

Countdown to Chaos

- **Dec. 15, 2016**: James Comey, John Brennan, and several other U.S. officials ask to unmask a U.S. person in intelligence reporting who turns out to be Flynn.
- **Dec. 23, 2016**: Samantha Power asks to unmask a U.S. person in intelligence reporting who turns out to be Flynn.
- **Dec. 27, 2016**: James Clapper asks to unmask a U.S. person in intelligence reporting that turns out to be Flynn.[163]

In the middle of the flurry of unmasking that took place as detailed by the Senate Select Committee on Intelligence Report above, a very important series of events unfolded. On December 6, 2016, outgoing President, Barack Obama, in a meeting of the National Security Council instructed Director of National Intelligence James Clapper "…to have the Intelligence Community prepare a comprehensive report on Russian interference in the 2016 presidential election…"[164] The President requested this product be completed by the end of his Administration, January 20, 2017. **"The presidential tasking also requested recommendations on how to prevent interference in the future and how to strengthen electoral systems."** [165] Director Clapper later testified to the Senate Intelligence Committee regarding the order for this Intelligence Community Assessment (ICA): **"I don't think we would have mounted the effort we did probably, to be honest, in the absence of presidential direction,** because that kind of cleared the way on sharing all the accesses."[166]

---

[163] https://www.hsgac.senate.gov/imo/media/doc/CFH%20Timeline%20w%20Updates%2020201203%20%28FINAL%29.pdf
[164] https://www.intelligence.senate.gov/sites/default/files/documents/Report_Volume4.pdf
[165] https://www.intelligence.senate.gov/sites/default/files/documents/Report_Volume4.pdf
[166] https://www.intelligence.senate.gov/sites/default/files/documents/Report_Volume4.pdf

CHAPTER 9

This report must impress to the highest degree possible, that according to information later declassified about this time period and the intelligence upon which President Obama and each of the IC agencies were acting upon, all agencies knew the information they were reviewing, later referred to as "The Steele Dossier," as well as other information from multiple sources about Russian interference with the campaign of incoming President Trump, was false. Colonel John Mills (Ret.), former member of the National Security Council at the White House, and senior Department of Defense representative for the Comprehensive National Cybersecurity Initiative (CNCI), was a direct participant in events surrounding the drafting of the ICA commissioned by President Barack Obama on December 6th. Of the incidents Col. Mills stated in one of several interviews:

> "A few days after the election I was called on the top-secret phone by a peer who urged me that it was most important that I participate in the creation of this document, an Intel Community Assessment, to finalize the Russia story, and potentially block or delay the inauguration of Trump in January, and he was absolutely giddy with excitement over this. It was absolutely stunning that I would be approached on that, and I could not believe it. But I, we, ran the process. In the process the document comes back to the department of an agency for final approval. I was one of the senior reviewers before it went to the Secretary of Defense. I went through it. There was essentially nothing in the body of this very classified document that gave any evidence that Trump was a Russian asset. Yet the executive summary said, "Trump was a Russian asset." I was told, "Stand down, no need to complete the staffing of the package, the Secretary of Defense has already signed off because Comey and Brennan are personally

'hands on keyboard' writing this document." You never get a Director of Central Intelligence or the FBI personally writing documents and typing documents. Well, as we know from the summer of 2020 with Ric Grenell and John Ratcliff – their declassification – we now know that Comey and Brennan knew the story, the Russia story, was fake in the in summer of '16. So I was staffing a fake document, which I did not know at the time. Comey and Brennan were lying. It's a false statement by a U.S. official, 18 U.S. Code, so I was asked to be part of this. And this was where I realized I needed to get to Durham, and I needed to get my information to Durham.

Paul Greaney [interviewer]: "And you knew that it was Comey and Brennan writing this because it was your boss at the DoD that told you, is that correct?"

Mills: "That's right,... I was told Comey and Brennan are personally doing this. [There was] no need to staff it any further. Ash Carter has already signed because Comey and Brennan are 'personally hands on keyboard' preparing this document. And I'm going, "That's unprecedented... That never happens..."[167]

Two extremely important points need to be discussed regarding the Intelligence Community Assessment ordered by President Obama at this time. Reiterating the first – **the information the ICA was being drafted upon was known to be false.** A second exceptionally important point is that **the directive requested specifically that the IC bring to the president specific proposals**

---

[167] https://www.theepochtimes.com/dod-green-lighted-fake-trump-russia-doc-in-2015-ret-colonel-john-mills_4693981.html

CHAPTER 9

regarding fortifying the American election system. The Senate Intelligence Report states:

> "...the purpose of the ICA was not to present a comprehensive historical perspective, and that the authors were working under significant time constraint, yet the direction received from the President asked for context for the 2016 election by looking at foreign interference in the 2008 and 2012 elections."[168]

While the ICA was being drafted, a significant Executive Order was also being written, and on December 28, 2016, Barack Obama would sign EO 13757.[169] Titled "Taking Additional Steps to Address the National Emergency With Respect to Significant Malicious Cyber-Enabled Activities" this executive order amended EO 13694 signed by Obama in 2015. Executive Order 13757 specified elections within the scope of the original declaration of a national emergency stating "... tampering with, altering, or causing a misappropriation of information with the purpose or effect of interfering with or undermining election processes or institutions..."[170] With this context, it is never overstated with respect to the events of the outgoing Obama Administration, that the information used to draft this EO and the ICA was known to be false.[171] In addition, worthy of a reminder at this point within this report is the fact that in February 2013, Obama had also signed an

---

[168] https://www.intelligence.senate.gov/sites/default/files/documents/Report_Volume4.pdf

[169] https://www.federalregister.gov/documents/2017/01/03/2016-31922/taking-additional-steps-to-address-the-national-emergency-with-respect-to-significant-malicious

[170] https://www.federalregister.gov/documents/2017/01/03/2016-31922/taking-additional-steps-to-address-the-national-emergency-with-respect-to-significant-malicious

[171] https://www.hsgac.senate.gov/imo/media/doc/2020-04-16%20RHJ-CEG%20to%20FBI%20(Crossfire%20Hurricane%20Intel%20Memos).pdf

Countdown to Chaos

executive order titled **"Improving Critical Infrastructure Cybersecurity"** which **specified the groundwork for information sharing framework and governance.** These executive orders were delicately designed over time and implemented with precision planning to move real control of the United States election system squarely under the direction and governance of the Executive Branch of the federal government of the United States as this report will further explain.

The day after the signing of EO 13757, on December 29, 2016, the Office of the Director of National Intelligence (ODNI – James Clapper, Director) and the Department of Homeland Security (DHS – Jeh Johnson, Secretary), released a public statement:

> "The intelligence community is confident the Russian Government directed the recent compromises of e-mails from U.S. persons and institutions, including from U.S. political organizations, and that the disclosures of alleged hacked e-mails on sites like DCLeaks.com and WikiLeaks are consistent with the Russian-directed efforts. ...Russian intelligence services have also undertaken damaging and disruptive cyber-attacks, including **on critical infrastructure**..."[172]

This statement mirrored the USIC statement made just months prior on October 7, 2016 and outlined in chapter eight. Also discussed in depth in the previous chapter, the assessment of the WikiLeaks DNC server hack came from CrowdStrike, and specifically Shawn Henry, who was called upon by Michael Sussman, to make that determination.[173] This report has previously reported in Chapter 8, that during the time Mr. Henry provided information to

---

[172] https://www.dni.gov/index.php/newsroom/press-releases/press-releases-2016/item/1616-joint-dhs-odni-fbi-statement-on-russian-malicious-cyber-activity

[173] https://intelligence.house.gov/uploadedfiles/sh21.pdf

CHAPTER 9

both the DNC and the FBI, he may have been a compromised actor with regard to the topic of anything relating to Donald Trump. The details of Shawn Henry's comment in London create serious problems for CrowdStrike in its capacity as a key government contract holder, having Mr. Henry not only representing the company, but also having a key technical position regarding direction of policy and product. And again, all Russian information reported now by the ODNI and the DHS in this statement was also based upon information known to be false. Was Mr. Henry part of a wide domestic misinformation campaign, and did his position at CrowdStrike expose the national election infrastructure to bias at a very high technical level?

In the timeframe of a single day once again, on December 30, 2016, the Intelligence Community Assessment (ICA), directed by President Obama on December 6, 2016, was completed and delivered as "Memorandum for the President". The report reflected false intelligence collected regarding Russian interference in the 2016 election as well as allegedly from the Trump campaign.[174] The ICA consisted of CIA, NSA, and FBI, reporting to ODNI, and as stated by former National Security Council member Colonel John Mills (Ret.), the executive summary of this report was personally written by CIA director John Brennan, and FBI Director James Comey.[175]

On January 5, 2017 according to the Senate Select Committee on Intelligence report on Russian interference, a now infamous meeting took place in the Obama White House ahead of the Congressional Electoral College vote:

---

[174] https://www.intelligence.senate.gov/sites/default/files/documents/Report_Volume4.pdf

[175] https://www.theepochtimes.com/dod-green-lighted-fake-trump-russia-doc-in-2015-ret-colonel-john-mills_4693981.html

Countdown to Chaos

- "**Jan. 5, 2017**:
    - Denis McDonough, Chief of Staff to President Obama, asks to unmask a U.S. person in intelligence reporting who turns out to be Flynn.
    - Clapper, NSA Director Adm. Michael Rogers, Brennan, and Comey brief the ICA report to Obama and his national security team, including Vice President Biden."[176]

According to additional information uncovered since the meeting that became discovered by later incoming intelligence sources, additional individuals in the White House meeting included National Security Advisor Susan Rice, Deputy Attorney General Sally Yates, and Vice President Joe Biden.[177] As at the time of authoring this report this meeting continued to be part of the open Durham Investigation, it is included here for reference to people, dates, and times to consider with all other information within the full context of this report.

However, very importantly, also well within the scope of the topic of this report, likewise on January 5, 2017, the Obama Administration released the classified version of the ICA report titled "Assessing Russian Activities and Intentions in Recent US Elections."[178] A key takeaway from the report is after some interagency debate, the ICA would include known false information known as "the Steele Dossier" as "Annex A." **With this information, President Obama would act on recommendations**

---

[176] https://www.hsgac.senate.gov/imo/media/doc/CFH%20Timeline%20w%20Updates%2020201203%20%28FINAL%29.pdf
[177] https://www.theepochtimes.com/attorney-general-says-new-strzok-notes-described-obama-white-house-meeting_3404650.html
[178] https://www.intelligence.senate.gov/sites/default/files/documents/Report_Volume4.pdf

CHAPTER 9

from the Intelligence Community to "fortify U.S. elections." That action took place the very next day.

On January 6, 2017, the United States Congress officially certified Donald Trump the winner of the Presidency of the United States, despite official Democrat objections to the certification.[179] On the same day, **Jeh Johnson, Obama's Secretary of the Department of Homeland Security, "designated U.S. election systems as part of the nation's critical infrastructure"**[180,181] The significance of this designation to the country may have been overlooked at the time. However, in light of the looking glass the reader sees through with the information here presented, and the information yet to follow, **the designation cemented what amounted to a federal takeover of U.S. elections, and the Department of Homeland Security was now the official manager and "governing authority" of them.** The U.S. Elections Assistance Commission issued a brief about the designation. It states:

- "Critical infrastructure is a DHS designation established by the Patriot Act."
- "DHS, the department responsible for critical infrastructure, was established by the Homeland Security Act in 2002."
- "In order to fulfill its responsibilities under the Patriot Act, DHS uses the National Infrastructure Protection Plan (NIPP) as the foundational document, or "rule book," for how to develop sector-specific critical infrastructure plans."
- "In addition to the Patriot Act and NIPP, a third piece of **critical infrastructure governing authority comes from Presidential Policy Directive 21 (PPD-21).** Released on

---

[179] https://www.cnn.com/2017/01/06/politics/electoral-college-vote-objections/index.html
[180] EPIC-17-03-31-DHS-FOIA-20191113-CISA-Production-Reprocessed.pdf
[181] https://www.eac.gov/sites/default/files/eac_assets/1/6/starting_point_us_election_systems_as_Critical_Infrastructure.pdf

Countdown to Chaos

February 12, 2013, PPD-21 established the Federal Government's "strategic imperatives" in its approach to the nation's critical infrastructure. It established the current critical infrastructure sectors and identified each sector's **Sector Specific Agency (SSA)**, which is the agency charged with structuring and managing the sector."

- "Once DHS creates a sector, the SSA structures it and helps it self-organize, a requirement of the NIPP. With regard to election systems, this means that members of the election community come together to join and manage the various components that make up this sector. After the critical infrastructure sector is formally established and organized, **the SSA is charged with managing it.**"

- "Sector Coordinating Councils (SCCs): These are "**self-organized, self-run, and self-governed private sector councils** consisting of owners and operators and their representatives, who interact on a wide range of sector-specific strategies, policies, activities, and issues. SCCs serve as principal collaboration points between the government and private sector owners and operators for critical infrastructure security and resilience policy coordination and planning and a range of related sector-specific activities."

- "**Government Coordinating Councils (GCCs):** These consist of 'representatives from across various levels of government (including Federal and State, local, tribal and territorial), as appropriate to the operating landscape of each individual sector, these councils enable interagency, intergovernmental, and cross-jurisdictional coordination within and across sectors and partner with SCCs on public private efforts.'"

- "Another key component of operating a critical infrastructure sector is to ensure clear, strong lines of communication between the SSA, Co-SSA, coordinating

councils, and stakeholders. This can include creation of the following:
- Information Sharing and Analysis Centers (ISACs)
- Information Sharing and Analysis Organizations (ISAOs)"
- "ISAOs offer a more flexible approach to self-organized information sharing activities amongst communities of interest such as small businesses across sectors: legal, accounting, and consulting firms that support cross-sector clients, etc." Essentially, ISAOs allow for more widespread information sharing across sectors and among interested individuals regardless of clearance, knowledge level, or inclusion in a critical infrastructure sector."
- "**Information about security and vulnerabilities** that is shared under the restrictions of the Critical Infrastructure Information Act is considered Protected Critical Infrastructure Information (PCII). **PCII is not subject to the many disclosure regulations, such as those found in the Freedom of Information Act and its state-level counterpart**. This protection allows the critical infrastructure community to discuss vulnerabilities and problems without publicly exposing potentially sensitive information. For those participating in election sector coordinating councils **this protection means that some information communicated between DHS and the coordinating councils can be protected**. This limits the potential for sensitive election security information to be made public and protects potentially sensitive material from being misconstrued or used for nefarious purposes."
- "The EAC has requested DHS name the commission as Co-SAA. This designation is important to ensure that state and local election officials and administrators have an informed federal advocate working directly with DHS as the department determines what resources and services are

Countdown to Chaos

needed to protect U.S. election systems and how these resources will be distributed."[182]

In testimony by Jeh Johnson reported in Volume 1 of the Senate Select Committee on Intelligence Report on Russian Collusion, just the idea of the designation of elections as critical infrastructure by the DHS was met with strong resistance from the states. The full quote from this testimony read:

> "States also reported that the [DHS] call did not go well. Several states told the Committee that the idea of a critical infrastructure designation surprised them and came without context of a particular threat. **Some state officials also did not understand what a critical infrastructure designation meant, in practical terms, and whether it would give the federal government the power to run elections**. DHS also did not anticipate a certain level of suspicion from the states toward the federal government. As a State 17 official told the Committee, 'when someone says 'we're from the government and we're here to help,' it's generally not a good thing.'"[183]

The report further comments:

> "One of the most controversial elements of the relationship between DHS and the states was the decision to designate election systems as critical infrastructure. Most state officials relayed that they were surprised by the designation and did not understand what it meant; **many also felt DHS was not**

---

[182] https://www.eac.gov/sites/default/files/eac_assets/1/6/starting_point_us_election_systems_as_Critical_Infrastructure.pdf

[183] https://www.intelligence.senate.gov/sites/default/files/documents/Report_Volume1.pdf

CHAPTER 9

open to input from the states on whether such a designation was beneficial"...and "remained suspicious that the designation is a first step toward a federal takeover of elections."[184]

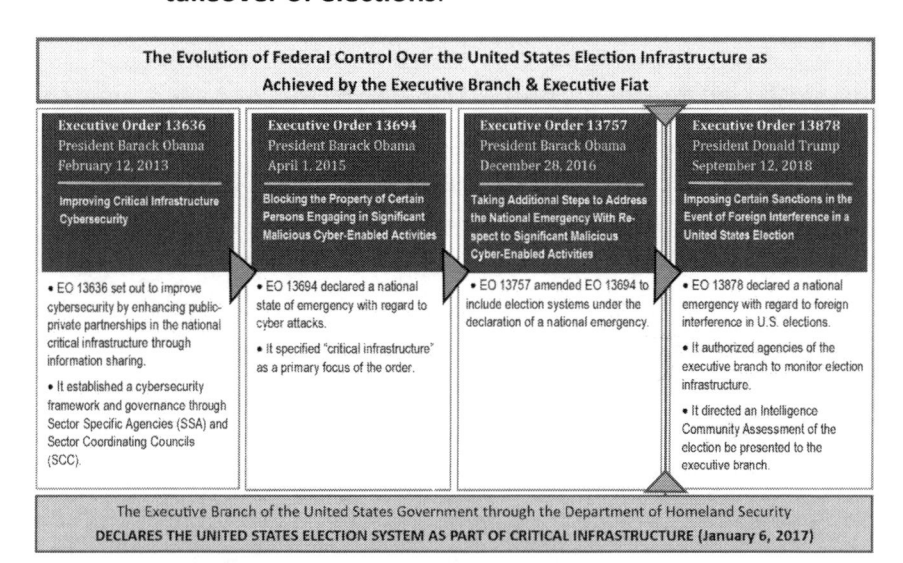

The Evolution of Federal Control Over the United States Election Infrastructure as Achieved by the Executive Branch & Executive Fiat			
Executive Order 13636 President Barack Obama February 12, 2013	**Executive Order 13694** President Barack Obama April 1, 2015	**Executive Order 13757** President Barack Obama December 28, 2016	**Executive Order 13878** President Donald Trump September 12, 2018
Improving Critical Infrastructure Cybersecurity	Blocking the Property of Certain Persons Engaging in Significant Malicious Cyber-Enabled Activities	Taking Additional Steps to Address the National Emergency With Respect to Significant Malicious Cyber-Enabled Activities	Imposing Certain Sanctions in the Event of Foreign Interference in a United States Election
• EO 13636 set out to improve cybersecurity by enhancing public-private partnerships in the national critical infrastructure through information sharing. • It established a cybersecurity framework and governance through Sector Specific Agencies (SSA) and Sector Coordinating Councils (SCC).	• EO 13694 declared a national state of emergency with regard to cyber attacks. • It specified "critical infrastructure" as a primary focus of the order.	• EO 13757 amended EO 13694 to include election systems under the declaration of a national emergency.	• EO 13878 declared a national emergency with regard to foreign interference in U.S. elections. • It authorized agencies of the executive branch to monitor election infrastructure. • It directed an Intelligence Community Assessment of the election be presented to the executive branch.
The Executive Branch of the United States Government through the Department of Homeland Security **DECLARES THE UNITED STATES ELECTION SYSTEM AS PART OF CRITICAL INFRASTRUCTURE** (January 6, 2017)			

On January 10, 2017, key players in the Russian collusion narrative were dispatched to Capitol Hill to testify in front of the Senate Select Committee on Intelligence in two separate hearings. Testifying to that committee were Admiral Rogers, CIA Director John Brennan, FBI Director James Comey, and Director of ODNI, James Clapper. These four were key architects of the Intelligence Community Assessment (ICA) that was released just days before,[185] and were also integrally involved in the flurry of domestic intelligence gathering as outlined in the previous chapter. As they would for months and years into the future, the narrative this group presented to the Senate Committee was that there was no

---

[184]

https://www.intelligence.senate.gov/sites/default/files/documents/Report_Volume1.pdf

[185]

https://www.intelligence.senate.gov/sites/default/files/documents/Report_Volume4.pdf

Countdown to Chaos

doubt Russia interfered in the 2016 Presidential Election, even though at that very point in time, that testimony could now be construed as perjury, as this report repeatedly states, the Intelligence Community knew the information they were presenting was uncorroborated and fake.[186]

When all facts presented within this report are critically evaluated, the reader would have to give serious thought to the idea that with each of the executive orders signed by Barack Obama during his presidency, and likely his personal directive to Jeh Johnson at the Department of Homeland Security to declare U.S. elections as national critical infrastructure, his pronouncement as he first came into office that, "We are five days away from fundamentally transforming the United States of America," was truly a mission accomplished. The steps undertaken by the executive branch of the federal government of the United States of America changed the entire election system, moving a very significant portion of the "manner" in which elections are held under control of that branch.

The most critical characteristic of management of elections, which is they are to be overseen by non-policy making or elected individuals (i.e. Boards of Supervisors, Election Boards, etc.), became nearly entirely nullified. These actions by the Obama Administration make the U.S. election system enslaved to the stroke of an executive's pen in writing executive orders to direct or change any part of the system managed under the Department of Homeland Security, CISA, and other agencies controlling national critical infrastructure. Furthermore, these actions remove the federal arbiters of election disputes and fraud out of the realm of independence from the process and give federal agencies an active role in election administration. In an article by Victor Davis Hansen

---

[186] https://www.hsgac.senate.gov/imo/media/doc/2020-04-16%20RHJ-CEG%20to%20FBI%20(Crossfire%20Hurricane%20Intel%20Memos).pdf

CHAPTER 9

published on Politico.com on October 1, 2013, the columnist made the following commentary:

> "…We live in an age when a president can arbitrarily nullify a law, like Obamacare's employer mandate; ignore it, like the Defense of Marriage Act; or simply create it, as with partial blanket amnesties. Various wars — on coal, guns, non-union businesses, and political opponents — are waged by executive action. For now, the logic is that the president's means are justified by the exalted ends that he professes. Obama has set the precedent of a president creating, ignoring, or defying laws as he sees fit to forward a progressive agenda."[187]

This article was penned after EO 13636 cited above, but well before what would transpire over the upcoming years and critical weeks just prior to the end of Obama's presidency. However, his comment is valid and carries serious weight when read in the context of elections and the information presented within this report. It is critical that the actions taken by Obama on elections are shared with every American citizen and elected official, and for the sake of freedom, the structure he created must be changed or somehow circumvented.

Moving ahead in time, on May 17, 2017, former FBI Director, Robert Mueller was appointed Special Counsel in the Russian collusion investigation named "Crossfire Hurricane."[188] In sworn testimony at a later date, special agent William Barnett stated under oath for the record that the appointment of Mueller "changed everything." Mr. Barnett testified that the focus of the

---

[187] https://www.realclearpolitics.com/articles/2013/10/01/obama_transforming_america_120170.html

[188] https://www.cbsnews.com/news/doj-appoints-special-counsel-in-wake-of-comey-developments/

Countdown to Chaos

investigation shifted to one of "Get Trump," with one of the modes being to entrap Gen. Michael Flynn.[189] Congruent with Agent Barnett's report that the intelligence structure was working to "get Trump" within the FBI, agencies throughout the federal bureaucracy quietly moved forward with the continued election cyber infrastructure.

A CISA communique dated January 18, 2018, confirmed that the DHS officially remained the Sector Specific Agency stating:

> "The Department of Homeland Security (DHS) designated election infrastructure as critical infrastructure on January 6, 2017. The designation created the Election Infrastructure Subsector (EIS) under the Government Facilities sector, with DHS as its Sector Specific Agency (SSA)."

> "The ETF is also developing a series of analytical products to improve understanding of systems, processes, and implementation of election infrastructure to inform risk analysis efforts. Products will be informed, coordinated, and validated by key ETF partners such as the U.S. Election Assistance Commission (EAC), National Association of Secretaries of State (NASS), National Association of State Election Directors (NASED), and local election officials, as appropriate. Following the National Infrastructure Protection Plan partnership model, the EIS will have two forums for collaboration and information sharing: the EIS Government Coordinating Council (GCC), representing the public-sector election community, and

---

[189] https://storage.courtlistener.com/recap/gov.uscourts.dcd.191592/gov.uscourts.dcd.191592.249.0.pdf

CHAPTER 9

the EIS Sector Coordinating Council (SCC), representing the private-sector election community." [190]

In addition to the Department of Homeland Security making the incredibly significant designation of "CRITICAL INFRASTRUCTURE" for elections in January of 2017, and on the same day as the well documented Obama White House meeting of January 5, 2017, the Intelligence and National Security Alliance (INSA), a private intelligence organization closely connected to White House meeting attendees, James Clapper and John Brennan, published a white paper that had been authored between the time of the November election and the January White House meeting. Titled "PROTECTING THE HOMELAND: Intelligence Integration 15 Years After 9/11,"[191] the focus of the paper was solely information sharing with SLTTs through public-private partnerships and the creation of "fusion centers" for information sharing in real time. Regarding fusion centers the report states, "Fusion Centers need relationships and communication with other Fusion Centers to ensure horizontal sharing, as well as a strong federal presence to facilitate vertical sharing."[192] The four points outlined in the executive summary are:

1. "The Office of Director of National Intelligence (ODNI) could have a clearer and more robust role as the coordinating body for homeland intelligence priorities and activities and the integration of homeland intelligence into national intelligence priorities and activities."

190
https://www.cisa.gov/sites/default/files/publications/Issue%201%20Communique_0.PDF
[191] https://www.insaonline.org/wp-content/uploads/2017/04/INSA_WP_ProtectHomeland.pdf
[192] https://www.insaonline.org/wp-content/uploads/2017/04/INSA_WP_ProtectHomeland.pdf

Countdown to Chaos

2. "Interagency mechanisms that foster collaboration and information sharing amongst Enterprise partners offer best practices to work across the statutory and organizational boundaries and should be expanded and strengthened."
3. "Information sharing efforts with SLTT entities would benefit from systematically informing them of current national priorities and information needs, streamlining the systems they use to receive federally provided information, and providing a process and mechanism for them to share relevant information with federal partners."
4. "Sharing government information with the private sector must now shift toward developing a truly reciprocal relationship, which requires the identification of sharing mechanisms that facilitate an interactive feedback loop between the government and the private sector and a more integrated government approach to meeting private sector requirements to protect critical infrastructure."[193]

Page fifteen of the INSA white paper lays out recommendations for the incoming Trump Administration. The sum of the recommendations will have a stark familiarity with Executive Order 13848 signed by Donald Trump in 2018. The recommendations in the 2017 INSA white paper include:

1. "The next Administration should clarify the DNI's role in coordinating and integrating all aspects of national intelligence and review the IRTPA and other intelligence statutes, regulations, EO's and related policies to ensure their consistency and adequacy for this purpose."
2. "The Office of the Director of National Intelligence should integrate the Homeland Threat Framework into the National Intelligence Priorities Framework as a means to

---

[193] https://www.insaonline.org/wp-content/uploads/2017/04/INSA_WP_ProtectHomeland.pdf

identify key national security threats to the homeland and align intelligence collection requirements and analytic priorities accordingly."
3. "The Director of National Intelligence, in close coordination with the DHS Under Secretary for Intelligence and Analysis and the FBI National Security Branch Executive Assistant Director, should designate a NIM [National Intelligence Manager] for the Homeland and an NIO [National Intelligence Officer] for the Homeland, and seek to include key non-Title 50 representatives on the NIM Staff. The new NIO should create a Program of Analysis for homeland intelligence and commission an NIE [National Intelligence Estimate] based on the threats contained in the Homeland Threat Framework."
4. "The Office of the DNI should clarify the roles of and guidance to the Domestic DNI Representatives, to include the appropriate mechanisms and procedures for interacting with non-Title 50 partners."
5. "The Program Manager of the Information Sharing Environment (PM-ISE) should work with other elements of the ODNI and the IC to develop a repeatable process for sharing national information needs with SLTT and private sector partners and receiving information from those partners. PM-ISE should also work to reduce the burden on SLTT of multiple, noncompatible systems for accessing federally provided information."[194]

These public-private structures that were built on top of the massive cyber network infrastructure previously laid and continually built by the DHS, clearly commandeered elections from the Constitutional purview of the state legislatures and placed them squarely under the DHS as the "governing authority". The

---

[194] https://www.insaonline.org/wp-content/uploads/2017/04/INSA_WP_ProtectHomeland.pdf

Countdown to Chaos

DHS then layered a number of other sub-sector councils beneath it to further tie up the structure and governance of elections and populated these councils with individuals elected from within closely held pools of candidates for executive committee positions.

On January 6, 2017, with the inauguration of President Trump, John Brennan left the office of Director of the Central Intelligence Agency. As Brennan left, he was involved with some events and activities later investigated as "Crossfire Hurricane," some of which has been discussed in the previous chapter. Those events would continue to swirl about the incoming Trump administration, which included the propagation of a narrative by John Brennan, James Clapper, James Comey, and Michael Rogers that the Russians interfered in the 2016 election.[195] In an interview on August 17, 2018, well after his departure from the CIA, Brennan appeared in an interview on the cable network MSNBC where he explained to Rachel Maddow that at the time of his departure in January of 2017, the CIA had a need to hand over information "incidentally collected" on U.S. citizens that "was of great relevance to the FBI." To facilitate the continuity of intelligence collection, and because he had "unresolved questions" in his mind about Russian efforts, Brennan divulged that they created a fusion center:

> **Brennan:** "...we were picking things up that was of great relevance to the FBI. We wanted to make sure that they were there so they could piece it together with whatever they were collecting domestically here."
>
> **Maddow:** "So it was an intelligence sharing operation."
>
> **Brennan:** "Absolutely. Right. We put together a fusion center at CIA with the NSA and FBI officers together with

---

[195] https://edition.cnn.com/2017/01/10/politics/donald-trump-intelligence-report-russia/index.html

CHAPTER 9

CIA to make sure that those proverbial dots would be connected."[196]

This admission of "incidental collection" of information on American citizens is important at this point regarding understanding what the Deep State may have been in the middle of undertaking. First, John Brennan used his favorite mechanism, the fusion center, as a dedicated intelligence collection outlet on the Trump/Russia election collusion theory. This report will demonstrate in detail why the fusion center is key to the federal government in its push for, then use of it, as a federal election security mechanism. Furthermore, as outlined earlier this this chapter, every allegation of Russian hacking made by federal government during this phase of the historical timeline always redirected the conversation back to American election security, with the operational solutions always being run and managed by the federal government, specifically the Department of Homeland Security.

This report noted at the end of chapter seven that already in 2015, nearly immediately after Donald Trump declared his candidacy, a self-identified CIA whistleblower (former contractor) filed an official report with the FBI. The report included physical evidence along with his testimony given in a three-hour-long interview in Washington D.C. According to a later court filing, in this individual's interview he stated that he had additional evidence regarding intelligence agencies not just spying on private citizens, but that they were specifically targeting candidate Donald Trump. This witness claimed he was able to soundly make the allegations because he personally participated in the collection process. This report will withhold the name of the whistleblower as this person and physical evidentiary facts yielded to the FBI are either unavailable for inspection or difficult to fully vet, however, court

---

[196] https://youtu.be/UV7-ZdDGijY?t=1170

Countdown to Chaos

filings at this point in 2017 yield important data points that should be included in this report.

On June 5, 2017, Attorney Larry Klayman filed a lawsuit in Federal District Court in Washington D.C. on behalf of himself and the self-identified whistleblower against James Comey, the FBI, Mike Rogers, the NSA, John Brennan, Mike Pompeo, the CIA, James Clapper, Dan Coats, and Barack Obama. Of interest to this report are these claims in this filing:

> "V. FACTS
>
> 18. Defendants have continued to engage in ongoing illegal, unconstitutional surveillance of millions of Americans, including prominent Americans such as the chief justice of the U.S. Supreme Court, other justices, 156 judges, prominent businessmen and others such as Donald J. Trump, as well as Plaintiffs themselves.
>
> 20. On information and belief, Defendants' ongoing illegal, unconstitutional surveillance continues to occur in numerous ways, including but not limited to, bulk telephony metadata collection similar to the now "discontinued" Section 215 of the USA PATRIOT ACT as well targeted "PRISM" collection under Section 702 of the Foreign Sovereignties Immunity Act. Additional, specific mechanisms employed by Defendants will be set forth in discovery.
>
> 24. Accordingly, the FISC took Defendant Comey and the FBI to task in the Order, finding that "[t]he Court is nonetheless concerned about the FBI's apparent disregard of minimization rules and whether the FBI may be engaging in similar disclosures of raw Section 702 information that have not been reported."

CHAPTER 9

40. On or around December 21, 2015, Plaintiff [name withheld] was interviewed under oath at the FBI field office in Washington, D.C. There, over the course of a three-hour interview, recorded on video, with agents Walter Giardina and William Barnett, Plaintiff [name withheld] meticulously laid out the NSA, CIA, and DNI's pattern and practice of conducting illegal, unconstitutional surveillance against millions of Americans, including prominent Americans such as the chief justice of the United States Supreme Court, other justices, 156 judges, prominent businessmen and others such as Donald J. Trump, as well as Plaintiffs themselves."[197]

Of interest in this filing are first, that the accusers allege the named federal agencies, the FBI, NSA, and the CIA were spying on not just normal Americans, but they were targeting Donald Trump. Of importance is the timeframe in which the allegations of this government contractor take place. The surveillance he discloses purportedly took place at a specific time that will find some validation via evidence from the Office of Special Counsel, John Durham, some outlined in the previous chapter. Secondly, the filing describes with specificity methods the agencies were purported to have used including bulk telephony metadata collection. Upon filing of this case, Director Comey was already under investigation over FISA warrant abuse.[198] All of these allegations will bear extraordinary weight and potential confirmation later in this report when further corroborating details will be divulged by U.S. Attorney John Durham in the federal district court case against Attorney Michael Sussman. And finally, this filing details one of the special agents to interview the self-identified whistleblower and co-plaintiff in this case was FBI special

---

[197] https://regmedia.co.uk/2017/06/08/01-main.pdf
[198] https://www.justice.gov/storage/120919-examination.pdf

Countdown to Chaos

agent William Barnett from the Washington D.C. office. This report stated just pages prior to this, special agent Barnett became a key person to make a sworn statement to the Department of Justice in 2020 both testifying that the Intelligence Community was out to "get Trump" during the Crossfire Hurricane operation and to make statements about the Crossfire Hurricane operation that ultimately exonerated General Michael Flynn whom the agencies had pulled into the Russian election collusion narrative, illegally unmasking General Flynn in their intelligence collection processes.

On September 13, 2017, the defendants in this case filed a motion to dismiss the case. Of importance within this filing by attorneys for all the defendants are the following data points:

- "As an initial matter, the Individual-Capacity Defendants enjoy qualified immunity...
- The Government Defendants have demonstrated that the plaintiffs' allegations are insufficient to establish their standing to bring their surveillance claims.
- The plaintiffs' speculative and conclusory allegations of a government conspiracy are especially implausible in light of the presumption of regularity afforded to official acts of government agencies.
- The bulk collection of telephony metadata is, as the Government Defendants have explained, now prohibited by the USA FREEDOM Act, Pub L. No. 114-23 §§ 103, 109, 129 Stat. 268, 272, 276; 50 U.S.C. § 1861(c)(3). And the plaintiffs once again have not pled any facts to overcome the presumption of regularity and show that the government is disregarding express legal limits on its surveillance authority...Indeed, the plaintiffs have made no factual allegations from which a court could reasonably conclude that such a clandestinely-resurrected program even exists.

CHAPTER 9

- "The complaint in this case contains no factual allegations of unlawful surveillance sufficient to establish the plaintiffs' standing."[199]

Of importance in this motion to dismiss is that the defendants, James Comey, the FBI, Mike Rogers, the NSA, John Brennan, Mike Pompeo, the CIA, James Clapper, Dan Coats, and Barack Obama did not argue the facts held within the content of the physical evidence turned over to the FBI during the interview of the self-identified whistleblower on December 21, 2015. Instead, defendants' counsel simply stated that the "allegations are insufficient," "speculative," and that the surveillance these agencies was being accused of was not shown by the plaintiffs to "overcome the presumption of regularity and show that the government is disregarding express legal limits on its surveillance authority." The defendants' motion to dismiss began with its basis in the defendants' individual claims of "qualified immunity," in addition to their argument against the plaintiffs' standing in bringing forth the case. The methods of collection named by the plaintiffs are defended on the basis of legal technicalities by the defendants, then calling the allegations "speculative...conspiracy theory." None of the physical evidence which was reported to have included dozens of hard drive images was given any attention or defense.

This report finds these allegations and their defense of interest as first it shows a pattern that began to emerge with regard to intelligence collection by the Intelligence Community. These operations alleged since 2013 by Edward Snowden, often received the standard blanket denial. This case reintroduces such allegations against the Deep State, and without access to the evidence turned over by the individual who met with special agent

---

[199]

https://ia800807.us.archive.org/34/items/gov.uscourts.dcd.187032/gov.uscourts.dcd.187032.36.1.pdf

Countdown to Chaos

William Barnett, the complete facts of the actions of the FBI, NSA, and CIA in this case cannot be discovered. However, this case helps validate Snowden at the least. Then, from 2015 and onward beginning with the meeting of this "whistleblower" with FBI special agent Barnett this court filing adds further validation to the forthcoming allegations that would be made by U.S. Attorney John Durham in the case United States v. Michael Sussman, as the alleged domestic spying activities in that case become isolated upon presidential candidate Donald Trump, the U.S. elections, and later included the Office of the President of the United States.

This report has presented facts also showing during this period the Executive Branch under Barack Obama began writing a series of executive orders authorizing information sharing (Chapter 7) which included formation and use of such tools as the Brennan/Clapper established fusion centers. The use of fusion centers as a critical tool of federal government, their use in elections, their use for intelligence collection, and their long history of abuse will be explained in detail in Chapter 12 of this report. However, considering the facts presented to this point, including multi-sourced evidence the federal government surveilled and collected intelligence targeting not only normal Americans but also of particular interest, political candidates and campaigns, the questions necessary to ask become: As the CIA/NSA/FBI fusion center personally divulged by former CIA Director John Brennan was set up to collect Trump, Russia, and election related intelligence, what information was collected, and was it shared anywhere else in the vast information sharing network related to elections? **Was this CIA/FBI/NSA fusion center running within the walls of the CIA active, operational, and live within the HSIN network on Election Day 2020?**

As the federal complaint filed by Attorney Larry Klayman against the federal agencies was dismissed, the country will never know what the information contained within the physical evidence turned over to the FBI may have produced with regard to these remarkable allegations. Additionally, the act of turning over such sensitive information to the FBI, in light of all evidence presented in this report, yields the possibility that the plaintiffs in this case may have handed over key evidence directly to the accused, and that the accused may have had culpability in a number of events for which this evidence may have been important to see. It is the connection of these allegations in each of these cases, particularly of the "whistleblower" case and the Durham case, to elections that is of remarkable importance to this report. The idea that such activities happen without a connection to elections as alleged by Edward Snowden is alarming enough; however, the connection of domestic espionage undertaken by governmental agencies potentially aimed at U.S. elections is an earth-shattering discovery that has the ability to turn Watergate, an event in history most considered the greatest, most egregious political scandal to ever unfold in America, into a mere asterisk behind what facts may be recorded by history about events that took place during the summer of 2016 then further to the 2016 and the 2020 Presidential Elections.

Former CIA Director John O. Brennan continued to drive his "Russian hack of the election" narrative for months and years after his departure, right up to the weeks preceding the 2020 Presidential Election. There will, however, be one point later in this report, where Mr. Brennan and Mr. Clapper's mouths will become all but sealed on the matter.

In the wake of continual drumbeat of the narrative of Russian interference in the 2016 election built by people like Brennan, Clapper, and Comey, an acting Deputy Undersecretary of DHS, Jeannette Manfra, testified at the Senate Committee on Select Intelligence in 2016, that the DHS did not conduct any forensic analysis of voting machines. DHS's prepared testimony at that hearing included the statement that it is "likely that cyber

Countdown to Chaos

manipulation of U.S. election systems intended to change the outcome of a national election would be detected."[200] This statement is interesting to read within the context of what the former intelligence heads were simultaneously claiming, however, it becomes important moving forward for the Department of Homeland Security to continue to build and maintain what it can sell to SLTTs as a substantial, secure, and effective cyber security infrastructure integrating in monitoring services, particularly after the originating system suffered two scathing audits, the most significant coming from the GAO as reported in January 2016.

On October 17, 2017, the Election Infrastructure Government Coordinating Council was formed.[201] The formation and adoption of the EI GCC Charter was done under the coordination of the Department of Homeland Security with the EAS having a significant role in the process. Membership of the initial council was published on the EAS website.[202] The initial Executive Committee of the EI GCC is:

> **Hon. Connie Lawson**, Indiana Secretary of State, NASS President
>
> **Dr. Judd Choate**, Director of Elections, Colorado, NASED Immediate Past President
>
> **Mr. Noah Praetz**, Director of Elections, Cook County, Illinois, Election Center Representative
>
> **Hon. Thomas Hicks**, Chairman, U.S. Election Assistance Commission

---

[200] https://www.intelligence.senate.gov/sites/default/files/documents/Report_Volume1.pdf
[201] https://www.nased.org/news/2018/4/16/an-open-letter-to-american-voters-from-the-executive-committee-of-the-government-coordinating-council
[202] https://www.eac.gov/news/2017/10/14/elections-government-sector-coordinating-council-established-charter-adopted

CHAPTER 9

Hon. Robert Kolasky, Deputy Under Secretary (acting) for National Protection and Programs Directorate, U.S. Department of Homeland Security

As a matter of investigation, the author and researcher of this report attempted to check party affiliation of quasigovernment agency appointments at each point along the way in this report. The only affiliation easily found in the list above was that of Connie Lawson, who appeared to be a long time Republican in the state of Indiana.

In an open letter to American voters dated about six months after its formation, the EI GCC stated:

> "The Council marks the first of its kind **collaboration between federal, state and local officials to secure elections. We are formalizing information sharing protocols** to ensure timely and actionable threat information reaches all election officials so they can respond to threats as they emerge.
>
> Our Council has guided the delivery of direct resources from DHS to support state and local election officials including onsite risk and vulnerability assessments, as well as a variety of other services and trainings to support election officials. While Council members and state election officials were in D.C., we **participated in classified briefings given by FBI, DHS, and officials from the Office of the Director for National Intelligence.** This was an important first step."[203]

An important point of scrutiny appears within the information discussed in the EI GCC open letter when compared to information in an archived official post by CISA from a later date about a similar

---

[203] https://www.nased.org/news/2018/4/16/an-open-letter-to-american-voters-from-the-executive-committee-of-the-government-coordinating-council

meeting.[204] Evidence in the archived report suggests the classified portion of briefings provided to EI GCC members surrounded information regarding the Albert Monitoring Services, CrowdStrike, and the CIS managed cyber security services provided through the DHS. This deduction fits with the testimony given by CrowdStrike's Shawn Henry to an Executive Session of the Permanent Select Committee on Intelligence of the U.S. House of Representatives outlined in the previous chapter, when Mr. Henry alluded to the CrowdStrike Falcon platform being involved in classified programs within the federal government. A reasonable question to ask about this evidence, is that if elections are truly under the purview of the state and local governments, then why is part of the management of the elections under classified status by the federal government? This is yet additional evidence that elections in the United States, as they were altered in 2017 by deeming them "critical infrastructure" violate Articles I & II of the Constitution and the 10th Amendment of the Constitution in the Bill of Rights.

In an event that will prove to be of serious consequence a few years into the future from this point in time within this report, stepping back in time for continuity of previous information presented, in about April 2017, "A former security adviser at the IT monitoring and network management company SolarWinds Corporation said he warned management of cybersecurity risks and laid out a plan to improve it that was ultimately ignored. In a 23-page PowerPoint presentation reviewed by Bloomberg News, Ian Thornton-Trump recommended to company executives in 2017 that SolarWinds appoint a senior director of cybersecurity, and said he told them that "the survival of the company depends on an internal

---

[204] https://www.fbcoverup.com/docs/library/2018-10-02-DHS-HOLDS-CLASSIFIED-BRIEFING-FOR-PRIVATE-SECTOR-ELECTION-COMPANIES-incl-Dominion-ESS-Scytl-Smartmatic-Press-Release-Natnl-Protectn-and-Progs-Directorate-CISA-Oct-02-2021.pdf

CHAPTER 9

commitment to security."[205] Readers of this report should recognize SolarWinds and already know the significance of this entry into the timeline being reported. The fallout from this warning takes place over the next couple of years and is detailed in Chapter 10 to follow.

---

[205] https://www.bloombergquint.com/business/solarwinds-adviser-warned-of-lax-security-years-before-hack

Countdown to Chaos

CHAPTER 10

Chapter 10

EI-SCC, EI-ISAC, IT-ISAC, Executive Order 13848, Help America Vote Act, CISA Cybersecurity Summit, SolarWinds (2018-2019)

After the election of President Donald Trump, the federal government's absorption of the states' responsibilities to conduct all elections moved in fast forward and at breakneck speed. The quasi-governmental agencies were built in layers with carefully hand-selected leadership. The public-private partnerships also became propagated with companies and individuals which would build a virtual federal firewall around the Constitution and the key to freedom of the citizens – their individual voting rights. The formation of an ISAC at this point had a blueprint, and with nearly every state in the nation already signed up to share all their information through the MS-ISAC structure, the EI-ISAC structure would become the entity every career government insider may have been praying for. This report will show how the EI-ISAC became a behemoth entity spawned from smaller experiments in government control over state and local information. The information to follow shows the further evolution of the federalization of elections, keeping in mind that **when the Department of Homeland Security retained the role of Sector Specific Agency over elections when elections became "critical infrastructure" on January 5, 2017 under Barack Obama, the DHS became the "governing authority" over elections.**

The transformation of the federalizing of the election system continued on February 15, 2018, when the Election Infrastructure Subsector Coordinating Council was formed (EI-SCC) and its charter adopted. The formation of the EI-SCC was one of the required pieces of structural framework that was to be built after elections were designated "critical infrastructure" by DHS Secretary Jeh

Countdown to Chaos

Johnson on January 5, 2017.[206] A worthwhile side note at this point, in light of the 2013 Executive Order 13636 establishing a cybersecurity framework through Sector Coordinating Councils, is that the definition of the word "soviet" literally is translated as "council".[207] The author of this report found this an interesting factoid in light of the vast network of councils that the Department of Homeland Security amassed under the creation of areas of "critical infrastructure." Is the DHS structure of information sharing though a vast network of councils by definition a soviet union of sorts? This question will be left rhetorical food for thought.

The charter of the EI-SCC and shortly after the EI-ISAC might be the most alarming affronts to the U.S. Constitution with regard to local operation and management of elections discovered in the research of this report. The charter of the EI-SCC, approved on February 15, 2018 states the purpose of the organization is "to clarify and inform the organizational structures, function, and operating procedures for the organization..."[208] and "The EI-SCC will serve as the principal asset owner interface with other private critical infrastructure sectors as well as with the Department of Homeland Security (DHS), the U.S. Election Assistance Commission (EAC), the state, local and tribal governments (SLTTs), and the Election Infrastructure Subsector Government Coordinating Council (EI-GCC)."[209]

The objectives and scope of the activities to be undertaken by the EI-SCC read like a list of election management activities. The most alarming "activity" is that **this council will act as ACT AS A**

---

[206] https://www.eac.gov/sites/default/files/eac_assets/1/6/starting_point_us_election_systems_as_Critical_Infrastructure.pdf
[207] https://encyclopedia2.thefreedictionary.com/soviet
[208] https://www.cisa.gov/sites/default/files/publications/govt-facilities%20-EIS-scc-charter-2018-508.pdf
[209] https://www.cisa.gov/sites/default/files/publications/govt-facilities%20-EIS-scc-charter-2018-508.pdf

CHAPTER 10

REPRESENTATIVE for those entities in the election subsector. The full list of activities is:

- **Serve as the primary liaison** between the election subsector and federal, state, and local agencies, including the Department of Homeland Security (DHS), concerning private election subsector security and emergency preparedness issues;
- **Facilitate sharing of information** and intelligence about physical and cyber threats, vulnerabilities, incidents, and potential protective measures;
- **Coordinate with DHS and the EIS GCC** to develop, recommend, and review sector-wide plans, procedures, and effective practices in support of infrastructure protection, including training, education, and implementation;
- **Represent the election subsector** in discussions with other infrastructure sectors, as well as with the EIS GCC, on matters of threat, security, risk analysis, emergency preparedness and response, and other related matters;
- **Identify and communicate priorities**, obstacles or impediments to effective critical infrastructure security and resilience protection programs and develop/recommend to appropriate authorities actions to mitigate them;
- **Provide a mechanism** to ensure that the specialized knowledge and expertise of sector operators, owners, and other pertinent representatives is available as a resource.[210]

Once again, designating election infrastructure as "critical infrastructure" was arguably the most monumental change to the American elections system ever in history. The designation created

---

[210] https://www.cisa.gov/sites/default/files/publications/govt-facilities%20-EIS-scc-charter-2018-508.pdf

Countdown to Chaos

the EI-SCC as "principal collaboration points between the government and private sector owners and operators for critical infrastructure security and resilience policy..."[211] Membership is "available to any owner or operator with significant business or operating interests in U.S. election infrastructure systems or services..." and may" include entities (companies, organizations, or components thereof) whose services, systems, products or technology are used by (or on behalf of) State or Local government in administering the U.S. election process."[212]

The EI-SCC is a self-governing body that "operates under the Critical Infrastructure Partnership Advisory Council (CIPAC) framework established by the Secretary of Homeland Security pursuant to section 871 of the Homeland Security Act of 2002 (6 U.S.C. §451)."[213] Each member of the EI-SCC receives one vote, and the body is further governed by a five-member executive committee.

The Constitution of the United States calls for elections to be free, fair, and transparent. Some key information regarding the EI-SCC, which has been delegated by the Department of Homeland Security to "represent the election subsector," is exceptionally tightly held. For example, "minutes, including records of votes, may be secured and electronically stored by the Secretariat. **Access to the records of the EISCC shall be limited to current EISCC membership.**"[214] In addition, the full membership list is kept with strict guidance as well. The charter states: "The Secretariat will

---

[211] https://www.eac.gov/sites/default/files/eac_assets/1/6/starting_point_us_election_systems_as_Critical_Infrastructure.pdf
[212] https://www.cisa.gov/sites/default/files/publications/govt-facilities%20-EIS-scc-charter-2018-508.pdf
[213] https://www.cisa.gov/sites/default/files/publications/govt-facilities%20-EIS-scc-charter-2018-508.pdf
[214] https://www.cisa.gov/sites/default/files/publications/govt-facilities%20-EIS-scc-charter-2018-508.pdf

CHAPTER 10

maintain the Council's CIPAC membership roster,"[215] while the charter does not detail any transparency or accessibility of the membership list to the voting public. However, the founding membership is provided in the charter.

The organizing members of the EI-SCC are:

- Associated Press (AP) Elections
- BPro, Inc.
- Clear Ballot Group
- Crosscheck
- Democracy Live
- Democracy Works
- Demtech Voting Solutions
- Dominion Voting Systems
- ELECTEC Election Services Inc.
- Election Systems & Software
- Electronic Registration Information Center (ERIC)
- Everyone Counts
- Hart InterCivic
- MicroVote General Corp.
- PCC Technology Inc.
- Pro V&V
- Runbeck Election Services
- SCYTL
- SLI Compliance
- Smartmatic
- Tenex Software Solutions
- Unisyn Voting Solutions
- VOTEC
- Votem
- VR Systems

Interesting additional evidence of failure to provide transparency to the public about the EI-SCC, the identities of the signers of the founding charter who sign as chair and vice chair, are redacted from the publicly posted charter document. After its formation,

---

[215] https://www.cisa.gov/sites/default/files/publications/govt-facilities%20-EIS-scc-charter-2018-508.pdf

Countdown to Chaos

the EI-SCC remained largely silent. The organization made curious appearances in the timeframe very close to the days before and after the 2020 Presidential Election. The content of the information published by the EI-SCC later in this report should be highly scrutinized in light of the intensely opaque nature of what is truly a quasi-governmental agency.

Only five months after its own establishment and charter, the Election Integrity Government Coordinating Council (EI GCC) formed by the Department of Homeland Security quickly established the Election Infrastructure Information Analysis Center (EI-ISAC) in March of 2018. The EI-ISAC charter states the entity "is a critical resource for cyber threat prevention, protection, response and recovery for the nation's state, local, territorial, and tribal (SLTT) election offices. The EI-ISAC is operated by the Center for Internet Security, Inc."[216] Within the description of the EI-ISAC mission resides the following details:

- "The mission of the EI-ISAC is to improve the overall cybersecurity posture of SLTT election offices, through collaboration and information sharing among members, the U.S. Department of Homeland Security (DHS) and other federal partners, and private sector partners are the keys to success."
- "The EI-ISAC provides a central resource for gathering information on cyber threats to election infrastructure and **two-way sharing of information** between and among public and private sectors…"
- "The EI-ISAC provides an election-focused cyber defense suite through its 24-hour watch and warning center, real-time network monitoring…"
- "The EI-ISAC works closely with DHS and is recognized by the GCC as the national ISAC for SLTT election offices to

---

[216] https://www.cisecurity.org/ei-isac/ei-isac-charter/

CHAPTER 10

coordinate cyber readiness and response. The EI-ISAC also works closely with other organizations, such as the National Council of ISACs, the National Association of Secretaries of State, the National Association of State Election Directors, the Election Center, and the International Association of Government Officials, as well as other public and private sector entities to build trusted relationships to further enhance our collective cybersecurity posture."[217]

Previous discussion and evidence in this report supports the description of the services provided in the mission of the EI-ISAC as those of the Albert Monitoring System described in detail in Chapter 6. Information listed in section titled "Principles of Conduct" of the charter includes the following dictates that members will:

- "Agree to share appropriate information between and among the Members to the greatest extent possible..."
- "Agree to collaborate and share across each of the critical sectors to reduce barriers in order to foster our collective mission..."
- "Agree to transmit sensitive data to other Members only through the use of agreed-upon secure method."[218]

Specifics of information sharing protocol outlined in the EI-ISAC charter includes this statement:

> "Notwithstanding the foregoing, all Data provided by Members may be shared with EI-ISAC's federal partners (including, without limitation, the U.S. Department of Homeland Security), and may be shared with other

---

[217] https://www.cisecurity.org/ei-isac/ei-isac-charter/
[218] https://www.cisecurity.org/ei-isac/ei-isac-charter/

Members provided that the Data is anonymized and not attributable to any individual Member."[219]

To ramp up on the scope and mission of the EI-ISAC, beyond the EI-ISAC charter, the Center for Internet Security and EI-ISAC published a Year in Review report for 2018. As information sharing was the primary reason for the formation of the EI-ISAC, points about information sharing are plentiful in this document and should be thoroughly reviewed. Within this report is information about the Homeland Security Information Network (HSIN) which was introduced briefly in Chapter 5 of this report with the evolution of the EINSTEIN program. The HSIN is a complete federal cyber network encompassing the participants from the entirety of the ISAC realm. The HSIN is part of the "information sharing environment" codified by 6 U.S. Code § 485.[220] Now that elections are "critical infrastructure" the EI-ISAC is a "node" in the federal information technology network built and managed by the HSIN. The DHS website states the scope of HSIN clearly with regard to elections:

> "DHS' Cybersecurity and Infrastructure Security Agency and the Elections Infrastructure Information Sharing and Analysis Center teamed with HSIN to operate web-based Cyber Situational Awareness Rooms, which allowed live monitoring of election security threats and enabled interagency officials to quickly collaborate on analysis and incident response."[221]

The report details specifications of the initial Pilot Program for the year 2018. The 2018 Year in Review Pilot report states:

---

[219] https://www.cisecurity.org/ei-isac/ei-isac-charter/
[220] https://www.law.cornell.edu/uscode/text/6/485
[221] https://www.dhs.gov/hsin-annual-report

CHAPTER 10

- "...pilot that included representatives from seven states (Colorado, Indiana, New Jersey, Texas, Utah, Virginia, Washington) and two local election organizations (Travis County, Texas; Weber County, Utah)."
- "The pilot program called for the deployment of "Albert," the MS-ISAC's Intrusion Detection System (IDS), on every pilot state's elections network to protect the voter registration database if it was not covered by an existing Albert sensor."
- "Albert deployments proved to be a challenge, with only five of the seven states successfully incorporating Albert sensors by the end of the pilot phase. The remaining two states were not far behind – one state went online the day after the pilot closed, and the final pilot sensor was installed and running by early March."
- "On February 15 the EIS-GCC reviewed the pilot's current efforts and future plans, and voted in favor of the formal creation of the EI-ISAC, operated by CIS alongside the MS-ISAC."[222]

Key information sharing statements made within the 2018 EI-ISAC Year in Review include:

- "In addition, working **with the FBI's** Cyberhood Watch provided the EI-ISAC with an opportunity for bidirectional sharing of valuable threat information, while other **partners like Democracy Works furnished information to assist with outreach to local elections offices**."
- "Nearly half of the EI-ISAC Membership provided the SOC with their public-facing IP address, ranges and domains for passive monitoring and monthly vulnerability notifications by the Vulnerability Management Program.

---

[222] https://www.cisecurity.org/ei-isac/ei-isac-charter/

Countdown to Chaos

- "Using the HSIN platform as a foundation, the EI-ISAC stood up an online portal specifically for the Election Infrastructure Subsector, seeding it with a library of all EI-ISAC published documents as well as discussion boards for members to collaborate."
- "...the EI-ISAC [set out] to prove its ability to achieve something the election infrastructure community had repeatedly identified as a key goal: **Effective collaboration and communication across agencies and organizations <u>on Election Day</u>.**"
- "...the EI-ISAC and DHS executed a community-wide communication plan so that appropriate parties would be notified about incidents and trends; federal agencies and partner organizations would be able to efficiently and securely exchange information; and state and local elections offices would have timely reporting streams and mechanisms."
- "...**fusion centers** ... developed new, internal reporting streams for information-sharing..."
- "**National Cyber Situational Awareness Room (NCSAR)** - The NCSAR HSIN room was opened to EI-ISAC members and partners on October 31 for 12 hours each day and transitioned to a 24-hour resource on November 4 for the duration of the week of the general election. Over the two-week span, and especially on November 6."
- "On Election Day, the goal of the EI-ISAC was collaboration: both facilitating it among our members, and also between our members and various representatives at the federal government level."[223]

With the federal government now free to have their hands practically anywhere in the election system, the EI-ISAC 2018 Year

---

[223] https://www.cisecurity.org/wp-content/uploads/2019/02/EI-ISAC-2018-YIR.pdf

CHAPTER 10

In Review outlines **the placement of federal intelligence officers throughout its election fusion centers and other federal agencies**:

- "DHS embedded a DHS Intelligence & Analysis representative at the EI-ISAC headquarters for more than a month prior to the election..."
- "At the end of October, an elections focused Intelligence Analyst from the EI-ISAC was detailed at NCCIC in Washington, D.C., to assist with federal communication with EI-ISAC headquarters."
- "The elections-focused Intelligence Analyst remained at the NCCIC, joining the ISAC liaison. This facilitated intelligence-sharing with the federal and private sector partners seated at the NCCIC, including DHS I&A and the FBI."
- "...two ISAC staff were positioned at the National Fusion Center Association (NFCA)... EI-ISAC representatives were able to get a pulse on what fusion center partners were reporting..."
- "On Election Day 2018, an additional HSIN situation room was opened and managed by the ETF. While the EI-ISAC NCSAR remained active, 225 federal employees were kept informed through this additional channel."[224]

The information outlined and highlighted here from the EI-ISAC bears a shocking resemblance to the white paper published by INSA in November 2016 titled "PROTECTING THE HOMELAND: Intelligence Integration 15 Years After 9/11."[225] Details about INSA, its connections and involvement with presidential administrations is briefly outlined previously in Chapter 9 of this report.

---

[224] https://www.cisecurity.org/wp-content/uploads/2019/02/EI-ISAC-2018-YIR.pdf
[225] https://www.insaonline.org/wp-content/uploads/2017/04/INSA_WP_ProtectHomeland.pdf

Countdown to Chaos

The EI-ISAC 2018 Year in Review also outlines the Albert Monitoring system in fairly wide terms, but highlighted the organization's massive push to get the IDS out into the SLTT election cyber environments quickly in order to be fully operational for the 2018 midterm election. Information about Albert included in the report included:

- "The pilot program called for the deployment of "Albert," the MS-ISAC's Intrusion Detection System (IDS), on every pilot state's elections network to protect the voter registration database if it was not covered by an existing Albert sensor."
- "The EI-ISAC expanded this initiative to cover the voter registration databases of any state or territory where the voter registration database was not already covered by an existing sensor, as well as to place sensors in 42 of the most populous local election jurisdictions in which voter registration data were hosted on local hardware."
- "By Election Day 2018 "approximately 90 percent of all voters in the United States would cast a ballot in a jurisdiction or state monitored by Albert... 45 states, one territory, and 84 local jurisdictions (18 of which were federally funded) had Albert sensors protecting their voter registration data."
- "...when these sensors are deployed nationwide, experts at the ISAC are able to track trends and intrusions and then share that information with election organizations at both the state and local level to better prepare them for the challenges that lie ahead. According to CIS President and CEO John Gilligan, "When you start to get dozens, hundreds of sensors, like we have now, you get real value."

A point that the report makes clear was that in context of the initial rollout of the Albert IDS system created by the DHS and offered initially by MS-ISAC since 2011, the rollout in 2018 prior to the

CHAPTER 10

midterm elections was, by the report's own testimony, rushed to say the least. Not only did the EI-ISAC team streamline the ordering and logistical process, but they reported "extensive outreach and technical support efforts" in order to reach the goal of implementing all the federally funded monitors. Considering the two failing federal government audits surrounding the EINSTEIN system from where the Albert monitor was born, the hasty rollout of an intrusion detection system inside an environment as sensitive as the American election system, and the details provided about this issue in this report, every American voter has definite cause for serious concern as to the soundness of the election system as well as cause for serious concern regarding whose "ears and eyes" are within the system and why.

One of the most peculiar facts of note in the EI-ISAC 2018 Year in Review is the admission that one of the "supporting partners" of this information sharing public-private partnership was the International Association of Government Officials (IGO).[226] The direction this discovery would take would redirect the scope of this paper and will require more investigation which this paper will not do, however, a quick examination of their website finds their vision quote as "The leading organization for local officials, fostering excellence in public service through education, innovation, and networking," while their mission states "Equipping Clerks, Election Officials, Recorders and Treasurers with professional training and leadership development..." Critically noteworthy, the homepage of their website very prominently lists Dominion Voting Systems and Election Systems & Software (ES&S) as sponsors.[227]

"On Friday, March 23, [2018], President Donald J. Trump signed the Consolidated Appropriations Act of 2018 (the Act) into law. The Act

---

[226] https://www.cisecurity.org/wp-content/uploads/2019/02/EI-ISAC-2018-YIR.pdf
[227] https://iaogo.org/

Countdown to Chaos

included $380 million in grants, made available to states to improve the administration of elections for Federal office, including to enhance technology and make election security improvements."[228] There can be little doubt these 2018 HAVA funds were likely the federal funds referred to in the EI-ISAC 2018 Year in Review that were used to implement the rollout of the Albert Monitoring System prior to the 2018 mid-term elections.

After over a year of members of the former administration of Barack Obama continually insisting the 2016 election had been hacked by the Russians, on June 23, 2017 the narrative continued when John Brennan in an interview given to the Senate Select Committee on Intelligence, stated:

> "We know that the Russians had already touched some of the electoral systems, and we know that they have capable cyber capabilities. So there was a real dilemma, even a conundrum, in terms of what do you do that's going to try to stave off worse action on the part of the Russians, and what do you do that is going to ... [give] the Russians what they were seeking, which was to really raise the specter that the election was not going to be fair and unaffected."[229]

And yet the conclusion of the final report of the Senate Select Committee on Intelligence released May 18, 2018, found that "The Russian government directed extensive activity, beginning in at least 2014 and carrying into at least 2017, against U.S. election infrastructure' at the state and local level. The Committee has seen no evidence that any votes were changed or that any voting

---

[228] https://www.eac.gov/payments-and-grants/2018-hava-funds-faqs
[229] https://www.intelligence.senate.gov/sites/default/files/documents/Report_Volume1.pdf

CHAPTER 10

machines were manipulated."[230] However, having been convinced there was some infiltration of state systems, such as the Illinois voter registration system, the Select Committee concluded that as part of their recommendations, the Albert Monitoring system should continue to be deployed as a part of the solution.[231]

On August 8, 2018, the Information Technology – Information Sharing and Analysis Center (IT-ISAC) and the Election Integrity Information Sharing and Analysis Center jointly announced the creation of the Election Integrity Special Interest Group (EI-SIG) in a press release stating the purpose of the group was "for election industry providers to guard their networks and assets against threats."[232] The press release further states:

- "The goal of the EI-SIG – or 'the SIG' – is **to scale up the sharing** that's happening through our companies within the private sector **to develop a 'Super-ISAC' capability,**" noted Kay Stimson, Chair of the Election Infrastructure Sector Coordinating Council and Vice President of Government Affairs for **Dominion Voting Systems.** "This proactive move will help industry understand broader threats to election IT systems and engage in peer-to-peer learning across sectors."[233]

---

[230] https://www.intelligence.senate.gov/sites/default/files/documents/Report_Volume1.pdf

[231] https://www.intelligence.senate.gov/sites/default/files/documents/Report_Volume1.pdf

[232] https://130760d6-684a-52ca-5172-0ea1f4aeebc3.filesusr.com/ugd/b8fa6c_765f03ef0e584e7ca6819b41b7d16847.pdf

[233] https://130760d6-684a-52ca-5172-0ea1f4aeebc3.filesusr.com/ugd/b8fa6c_765f03ef0e584e7ca6819b41b7d16847.pdf

Countdown to Chaos

- The IT-ISAC was established ... as **a central hub for anonymously sharing intelligence** about cybersecurity risks and threats to more effectively respond to risks and threats.
- The Elections Infrastructure Sector Coordinating Council, established in 2018, is a voluntary, self-organized and **self-governing body** representing more than two dozen private sector owners and operators of critical election infrastructure assets.[234]

It was this snippet of information, along with the 2019 CISA Cybersecurity Summit to appear in this report shortly, that began the research that this paper now encompasses. When this was first uncovered, the questions that needed to be asked and answered were:

- Why do American voting system companies need a special interest group under the cover of an ISAC?
- On what platform is EI-SIG information shared?
- What type of information is specifically shared by EI-SIG members and what is the limit of that sharing within the ISAC(s), if any?

After further understanding the ramifications of the formation of public-private partnerships, quasi-governmental agencies, and ISACs, these questions also need answering:

- Do the members of the EI-SIG have access to election night National Cyber Situational Awareness Rooms (NCSAR)?
- Do the member of the EI-SIG also have the same limits to liability as other EI-ISAC, MS-ISAC, and IT-ISAC members?

---

[234] https://130760d6-684a-52ca-5172-0ea1f4aeebc3.filesusr.com/ugd/b8fa6c_765f03ef0e584e7ca6819b41b7d16847.pdf

CHAPTER 10

- Do members of the EI-SIG also have the same protections as other ISAC members from Freedom Of Information Act (FOIA) requests?
- As members of the EI-SIG are also members if the EI-SCC, and are responsible for industry wide "representation" in connection with the Department of Homeland Security and all agencies to which they are connected, including the EAC, how can any audits of any elections in which any of these companies participate be valid if they are NOT performed by independent companies who do NOT share information with other ISAC members, are not present in NSCAR election night situation rooms, or other ISAC SOCs?

Members of the EI-SIG provided on the website are:

- Dominion Voting Systems
- Hart Intercivic
- Election Systems & Software (ES&S)
- Unisyn

This report is testament of the rabbit holes inside which these answers lie. The information necessary to answer these questions has driven the search for answers and focus of this paper. It has additionally yielded the continuous nagging question: How is the organization of each of these public-private partnerships, ISACs, SIGs, and other governance of elections under the Department of Homeland Security not a clear violation of the plenary power relegated to the state legislatures by the Constitution of the United States to determine the time and manner of elections, and how is it not a federal takeover of the American election process? This report aims to fully inform the American public the situation our federal government has quietly placed us in and let the PEOPLE determine the future of elections in this country. The EI-SIG will appear again in the future of this, prior to the 2020 general election, in a very interesting place, under very interesting

Countdown to Chaos

circumstances, with exceptionally interesting personalities that pose remarkably puzzling questions.

The next entry in the 2018 timeline happens on August 8, 2018, within the Senate Selection Committee of Intelligence report on Russian interference in the 2016 election which states for the record:

> "In a briefing before Senators on August 22, 2018, DNI Daniel Coats, FBI Director Christopher Wray, then DHS Secretary Kirstjen Nielsen, and then-DHS Undersecretary for the National Protection and Programs Division Christopher Krebs told Senators that **there were no known threats to election infrastructure**. However, Mr. Krebs also said that top election vulnerabilities remain, including the administration of the voter databases and the tabulation of the data, with the latter being a much more difficult target to attack." Relatedly, several weeks prior to the 2018 mid-term election, DHS assessed that "numerous actors are regularly targeting election infrastructure, likely for different purposes, including to cause disruptive effects, steal sensitive data, and undermine confidence in the election.'"[235]

As mentioned throughout this report, despite continual reports that the Russians did NOT directly threaten the election infrastructure, for years after the Obama administration and during the Trump administration, former Deputy National Security Advisor for Homeland Security and former CIA Director under Barack Obama, John Brennan, continually peddled that information. As this report outlines, John Brennan was, for all intents and purposes, the godfather of information sharing, public-private partnerships,

---

[235] https://www.intelligence.senate.gov/sites/default/files/documents/Report_Volume1.pdf

CHAPTER 10

and joint fusion centers. As such, the debate could soundly be undertaken to ask the question, "Was the singular goal of the ideology of John Brennan, James Clapper, and the like, to federalize and centralize the American election system?" This report has more information to consider in light of this question, with much of it appearing in the upcoming chapter twelve. The reader should make a real effort to read all referenced source material presented within this report in addition to all other material connected to this topic not included herein.

September 12, 2018 is another highly significant entry into the timeline of this report. On this date, President Donald J. Trump signed Executive Order 13848.[236] For weeks and months after the 2020 election, hardened supporters of President Trump wrongly hung their hopes on the notion that this EO was written with foreknowledge of nefarious activities in the upcoming 2020 Presidential Election, and that the EO was a blueprint for the apparently defeated incumbent president to challenge the results of the election and be pronounced the winner of the election. Understanding the timeline of events, the structures put into place, and the ramifications of each of these, the opposite impact of the EO was the alternative truth. Executive Order 13848, under the auspices of an emergency declaration, took the incredible power placed into the hands of the Department of Homeland Security as the sole manager and governing authority over elections after being designated "critical infrastructure" on January 6, 2017, by Obama's DHS Secretary, Jeh Johnson, and under its emergency authorization, **gave all federal departments connected to the DHS in its capacity of Election Infracture SSA (Sector Specific Agency) the order to monitor the 2020 election.** The extent to which that order was undertaken and the resulting events that became a part

---

[236] https://www.federalregister.gov/documents/2018/09/14/2018-20203/imposing-certain-sanctions-in-the-event-of-foreign-interference-in-a-united-states-election

Countdown to Chaos

of the historical record will be described later in this report. A blogpost published by The Conservative Treehouse does a good job of describing the proverbial corner Executive Order 13848 painted President Donald Trump into.[237] Reading of this information is recommended in context with the scope and evidence presented here later.

On Tuesday, November 6, 2018, the United States midterm elections were held. The Democrat party gained a total of 41 seats in the House of Representatives to return control of that chamber of Congress to the Democrat Party. It is noteworthy that among Democrat candidates for various seats throughout government in 2018 were an unusual number of former CIA officials.[238] Very interestingly, the 2018 midterm election was reported to have yielded the highest voter turnout since 1914. The EI-ISAC 2018 Year In Review reported the SLTTs were served by 135 Albert monitors, the HSIN Situation Room, and hundreds of federal employees and intelligence officers.[239] While this statement will be harshly criticized, evidence here demonstrates that the 2018 midterm election was the first federalized election in U.S. history.

In February 2019, the EI-ISAC charter was adopted about one year after the organization of the ISAC.[240] Details of that charter were outlined earlier in this chapter. In conjunction with and referenced in the EI-ISAC charter, the Terms and Conditions of membership state that members WILL SHARE INFORMATION, and this is how the terms outline that agreement:

---

[237] https://theconservativetreehouse.com/blog/2021/09/08/white-house-extends-national-election-emergency-granting-authority-for-federal-intelligence-agencies-to-enter-state-election-databases-for-mid-term-election/
[238] https://www.cnn.com/2018/04/18/politics/intel-officers-running-against-trump-2018/index.html
[239] https://www.cisecurity.org/wp-content/uploads/2019/02/EI-ISAC-2018-YIR.pdf
[240] https://www.cisecurity.org/ei-isac/ei-isac-charter/

CHAPTER 10

- "The EI-ISAC has been established to facilitate the sharing of cyber and/or critical election infrastructure Data among EI-ISAC Members, and others as appropriate, in order to facilitate communication regarding cyber and/or election infrastructure readiness and response efforts. These efforts include, but are not limited to, disseminating early warnings of physical and cyber system threats, sharing security incident information between state, territorial, and local entities, providing trends and other analysis for security planning, and distributing current proven security practices and suggestions."

- "The EI-ISAC will be operated and supported by the Center for Internet Security, Inc., a not for profit corporation focused on enhancing the cyber security readiness and response of public and private sector entities, with a particular focus on state, local, tribal and territorial governments and critical infrastructure. EI-ISAC may also retain contractors from time to time to provide services to the EI-ISAC and its Members."

- "...The intent of the Data protection terms are to: (a) enable Member to make disclosures of Data to EI-ISAC while still maintaining rights in, and control over, the Data; and (b) set common information sharing protocol that will determine the extent to which Data can be shared with others. Nothing in these terms and conditions grants EI-ISAC or Member an express or implied license or an option on a license, or any other rights to, or interests in, the Data."

- "Notwithstanding the foregoing, unless a Member designates in writing that the Data in question cannot be shared or that such sharing is subject to stated restrictions, **all Data provided by Members may be shared with EI-ISAC's federal partners (including, without limitation, the U.S. Department of Homeland Security), and may be**

Countdown to Chaos

> **shared with other EI-ISAC members** provided that the Data is anonymized and not attributable to Member."

September 18-20, 2019, CISA (Cybersecurity and Infrastructure Security Agency) held its 2nd Annual National Cybersecurity Summit in National Harbor, MD.[241] CISA's own description of the event on its website states:

> "The Department of Homeland Security, Cybersecurity and Infrastructure Security Agency (CISA) will bring together critical infrastructure stakeholders from around the world to a forum with presentations focused on emerging technologies, vulnerability management, incident response, risk mitigation, and other current cybersecurity topics at the 2nd Annual National Cybersecurity Summit. The Summit provides the opportunity for Federal, state, local, tribal, and territorial agencies, private sector organizations, and international partners to highlight successes and opportunities for collective action.
>
> It is intended to be an inclusive event and will be particularly valuable for senior leaders, CISOs, general counsels, practitioners, and policy experts in public and private sector organizations, academia, and international entities who have shown a commitment to advancing cybersecurity and infrastructure protection risk management discussions."[242]

The most intriguing piece of intelligence to come out of this summit, with the exception of the PDF file of the agenda,[243] is the abject disappearance of all existence of Day 2 of the summit –

---

[241] https://us-cert.cisa.gov/event/2019-cisa-cybersecurity-summit
[242] https://us-cert.cisa.gov/event/2019-cisa-cybersecurity-summit
[243] https://us-cert.cisa.gov/sites/default/files/2019-09/2019_Cybersecurity_Summit_Agenda_S508C_13.pdf

CHAPTER 10

September 19, 2019. This report uncovered every piece of the information studied and provided within this report after undertaking an investigation into the fact that while Day 1 and Day 3 of the summit were widely available for review online, Day 2 was unretrievable. The author tried every mode of internet search possible to find it, including searches through foreign video and image search engines, and through multiple social media sources. There is not a single video or image of this Day to be found on the internet to the date of the writing of this report. The presentation of interest on September 19, 2020, in Breakout 5 of Maryland Ballroom A, of the National Harbor Room held at Gaylord at National Harbor, Maryland was titled:

"Protect 2020 - What the Elections Industry is Doing to Secure the 2020 Elections"

The description of the seminar was listed as: "Behind the scenes, the vendor community is working to protect the 2020 elections. Learn how they are coordinating on vulnerability disclosure and other mitigation actions to ensure the integrity of the democratic process. Moderator: Peder Jungck, BAE Systems"[244] Panelists for the presentation were:

- Eric Coomer, Director of Product Strategy and Security, Dominion Voting Systems
- Sam Derheimer, Director of Government Affairs, Hart InterCivic
- Brian Hancock, Unisyn Voting
- Chris Wlaschin, Vice President Systems Security and CISO, Election Systems and Software

This same group of presenters are also featured prominently on the IT-ISAC's EI-SIG website, featuring a virtual chat of the men talking

---

[244] https://us-cert.cisa.gov/sites/default/files/2019-09/2019_Cybersecurity_Summit_Agenda_S508C_13.pdf

Countdown to Chaos

about moving forward with securing voting systems. It is a very curious data point that the preeminent federal cyber agency, CISA, would scrub the internet of an entire day of its annual cyber conference. Not a photo or video of any sort exists of Eric Coomer at the 2019 CISA Cybersecurity Summit. The action alone is simply evidence, not of proof of any particular correlation, but basically intriguing information for consideration that CISA found it necessary to purge either the content or the presenters from their platform.

To the date of this report, it is the presenter, Eric Coomer, that made further headlines, being sued by a number of people after the 2020 Presidential Election, that may be the reason for the information to have disappeared. Stories about the circumstances surrounding that action are scantly available on the internet to date as well, coming under a flurry of censorship after the 2020 election. However, for the record here, Snopes ran an explanation coined as "Unproven"[245] which can be reviewed for context. It is, however, as one views the content, an important point to present in this report. Mr. Coomer's deposition appears later in the timeline of these events, and Mr. Coomer's own words should cause the Snopes story to be changed from "Unproven" to at least partly "Verified."

As 2019 wrapped up, the world was changing. China was under the watch of the intelligence community and others as the SARS-CoV-2 virus began its march around the globe.[246] On September 12, 2019, the first snippet of code was embedded into government systems running SolarWinds Orion platform. This incident begins what will be reported later as the greatest cyber hack in American history:

---

[245] https://www.snopes.com/fact-check/eric-coomer-dominion-trump/
[246] https://news.yahoo.com/suspected-sars-virus-and-flu-found-in-luggage-fbi-report-describes-chinas-biosecurity-risk-144526820.html

CHAPTER 10

"The attack began with a tiny strip of code. Meyers traced it back to Sept. 12, 2019. 'This little snippet of code doesn't do anything,' Meyers said. 'It's literally just checking to see which processor is running on the computer, if it is a 32- or 64-bit processor and if it is one or the other, it returns either a zero or a one.'

The code fragment, it turns out, was a proof of concept — a little trial balloon to see if it was possible to modify SolarWinds' signed-and-sealed software code, get it published and then later see it in a downloaded version. And they realized they could. 'So at this point, they know that they can pull off a supply chain attack,' Meyers said. 'They know that they have that capability.'

After that initial success, the hackers disappeared for five months. When they returned in February 2020, Meyers said, they came armed with an amazing new implant that delivered a backdoor that went into the software itself before it was published."[247]

On December 20, 2019, the Consolidated Appropriations Act of 2020 passed, appropriating $425M to states for expenditures including upgrade of election-related computer systems to address cyber vulnerabilities identified through the Department of Homeland Security.[248] As the country worked toward the upcoming 2020 election, additional money was passed and sent through the DHS to continue to build and reinforce the massive cyber network infrastructure that had been quietly built to connect as many election precincts to the federal network as possible through the Albert Monitor System and the HSIN. The 2020 election will be the first Presidential election in the history of the

---

[247] https://www.npr.org/2021/04/16/985439655/a-worst-nightmare-cyberattack-the-untold-story-of-the-solarwinds-hack
[248] https://www.congress.gov/bill/116th-congress/house-bill/1158/text

Countdown to Chaos

United States that will have a federal agency, the Department of Homeland Security, act as "governing authority" over the entire election infrastructure. The 2020 election will prove to be one fraught with unrest and unanswered questions. This report will align the facts of the federal programs put into place with facts reported to multiple sources on election day within the summary of the report.

Chapter 11

EDR Monitoring Beyond Albert, RABET-V Pilot System, The 2020 Presidential Election, SolarWinds (2020)

The year 2020 was a year that will go down in history for being one of the most tumultuous and poignant moments in world history. The year began with a struggle between the World Health Organization (WHO) and the Trump Administration regarding a travel restriction mandate for travel into and out of the United States from China. Later, the mandate would extend to limit travel to and from European nations as well. At the same time, in January, House Leader Nancy Pelosi was delivering articles of impeachment against President Trump to the Senate. While geopolitical winds were whipping, the CIS and DHS continued their work on the Albert Monitoring System.

In February 2020, CIS launched the "CIS SLTT Endpoint Protection Concept of Operations (CONOPS) (Elections Infrastructure Pilot)". This purpose of the pilot was to test an expansion of endpoint protection platforms (EPP), endpoint detect and response (EDR) programs, and a next generation antivirus package.[249] The information provided potential participants stated the following about the program in its request for information (RFI):

> "The EI-ISAC is currently conducting an EDR pilot and has deployed agents on election infrastructure systems. Pilot activities started in February 2020 and will end in July 2021. During the pilot, **EDR agents from a single vendor (CrowdStrike)** were deployed to thousands of endpoints, which span across several hundred election entities. The EI-ISAC's primary role during the pilot is to

---

[249] https://www.cisecurity.org/wp-content/uploads/2021/02/2021-02-24-EPP-RFI-FINAL.pdf

Countdown to Chaos

> act as a Managed Security Service Provider (MSSP). The CIS Security Operations Center (SOC) receives threat telemetry data from all of the EDR agents from the commercial service provider's virtual private cloud using a well-formed API. ... In addition to analyzing threat data, the CIS SOC is responsible for 'deny/allow' list management and 'indicators of actions rule' tuning. The EDR pilot vendor's portal also enables the CIS Device Engineering team to onboard new pilot participants and to manage all deployed EDR agents."[250]

In the section titled "Mandatory EPP Product Requirements" the following points are noteworthy requirements of participating systems:

- "Capability that includes signatureless protection and use of behavioral-based methods that use Machine Learning and/or Artificial Intelligence learned algometric models for threat detection and blocking."
- "Capability of the EPP agent to gather and retain gathered endpoint activity metadata in a CIS specified centralized storage location for later examination."
- "Capability to send captured EPP log data to a CIS specified log collection platform in a standard log format such as syslog, CSV, or JSON."
- "Capability to use "zero touch" provisioning to rapidly implement the EPP agents on SLTT organizational devices. Installing, configuring, and operationalizing many locations must be accomplished in a short period of time. Specifically, this should happen in hours, not days or weeks."

---

[250] https://www.cisecurity.org/wp-content/uploads/2021/02/2021-02-24-EPP-RFI-FINAL.pdf

CHAPTER 11

- "**Capability to uninstall all vendor EPP related components rapidly from SLTT organization endpoints. This agent removal must support many locations.**"
- "Capability to provide federated controls for the purposes of limiting or granting access to SLTT EPP data (e.g., alerts, event data, and forensics) within a multi-level hierarchical structure that is controlled by CIS."
- "Capability for CIS and SLTT organizations to perform ad hoc queries on the EPP data being captured for their respective organizations. - The EPP capability should be able to capture, store, index, and correlate realtime endpoint data in a searchable repository from which CIS can generate ad-hoc reports, alerts, dashboards, and visualizations for any specific SLTT organization, organizational subcomponent, a combination of CIS specified organizations, or all SLTT CIS supported organizations."
- "Capability of the EPP tool to easily integrate with other security and operations tools, such as a SIEM, SOAR, additional EPPs, and network sandboxes. This includes access via mature product APIs to allow CIS applications, as well as other COTS products, and access to the EPP-generated data and EPP security events."
- "AWS or Azure GovCloud instances of the platform must be available."[251]

In addition, to the system requirements above, CIS had a list of "desired" capabilities as well. They included:

- "**Not require a reboot of endpoint devices after installation or removal of the endpoint agent or for periodic commercially released updates and upgrades.**"

---

[251] https://www.cisecurity.org/wp-content/uploads/2021/02/2021-02-24-EPP-RFI-FINAL.pdf

Countdown to Chaos

- **"Use of machine learning and artificial intelligence** capabilities to enhance detection of threats."
- "A "device control" component for controlling and monitoring the external devices connected to a monitored endpoint."
- "A real time response capability to allow Cyber Incident Response Team (CIRT) members to conduct live investigations into machines that are potentially compromised by malicious actors."

Finally, from this RFI was a list of requirements if the SLTT entity wished to add the antivirus package. This list included:

- "Ability for vendor's Antivirus capability for SLTT endpoints to be centrally monitored and managed by CIS."
- "Capability to automatically uninstall a competitor's well-known COTS Antivirus or EPP software on specified SLTT endpoints."
- **"Capability to automatically uninstall the proposed Antivirus capability** from specified endpoints without adversely affecting the endpoint, other endpoint applications or end-user experience."
- **"Capability to disable the existing Antivirus capability on the endpoint**, or re-enable and reconfigure the existing Antivirus to run as the secondary Antivirus solution and the proposed Antivirus solution to operate as the primary Antivirus capability."

The key takeaways from the information presented for this CIS SLTT Endpoint Protection Concept of Operations (CONOPS) (Elections Infrastructure Pilot) include that the platform was created to work remotely, invisibly, live in real-time, remote access was to have full access to the endpoint, run through the cloud, use machine learning/artificial intelligence, and the remote user would have the ability to make changes at will, live in real-time on the endpoint.

CHAPTER 11

The importance of yielding these capabilities over to remote, unseen, federal, or quasigovernment agency agents cannot be overstated. The access and capabilities granted to federal agencies by the use of this EDR system was limitless and the results of what would happen in cyberspace would be completely invisible to the state and local administrators of the election systems which would be running these parallel EDR systems.

When local elections officials have machines certified for an election, it is always imperative that those machines, systems, and equipment DO NOT CHANGE prior to or during the election. A full review of the scope of systems and platforms being implemented by federal programs in this report and these additional capabilities that were expanded on election infrastructure as described above, raise serious questions once again over the management and oversight of elections that constitutionally belongs to the states. This also raises the question of certification of systems. If, as this report demonstrates, the remote capabilities of monitoring and mitigation services have the ability to reach devices in the election environment that include the voter registry, poll pads, and as state contracts testified, reach the voting systems[252], how can any system's certification have any meaning? As these election environments can be altered in real time, and unknowingly to anything or anyone with exception of another machine by means of artificial intelligence, how can any system using this technology be considered certified for the election?

When coupled with the HSIN live situation room (NCSAR), this access of election environments opens the entire process, down to the very precinct level, to invisible individuals and agencies, including federal agents and intelligence agencies. Federal agents

---

[252] https://www.ohiosos.gov/globalassets/elections/directives/2019/dir2019-08.pdf?__cf_chl_jschl_tk__=pmd_PqdUeUMq.hWsh5t7hSZySi7kvJdgOPtCD0SgmjkQsG0-1633723399-0-gqNtZGzNAnujcnBszQhl

and agencies have invisible access to the entire process for which it is the local authorities who are constitutionally first to have jurisdiction and management of the process to begin with. The problems with this election structure are numerous and exceptionally serious. Consider, for example, when the list of organizations and individuals that become a DIRECT part of the election process is compiled, there leaves little or any independent agencies to oversee or audit any of the process. These issues are of highest importance to further discover and address.

On February 6, 2020, the Government Accountability Office released what would be the third review of the network infrastructure and monitoring systems set up by CISA and the DHS.[253] In its report titled "DHS Plans Are Urgently Needed to Address Identified Challenges Before the 2020 Elections" the GAO states:

- "Since the 2017 designation of election infrastructure as critical infrastructure, the Department of Homeland Security (DHS), through its Cybersecurity and Infrastructure Security Agency (CISA), has assisted state and local election officials in securing election infrastructure through regional support and assistance, education, and information sharing."
- **CISA is not well-positioned to execute a nationwide strategy for securing election infrastructure prior to the start of the 2020 election cycle.** Further, CISA's operations plan may not fully address all aspects outlined in its strategic plan, when finalized.
- **CISA's unfinished planning means the agency may be limited in its ability to execute a nationwide strategy for securing election infrastructure.**

---

[253] https://www.gao.gov/assets/gao-20-267.pdf

CHAPTER 11

- CISA has not fully assessed and documented how it will address challenges identified in prior assessments, which limits the ability of CISA to address these challenges in its current efforts. [254]

This assessment was done in response to "the Conference Report (H. Rep. No. 116-9) accompanying the 2019 Consolidated Appropriations Act [which] included a provision for GAO to examine how DHS is implementing key responsibilities to help protect the election infrastructure and the reported benefits and challenges of such efforts."[255] As such, the GAO made three recommendations in early 2020, two of which remain open up to the completion of this report. They are:

- "The CISA Director should ensure that the operations plan fully addresses all lines of effort in the strategic plan for securing election infrastructure for the upcoming elections."
- "The CISA Director should document how the agency intends to address challenges identified in its prior election assistance efforts and incorporate appropriate remedial actions into the agency's 2020 planning."[256]

This audit and review would be the third time oversight of the program built by CISA, the DHS, and the CIS, was reported to be insufficient. Without being able to deliver on its cybersecurity promises, this system once again became nothing more than a grand national cybernetwork infrastructure linking all the United States' election systems together, and as this report has presented at multiple points, this cyber infrastructure was and is managed by

---

[254] https://www.gao.gov/assets/gao-20-267.pdf
[255] https://www.gao.gov/assets/gao-20-267.pdf
[256] https://www.gao.gov/assets/gao-20-267.pdf

Countdown to Chaos

the Executive Branch of the United States government and was riddled with vulnerabilities.

In the middle of February, on the 12th, 2020, the Department of Homeland Security issued a privacy impact statement. Historically these statements show up when a change to cyber data flows could potentially impact private information or other sensitive information that the network manages. The impact statement dated February 12, 2020 is titled "Privacy Impact Assessment for the Continuous Monitoring as a Service (CMaaS)."[257] The abstract of this PIA states the following:

> "The Department of Homeland Security (DHS), Chief Information Security Office (CISO) is leading the **DHS enterprise-wide deployment of Continuous Diagnostics and Mitigation (CDM) tools under the Continuous Monitoring as a Service (CMaaS) Program** to support the agency specific efforts to implement adequate, risk-based, and cost-effective cybersecurity across DHS. CMaaS provides continuous monitoring, diagnostics, and mitigation capabilities designed to strengthen the security posture of DHS and its Components, systems, and networks through the establishment of a suite of functionalities that **enable network administrators to know the state of their respective networks <u>at any given time</u>**. CMaaS further informs Chief Information Officers (CIO) and Chief Information Security Officers (CISO) on **the <u>relative risks</u> of cybersecurity threats**, and makes it possible for Department personnel to identify, prioritize, and mitigate vulnerabilities. This Privacy Impact Assessment (PIA) is being conducted to cover the first two phases of the program (Asset Management and

---

[257] https://www.dhs.gov/sites/default/files/publications/privacy-pia-dhs082-cmaas-february2020.pdf

CHAPTER 11

Identity and Access Management) and addresses the privacy risks associated with the deployment and operation of the CDM Agency Dashboard."[258]

Key points within the overview and body of this document include the following:

- "The Department of Homeland Security (DHS) is in the process of implementing the Continuous Monitoring as a Service (CMaaS) Program, which includes tools, sensors, and integration support services that support the planning, provisioning, configuration, operation, and management of tools, sensors, dashboards, and data feeds, to facilitate Continuous Diagnostics and Mitigation (CDM) governance." [This statement includes a reference provided here in the footnotes].[259]
- "The goal of CDM is to enable federal civilian departments and agencies to expand their continuous diagnostic capabilities for securing their computer networks and systems by increasing their network sensor capacity, automating sensor collections, and prioritizing risk alerts.""
- "Additionally, the implementation of CMaaS provides the following benefits:
    - **CMaaS deployed as a centralized service** (through the existing on-premise cloud at DHS Data Centers) to all DHS IT assets residing in a federated infrastructure model.
    - Tools and sensors implemented in a federated model providing Component-level service, capabilities, automation, dashboards, and limited customizations.

---

[258] https://www.dhs.gov/sites/default/files/publications/privacy-pia-dhs082-cmaas-february2020.pdf
[259] https://www.dhs.gov/topic/privacy

Countdown to Chaos

- o Endpoint sensors on supported operating systems deployed throughout Component networks feeding near-real time data to CMaaS tools.
- o Centralized management of the Component federated sensors, tools, automation, dashboards, and data.
- o Department reporting capabilities and the ability to interface and interoperate with all Department and Component Security Operations, Network Operations, Ongoing Authorization, and Common Operating Picture programs and efforts."

- "Asset Management data is used to identify all the hardware components and associated software, configuration settings, and vulnerabilities in the network environment and develop mitigation plans to address risks. Identity and Access Management data is used to identify risky conditions to users, the access (including privileged access) that each user has, each user's training, and the user's credential levels."
- "The Agency Dashboard and Splunk are configured to complete queries to identify and detect unexpected behavior based on hardware assets, software assets, configuration settings, and privilege/credential management."
- "Each Component is responsible for the deployment of the tools and sensors it uses on its network. Additionally, each Component, through role-based access, has access to its own data on the CDM Agency Dashboard. Those with the appropriate need-to-know, to include DHS CISO personnel may require access to all of the component data on the dashboard."[260]

---

[260] https://www.dhs.gov/sites/default/files/publications/privacy-pia-dhs082-cmaas-february2020.pdf

CHAPTER 11

One finding within this report that is worthy of noting and referring to, is that the SolarWinds platform as installed within its enterprise-wide deployment throughout the Department of Homeland Security environment is listed with settings in the "Master User Record" as being included in the "PRIVType" NETADMIN consoles.[261] This alone should raise eyebrows, but consider this along with these two facts uncovered by news sources that appear at this point in the timeline of this report:

- "When they [hackers] returned in February 2020, Meyers said, they came armed with **an amazing new implant that delivered a backdoor** [Sunburst] that went into the software itself before it was published."[262]
- "The hack began as early as March this year [2020] when hackers snuck malicious code into recent versions of SolarWinds' premier software product, Orion."[263]

In the context of the full timeline yet to be revealed in this report, there are multiple questions that arise from these findings, and the critical discoveries in the future. The big picture of the super cyber election infrastructure gets amazingly complex and dramatic as time approached the end of 2020.

On June 3, 2020, CISCO Systems announced a vulnerability in its NetFlow Version 9 packet processor used by DHS monitoring systems. Rating the vulnerability as "HIGH," Cisco explained the issue on its website in the following terms:

---

[261] https://www.dhs.gov/sites/default/files/publications/privacy-pia-dhs082-cmaas-february2020.pdf
[262] https://www.npr.org/2021/04/16/985439655/a-worst-nightmare-cyberattack-the-untold-story-of-the-solarwinds-hack
[263] https://www.dailymail.co.uk/news/article-9076045/SolarWinds-adviser-warned-cybersecurity-risks-2017-Russian-hack.html?ito=email_share_article-factbox

Countdown to Chaos

> "A vulnerability in the Flexible NetFlow Version 9 packet processor of Cisco IOS XE Software for Cisco Catalyst 9800 Series Wireless Controllers could allow an unauthenticated, remote attacker to cause a denial of service (DoS) condition on an affected device."[264]

Cisco's NetFlow was and is utilized by the Albert Monitoring System. The CIS website highlights its part in the system used by SLTTs inside the election system environment.[265] This event is mentioned at this point in this report to maintain the chronology of the timeline, however, its further significance will be discussed in the next chapter.

On August 4, 2020, President and CEO of the Center for Internet Security (CIS), John Gilligan, testified to a House Subcommittee on Cybersecurity, Infrastructure Protection, & Innovation Committee on Homeland Security. In the testimony Mr. Gilligan pointed out that the newly formed EI-ISAC was created in response to "the interference in the 2016 election."[266] About Albert monitors Gilligan shared:

- "As part of the initial [EI-ISAC] launch, CIS was also tasked with deploying a network of Albert sensors to all 50 state election offices and the five largest counties in states that have bottom-up and hybrid voter registration processes. Since then, all 50 states have deployed and many states have leveraged HAVA funding to procure additional Albert sensors for every county election office. CIS now processes data from 269 Albert sensors monitoring state and local

---

[264] https://tools.cisco.com/security/center/content/CiscoSecurityAdvisory/cisco-sa-iosxe-fnfv9-dos-HND6Fc9u
[265] https://www.cisecurity.org/services/albert-network-monitoring/
[266] https://homeland.house.gov/imo/media/doc/Testimony%20-%20Gilligan.pdf

CHAPTER 11

election networks, which support online elections functions such as voter registration and election night reporting..."

- "Starting with the 2018 primaries and mid-term elections, the EI-ISAC has hosted the Election Day Cyber Situational Awareness Room, an online collaboration forum to keep elections officials aware of cyber and non-cyber incidents and potential cyber threats for any statewide or national election. More than 600 elections officials, federal partners, and election vendors have participated in these forums. It is expected that participation in the situation room will likely grow to all 50 states for the November 2020 General Election."
- "Rapid Architecture-Based Election Technology Verification (RABET-V), focuses on the need for internet-connected election technology to be responsive and adapt quickly to changes in the threat landscape. RABET-V is addressing this with a process model that provides assurances of security, reliability, and functionality in a risk-based, flexible, change-tolerant process. We are currently piloting this process with several election technology vendors and a steering committee consisting of the Election Assistance Commission, DHS CISA, Federal Voting Assistance Program, and the States of Wisconsin, Ohio, Maryland, Texas, Pennsylvania, and Indiana. We anticipate a report following the November General Election."[267]

In a bit of a stunning admission forever memorialized in the Congressional Record, Mr. Gilligan states:

> "When you look back on it, the **post-2016 response to securing our elections is an excellent example of a successful public-private partnership**. The recognized

---

[267] https://homeland.house.gov/imo/media/doc/Testimony%20-%20Gilligan.pdf

shortfalls in 2016 have helped highlight a national crisis that has been responded to by many organizations working together. **NASS, NASED, the Election Center, IGO and their respective members remain central in running American elections.**"[268]

The federalization of much of the American government process has long been a dream of many in the progressive realm of political ideology. After the 2016 election of Donald Trump, all evidence suggests that any federal agency and individuals in positions of power able to influence key decision making, the process of federalization and centralization had been completed, and those orchestrating it were ready to admit it as we see by the admission of Mr. Gilligan in this testimony.

The RABET-V Pilot program (The Rapid Architecture-Based Election Technology Verification) described by CIS President, John Gilligan, in his House testimony was rolled out in February 2020. States that joined the CIS in this rollout as part of the steering committee were Wisconsin, Pennsylvania, Ohio, Texas, Maryland, and Indiana. The RABET-V Program was described by CIS as "an election technology verification process that supports rapid product changes by design,."[269] with a focus on electronic pollbooks, the election-night reporting system, and the election management systems (EMS). The RABET-V program was yet another layer of election management services being endorsed by federal agencies such as the NASS, and NASED, and being provided by and implemented through the CIS, and ultimately through the Department of Homeland Security.

---

[268] https://homeland.house.gov/imo/media/doc/Testimony%20-%20Gilligan.pdf
[269] https://www.nass.org/sites/default/files/2021 01/cis white paper nass winter21.pdf

CHAPTER 11

On August 31, 2020, former CIA Director John Brennan, popped his head out into the election landscape when he penned an op-ed for the *Washington Post*.[270] In his piece, Mr. Brennan, even though intelligence officials had testified and Congressional investigations had concluded that there was no significant Russian influence in the previous 2016 election, immediately came out of the chute and built this opinion article on "Russian interference in our elections." Mr. Brennan practically declared a personal war on President Trump in print ahead of the election stating:

> "In 2020, however, the situation is far different, as President Trump has shown utter contempt for the independence, objectivity and apolitical integrity of the intelligence community. And, since he has made no secret of his intention to do whatever necessary to stay in office beyond January 2021, there should be no doubt in anyone's mind that he will attempt to suffocate the flow of any intelligence to Congress that could upend his ruthless ambition."

Throughout the *Washington Post* piece, Brennan held onto and reasserted the falsely peddled narrative that embroiled Brennan, Clapper, Comey, Rice, Yates, Obama, Biden and the FBI into what turned into the Crossfire Hurricane investigation, and then exposed his erroneous position in the subsequently filed Senate Intelligence Committee. Key comments of interest by John Brennan in this piece in context with this report were:

- "In my more than 30 years of government service, I had witnessed some members of both political parties engage in **unethical behavior by misusing intelligence**, and I wanted to avoid that happening on the eve of a closely contested presidential election."

---

[270] https://www.washingtonpost.com/opinions/2020/08/31/john-brennan-trump-national-intelligence-congress/

Countdown to Chaos

- I personally conducted all the [Gang of 8] briefings. Most of the eight immediately recognized the gravity of Russian efforts. A notable exception was Sen. Mitch McConnell (R-Ky.), who insinuated that the CIA was working with the Obama administration to prevent Trump from getting elected."[271]

John Brennan was a key ideological architect of the public-private partnership structure that included ISACs, the CIS, federal fusions centers, and ultimately the federal government's takeover of the management of American elections. In late 2020, his resulting cyber structure architecture would be tested.

On September 28, 2020, members of the EI-SCC, the Election Infrastructure Subsector Coordinating Council, who were responsible for the formation of the public-private backbone of the EI-ISAC after the Jeh Johnson declared elections "critical infrastructure", published a statement shared by voting machine company Hart Intercivic. Titled "Election Technology Providers Urge Patience on Election Day,"[272] the executive committee of the EI-SCC preemptively warned American voters that counting of mail-in votes will delay the results of the 2020 election and official results could take up to 30 days. The executive committee of the EI-SCC who signed the statement was:

2020 EI-SCC Executive Committee:

- Brian Hancock, Chair (Unisyn Voting Solutions)
- Sam Derheimer, Vice Chair (Hart InterCivic)
- Ericka Haas, (ERIC) Maria Bianchi, (Democracy Works)
- Chris Wlaschin, (ES&S)

---

[271] https://www.washingtonpost.com/opinions/2020/08/31/john-brennan-trump-national-intelligence-congress/
[272] https://www.hartintercivic.com/eisccelectiondaystatement/

CHAPTER 11

The statement includes a comment already made earlier in August of 2020: "As CISA Director Christopher C. Krebs told event attendees at the Black Hat Information Security Conference earlier this year, delayed results will be a sign of careful counting — not of nefarious motives and widespread fraud."[273] The final admonition of the EI-SCC is, "The EI-SCC Executive Committee strongly reiterates this message and encourages the voting public to exercise patience and allow the official vote tallying and certification processes play out as intended in every State. Remember to rely on state and local election officials as your trusted sources for official election results." [274]

On October 1, 2020, John Brennan joined 50 other former intelligence officials and signed a letter that the news of a laptop reported to be owned by Hunter Biden (and later conclusively confirmed to be true), was in their assessment, part of a Russian disinformation campaign. In a later report about the letter in the *Washington Examiner*, another former official makes a comment about Brennan appearing at this point in time:

> "A former national security official who was asked to sign the letter but declined to do so told the *Washington Examiner* that Brennan's involvement with the letter was problematic because of his anti-Trump commentary and repeated claims of Trump-Russia collusion, and Brennan's name on the letter made it look like he was running a "rear guard action" as a favor to Biden to push back against a problematic story for the Biden campaign just before an election, saying Brennan was "too political" to be involved with a letter like this. The former official said Brennan "has Biden's ear" and it looked like Brennan worked to get his favored people in place once

---

[273] https://www.hartintercivic.com/eisccelectiondaystatement/
[274] https://www.hartintercivic.com/eisccelectiondaystatement/

Countdown to Chaos

Biden won, including Brennan's former deputies ending up as deputy CIA director and director of national intelligence."[275]

On October 7th 2020, John Brennan used his Twitter account[276] to make another assertion regarding the intelligence community's allegations that Trump colluded with Russia. He said:

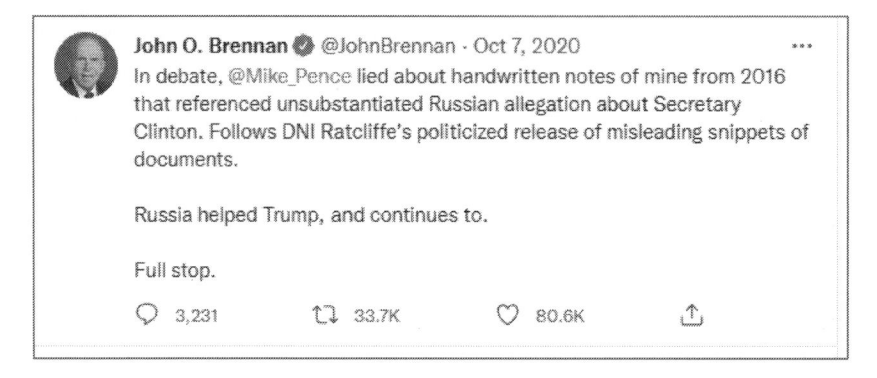

> **John O. Brennan** @JohnBrennan · Oct 7, 2020
>
> In debate, @Mike_Pence lied about handwritten notes of mine from 2016 that referenced unsubstantiated Russian allegation about Secretary Clinton. Follows DNI Ratcliffe's politicized release of misleading snippets of documents.
>
> Russia helped Trump, and continues to.
>
> Full stop.
>
> 3,231   33.7K   80.6K

The significance of each statement John Brennan and any others made on this topic will become shockingly clear with more information to be presented in chapter fifteen of this report.

The last event of note prior to the November 3rd, 2020 election, was an upgrade that is made to every voting machine in Georgia during the first week of October, 2020. It is on a date during that time that Dominion Voting Systems representative, Eric Coomer, completed a software upgrade to all 34,000 Dominion Voting machines in the state of Georgia.[277]

---

[275] https://www.washingtonexaminer.com/news/intel-officials-silent-letter-russian-involvement-hunter-biden-laptop-saga?utm_source=msn&utm_medium=referral&utm_campaign=msn_feed

[276] https://twitter.com/JohnBrennan/status/1314034940321898498?ref_src=twsrc%5Etfw

[277] https://www.newspapers.com/clip/63955060/coomer-pre-election-update-to-software/

CHAPTER 11

On November 3, 2020, America went to the polls to vote in person. Because of the declared COVID pandemic, a record-breaking number of ballots would be cast by mail which had a significant impact on the management of the election. Seven hundred fifty-one Albert monitors were deployed throughout all fifty states. In addition, the Department of Homeland Security ran the HSIN Cyber Situational Awareness Room, and the CIS SOC (Center for Internet Security – Security Operations Center). As predicted, the counting of mail-in absentee ballots extended the counting period. While most states were declared by the end of the evening on November 3rd, the states of Georgia, Pennsylvania, Michigan, Wisconsin, Nevada, and Arizona would remain outstanding for days after Election Day. As a result, the second election conducted under the governing authority of the Department of Homeland Security and the federal government, would record the greatest American voter turnout rate in over one hundred years, breaking the record turnout rate of the first federalized election of 2018.[278]

After the ballots were officially certified, Joe Biden would be declared the winner of the 2020 Presidential race. And while the state and local governments set up voting booths in their precincts and tallied votes at the precinct level, the federal government was involved in every single piece of the events of the day as the Department of Homeland Security had deployed 751 Albert Monitoring Systems in all fifty states for the 2020 election.[279] An official report required to be filed in answer to EO 13848, titled "Foreign Interference Targeting Election Infrastructure or Political Organization, Campaign, or Candidate Infrastructure Related to the 2020 US Related to the 2020 US Federal Elections," federal agencies including the DHS, FBI, CISA, and the Department of

---

[278] https://electionlab.mit.edu/research/voter-turnout
[279] https://learn.cisecurity.org/CIS-YIR-2020

Countdown to Chaos

Justice, would be declassified and released to the general public in March 2021. The details of the report state:

- "The impact to covered infrastructure was evaluated by considering, among other information, FBI forensic analyses; CISA cyber incident response activities, risk analysis, and stakeholder information; IC reporting; and open-source reporting."
- "We—the Department of Justice, including the FBI, and Department of Homeland Security, including CISA—have no evidence that any foreign government-affiliated actor prevented voting, changed votes, or disrupted the ability to tally votes or to transmit election results in a timely manner; altered any technical aspect of the voting process; or otherwise compromised the integrity of voter registration information of any ballots cast during 2020 federal elections."
- "We are aware of multiple public claims that one or more foreign governments—including Venezuela, Cuba, or China—owned, directed, or controlled election infrastructure used in the 2020 federal elections; implemented a scheme to manipulate election infrastructure; or tallied, changed, or otherwise manipulated vote counts. Following the election, the Department of Justice, including the FBI, and the Department of Homeland Security, including CISA, investigated the public claims and determined that they are not credible."
- "We have no evidence—not through intelligence collection on the foreign actors themselves, not through physical security and cybersecurity monitoring of voting systems across the country, not through post-election audits, and not through any other means—that a foreign

CHAPTER 11

government or other actors compromised election infrastructure to manipulate election results."[280]

Very important takeaways from this report are that clearly the federal agencies lay full claim on the management of the elections as this report outlines. It is paramount to note that at no point in the report do ANY of the state level complaints of voter integrity issues, affidavits, or other reported irregularities get addressed. The federal government clearly overtook the operation of the election and viewed it only through that looking glass, and the scope of the official report to the Executive Branch was only in answer to Executive Order 13848 as earlier outlined in this report. The "postmortem" of the 2020 election in light of EO 13848 is also a very important study to undertake. This report cites a blogpost commentary made about the fallout from that executive order in light of the federal cybernetwork superstructure the government built and the DHS took control over as its "governing authority." The event the article is written in response to will be reviewed in chapter thirteen, however the topic of the 2020 election is addressed within it and is applicable to this discussion at this point in the timeline.[281]

Even as state legislators throughout the United States took to their chambers and to courts in the months of November and December 2020 in attempts to properly assert the Constitutional power provided their state legislatures, the full power of the federal government provided through the declaration of elections as "critical infrastructure" came to bear on each and every state and every single voter as case by case was dismissed, primarily on standing. As outlined, the declaration of elections as critical

---

[280] https://www.dhs.gov/sites/default/files/publications/21_0311_key-findings-and-recommendations-related-to-2020-elections_1.pdf
[281] https://theconservativetreehouse.com/blog/2021/09/08/white-house-extends-national-election-emergency-granting-authority-for-federal-intelligence-agencies-to-enter-state-election-databases-for-mid-term-election/

Countdown to Chaos

infrastructure made the Department of Homeland Security the governing authority over the elections, and the EI-SCC, the representative body of the election participants (i.e. the SLTTs). In fact, it was the EI-SCC that issued the declaration via CISA Director, Chris Krebs, that "The November 3rd election was the most secure in American history."[282]

Consider this entire statement in context once again. This statement, "The November 3rd election was the most secure in American history,"[283] was made on November 12, 2020. The organizations conjoining on the statement were all federal agencies or quasi-governmental agencies. The names on the statement at the executive leadership level were:

- Election Infrastructure Government Coordinating Council (GCC) Executive Committee
- Cybersecurity and Infrastructure Security Agency (CISA)
- Assistant Director Bob Kolasky, U.S. Election Assistance Commission Chair
- Benjamin Hovland, National Association of Secretaries of State (NASS) President
- Maggie Toulouse Oliver, National Association of State Election Directors (NASED) President
- Lori Augino, and Escambia County (Florida) Supervisor of Elections
- David Stafford – and the members of the Election Infrastructure Sector Coordinating Council (SCC) – Chair Brian Hancock (Unisyn Voting Solutions), Vice Chair Sam Derheimer (Hart InterCivic), Chris Wlaschin (Election

---

[282] https://www.cisa.gov/news/2020/11/12/joint-statement-elections-infrastructure-government-coordinating-council-election
[283] https://www.cisa.gov/news/2020/11/12/joint-statement-elections-infrastructure-government-coordinating-council-election

CHAPTER 11

Systems & Software), Ericka Haas (Electronic Registration Information Center), and Maria Bianchi (Democracy Works)

An exceptionally important list of names for review in the context of the statement of "The November 3rd election was the most secure in American history,"[284] is the list of members of the EI-SCC that were the council that set up the EI-ISAC. The EI-ISAC was the final piece of the cyber networking puzzle that allowed the federal agencies and intelligence officials (i.e. the FBI, CIA, DHS, CISA, etc.) to all monitor and covertly access the election systems in real time within the local election environments themselves, accessing endpoints including the pollbooks, election management systems, and voter registration databases. At the time of the published statement, states were in the process of collecting literally thousands of affidavits of election witnesses, judges, monitors, and individual voters reporting what they all described as blatant election fraud. The list of people endorsing the now infamous statement about the purported security of the 2020 election was[285]:

Associated Press (AP) Elections

BPro, Inc.

Clear Ballot Group

Crosscheck

Democracy Live

Democracy Works

Demtech Voting Solutions

Dominion Voting Systems

ELECTEC Election Services Inc.

Election Systems & Software

Electronic Registration Information Center (ERIC)

Everyone Counts

---

[284] https://www.cisa.gov/news/2020/11/12/joint-statement-elections-infrastructure-government-coordinating-council-election
[285] https://www.cisa.gov/sites/default/files/publications/govt-facilities%20-EIS-scc-charter-2018-508.pdf

Countdown to Chaos

Hart InterCivic	Smartmatic
MicroVote General Corp.	Tenex Software Solutions
PCC Technology Inc.	Unisyn Voting Solutions
Pro V&V	VOTEC
Runbeck Election Services	Votem
SCYTL	VR Systems
SLI Compliance	

In issuing the statement, CISA, the DHS, and all agencies corresponding with the issuance of the release blatantly marginalized the authority of the states. In fact, in an election in which mail-in voting was used in historically record numbers, federal agencies patently ignored pressing issues coming from counties and states that were arising on a day-by-day and hour-by-hour basis with regard to serious questions about election issues such as chain of custody, voter registrations, ballot validity, and the rewriting of state election laws prior to the election. The federal government superstructure asserted itself as the authority over the election as the DHS, in its position as SSA, and in a very carefully crafted, made a the shocking, blunt, short statement endorsed by the public-private partnership quasigovernmental agencies and other federal agencies. Then, without any input from states struggling with election anomalies, the statement was immediately pushed out to the American public using EI-SCC member, The Associated Press.

For years following the 2016 election, right up to the weeks before the 2020 election, as already prefaced in earlier chapters of this report, the Intelligence Community and former intelligence officers John Brennan and James Clapper relentlessly preached that Russians were a serious threat to the election, declaring they believed Russians to be perpetrating operations just weeks before

CHAPTER 11

it, **even though information declassified by former acting Director of National Intelligence, Ric Grenell, as well as information given to the CIA in 2016 reported in later federal filings by John Durham, shows both men knew this premise to be absolutely false.**[286] Both Brennan and Clapper would now disappear from the scene and would remain silent about the security of the 2020 election, even as physical evidence from all over the country emerged alleging election fraud.

A historical review of the facts surrounding the assertion of Russian interference by the Brennan/Clapper crowd at different points throughout the years, and then the subsequent, ultimate proof that the assertions were blatant lies as laid out in the case of The United States v. Michael Sussman, causes some question as to whether the mention of the words "Russian interference" were used as a smoke screen in those years previously. Or, perhaps the scenario was one that could be used as excuse should their cyber superstructure fail in some way or another to function as they had planned. There is, in fact, historical evidence that simply laying the blame of anything by naming and declaring a nation's guilt, has been a tool used for influence and was used as such in the Australian NotPetya hack case.[287]

This report must yet again reiterate that when the Obama Secretary of the Department of Homeland Security, Jeh Johnson, declared U.S. elections part of the critical infrastructure just two short weeks before leaving office in 2017, the DHS became the governing authority over American elections and the EI-SCC, whose partial membership was just listed, were and are the representatives of the election "players" (i.e. the county clerks, boards of elections, secretaries of state, etc.). On November 16,

---

[286] https://www.hsgac.senate.gov/imo/media/doc/2020-04-16%20RHJ-CEG%20to%20FBI%20(Crossfire%20Hurricane%20Intel%20Memos).pdf
[287] https://www.zdnet.com/article/blaming-russia-for-notpetya-was-coordinated-diplomatic-action/

Countdown to Chaos

2020, a news story was published by the *Epoch Times* about the CISA statement and the group endorsing the claim. (The news story includes a screenshot of the EI-SCC membership that also included Amazon Web Services (AWS) and others.) The *Epoch Times* story stated:

> "After allegations emerged that called into question the integrity of voting machines produced by Dominion Voting Systems, the Cybersecurity and Infrastructure Security Agency (CISA)—part of the Department of Homeland Security—issued a statement on Nov. 12 disputing the allegations, saying 'the November 3rd election was the most secure in American history.'
>
> What the agency failed to disclose, however, is that Dominion is a member of CISA's Election Infrastructure Sector Coordinating Council, one of two entities that authored the statement put out by CISA.
>
> In addition, Smartmatic, a separate voting machine company that has been the subject of additional concerns, is another member."[288]

On November 17, 2020, President Donald Trump fired CISA Director, Chris Krebs, for the statements he released regarding the 2020 election.

Events were on a collision course for each other. The federal government agencies, after staking the claim that the 2020 election was the most secure in American history, would come in direct

---

[288] https://www.theepochtimes.com/dominion-part-of-council-that-disputed-election-integrity-concerns-in-dhs-statement_3581659.html?utm_source=newsnoe&utm_medium=email&utm_campaign=breaking-2020-11-16-5

CHAPTER 11

conflict with audits and data from the states. This information will be presented in this timeline in chapter thirteen.

The struggle continued in court cases through the meeting of the Electoral College and continues to this writing of this report. With a review of the timeline here presented, there is no doubt the role the states had for over two hundred years in running the election process was overtaken by the federal government structure of the United States in 2018 and 2020.

Countdown to Chaos

CHAPTER 12

Chapter 12
TIME OUT TO FOCUS ON:
National Fusion Centers (2001 - present)

When the election came into microfocus in 2020, and with the addition of the information presented within this report, it is imperative to take a moment to take a very close look at the fusion center system in America. Cleary, according to the 2018 EI-ISAC Year in Review, the fusion centers were a mode of information sharing within the public-private partnership model and became a key component of the management of the 2018 mid-term elections through the Homeland Security Information Network (HSIN).[289]

The investigation of the fusion centers for this report aimed to answer the following questions:

- What is the history of fusion centers?
- Under what governing authority are fusion managed?
- How are they funded?
- What is the standard for staffing the centers?
- Are those running fusion centers to be trusted?
- Is election data information traffic classified or unclassified information?
- Who holds the ultimate responsibility and liability for violations of civil rights, or violations to the U.S. Constitution when they occur within the structure of a fusion center?

---

[289] https://www.cisecurity.org/wp-content/uploads/2019/02/EI-ISAC-2018-YIR.pdf

Countdown to Chaos

- Are fusion centers simply a perfect amalgamation of state and federal entities to keep both accountability and transparency cloaked in bureaucratic secrecy?

When the Obama Administration established elections as critical infrastructure in 2017, he established their management within the Department of Homeland Security. Because that management by DHS was implemented through multiple ISAC's integral utilization of national fusion centers and the HSIN, a close inspection of that system is warranted in the scope of the handling of election data and management. The information to follow should open an important debate supporting the concept that the chain of custody of ballots should very much also include the chain of custody of all data information traffic, transmission, and access.

What is the history of fusion centers?

While most sources identify the establishment of fusion centers as following the September 11, 2001 terror attacks, there is evidence the concept began as early as 1997 by a group called "Terrorism Early Warning Group Expansion Project" founded in Los Angeles.[290] The citation accompanying this information suggests that this group intelligence gathering concept eventually migrated to the Department of Homeland Security. This appears to be a plausible beginning to the idea of the consolidation of high-tech monitoring of community events.

The details of 6 USC 607 Section 2006, specifies the establishment of fusion centers for law enforcement use in terror prevention. The activities of the fusion centers began with "information sharing and analysis."[291] While the primary establishment of fusion centers was for law enforcement, they experienced the "mission creep" of their new recharacterization for election monitoring after the 2016

---

[290] https://www.terrorism.org/historic-projects/
[291] https://www.congress.gov/110/plaws/publ53/PLAW-110publ53.pdf

CHAPTER 12

Presidential Election, when elections were added to "critical infrastructure" by President Obama and DHS Secretary Jeh Johnson on their way out of office in 2017. As there are no audits or oversight reviews of fusion centers' performance in monitoring elections available, the review for this report will rely on information from the approximately fifteen years of established practices of fusion centers up to their use in the 2018 and 2020 elections to apply to the concept of their use for monitoring elections on behalf of the federal government via the EI-ISAC and the HSIN.

The executive summary of a 2013 report by The United States House of Representatives Committee on Homeland Security titled "Majority Staff Report on the National Network of Fusion Centers" published a very simple definition of "fusion center". It stated that after the terror attacks in 2001, "The Implementing Recommendations of the 9/11 Commission Act of 2007 (Pub. L. 110-53) defines fusion centers as: "a collaborative effort of 2 or more Federal, State, local, or tribal government agencies that combines resources, expertise, or information..."[292]

Regarding the origin of both the physical establishments and policies of fusion centers, to this day, a document published by both the Department of Homeland Security and the Department of Justice in 2004, titled "Fusion Center Guidelines – Developing and Sharing Information and Intelligence in a New Era"[293] is cited by the National Fusion Center Association as the developmental document for the emergence of national fusion centers all over the United States. The National Fusion Center Association (NFCA) itself, was later established in 2010 with its mission declared as:

---

[292] https://www.archives.gov/files/isoo/oversight-groups/sltps-pac/staff-report-on-fusion-networks-2013.pdf

[293] https://bja.ojp.gov/sites/g/files/xyckuh186/files/media/document/fusion_center_guidelines_law_enforcement.pdf

Countdown to Chaos

> "...to represent the interests of state and major urban area fusion centers, as well as associated interests of states, tribal nations, and units of local government, to promote the development and sustainment of fusion centers to enhance public safety; encourage effective, efficient, ethical, lawful, and professional intelligence and information sharing; and prevent and reduce the harmful effects of crime and terrorism on victims, individuals, and communities."[294]

The same report also makes it clear that the fusion centers are an integral part of the Homeland Security Information Network (HSIN). This interconnected agency system was utilized in the 2018 midterm election and was highlighted on pages 66-67 of this report. Certainly, the capabilities of the communications and information sharing were improved and enhanced for the 2020 election as the Albert Monitoring System integration grew significantly in that timeframe. A recent FEMA report published in February 2021 outlines 80 fusion centers are currently operational within the United States.[295]

The establishment of fusion centers was met with resistance from groups such as the American Civil Liberties Union, the media, and academia. These organizations have published reviews cited in areas of discussion to follow. A few official reviews of these centers publish findings that excoriate fusion centers for a wide range of general inadequacies, violations, and waste. In one review by the United States Senate Permanent Subcommittee on Homeland Security and Governmental Affairs published October 3, 2012, the body castigated the Department of Homeland Security for multiple insufficiencies of the fusion centers. The executive summary of the report stated:

---

[294] https://nfcausa.wpengine.com/wp-content/uploads/2020/10/2018-to-2021-National-Strategy-for-the-NNFC7715.pdf
[295] https://www.fema.gov/sites/default/files/documents/FEMA_2021-Preparedness-Grants-Manual_02-19-2021.pdf

CHAPTER 12

> "**The investigation identified problems with <u>nearly every</u> significant aspect** of DHS's involvement with fusion centers...
>
> Regarding the centers themselves, the Subcommittee investigation learned that a 2010 assessment of state and local fusion centers conducted at the request of DHS found widespread deficiencies in the centers' basic counterterrorism information-sharing capabilities. DHS did not share that report with Congress or discuss its findings publicly. When the Subcommittee requested the assessment as part of its investigation, **DHS at first denied it existed, then disputed whether it could be shared with Congress**, before ultimately providing a copy...
>
> The Subcommittee investigation found that the fusion centers often produced irrelevant, useless or inappropriate intelligence reporting to DHS... Yet amid all the Congressional oversight, some of the worst problems plaguing the Department's fusion center efforts have gone largely undisclosed and unexamined.
>
> ... They [DHS officials and members of the Intelligence Community] have also admitted that DHS's own practices have fallen well short of what is necessary for an effective intelligence enterprise." [296]

The findings by the Senate Permanent Subcommittee were extensive and additional findings will be included within the information to follow.

---

[296] https://www.hsgac.senate.gov/imo/media/doc/10-3-2012%20PSI%20STAFF%20REPORT%20re%20FUSION%20CENTERS.2.pdf

Countdown to Chaos

Under what governing authority are fusion centers managed?

While most sources including a 2017 report by the Department of Justice Inspector General[297] agree that fusion centers are owned by state and local governments, according to the Department of Justice and DHS publication, "Fusion Center Guidelines – Developing and Sharing Information and Intelligence in a New Era,"[298] fusion centers are governed individually by a representative structure comprised of law enforcement, public safety, and private sector partners of each individual center. With 79 fusion centers established at the time of the 2018 midterm elections, seventy-nine individual structures of governance were running seventy-nine individual fusion centers in addition to sharing and reporting to and with the National Fusion Center Association. [299] (The 2021 FEMA report[300] would suggest 80 fusion center sites were running during the 2020 Presidential Election). The cited DoJ/DHS publication further states:

> "Executive committees set policy, make critical decisions, and commit resources. Operational committees may be asked to focus on specific policies, such as purge and retention or privacy. Technical committees will focus on technical standards, critical infrastructure operation, and security. Under these committees, subcommittees may be used to conduct detailed research and analysis, ultimately to bring

---

[297] https://www.oversight.gov/sites/default/files/oig-reports/OIG-17-49-Mar17.pdf
[298] https://bja.ojp.gov/sites/g/files/xyckuh186/files/media/document/fusion_center_guidelines_law_enforcement.pdf
[299] https://www.cisecurity.org/wp-content/uploads/2019/02/EI-ISAC-2018-YIR.pdf
[300] https://www.fema.gov/sites/default/files/documents/FEMA_2021-Preparedness-Grants-Manual_02-19-2021.pdf

CHAPTER 12

recommendations to the governing body for review and endorsement"[301]

Each fusion center was established to completely self-run, self-govern, and incredibly, self-monitor as the oversight body for all activities within each of the established fusion centers. According to the DoJ/DHS publication above, this structure to be set up as follows: "Fusion centers should consider establishing an oversight committee that reports directly to the governance body." [302] Information will be presented within this chapter to demonstrate the abject failure of this structure historically, with fusion centers earning reputations as hotbeds for domestic spying. In a 2008 report the American Civil Liberties Union (ACLU) stated the following in its executive summary:

> "The participation of agencies from multiple jurisdictions in fusion centers allows the authorities to manipulate differences in federal, state and local laws to maximize information collection while evading accountability and oversight through the practice of 'policy shopping.'"[303]

Published evidence suggests that established committees of self-oversight within fusion centers do on occasion, request audits from other authorities, to include federal and state entities. Published in 2014, a joint report by the Inspectors General of the Intelligence Community, Department of Homeland Security, and Department of Justice, titled "Review of Domestic Sharing of Counterterrorism Information"[304] is one, and a 2013 report by The United States

---

[301] https://bja.ojp.gov/sites/g/files/xyckuh186/files/media/document/fusion_center_guidelines_law_enforcement.pdf
[302] https://bja.ojp.gov/sites/g/files/xyckuh186/files/media/document/fusion_center_guidelines_law_enforcement.pdf
[303] https://www.aclu.org/report/whats-wrong-fusion-centers-executive-summary?redirect=cpredirect/32966
[304] https://www.oversight.gov/sites/default/files/oig-reports/OIG-17-49-Mar17.pdf

Countdown to Chaos

House of Representatives Committee on Homeland Security titled "Majority Staff Report on the National Network of Fusion Centers" referenced earlier is another. [305] These, in addition to the findings from the 2012 report from the Permanent Senate Subcommittee, will be referenced further in this chapter along with other independent reviews of the fusion center structure.

How are fusion centers funded?

An inspection of the funding of fusion centers is a very important area of review here, following governance. Each source of funds funneled into fusion centers expects some sort of accountability for funds allocated. For example, the Department of Justice Inspector General reported that federal funds allocated must be used for federal salaries and infrastructure:

> "Direct federal expenditures are primarily salaries and benefits for federal personnel assigned to or directly supporting fusion centers, but also include federal information technology systems deployed to fusion centers, security clearances sponsored by federal agencies, and training and other resources specifically intended to help fusion centers build and sustain capabilities."[306]

In the report by the United States Senate Permanent Subcommittee on Homeland Security and Governmental Affairs published October 3, 2012, funding was also addressed. That report mentions:

---

[305] https://www.archives.gov/files/isoo/oversight-groups/sltps-pac/staff-report-on-fusion-networks-2013.pdf
[306] https://www.oversight.gov/sites/default/files/oig-reports/OIG-17-49-Mar17.pdf

CHAPTER 12

> "Today, DHS provides millions of dollars in Federal grant funds to support state and local fusion center efforts. It details personnel to the centers, and offers them guidance, training and technology...DHS funds state and local fusion centers through its Federal Emergency Management Agency (FEMA) grant programs. DHS provides information, logistical support, technology and personnel to the centers through its State and Local Program Office (SLPO), part of its Office of Intelligence and Analysis (I&A). DHS personnel also draft intelligence reports based on information received at fusion centers..."[307]

This question of both funding and management of elections becomes even further confused by the fact that fusion centers are a location of information sharing for the EI-ISAC and MS-ISACs. These agencies are quasi-governmental, voluntarily, but largely managed and funded by the Department of Homeland Security. The list of funding going to fusion centers spans multiple sources from federal general funds, DHS grant funds, FEMA grand funds, the Department of Justice funds[308], state funds, to a wide range of private funding. "Led by a former DHS grants official who lobbies for increased federal funding for fusion centers, the NFCA receives funds from Microsoft, ESRI, Thomson-Reuters, Mutualink and other firms that want business with fusion centers."[309] The extent to which Microsoft provides funding and implements technology, while not completely surprising by the nature of their corporation,

---

[307] https://www.hsgac.senate.gov/imo/media/doc/10-3-2012%20PSI%20STAFF%20REPORT%20re%20FUSION%20CENTERS.2.pdf
[308] https://www.dhs.gov/xlibrary/assets/privacy/privacy_pia_ia_slrfci.pdf
[309] https://www.csoonline.com/article/2223440/microsoft-provides-fusion-center-technology-and-funding-for-surveillance.html

Countdown to Chaos

is eye opening when considering the company also funds and supports NATO fusion centers.[310]

In the light of the era of information sharing, the access, control, and accountability wrapped up in fusion centers via funding is a nothing less than convoluted mess when it comes to the topic of management of elections. The nature of complex operations taking place within the fusion structure framework and the fabric of state and federal staff operating within them creates a nearly impossible situation for anyone to verify who is responsible for any operations.

Rather than following the money, perhaps finding an answer to the question of what entity is directly responsible for managing elections within the fusion centers might best be found in receiving acknowledgment from one of the entities within the system willing to take full responsibility for this massive cyber super structure. If the state is not the primary fund or staff source of a fusion center, then the candidates who might be responsible for the system would come from those sourcing federal funds, federal grants, or other private funds. If one of these entities would arise from this multi-layered system of management, then not only would the voters have a target for redress of grievances, but the answer of constitutionality of the system could be better addressed.

Furthermore, if the lead on the monitoring is done by federal employees, and the information is not made available to state entities then the management of election data appears to fall under federal control. A current example of such a situation might be the inability of the Arizona State Senate to secure the router and Splunk logs for Maricopa County, Arizona[311]. This stalemate

---

[310] https://www.csoonline.com/article/2223440/microsoft-provides-fusion-center-technology-and-funding-for-surveillance.html
[311] https://www.azag.gov/sites/default/files/docs/complaints/sb1487/21-002/LT_AG_re_Legislative_Subpoena_8-18-21-c.pdf

CHAPTER 12

suggests that the federal government may have jurisdiction over that information and the federal government was, in fact, managing election data transfer. This may be a direct violation of the constitution enumerating the management of federal elections to the states.

What is the standard for staffing the centers? Are those running fusion centers to be trusted?

Upon establishment, the Department of Homeland Security and Department of Justice envisioned fusion centers in its publication titled "Fusion Center Guidelines" to be staffed by a core of civilian individuals for administration duties and to maintain continuity. This core staff was hoped to be "dedicated to specific functions, such as administration, information technology, communications, and graphics."[312] Another level of staffing was imagined to be "subject-matter experts from law enforcement, public safety, and the private sector," in addition to "legal counsel dedicated to the fusion center to help clarify laws, rules, regulations, and statutes governing the collection, maintenance, and dissemination of information and liaison with the development of policies, procedures, guidelines, and operational manuals."[313]

Within these areas of personnel and staffing at fusion centers lies the necessity of appropriately staffing positions that require security clearances. Because staffing is key to the preservation of accurate intelligence gathering and the appropriate handling of other sensitive information, any fusion center could potentially be polluted by poor staffing. In a February 2021 FEMA publication, the agency stated:

---

[312]https://bja.ojp.gov/sites/g/files/xyckuh186/files/media/document/fusion_center_guidelines_law_enforcement.pdf
[313]https://bja.ojp.gov/sites/g/files/xyckuh186/files/media/document/fusion_center_guidelines_law_enforcement.pdf

> "All fusion center **analytical personnel** must demonstrate qualifications that meet or exceed competencies identified in the Common Competencies for state, local, and tribal intelligence analysts, which outlines the minimum categories of training needed for intelligence analysts. A certificate of completion of such training must be on file with the State Administrative Agency (SAA) and must be made available to the recipient's respective FEMA HQ Preparedness Officer upon request."[314]

Despite the vision established for fusion centers, history shows these state and locally owned, but primarily federally funded amalgamations of information collection, analysis, and dissemination are **riddled with inadequate personnel and protocols**. In an extensive review referred to earlier completed by the United States Senate Permanent Subcommittee on Homeland Security and Governmental Affairs and published October 3, 2012, regarding staffing within the centers, the Senate found that:

- "DHS did not sufficiently train its fusion center detailees to legally and effectively collect and report intelligence.
- DHS-assigned detailees to the fusion centers forwarded 'intelligence' of uneven quality – oftentimes shoddy, rarely timely, sometimes endangering citizens' civil liberties and Privacy Act protections...
- Short-staffing and reliance on contract employees hampered reporting efforts.
- DHS required only a week of training for intelligence officials before sending them to state and local fusion

---

[314] https://www.fema.gov/sites/default/files/documents/FEMA_2021-Preparedness-Grants-Manual_02-19-2021.pdf

CHAPTER 12

centers to report sensitive domestic intelligence, largely concerning U.S. persons.
- Reporting officials aren't evaluated on the quality of their reporting.
- Officials who routinely authored useless or potentially illegal fusion center intelligence reports faced **no sanction or reprimand**.
- DHS officials said they relied on contract employees to perform these sensitive tasks, some of whom they believed to be **undertrained or poor performers**. And for most of its existence, the office lacked basic documentation outlining its policies and practices, such as Standard Operating Procedures or a Concept of Operations, which should have clearly defined functions, roles and responsibilities in the reporting process" [315]

Thus, the question of who is staffing these centers directly effects each individual citizen in America for many reasons. However, when you add elections to the equation of the functions of fusion centers, the extent of information handling and analysis becomes so wide in scope and has so many different individuals that might have access to that information, that it is almost impossible for any person responsible for the election integrity at the state legislative or secretary of state level to have any confidence in the security of the chain of custody of election data information traffic. **An understanding of the network cyber structure created by CISA and the DHS creates the concept that the live monitoring of elections in real time, whether it be access to poll pads, voter registration, election officer networks, polling locations, or vote tabulation systems, is nothing shy of peeking into the ballot box for those with technical capability to do so.**

---

[315] https://www.hsgac.senate.gov/imo/media/doc/10-3-2012%20PSI%20STAFF%20REPORT%20re%20FUSION%20CENTERS.2.pdf

Countdown to Chaos

To add insult and injury to the topic of election data information traffic flowing through election fusion centers, one cannot ignore that each sector of personnel operating at a fusion center has a representative union. These include police, firefighters, state employees, and federal employees. Each of these public unions has a history of endorsing candidates for public office. Thus, the people and entities responsible for election data could be driven by unions with deep vested interests in the outcome of an election, with some areas, precincts, or markets being very heavily more politically driven than others.

Boards of elections or boards of supervisors do not organize unions. These entities are to be run by individuals equally representing both major political parties. With so much at stake in each election, how can the flow of election data information traffic through fusion centers staffed by hundreds, perhaps thousands of potentially unionized employees each election cycle, guarantee that every component and all data streams accessible during an election are kept under strict confidentiality and secrecy? The details of the wide range of capabilities and reach of The Albert System in Chapter 6 bring the seriousness of this question into stark focus. Every connected system in the EI-ISAC cyber super structure exposes every area of the election infrastructure to individuals contracted to monitor the information in real time. **Thus, the chain of custody of ballots cannot simply include the handling of physical ballots. Chain of custody in an election must consider the chain of custody of all election data information traffic at every moment an election is run** from early voting through final tabulation.

Who holds the ultimate responsibility and liability for violations of civil rights, or violations to the U.S. Constitution when they occur within the structure of a fusion center?

CHAPTER 12

This question is one that dovetails directly with the questions of funding and accountability previously addressed. The legal liability for the rights of each individual citizen that lies within the context of the fusion center structure is of critical importance for many reasons not only on the topic of policing and security, but also equally if not more importantly on the topic of elections. The Department of Homeland Security in a Privacy Impact Assessment dated December 11, 2008, stated in its own words that **"fusion centers engender a range of concerns about privacy, from broad mischaracterizations of them as 'mini-spy agencies...'"**[316] However, the reference of fusions centers using the term "mini-spy agencies" may not be hyperbole, as the information to follow will explain. For example, in yet another report prepared for Congressional Committees in 2008, written by the Congressional Research Service and titled, "Fusion Centers: Issues and Options for Congress," the CRS makes the following statement regarding fusion centers:

> "The argument is that the further law enforcement, public safety and private sector representatives get away from a criminal predicate, **the greater the chances that civil liberties may be violated**. Furthermore, it could be argued that **one of the risks to the fusion center concept is that individuals who do not necessarily have the appropriate law enforcement or broader intelligence training will engage in intelligence collection that is not supported by law**."[317]

These statements are the opening salvo as to why the flow of election data through fusion centers staffed with multiple levels of personnel from federal agencies, federal intelligence organizations,

---

[316] https://www.dhs.gov/xlibrary/assets/privacy/privacy_pia_ia_slrfci.pdf
[317] https://sgp.fas.org/crs/intel/RL34070.pdf

Countdown to Chaos

state, and local governments, with a myriad of different expertise and security clearances is at minimum a poor decision regarding chain of custody of election data, and at worst, an incredible Constitutional dilemma regarding the management of elections.

Since their inception, questions stemming from the public of civil liberties and protections surrounding fusion centers have been extensive and wide ranging. The American Civil Liberties Union published several reports in the early years of the development of fusion centers. One such report enumerated stories of domestic spying from nearly every state in the union and Washington D.C..[318] One story cited by the ACLU report but no longer available for review online was titled "Maricopa County Sheriff Department Surveils Political Enemies." This story was originally published by *The Los Angeles Times* in 2010. In yet another story out of Illinois published behind a paywall at *The Washington Post*, a headline read "Activists Cry Foul Over FBI Probe." This story was further described with this partial tease: "Peace activists and labor organizers who were the target of large-scale FBI raids in September, 2010, and who believe they [were] being improperly targeted as a result of their political activism and speech..."[319] Each of the incidents and stories in the ACLU report highlights the slippery slope an unfettered flow of information has in the hands of large numbers of analysts not only for the insurance of the integrity of the information and the preservation of constitutional rights but also for the temptations that the American political divide presents to any person in such a position of power and access. Many would consider the activities reported upon in the ACLU article to be covered by the definition of "spying".

---

[318]https://www.aclu.org/sites/default/files/field_document/spying_on_first_amendment_activity_12.19.12_update.pdf
[319] https://www.aclu.org/files/assets/policingfreespeech_20111103.pdf

CHAPTER 12

In a story published by *The Cato Institute*, titled "We're All Terrorists Now" by David Rittgers, a laundry list of activities reportedly surveilled by fusion centers is one steeped in partisan political activism.[320] The areas mentioned in the article which were under the watchful eye of area fusion center personnel included pro-life and pro-abortion positions, environmentalism, Second Amendment issues, as well as surveillance of specific politicians. If fusion centers are monitoring activities focused on such subjects, it is difficult to argue that the centers could remain bipartisan and policy neutral in any of the eighty locations, and particularly more difficult in the monitoring of high stakes elections. Integrity becomes conceivably much harder for those staffing centers with full access to elections when much of the staff have their analyst fingertips inside the election information sharing system. The fact that most of the staff in these centers are or can be represented by unions that publicly endorse specific candidates, again adds much weight to bear upon the question of the integrity of election data information transfer.

In a white paper from 2012 published by *The Constitution Project* titled "Recommendations for Fusion Centers – Preserving Privacy and Civil Liberties While Protecting Against Crime and Terrorism," the information integrity and liability issues were discussed as part of its report of a wider scope. The paper reported:

> "Accountability is crucial to both protecting privacy and civil liberties and ensuring that institutions operate effectively. Yet, several features of fusion centers contribute to a lack of accountability. First, the rapid pace of advances in information technology and the nation's limited experience with the fusion center concept may make it difficult for policymakers to

---

[320] https://web.archive.org/web/20110415064139/http://www.cato-at-liberty.org/we%E2%80%99re-all-terrorists-now/

Countdown to Chaos

understand the nature and consequences of fusion center activity. Some fusion center employees may be aware of the latitude that can result from this lack of understanding; in the words of one analyst, fusion centers are 'a sort of 'wild west' . . . in that they can use a variety of technologies before 'politics' catches up and limits options.'"[321]

The Constitution Project white paper then goes on to also describe an incident by a private federal contractor while unnamed in *The Constitution Project* report, was previously reported in this investigation as The Analysis Corporation of which John Brennan served as the Chief Executive Officer during the incident. The white paper describes the importance of audit tracking of fusion center activity, reporting the circumstance as follows:

"In early 2008, a State Department auditing system determined that private contractors had improperly accessed the passport files of presidential candidates Hillary Clinton, Barack Obama and John McCain. Several of the contractors were disciplined for their actions."[322]

As *The Constitution Project* paper pulls the contractor, The Analysis Corporation, into the framework of fusion centers, this incident takes on greater weight in the scope of this report as this incident now has connective tissue in the history of fusion centers during the deliberate build up to their use in the election system as critical infrastructure. The answers to the question of who is present inside these fusion centers during elections also becomes more and more troubling as this structure is more closely investigated. *The Constitution Project* white paper records yet another similar incident in the review of fusion centers highlighting:

---

[321] https://archive.constitutionproject.org/pdf/fusioncenterreport.pdf
[322] https://archive.constitutionproject.org/pdf/fusioncenterreport.pdf

CHAPTER 12

> "Later in the [2008] election season, Ohio state government employees made a number of intrusive searches in state databases for information regarding Joe Wurzelbacher, the public John McCain supporter more commonly known as "Joe the Plumber." Audits of these searches enabled investigators to determine that a number were legitimate, but also that several were unauthorized and improper. Several employees reportedly were disciplined, one resigned, and another was placed under criminal investigation." [323]

The nature of these reports paints the environment within fusion centers as far from being bipartisan, and clearly the center employees are not immune to illegally accessing information while some have been proven to be guilty of blatant spying.

In the review by the United States Senate Permanent Subcommittee on Homeland Security and Governmental Affairs and published October 3, 2012 referred to in previous sections of this chapter, the subcommittee found:

- "[Fusion centers] potentially violated Department guidelines meant to protect Americans' civil liberties or Privacy Act protections...
- In 2009, DHS instituted a lengthy privacy and civil liberties review process which kept most of the troubling reports from being released outside of DHS; however, it also slowed reporting down by months, and DHS continued to store troubling intelligence reports from fusion centers on U.S. persons, possibly in violation of the Privacy Act.

---

[323] https://archive.constitutionproject.org/pdf/fusioncenterreport.pdf

Countdown to Chaos

- Some terrorism-related "intelligence" reporting was based on older **news releases or media accounts**.
- DHS **required only a week of training** for intelligence officials before sending them to state and local fusion centers to report sensitive domestic intelligence, largely concerning U.S. persons.
- Officials who routinely authored useless or potentially illegal fusion center intelligence reports faced **no sanction or reprimand**." [324]

About sensitive and classified information handling by staff inside fusion centers, within a March 2017 joint report by the Inspectors General of the Intelligence Community, Department of Homeland Security, and Department of Justice, the executive summary stated in one of a number of repudiations, that:

> "At DHS, a lack of unity in its Intelligence Enterprise, issues in the field related to staffing and ***access to classified systems and facilities,*** as well as problems with intelligence reporting processes, have made the DHS Intelligence Enterprise less effective and valuable to the IC than it could be."[325]

Failure in the general handing of both sensitive and classified information and the troubling lack of liability for those guilty of direct violations of and breaches into sensitive or classified information is a serious issue not only for policing but it is a watershed issue in the country when election integrity comes into the equation.

---

[324] https://www.hsgac.senate.gov/imo/media/doc/10-3-2012%20PSI%20STAFF%20REPORT%20re%20FUSION%20CENTERS.2.pdf
[325] https://www.oversight.gov/sites/default/files/oig-reports/OIG-17-49-Mar17.pdf

CHAPTER 12

In a 2009 report from Vanderbilt University Department of Human and Organizational Development titled "The Emerging Politics of DHS Fusion Centers", authors Torin Monahan and Neal A. Palmer discussed the growing problems fusion centers were fomenting surrounding information handling and civil rights. They state:

> "Rather than the risk of an authoritarian state – or Big Brother – trampling civil liberties, a greater and more likely threat is the systematic generation, integration, and sharing of vast quantities of personal data that can be harnessed to sort, control, and discriminate against people or groups (O'Harrow, 2005; Lyon, 2003b; Regan, 2004; Gandy, 2006). This is not to say that state-led surveillance operations do not violate the rights of people: they clearly can and do. Instead, this orientation highlights the fact that routine surveillance, in the form of data-collection and data-mining, is key to the operations of private companies, and that these organizations can also impinge upon the rights of people or collaborate with government agencies to do so... Far from being restricted to the sharing of data among government agencies, fusion centers also facilitate cooperative efforts among government agencies and private industries, although the details of these relationships are shrouded in secrecy (Monahan, 2009b)."[326]

While the scope of the Vanderbilt paper addresses fusion centers mainly used for policing and threats to the homeland, the point regarding information access and sharing is relevant here. The addition of fusion centers to elections as critical infrastructure adds an uninspected node in the chain of custody of election data information traffic. The questionable history of fusion center

---

[326] https://publicsurveillance.com/papers/FC-SD.pdf

Countdown to Chaos

policies, staffing, funding, and effectiveness is highly relevant and deserves review of their use in the both the 2018 and 2020 elections. If a staff member of a fusion center data mines within an election system, the list of individuals who the information could be shared with under the umbrella of both the fusion center structure and the ISAC structure is vast. By the time a data breech of election information could be detected, the damage done within the information structure has the potential to be historic in not only the nature of such an act but also historic in the time frame in which anything could be discovered or rectified.

A review of the governance, liability, and representation within the national fusion centers presented demonstrates a serious intermingling of individuals from organizations, federal, state, and local, that not only execute policy, but these agencies all potentially can influence it. Further, evidence shows (Chapter 6 – The Albert Monitoring System) that the level of digital access and intelligence for those with the expertise and clearance to cyber infrastructure is so great, there is practically no limit to access of any portion of the election systems at any point in time during an election. The addition of artificial intelligence to the Albert architecture also opens the door to the possibility of unquestionable or unknowable activities happening within the data flow.

As stated in an earlier section of this chapter, the purpose of state and local governments having non-partisan boards of elections to administer and govern the logistics of elections is to keep the process of election administration out of the hands of one political party or another (as all boards should have equal numbers of members from both parties that all serve a limited term), and to have the logistics in the hands of a group of individuals not connected to any other area of the three branches of government. This protocol exists, not just to prevent bias or fraud in an election, but also to limit the chance members of such boards might make

CHAPTER 12

decisions or mobilize actions via elections that could affect policy or that could be driven by policy directives.

To again address the exceedingly important topic of liability within the fusion center monitoring apparatus, according to the Department of Justice and DHS publication "Fusion Center Guidelines – Developing and Sharing Information and Intelligence in a New Era," the recommended solution for liability issues is to have each fusion center complete MOUs (Memorandum of Understanding), and NDA (Non-Disclosure Agreements) to assist in governing centers and shielding liability. The publication states:

> "It is recommended that fusion centers be governed and managed in accordance with an MOU. An MOU, a necessary tool for information sharing, defines the terms, responsibilities, relationships, intentions, and commitments of each participating entity; the agreement also provides an outline of the who, what, where, when, why, and how of the project. Partners should commit to the program policies by signing the MOU. In addition to MOUs, some initiatives utilize agency, individual, and data sharing user agreements." [327]

The issue of liability for information sharing and the protections afforded those participating in the structure was addressed by a Department of Homeland Security spokesperson in 2009. In an article published by the *Centre for Crime and Justice Studies* the DHS official, Matthew Skonovd was mentioned in the text of the article on the topic:

> "If industry partners in Fusion Centres do not have appropriate classified clearance levels, Skonovd hinted

---

[327] https://bja.ojp.gov/sites/g/files/xyckuh186/files/media/document/fusion_ce nter_guidelines_law_enforcement.pdf

Countdown to Chaos

that there are always 'work arounds' to facilitate sharing, such as having individuals sign 'non-disclosure agreements'. Industry representatives on the panel added that their companies were in a good position to co-operate with DHS because the US Safety Act of 2002 protected them from liability if they did so. Since then, the passage of an amended Foreign Intelligence Surveillance Act in 2008 granted retroactive immunity to telecommunications companies that illegally shared data on individual customers with federal intelligence agencies, confirming that businesses will likely be shielded from liability when sharing with Fusion Centres or any other government organisations."[328]

In yet another white paper by Krista Craven, Torin Monahan and Priscilla Regan of Guilford College, the University of North Carolina at Chapel Hill, and George Mason University, on the topic of fusion centers the abstract states:

"The fraught history of surveillance programs in the United States, for instance, illustrates that government agencies mobilize discourses of exceptional circumstances to engage in domestic and foreign spying operations without public awareness or oversight... On one hand, in justifying state surveillance, government representatives claim that the public should trust police and intelligence communities not to violate their rights; on the other hand, the very act of engaging in secretive surveillance operations erodes public trust in government, especially when revelations about such programs come to light without any advance notice or consent."[329]

---

[328] https://publicsurveillance.com/papers/FC-CJM.pdf
[329] https://publicsurveillance.com/papers/FC_Compromised_Trust.pdf

CHAPTER 12

One author of the above piece, Torin Monahan, wrote an article in 2009 titled "The Murky World of Fusion Centers." In this article published by the *Centre for Crime and Justice Studies* the author writes:

> "According to Robert O'Harrow Jr, who is an investigative journalist at the Washington Post, these centres are sifting through drivers' license records, identity-theft reports, financial information on individuals, firearms' licenses, car-rental information, top-secret FBI databases and more. This is all being done in partnership with private sector 'data brokers', such as 'Entersect, which claims it maintains 12 billion records on about 98 per cent of Americans' (O'Harrow Jr, 2008). There are no clear mechanisms for oversight or accountability with Fusion Centres, in spite of the fact that private companies are likely obtaining unprecedented access to government data on individuals, and vice versa."[330]

With each fusion center tasked with monitoring election data and structured as an independently governed and run entity, no secretary of state, county clerk, or election board, can see, audit, verify, or guarantee that the information monitored, reviewed, or shared by the fusion centers, maintains any semblance of its original integrity as access to these centers by personnel is limited to those with the appropriate clearances, and evidence shows the DHS and partners within the fusion system have not historically been transparent with the operations within the center walls. In addition, information presented earlier in this report demonstrated that membership to the MS-ISAC or EI-ISAC already offered enhanced protection from public access to information via the Freedom of Information Act (FOIA). Truly, the only way any

---

[330] https://publicsurveillance.com/papers/FC-CJM.pdf

Countdown to Chaos

American could have any idea of the integrity of any election when considering the chain of custody of the data flow would be with an audit of every single ballot in every single precinct in any questionable locales. The Maricopa County Arizona audit is the first audit of this type, begun in April of 2021. The results of that audit were so extensive, that data was still being analyzed nearly a year after collection of the ballot evidence began.

Access to election data traffic of any kind should be recognized within the election system as an incredibly important area of chain of custody. Not only should inspection of that data traffic chain of custody be available to the voting public, but every individual with any access to that information should also be required to be officially trained, credentialed, logged as a portion of the chain of custody, and held ultimately criminally responsible for violations occurring within the area of the system they operate. In addition, an argument could be made that if an entity such as a fusion center or ISAC is monitoring election data, an independent group should be able to observe and audit the operations and protocols of such a monitoring system in real time while members of the fusion center staff and ISAC groups operate during an election.

Ultimately, when considering the full extent to which election data was "governed" in the 2018 and 2020 elections, and the understanding that the quasigovernmental agencies that are fusion centers were primarily staffed by an amalgamation of state, local, federal, and private entities, the answer to the question of liability with regard to information management and security that this report poses is not clear to any extent whatsoever. The information detailed within this chapter only clouds the question of liability for civil liberties, equal protection, and chain of custody of ballots surrounding elections. It also very much confounds questions regarding election management, the scope of information sharing, and constitutionality of the American election

CHAPTER 12

system as was reconstructed by Barack Obama and the Department of Homeland Security since the 2016 election.

Is election data information traffic classified or unclassified information?

This report has presented information that demonstrates a portion of the election infrastructure, specifically the Albert Monitoring System and systems stemming from Albert, is in fact considered classified. However, information presented in the National Association of Secretary of States' 2019 Cyber Resource Guide explains the election data traffic is possibly only considered "sensitive" but not "classified." Yet, within the discussion of fusion centers and their part in the Homeland Security Information Network, the 2019 NASS guide lays out the ease to which the "sensitive" election data is accessed:

> "Homeland Security Information Network (HSIN) State and local election officials can register with the Homeland Security Information Network (HSIN). HSIN is DHS's official system for the trusted sharing of sensitive but unclassified information between federal, state, local, territorial, tribal, international and private sector partners. EI-ISAC Cyber Situational Awareness Rooms for election officials are hosted through HSIN. However, EI-ISAC members can access the Cyber Situational Awareness Rooms through the EI-ISAC and are not required to be separately registered with HSIN."[331]

Notable in the quote above is the fact that there are "international partners" in the HSIN network. This is worthy of note for this report

---

[331] https://www.nass.org/sites/default/files/Cybersecurity/10.11_NASS_Cyber_Resource_Guide.pdf

Countdown to Chaos

but beyond the topic of this chapter. However, further to this quote, in light of the historical concerns regarding the integrity of activities that are undertaken in area fusion centers, the information above suggesting election data traffic flow IS NOT classified is an area of concern that rises near the top of issues that this report presents and holds nearly as much weight as the constitutional issue of management of elections by state legislatures. The fact that election data traffic may not be classified, leaves access to the information to far too many individuals within the system. Complete transparency must meet these issues and this structure must be exposed and clarified to all officials in the legislatures of all fifty states. In addition, every voting citizen for whom state representatives speak must know these issues and clearly voice their positions on them to their legislators.

Are fusion centers simply a perfect amalgamation of state and federal entities to keep both accountability and transparency cloaked in bureaucratic secrecy?

Each and every layer a quasi-governmental agency adds onto any area of government adds layers of procedural red tape, complicated protocols, and dims the transparency of government activities to the citizens for which governments are to be beholden to and in service of. In the matter of elections, the issue of management of elections is a serious constitutional topic. As highlighted at the very beginning of this report, the Constitution of the United States in Articles I and II known as "The Elections Clause"[332] dictates that "The Times , Places and Manner of holding Elections for Senators and Representatives, shall be prescribed in

---

[332] https://constitutioncenter.org/interactive-constitution/interpretation/article-i/clauses/750

CHAPTER 12

each State by the Legislature".[333] This specific topic was addressed in a recent article about fusion centers and the 2020 election published by *Thenewamerican.com* by Joe Wolverton, II, titled "Colorado Election Security in the Hands of DHS Fusion Center."[334] In the article, Wolverton explains that after the Colorado Secretary of State Jena Griswold announced the formation of a joint task force to include the DHS and their state fusion center to handle the 2020 election, there was pushback from many, both in the state and nationally, citing the constitutional concerns. In the article Wolverton writes, "There are many in Colorado and beyond who may find troublesome this transfer of supervision of election from the state legislature to the federal intelligence and surveillance bureaucracy." At the core of the move by Griswold was that she "created the Rapid Response Election Security Cyber Unit (RESCU), a group of local law-enforcement agents who plan to coordinate with federal intelligence and Homeland Security agents to protect 'Colorado's elections from cyberattacks, foreign interference, and disinformation campaigns.'"[335] The Chief Information Officer for the Colorado Secretary of State's office issued a statement on the issue: "We have individuals in our offices that have clearances at the secret level, so that we can have conversations with DHS, FBI, with ODNI, so that we can get that information, even before it may have been declassified and made available publicly. We're able to get that information and just sort of factor it into how we think about things." [336]

---

[333] https://www.eac.gov/sites/default/files/eac_assets/1/1/U.S.%20Constitutional%20Provisions%20on%20Elections.pdf
[334] https://thenewamerican.com/colorado-election-security-in-the-hands-of-dhs-fusion-center/
[335] https://thenewamerican.com/colorado-election-security- in-the-hands-of-dhs-fusion-center/
[336] https://thenewamerican.com/colorado-election-security-in-the-hands-of-dhs-fusion-center/

Countdown to Chaos

The issues in the article speak directly to the plethora of issues created by the use of fusion centers in the election structure. The addition of fusion centers is by no means a one-dimensional move. The layer of oversight by any entity outside of any structure directly approved and supervised by the state legislature and tested for constitutionality must be closely examined and audited. The issue is, to what extent do the legislature, voter integrity groups, or individual voters have any access to election data or election data handling protocols for review or audit? The audit of Maricopa County, Arizona has already highlighted the serious issue of the inability of the State Senate of Arizona, under a state subpoena, to be given the ability to review the Maricopa County router and Splunk logs that were running on the election system environment during the 2020 election. If the State Senate of Arizona, who has the plenary power under the Constitution the of United States to run the election, is unable to review and audit critical information in the state election system architecture with a subpoena, how could anyone expect to have any transparency from any quasi-governmental agency or any other entity within the critical infrastructure system built by the DHS? Furthermore, how can any voter have any confidence in such an opaque process?

This report has provided documentation showing the layer of additional protection from FOIA that is afforded members of both the MS-ISAC and the EI-ISAC. This shield became a much more virulent layer of protection after elections were declared Critical Infrastructure. [337] When the ownership of a fusion center is the state and local governments, the funding is primarily provided through federal budgets, federal agency grants, other agencies, and private funding, FOIA requests become extremely complicated

---

[337]https://www.eac.gov/sites/default/files/eac_assets/1/6/starting_point_us_election_systems_as_Critical_Infrastructure.pdf

CHAPTER 12

if not impossible. In a white paper referred to earlier by *The Constitution Project*, the issue of transparency is addressed:

> "Indeed, in some instances, **federal agencies like the FBI have reportedly required states to exempt fusion centers from their open government laws as a condition to allowing those fusion centers access to important federal law enforcement databases**—a troubling practice that implicates issues of federalism as well as transparency."[338]

In any situation in which an election is close, such as in the 2020 Presidential Election, the multilayered quasigovernmental superstructure creates either a circle of protection for those in the machinery of the system, or circular firing squad for each and every employee, agent, or officer, to try to pin blame for errors, omissions, and violations upon another entity within the system. The evidence of this assertion is playing out as Senators, integrity groups, and voters watch and wait for results from the first complete audit of an election system in the history of the United States of America. What happens in Maricopa County, Arizona will have implications for every American voter for decades or centuries to come. If the ISAC edifice, fusion center structure, and critical infrastructure architecture prove anything, it is that the American election system has been placed into a deep dark hole of bureaucratic layers of red tape and secrecy which was constructed in 2017 by the Obama Administration and an Obama executive fiat.

Because the topic of election integrity is white hot, as this report was being written, stories, court cases, facts, and firsthand accounts would continually beg to have their facts covered within the evidence presented in these pages. As such, to close this chapter, another review of former CIA Director John Brennan's own words about a specific fusion center are important as they tie into

---

[338] https://archive.constitutionproject.org/pdf/fusioncenterreport.pdf

Countdown to Chaos

the events surrounding the aftermath of the 2016 election and may potentially have a material connection to the 2020 election. As presented in an earlier chapter, John O. Brennan appeared in an interview on April 17, 2018 on the cable network MSNBC where he explained to Rachel Maddow that at the time of his departure from his position as CIA Director in January of 2017, the CIA had a need to hand over information "incidentally collected" on U.S. citizens that "was of great relevance to the FBI." To facilitate the continuity of intelligence collection, and because he had "unresolved questions" in his mind about Russian efforts, Brennan divulged that they created a fusion center:

> **Brennan:** "...we were picking things up that was of great relevance to the FBI. We wanted to make sure that they were there so they could piece it together with whatever they were collecting domestically here."
>
> **Maddow:** "So it was an intelligence sharing operation."
>
> **Brennan:** "Absolutely. Right. We put together a fusion center at CIA with the NSA and FBI officers together with CIA to make sure that those proverbial dots would be connected."[339]

According to the information uncovered by the investigation surrounding this report, the fusion center set up at the firsthand direction of John Brennan inside the very walls of the CIA to share information freely between the CIA, the FBI, and the NSA was done for the sole purpose of collecting and managing information via domestic surveillance of 2016 candidate and later President Donald J. Trump as the agencies tried to build a case that Trump was colluding with Russia. Certainly logic would ascertain that the information collected as a result of domestic spying by federal agencies presented by John Durham in his case against Michael

---

[339] https://youtu.be/UV7-ZdDGijY?t=1170

CHAPTER 12

Sussman in the spring of 2022, likely found its way into the CIA Trump/Russia fusion center. During the oral arguments from the Durham case United States v. Michael Sussman, evidence presented and entered into the record included key messages shared between FBI agents. One of the messages Durham's case focused upon was between agents working on the Trump/Russia collusion case. The message commented about the evidence the agency was collecting stating, "People on the 7th floor [FBI] to include Director are fired up."[340] Later U.S. Attorney John Durham would present a body of the evidence which would prove the evidence being collected which was handed over to the agency by federal cyber contractor Rodney Joffe (Neustar Inc.) via DNC and Clinton attorney Michael Sussman was fabricated.

Evidence of fusion centers having been used as hot beds of spying in the past was presented in this chapter to set the table to demonstrate the danger of the direct use of such a mode of data management in the monitoring of U.S. elections. However, the admission that this CIA based fusion center was, according to the architect of such centers and the former director of national spying for America, John Brennan, absolutely shocking. Listening to Brennan in his own words, America is able to understand that a fusion center can be set up and used specifically as a domestic spy agency node. In this case the center was established with a mission of collecting domestic intelligence surrounding not just a political candidate, but the President of the United States, Donald J. Trump. Based upon the public admission of former CIA Director John Brennan, the creation and purpose of this fusion center is unquestionable fact and these facts are once again blatant red flags reporting to the American electorate why the federal government can in no way be charged with any aspect of running and managing

---

[340] https://www.govinfo.gov/content/pkg/CREC-2022-05-24/html/CREC-2022-05-24-pt1-PgS2647.htm

Countdown to Chaos

elections in the country, and fusion centers are an alarming and dangerous part of an out-of-control federal cyber network.

With the information presented in this chapter piled upon the information laid out in the rest of this investigation, the questions posed in the chapter this information was originally written in are worth reiterating. They are: As the CIA/NSA/FBI fusion center personally divulged by former CIA Director John Brennan was later proven to collect Trump, Russia, and election related intelligence, what information was collected, and was it shared anywhere else in the vast information sharing network related to elections? Was this CIA/FBI/NSA fusion center running within the walls of the CIA active, operational, and live within the HSIN network on Election Day 2020?

The evidence collected within this report shows unequivocally that the chain of custody of election information is broken, putrefied, un-auditable, unreliable, and in desperate need of reformation which includes returning it to its origin – the management of the electorate, the American people, within their states and specifically within their counties and precincts. This was how the Founders intended to preserve the consent of the governed and we the people, the electorate, need to demand the return of our Constitutional rights as they were written and intended.

Review of Fusion Center Facts:
- Fusion centers are an integral part of the HSIN (Homeland Security Information Network).
- Fusion centers are self-governed entities.
- Fusion centers were integrated into the election monitoring process in 2018 via the EI-ISAC.
- Members of the EI-ISAC utilize Albert Monitoring and other networking systems for election system monitoring and response.

CHAPTER 12

- Utilization of the Albert Monitoring and other network solutions provided by the EI-ISAC requires the systems within the networks to keep system ports open. [341]
- The Albert Monitoring System and other areas of the election system are classified by the DHS and the federal government.
- Election data traffic is considered "sensitive," not "classified."
- An unknown number of fusion center employees have security clearances and access to classified systems in the election environment.
- Fusion centers are staffed by different federal agencies including the FBI.
- Every employee working in fusion centers could potentially be represented by a union. Every union (police, firefighter, federal employees, and state employees) has regularly endorsed political candidates for public office.
- Fusion center employees have violated constitutional civil rights of American citizens in the past.
- Previous violations documented within fusion centers include employees spying on political adversaries.
- Former CIA Director John Brennan publicly disclosed the creation and use of a CIA/NSA/FBI fusion center within the walls of the CIA dedicated to sharing information collected regarding Trump/Russia domestic surveillance.

---

[341] https://www.marc.org/Government/Cybersecurity/assets/MS-ISAC_ServicesGuide_8-5x11_Print_v2.aspx

Countdown to Chaos

CHAPTER 13

Chapter 13

SolarWinds (Post Election 2020 - 2021)

The election between President Donald Trump and former Vice-President Joseph Biden was full of tension, drama, and mystery. It was an election as this report outlines, that changed elections in this country forever unless the American people understand what happened in 2018 and in 2020 and continue to struggle to have their lawful Constitutional rights returned. Election Day was not the end of this report, however. As days and weeks moved on after the election, many more significant events happened that have bearing on the subject matter of this report. The two very large, very significant events that apply first surround the company SolarWinds, and secondly encompass the national grassroots movement toward forensic auditing of physical ballots.

On November 18 and 19, 2020, the outgoing CEO of SolarWinds, Kevin Thompson, sold $15,000,000 of SolarWinds stock.[342] On that day in the world, this event would pass most people's news feeds without a second look. However, it was 2020, and nothing about 2020 was normal. Mr. Thompson began a transition out of the company but waited to announce his resignation until December 7, 2020.[343]

Additionally, on December 7, 2020, the same day the CEO formally announced his resignation, two major investors in SolarWinds, Silver Lake and Thoma Bravo, sold $280,000,000 worth of

---

[342] https://insiderpaper.com/solarwinds-hack-outgoing-ceo-sold-huge-amount-of-stock-in-nov/
[343] https://www.dailymail.co.uk/news/article-9076045/SolarWinds-adviser-warned-cybersecurity-risks-2017-Russian-hack.html?ito=native_share_article-masthead

Countdown to Chaos

SolarWinds shares.[344] The very next day, on December 8, 2020, IT security company FireEye, announced the discovery of a breach into their system as well as into government systems. Within the week, FireEye would understand the access into the systems was through the SolarWinds Orion platform.[345]

On December 14, 2020, SolarWinds filed an official SEC report about the Orion security breech. The statement reads in part:

> "SolarWinds has been advised that this incident was likely the result of a highly sophisticated, targeted and manual supply chain attack by an outside nation state, **but SolarWinds has not independently verified the identity of the attacker.**"[346]

Government agencies known to have been infiltrated by this hack included the Department of Homeland Security and the FBI. "Reuters reported that the incident was considered so serious that it led to a rare meeting of the US National Security Council at the White House..."[347]

On December 22, 2020, The Department of Homeland Security through the CIS issued mitigation instructions for network security administrators throughout the DHS system, including to the users

---

[344] https://www.dailymail.co.uk/news/article-9076045/SolarWinds-adviser-warned-cybersecurity-risks-2017-Russian-hack.html?ito=native_share_article-masthead

[345] https://www.dailymail.co.uk/news/article-9076045/SolarWinds-adviser-warned-cybersecurity-risks-2017-Russian-hack.html?ito=native_share_article-masthead

[346] https://www.sec.gov/Archives/edgar/data/0001739942/000162828020017451/swi-20201214.htm

[347] https://www.zdnet.com/article/microsoft-fireeye-confirm-solarwinds-supply-chain-attack/

CHAPTER 13

of the Albert Monitoring Systems.[348] It is crucial to reassert the importance of the extent of the deployment of the Albert Monitoring Systems. All fifty states were employing the Albert monitors on their systems during the 2020 Presidential Election, and in total 751 monitors were deployed on the state election infrastructures.[349] In addition, it is important to understand that evidence from and Ohio directive that addressed Albert services reported:

> "...Albert intrusion detection devices [applied] to the voting system, epollbook, voter registration system, and remote marking ballot device vendors that are operational in Ohio."[350]

Just into the new year, on January 5, 2021, in a "Joint Statement by the Federal Bureau of Investigation (FBI), the Cybersecurity and Infrastructure Security Agency (CISA), the Office of the Director of National Intelligence (ODNI), and the National Security Agency (NSA),"[351] with regard to the SolarWinds Orion attack, the federal intelligence agencies announce:

> "...an Advanced Persistent Threat (APT) actor, **likely Russian in origin**, is responsible for most or all of the recently discovered, ongoing cyber compromises of both government and non-governmental networks. At this time, we believe this was, and continues to be, an intelligence gathering effort. We are taking all necessary

---

[348] https://web.archive.org/web/20210116034200/https://www.cisecurity.org/ms-isac/solarwinds/
[349] https://learn.cisecurity.org
[350] https://www.ohiosos.gov/globalassets/elections/directives/2019/dir2019-08.pdf?_cf_chl_jschl_tk_=pmd_Bv28nbkvmVJdVHKOHhdxJw00Q6yErlYNQow5yvPV5jl-1629397494-0-gqNtZGzNAlCjcnBszQil
[351] https://www.cisa.gov/news/2021/01/05/joint-statement-federal-bureau-investigation-fbi-cybersecurity-and-infrastructure

> steps to understand the full scope of this campaign and respond accordingly..."[352]

Despite this announcement, neither SolarWinds, nor FireEye, the company making the original discovery of the breach, made this definitive determination, and continued to refer to the hack as originating from an outside "nation-state" without naming any one nation.

As a follow up to an event that happened on June 3, 2020, as described in Chapter 11 of this report, Cisco Systems announced a vulnerability in its NetFlow Version 9 packet processor used by DHS monitoring systems. Cisco explained the issue on its website in the following terms:

> "A vulnerability in the Flexible NetFlow Version 9 packet processor of Cisco IOS XE Software for Cisco Catalyst 9800 Series Wireless Controllers could allow an unauthenticated, remote attacker to cause a denial of service (DoS) condition on an affected device."[353]

Cisco's NetFlow was and is utilized by the Albert Monitoring System. The NIST National Vulnerability Database listed the risk as "high" stating, "A successful exploit could allow the attacker to cause a process crash that would lead to a reload of the device."[354]

Of significance regarding this situation is that Cisco's NetFlow platforms had previously been identified to be exploitable through the SolarWinds Orion system. The Albert Monitoring Systems being utilized in the election infrastructure, according to CIS and the DHS, were not only exposed to the SolarWinds hack during

---

[352] https://www.cisa.gov/news/2021/01/05/joint-statement-federal-bureau-investigation-fbi-cybersecurity-and-infrastructure

[353] https://tools.cisco.com/security/center/content/CiscoSecurityAdvisory/cisco-sa-iosxe-fnfv9-dos-HND6Fc9u

[354] https://nvd.nist.gov/vuln/detail/CVE-2020-3492

CHAPTER 13

2020, including during the 2020 Presidential Election, but these systems also were highly likely exposed by the Cisco NetFlow Version 9 vulnerability. Of interest within this discussion is that Dominion Voting Systems was known to have also utilized the SolarWinds Orion platform within their networks, although the company had attempted to delete evidence showing as much.[355] After the SolarWinds Orion attack, Dominion replaced the platform with Cisco NetFlow.[356] When CISA came out on November 18, 2020, declaring, "The November 3rd election was the most secure in American history,"[357] certainly CISA, DHS, FBI, and Dominion, (who was a member of the EI-SCC and a signature party to the CISA statement), were well aware of the June 2020 Cisco NetFlow vulnerability. In light of this, compounded with the SolarWinds hack, the statement by CISA has to be one of the greatest misstatements ever made. Additionally, the fact that Dominion REPLACED SolarWinds with Cisco Netflow is an interesting decision when considering the company's position as a member of the EI-SCC and the company's solidarity with the CISA statement.

In a book released in 2019 by *The Brookings Institute* titled, "Bytes, Bombs, and Spies- The Strategic Dimensions of Offensive Cyber Operations,"[358] the topic of cyber vulnerabilities is discussed in the introduction to the book as being something of an asset for the Intelligence Community to leverage. The book states:

> "The U.S. government's Vulnerabilities Equities Process, which determines whether software vulnerabilities discovered by intelligence agencies should be disclosed to private sector vendors so that they can be patched,

---

[355] https://spectrumgrp.com/john-mills/
[356] https://spectrumgrp.com/john-mills/
[357] https://www.cisa.gov/news/2020/11/12/joint-statement-elections-infrastructure-government-coordinating-council-election
[358] https://www.brookings.edu/wp-content/uploads/2018/10/978081573547_ch1.pdf

may also shift. Under the Obama administration, this process reportedly tilted toward disclosing vulnerabilities to companies. The rising use of offensive cyber operations may **shift the calculus toward stockpiling vulnerabilities instead so that they can be used by the U.S. government in subsequent offensive operations.** In addition, more open and vigorous support may be offered to efforts that promote exceptional access to encrypted files and communications for law enforcement and intelligence agencies."[359]

While researching each fact that emerged from the material presented within this report, a few curious data points caused more questions to be asked. One question that this report asked earlier is: Is it oversight, ignorance, or intent that platform upgrades contained key vulnerabilities in a system as widely used as the Cisco NetFlow platform is, and as widely as it is deployed to include most government systems, would emerge only months prior to key elections (both 2016 and 2020)? Certainly, upgrades to systems are vetted by large tech companies before rollout. However, the commentary in the book by *The Brookings Institute* validates the question of timing of such vulnerabilities and their appearance could be very worthy of further investigation. Another curiosity that arose after the research herein was documented was similarities in architecture of the Dominion networks and timing of the integration of platforms to those of the Albert Monitoring Systems. Is this stark similarity a result of information sharing through the CIS via EI-ISAC, planned for some intent or purpose, or merely a coincidence? These questions are valid and deserve legitimate answers to allay any concerns of cyber hacking or mismanagement of networks or other systems. As the Constitutional voting right of each and every American hinges on

---

[359] https://www.brookings.edu/wp-content/uploads/2018/10/978081573547_ch1.pdf

CHAPTER 13

every aspect of this massive cyber network, presumptions, dismissals, or weak hypothesis to address these issues are completely unacceptable.

Moving on in the timeline, on or about January 8, 2021, SolarWinds hired former CISA Director, Chris Krebs, and former Facebook chief security officer, Alex Stamos, as consultants to assist with the hack of government agencies through their Orion platform.[360] The timing of this move by SolarWinds should be carefully considered in the large picture of any connectivity of events between the 2020 Presidential Election and the SolarWinds hack.

On February 23, 2021, SolarWinds CEO, Sudhakar Ramakrishna, filed a written statement with the Senate Select Committee on intelligence. In his statement Mr. Ramakrishna never identified a single nation-state as the origin of the SolarWinds Orion hack.[361] This position was maintained months after the federal intelligence community named Russia as the source of the hack. The highly respected technical publication, ZDNet, published an article about the APT (Advanced Persistent Threat) moniker attached to the SolarWinds attacker, and stated in a brief article, "Sometimes naming and shaming nations-states for their hacking is part of a deliberate diplomatic strategy,"[362] further referring to a specific situation previously reported in Australia, in 2018.[363]

For the scope of this report, it is important to question why the intelligence community came out nearly immediately blaming the Russians for the SolarWinds Orion hack. Within the timeline here

---

[360] https://www.govconwire.com/2021/01/solarwinds-hires-consulting-firm-krebs-stamos-group-to-assist-in-cybersecurity-assessment/

[361] https://www.intelligence.senate.gov/sites/default/files/documents/os-sramakrishna-022321.pdf

[362] https://www.zdnet.com/article/apt-groups-arent-all-from-russia-china-and-north-korea/

[363] https://www.zdnet.com/article/blaming-russia-for-notpetya-was-coordinated-diplomatic-action/

studied, the same methodology happened in the circumstance surrounding the DNC server hack when former FBI Executive Director and president of CrowdStrike Services, Shawn Henry, attributed that hack to Russia, also within days. Similarly, just weeks before the 2020 Presidential Election, the entire intelligence community came out in its fifty-plus individual strong statement regarding the Hunter Biden laptop and attributed that intelligence to Russian hacking and disinformation.

What is known at the time of this report is that the party or parties directly responsible for the SolarWinds Orion hack, have not been definitively identified. The attribution of Russia to the hack of the DNC server by CrowdStrike Services' President Shawn Henry has now become part of the Durham investigation and initial indictment in the Crossfire Hurricane investigation. Finally, the laptop purported to be that of Hunter Biden, has also been understood to in fact be truth.[364] This report has demonstrated a pattern that emerged immediately before and after the election of Donald Trump in 2016 from the heads of the Obama Intelligence Community and others closely connected to those individuals. Evidence shows that when Russians were assigned blame in most every circumstance surrounding cyber intelligence within that timeframe, the blame was false. Further evidence declassified by acting Director of National Intelligence, Ric Grenell, in a letter to Senators Grassley and Johnson and previously discussed in this report and worthy of continual repeating is that not only was the Russian evidence proven to be false as peddled by Brennan, Comey, and Clapper, but they KNEW it was false and sold the falsified information as truth to both the entire government structure in addition to the American public.[365] As mentioned in the

---

[364] https://www.politico.com/newsletters/playbook/2021/09/21/double-trouble-for-biden-494411
[365] https://www.hsgac.senate.gov/imo/media/doc/2020-04-16%20RHJ-CEG%20to%20FBI%20(Crossfire%20Hurricane%20Intel%20Memos).pdf

CHAPTER 13

previous chapter, it is important to question whether these false charges were made with intent of moving further policy and what that could imply for any other areas these charges are found later as this investigation continues. Certainly, in light of their use in the ICA report to Barack Obama in January of 2017, **this false narrative was one factor that pushed the United States election system into federal control under the Executive Branch of government**.

On March 11, 2021, the report answering 2018 Executive Order 13848 titled "Key Findings & Recommendations From the Joint Report from the DoJ and DHS"[366] was released. The report exposed one of the key aspects for having EO 13848 signed by President Trump. After the DHS had declared elections "critical infrastructure," President Trump was forced to run the gauntlet between giving the intelligence community the proverbial keys to drive the incredible cyber network monitoring infrastructure it had built over the past decade and which had now overtaken the entire election system, by signing EO 13848, or to independently sidestep the intelligence community and risk being called a Russian co-conspirator against the country. The text of the DHS/DoJ report prefaces the findings with the following statement:

> **"The purpose of this report was solely to evaluate the impact of foreign government activity on the security or integrity of the covered infrastructure.** It did not address the effect of foreign government activity on public perception or the behavior of any voters, nor did it address the impact of non-state foreign actors like cybercriminals."[367]

---

[366] https://www.dhs.gov/sites/default/files/publications/21_0311_key-findings-and-recommendations-related-to-2020-elections_1.pdf
[367] https://www.dhs.gov/sites/default/files/publications/21_0311_key-findings-and-recommendations-related-to-2020-elections_1.pdf

Countdown to Chaos

While the majority of Trump supporters eagerly awaited this report in hope that it would open the door to help state level election fraud cases move forward, it did quite the opposite. The federalization of the election infrastructure gave the agencies overseeing it, specifically the Department of Homeland Security, the EI-GCC, the EI-SCC, CISA, and others, governing authority over the "critical infrastructure" of the election. As such, this report in answer to EO 13848 limited the scope of their review to their own cyber infrastructure and monitoring and the statement above verifies this.

The federalization of the elections allowed the intelligence community to ignore and marginalize the pleas of states to investigate their own reported incidences of election fraud and legislative malfeasance in the scope of the security of the election, and used every tool it had within its structure, including the Associated Press (foundational member of the EI-SCC) to attempt to end any questions surrounding any other circumstances being questioned about the 2020 Presidential Election. The joint report from the DoJ and the DHS state the following within their response to EO 13848:

- "For the purposes of this report, the term security refers to protecting information and information systems from unauthorized access, use, disclosure, and disruption. The term integrity refers to protecting against unauthorized modification or destruction of information..."
- "For the purposes of this report, the term security refers to protecting information and information systems from unauthorized access, use, disclosure, and disruption. The term integrity refers to protecting against unauthorized modification or destruction of information."
    o "Broad Russian and Iranian campaigns targeting multiple critical infrastructure sectors did compromise the security of several networks that

CHAPTER 13

managed some election functions, but they did not materially affect the integrity of voter data, the ability to vote, the tabulation of votes, or the timely transmission of election results."

- "We are aware of multiple public claims that one or more foreign governments—including Venezuela, Cuba, or China—owned, directed, or controlled election infrastructure used in the 2020 federal elections; implemented a scheme to manipulate election infrastructure; or tallied, changed, or otherwise manipulated vote counts. Following the election, the Department of Justice, including the FBI, and the Department of Homeland Security, including CISA, investigated the public claims and determined that they are not credible."
- "We have no evidence—not through intelligence collection on the foreign actors themselves, not through physical security and cybersecurity monitoring of voting systems across the country, not through post-election audits, and not through any other means—that a foreign government or other actors compromised election infrastructure to manipulate election results."
- "Since 2018, federal, state, local, and private sector partners nationwide worked together in unprecedented ways ... to support state and local officials in safeguarding election infrastructure..."[368]

This report was filed with the Executive Branch in March 2021. Once again, the contents of this report put the intelligence community on a collision course with an unforeseen action only a month into the future. The Department of Justice and the Department of Homeland Security would have these findings

---

[368] https://www.dhs.gov/sites/default/files/publications/21_0311_key-findings-and-recommendations-related-to-2020-elections_1.pdf

Countdown to Chaos

tested by the voters of Arizona, when in late April 2021, the Arizona State Senate would use its legislative authority to commission the first full forensic audit ever undertaken in American history.

Backing up in time, just a few months, on January 21, 2021, on the first full day of the Biden-Harris Administration, a report was delivered to the Oval Office by "The President's National Infrastructure Advisory Council." Described by CISA as a group which "includes executive leaders from private sector and state/local government who advise the White House on how to reduce physical and cyber risks and improve the security and resilience of the nation's critical infrastructure sectors,"[369] the paper was titled, "Actionable Cyber Intelligence: An Executive Led Collaborative Model."[370] Of particular interest about this report is first that the general focus of this report deals with hardening cyber infrastructure via ISACs, Sector Coordinating Councils, and public-private partnerships. Within the NIAC document are the following project points:

- "...the NIAC recommended that the President establish a Critical Infrastructure Command Center (CICC) to improve real-time sharing and processing of private and public risk data—including classified information—between co-located government intelligence analysts and cleared cyber experts from companies whose functions are integral to U.S. national security."
- "The CICC is not simply another cyber intelligence or information sharing mechanism; rather, it is an operations center intended to drive innovative, tactical, and rapid solutions to cyber threats affecting the infrastructure most critical to U.S. national security and the U.S. economy."

---

[369] https://www.cisa.gov/niac
[370] https://www.cisa.gov/sites/default/files/publications/NIAC%20Actionable%20Cyber%20Intelligence_FINAL_508_0.pdf

CHAPTER 13

- "Working side-by-side in a classified environment, government and industry experts can rapidly assess intelligence in real-time and then develop and communicate tactical measures to protect critical infrastructure systems."
- "Mitigation measures can be shared and disseminated to the broader infrastructure community using industry partnerships like Information Sharing and Analysis Centers (ISACs) and Sector Coordinating Councils (SCCs)."
- "Support rapid declassification of threat information and mitigations by identifying the minimal parts of intelligence needed for companies to act and share with sector partners and smaller entities (e.g., through ISACs and other mechanisms)."
- "Provide a platform that enables the private and public sector to perform confidential cyber correlation searches."

The second point of interest regarding this report is an individual listed as a "Working Group Interviewee" was:

Rodney Joffe, Senior Vice President, Security CTO, Neustar, Inc.; NSTAC member

The significance of Mr. Joffe's participation in this report to the Biden-Harris White House will become clearer in chapter fifteen of this report which highlights details found in a 2022 motion filed in U.S. District Court by U.S. Attorney John Durham.

Countdown to Chaos

Chapter 14

The Arizona Audit, EI-ISAC Appointments, Eric Coomer Deposition (2021)

In April 2021, the Arizona State Senate, under the leadership of Senate President Karen Fann, used the full legal power of Arizona law to commission a full forensic audit of the ballots and voting machines in Maricopa County, Arizona. While the ballots and machines were due to be turned over to independent auditors (The Cyber Ninjas) on April 23, 2021, a host of seventy-three democrat attorneys descended upon the city of Phoenix in an attempt to stop the audit.[371] It is noteworthy that Maricopa County was one of the pilot locations for the John's Hopkins pilot SOAR platform referred to as the Integrated Adaptive Cyber Defense framework (IACD) (see chapter 6 of this report). It is also noteworthy that the biggest legal fights in the audit were for the Board of Supervisors to turn over all the voting machines, which were supplied by the vendor Dominion Voting systems, and for the routers used in the election to be turned over as well. Understanding the cyber structure built by the DHS over the last decade or more, the router traffic would be critical forensic evidence to lay side-by-side with the physical ballot findings. The DHS, CISA, EI-ISAC, FBI and others sold a bill of goods to the states and counties in the name of critical cyber security. None of the systems had been fully tested since the GAO audits of the EINSTEIN system in 2016 and the GAO audit of 2020. This independent full forensic examination would yield a true situational picture of what billions of federal dollars had paid for, what the states were getting in return for turning over their data and systems to the EI-ISAC and the Department of Homeland

---

[371] https://www.thegatewaypundit.com/2021/04/democrats-sent-73-lawyers-az-know-breaking-president-trump-releases-statement-forensic-audit-maricopa-county-arizona/

Countdown to Chaos

Security, and ultimately what the federal system and structure was worth.

News outlet reports were not impartial during any portion of the audit, reporting the proceedings as a "fraudit", a "clown show", and "theater."[372] This report would once again like to state for the record that the Associated Press was part of the EI-SCC, the organization created to be representatives for the election community under the governing authority, the Department of Homeland Security. Additionally, the AP was a co-sponsor of the CISA statement declaring "The November 3rd election was the most secure in American history."[373] The Associate Press, rather than reporting on the facts regarding the audit proceedings on a daily basis, chose to run stories that could be described as opinion pieces.[374] When the American public reviews everything within the scope this report, the 2020 Presidential Election, and the audits that continue to unfold after the election, it will become apparent that with regard to audits, an independent auditing agency will be difficult to contract for any audits of the 2020 election across the country, as nearly every single entity endorsed by the EAC, including the EAC, became a part of the DHS structure and "governing authority" over elections beginning in 2017. When the Arizona State Senate contracted the firm, Cyber Ninjas, for a full forensic audit of the 2020 election in Maricopa County, Arizona, the firm was able to be defined as independent in the scope of the activities surrounding the execution of the election as there was no affiliation between the Cyber Ninjas company with the state of

---

[372] https://www.npr.org/2021/06/03/1000954549/experts-call-it-a-clown-show-but-arizona-audit-is-a-disinformation-blueprint
[373] https://www.cisa.gov/news/2020/11/12/joint-statement-elections-infrastructure-government-coordinating-council-election
[374] https://apnews.com/article/joe-biden-media-social-media-arizona-presidential-elections-9a68234adab79b0f8a55e189af5a16e4

CHAPTER 14

Arizona or any other federal agency involved in the election process. Arguments to the contrary are illogical.

In an attempt to assert the power of the federal government over the states' constitutional authority over elections, on June 11, 2021, United States Attorney General, Merrick Garland, indicated that the Justice Department would be "staffing up and will apply new 'scrutiny' to controversial audits looking for evidence of fraud in the 2020 election."[375] This announcement would follow a similar assertion in May 2021, when Garland warned Arizona against proceeding with a planned voter canvass as part of Arizona's full forensic audit. As a response to the attempted action by the United States Department of Justice, Arizona state Senator Wendy Rogers boldly stood up for Arizona's Constitutional rights under Articles I & II of the Constitution, and the Tenth Amendment of the Constitution, and warned AG Garland, "You will not touch Arizona ballots or machines unless you want to spend time in an Arizona prison."[376] The simple fact that the federal government tried to insert federal powers into the jurisdiction of the state with regard to the 2020 Presidential Election is stand-alone evidence and a data point within the scope of information presented within this report.

On September 24, 2021, the Arizona State Senate released the findings of the full forensic audit undertaken months beforehand. While there are many findings within the audit, including critical findings of over 16,000 duplicate physical ballots counted, and potentially nearly 300,000 other illegal ballots identified in the certified count, this report will focus solely on those findings which question the cyber portion of the election audit in order to keep

---

[375] https://www.washingtonexaminer.com/news/garland-charts-doj-collision-course-with-maricopa-county-election-audit

[376] https://wendyrogers.org/az-state-senator-wendy-rogers-to-ag-garland-you-will-not-touch-arizona-ballots-or-you-will-go-to-jail/

Countdown to Chaos

discussion in context with the Albert Monitoring System and other EPS systems employed by the DHS during the election.

The digital findings of the audit of the 2020 Presidential Election[377] were presented to the Arizona State Senate by Ben Cotton, founder of CyFIR. In considering the findings of CyFIR, it is important to read and understand it with the information provided in chapter six of this report. Evidence shows the CIS and DHS were monitoring the election live in Maricopa County using their Albert Monitoring System, further equipped with the DHS/John's Hopkins Integrated Adaptive Cyber Defense framework (IACD) which allowed live alterations to the election environment. Immediately at the beginning of the 2021 audit report, CyFIR reported the following devices and data were withheld from the Senate subpoena by the Maricopa County Board of Supervisors. **The items withheld** were:

- Routers and Network Related Data
- Poll Worker Laptops
- ICX Devices
- ICP Credentials to Validate Configuration Settings or Administrative Settings
- Other Devices Connected to Election Network
    - 192.168.100.1
    - 192.168.100.11[378]

Understanding the reach of the Albert Monitoring System, and its ability to literally work inside the election environment, the withholding of the above items is again both a data point and standalone evidence within the context of this report. The next

---

[377] https://c692f527-da75-4c86-b5d1-8b3d5d4d5b43.filesusr.com/ugd/2f3470_2a043c72ca3e4823bdb76aaa944728d1.pptx?dn=Cotton%20Presentation.pptx
[378] https://c692f527-da75-4c86-b5d1-8b3d5d4d5b43.filesusr.com/ugd/2f3470_2a043c72ca3e4823bdb76aaa944728d1.pptx?dn=Cotton%20Presentation.pptx

CHAPTER 14

page of the CyFIR audit report listed "Cyber Security Issues." They were:

- Failed to Perform Basic OS Patch Management
- Failed to Update AntiVirus Definitions
- EAC Certification Defense is NOT Valid In View of the Evidence
    - 4 .exe Files Created After Dominion Software Install
    - 45 .exe Files Modified After Dominion Software Install
    - 377 .dll Files Created After Dominion Software Install
    - 1053 .dll Files Modified After Dominion Software Install
- Log Management - Failed to Preserve Security Logs
- Credential Management – Shared Accounts and Common Passwords
- Failed to Establish and Monitor Host Baseline
- Failed to Establish and Monitor Network Communications Baseline[379]

The audit report further outlined an illegal two hard drive, dual-boot configuration on the system's adjudication endpoint. The second hard drive in that configuration contained NON-Maricopa County data. Additionally, CyFIR found the deletions of 865 directories and 85,673 Election Related Files on the EMS C:/ drive. The files were deleted between October 28 and November 5, 2020. Deletions discovered to the EMS D:/ drive were 9,571 directories and 1,064,746 election related files that were deleted between

---

[379] https://c692f527-da75-4c86-b5d1-8b3d5d4d5b43.filesusr.com/ugd/2f3470_2a043c72ca3e4823bdb76aaa944728d1.pptx?dn=Cotton%20Presentation.pptx

Page 259

Countdown to Chaos

November 1st, 2020, and March 16, 2021 (days before the equipment was subpoenaed to be turned over the auditors). [380]

The audit report found deletions from the HiPro scanners inside the election environment. CyFIR reported 304 directories and 59,387 files containing election data deleted from the HiPro scanner 1 on March 3rd, 2021. CyFIR found 1,016 directories and 196,463 files containing election data deleted from the HiPro scanner 3 also on March 3rd, 2021. From HiPro scanner 4, CyFIR found 981 Directories and 191,295 files containing election data deleted on March 3rd, 2021. [381]

The report described deletion of both election results and security logs understood to be a necessary component to be kept for the historical election record. Within the systems examined CyFIR also found:

- Clear Intentional Overwriting of the Security Logs by the EMSADMIN Account
    - 2/11/2021 – 462 Log Entries Overwritten
    - 3/3/2021 - 37,686 Log Entries Overwritten
    - 4/12/2021 – 330 Log Entries Overwritten
- Anonymous logins (both typical and atypical)
- EMS network connection attempts on boot
- Significant Internet History Recovered from Unallocated Space
    - EMS Server
    - EMS Client Workstations
    - Adjudication Workstations

---

[380] https://c692f527-da75-4c86-b5d1-8b3d5d4d5b43.filesusr.com/ugd/2f3470_2a043c72ca3e4823bdb76aaa944728d1.pptx?dn=Cotton%20Presentation.pptx
[381] https://c692f527-da75-4c86-b5d1-8b3d5d4d5b43.filesusr.com/ugd/2f3470_2a043c72ca3e4823bdb76aaa944728d1.pptx?dn=Cotton%20Presentation.pptx

CHAPTER 14

- o   REWEB 1601
- o   REGIS 1202
- EMS listening ports
    - o   Analysis Discovered 59 Ports That Were Open on the EMS Server at Boot
    - o   Unexpected High Port Listening Activity by Standard Windows Processes (winit.exe, dns.exe, dhcpserver)
    - o   IPV6 Enabled
    - o   Terminal Services are Enabled
    - o   Remote Access is Enabled

The dates of the deletions and overwrites are exceptionally important and should be cross-referenced with any access the CIS SOC or the DHS EI-ISAC National Cyber Situational Awareness Room (NCSAR) may have had within these time frames, or what these agencies may be found to have accessed. In light of the final Arizona audit report released in September 2021, the interim report data from the Arizona audit report given in July is important to the discussion in this report as well. In the July report, CyFIR's cyber expert reported the Maricopa County EMS system experienced 37,000 anonymous administrative queries which was "not normal Windows behavior." Cotton further stated, "the Maricopa County election system was "compromised" during the 2020 election. "An element of the election system was actually compromised or breached during the course of the November 2020 election…The registration server that was public facing did have unauthorized access to that. In cybersecurity terms, it was breached…The county issued a letter" regarding the problem."[382] Knowing the immense reach the Department of Homeland Security built around the election systems in both 2018 and 2020, in addition to the knowledge of the SolarWinds Orion attack, the

---

[382] https://nationalfile.com/breaking-37000-anonymous-queries-to-access-2020-election-in-arizona-do-not-follow-that-pattern-of-normal-windows-behavior/

Countdown to Chaos

findings in Arizona create a serious problem for DHS, CISA, et al. Technologists all know the router(s) in Arizona hold all the answers to the questions raised within this report and the Arizona Senate audit report. As such, the abject refusal of the Maricopa County Board of Supervisors to hand over the routers, is again, a data point and evidence that stands alone. The evidence within the router(s) can either exonerate or incriminate those responsible for or who had access to them during this timeframe.

Upon the writing of this report, every single agency inside the federal government that had awareness regarding the cyber structure running during the 2020 election have been absolutely silent about the findings in Maricopa County, Arizona. After more discovery for this report, one of the key individuals that should have full awareness about every component governing the Maricopa County, Arizona election environment is also current CISA Director, Jen Easterly, whose extensive experience throughout all areas of cyber in the military and government would give her a unique perspective as to the findings reported in the Arizona audit. Ms. Easterly's silence is a standalone evidentiary data point.

The last statements made about anything having to do with the cyber structure of the election was the joint DoJ/DHS report cited earlier as a response to Executive Order 13848,[383] and the combined statement by CISA, and other agencies stating, "The November 3rd election was the most secure in American history."[384] The critical piece to solve this audit puzzle would be access to the routers and Splunk logs the Senate has subpoenaed since the outset of the audit process. To date that information has not been turned over to the Senate. As a point of interest, EI-SCC

---

[383] https://www.dhs.gov/sites/default/files/publications/21_0311_key-findings-and-recommendations-related-to-2020-elections_1.pdf
[384] https://www.cisa.gov/news/2020/11/12/joint-statement-elections-infrastructure-government-coordinating-council-election

CHAPTER 14

member, the Associated Press, has not published a single story about these Arizona findings by Ben Cotton.

Critical thinking of all evidence involving the technical aspect of the audit in Maricopa County yields a very limited number of possibilities regarding the findings reported to the Arizona State Senate. They are:

1. The Department of Homeland Security, CISA, the EI-ISAC, the Albert Monitoring System running CrowdStrike Services, classified DHS activities, and other enhanced cybersecurity services **failed in the highest manner and degree possible.** The audit findings are evidence that the system employed by the DHS was completely useless and nothing more than an unconstitutional federal election cyber superstructure.
2. The federal agencies using the tools mentioned above were in fact aware (as the system was monitored live by these agencies and agents) of activities going on within the election structure on Election Day, and on days immediately surrounding that date, and **the agencies either ignored or misidentified the activity;** OR
3. The federal agencies mentioned above, running enhanced cybersecurity services, tools, monitoring, and oversight, including some classified activities, **were the source of or allowed the activities presented in the findings** by CyFIR in the Arizona audit.

These deductions MUST be considered in context of the grand picture composed by the Department of Homeland Security when created in January 2017 under Barack Obama and then DHS Secretary Jeh Johnson in federalizing the election structure. The state of Arizona and the American people need to be told what the truth is regarding these findings AND the system employed by the federal government.

Countdown to Chaos

As this report draws to a close, the timeline ticks to the current date and a few events are noteworthy. On September 7, 2021, the Biden White House extended the state of emergency to continue the Executive Order 13848 through the 2022 midterm elections.[385] The federal cyber security network that was employed in the 2018 and 2020 election, is now under Executive Order 13848 to fully monitor the 2022 midterm elections as well. **Executive Order 13848 is the ONLY Trump era executive order to be renewed by the Biden Administration.**

On September 21, 2021, CIS announces new MS-ISAC elections leadership team. While most of these appointments are made without party affiliation designation, and historically people filling appointed positions to quasigovernmental agencies have been found to have their party affiliations expunged from public searches, these appointments were found with affiliations still discoverable online. They were:

- Kathy Bookvar (D), former PA SoS, served during the 2020 Presidential Election
- Jared Dearing (D), KY State Board of Elections Director
- Marci Andino (I), South Carolina Elections Director

The appointments were also not without some controversy as Bookvar left her position of Secretary of State in Pennsylvania under heavy scrutiny regarding the integrity of the 2020 Presidential Election. However, the CIS website made the following statement on the appointments saying:

> "Former Pennsylvania Secretary of State Kathy Boockvar will head the CIS elections security mission as the Vice President of Election Operations and Support. Kentucky

---

[385] https://www.federalregister.gov/documents/2018/09/14/2018-20203/imposing-certain-sanctions-in-the-event-of-foreign-interference-in-a-united-states-election

CHAPTER 14

State Board of Elections Executive Director Jared Dearing will serve as the Senior Director of Elections Security. Longstanding South Carolina Elections Director Marci Andino will assume a leadership role as the Director of the Elections Infrastructure Information Sharing and Analysis Center® (EI-ISAC®)."[386]

The next timeline entry followed up on information earlier presented in this report about other fallout from the 2020 Presidential Election, on September 23, 2021, Eric Coomer, the Dominion Voting Systems executive who played an important role in the 2020 Presidential Election on behalf of Dominion, and who appeared as a representative of the EI-SIG at the 2019 CISA Cybersecurity Summit, was deposed in a case directly related to the election.[387] The deposition was reported to have been disastrous in both the content recorded and demeanor displayed by Mr. Coomer. In a stunning move the deposition was sealed by the judge in a "sua sponte" order. A source in the story attached was reported as saying:

> "The Judge issued this order sua sponte, which means that no one asked her to do this. She just did it on her own the day after Coomer gave a train-wreck deposition in which he was very clearly emotionally unstable, arrogant, and repeatedly failed to give direct answers to questions. He was clearly playing games and his testimony is simply not credible."[388]

---

[386] https://www.cisecurity.org/press-release/center-for-internet-security-announces-new-elections-leadership-team/
[387] https://www.worldtribune.com/judge-puts-protective-order-on-eric-coomer-testimony-in-deposition-by-sidney-powell/
[388] https://www.worldtribune.com/judge-puts-protective-order-on-eric-coomer-testimony-in-deposition-by-sidney-powell/

Countdown to Chaos

On October 11, 2021, the deposition testimony of Dominion Voting Systems' employee, Eric Coomer, was opened to the public.[389] In the testimony, Mr. Coomer admits that evidence presented from social media was in fact posted by him. This case continues in the discovery phase.

As if to add insult to injury, the following entry in the timeline of this report was also reported on October 11, 2021, when the Pentagon's first software chief, Nicolas Chaillan, resigned, stating the United States had already lost the cyber war. Not wanting to preside over a system he said was too far behind to be effective at fighting for and protecting the country, Chaillan believed, "Some US government cyber-defense systems are so dated, they are merely at "kindergarten level…"[390] This news broke just as the final comments were being written for this report, and only a week after the Arizona State Senate audit report, which added many other layers of failure to the 2020 election cyber structure.

While collecting and evaluating the facts presented about the cyber network superstructure built and maintained by the DHS and conjoining agencies, the failures of the EINSTEIN 3A system as exposed by the GAO, in addition to the Arizona State Senate audit report, and this informal testimony by Nicolas Chaillan, **the purpose of fast tracking the election network and monitoring system throughout all fifty states and territories appears to be less about the security upon which it was claimed to have been built, and far more about quickly building a cyber network super structure and access to it.**

---

[389] https://www.thegatewaypundit.com/2021/10/exclusive-coomer-deposition-released-verifies-antifa-facebook-posts-extreme-left-bias/?utm_source=Telegram&utm_medium=PostTopSharingButtons&utm_campaign=websitesharingbuttons

[390] https://nypost.com/2021/10/11/pentagon-software-chief-nicolas-chaillan-resigns/

CHAPTER 14

The information presented within this report should give every American an incredible motivation to organize and take action against one of the greatest threats against freedom, perhaps since the Revolution. America must activate to reclaim its election system from the federal government agencies and agents that now control its most sensitive operations.

Certainly, the contents of this report are clear evidence regarding the brilliance of the minds of Alexander Hamilton and James Madison as they penned *The Federalist Papers*. Truly a centralized election system cannot benefit the individual in the furthest reaches of the country. The evidence presented here also supports the worst musings of the op-ed written by economist Steve Landsburg and published in *The Wall Street Journal* which said:

> "**…Now imagine that the election in question is actually run by a federal agency or by some nationwide quasigovernmental authority** charged with collecting and aggregating the results from all 50 states. I don't know about you, but I might worry a bit about the pressure that could be brought to bear on that single authority."[391]

America does not need to imagine this scenario – America has now lived it, at least twice. Now America needs to understand what was just perpetrated upon it unconstitutionally, and we must, as a free society demand its correction. Every elected leader in the country swears an oath to uphold the Constitution. Now it can be stated that any and every elected official who knowingly built and transferred the election system to the Department of Homeland Security as "critical infrastructure," stands in clear violation of their oath, and voters should soberly consider removing each and every one of these officials and replacing them with Constitutional

---

[391] https://www.cato.org/blog/framers-wisely-left-election-practice-decentralized

Countdown to Chaos

representatives which will return the elections to the freedom loving people of this country.

Chapter 15

DHS Terror Warning, John Durham Filings, Neustar, Inc., Rodney Joffe, Hillary Clinton and "Spygate", DHS Disinformation Governance Board, Sussman Trial, The FBI (2022)

On February 7, 2022 the Department of Homeland Security issued a National Terrorism Advisory System Bulletin (NTAS).[392] The premise of this bulletin is a strong warning as to why the DHS (or any agency that can be agenda-driven) cannot be the governing authority over or even simply have any participatory part of elections. Within the bulletin the DHS states the following:

- "The United States remains in a heightened threat environment fueled by several factors, including an online environment filled with false or misleading narratives and conspiracy theories, and other forms of mis- dis- and mal-information (MDM) introduced and/or amplified by foreign and **domestic threat actors**.
- While the conditions underlying the heightened threat landscape have not significantly changed over the last year, the convergence of the following factors has increased the volatility, unpredictability, and complexity of the threat environment: (1) **the proliferation of false or misleading narratives, which sow discord or undermine public trust in U.S. government institutions**; (2) **continued calls for violence directed at U.S. critical infrastructure**; ...
- DHS and the Federal Bureau of Investigation (FBI) continue to share timely and actionable information and intelligence with the broadest audience possible. **This includes sharing**

---

[392] https://www.dhs.gov/news/2022/02/07/dhs-issues-national-terrorism-advisory-system-ntas-bulletin

information and intelligence with our partners across every level of government and in the private sector." [393]

This bulletin needs to be consumed along with the knowledge that in addition to the Obama Administration via DHS Secretary Jeh Johnson having declared elections "critical infrastructure," it is incredibly significant that very early in the Biden-Harris Administration, on May 11, 2021, the DHS organized "a new, dedicated domestic terrorism branch within the Department's Office of Intelligence & Analysis (I&A) to ensure DHS develops the expertise necessary to produce the sound, timely intelligence needed to combat threats posed by domestic terrorism and targeted violence. **I&A will also continue leveraging the National Network of Fusion Centers** and our deployed intelligence professionals who collect and analyze threat information alongside our state, local, tribal, territorial, and private sector partners **to increase timely and actionable information sharing in a dynamic threat environment.** "[394]

The magnitude of this bulletin is highly significant. When the DHS became the governing authority over elections in January 2017, the election infrastructure became extraordinarily complex, as do most things run by the federal government. With the February 7, 2022 bulletin, the DHS again chose to use the national network of fusion centers as the actionable point of intelligence collection for this NTAS bulletin. The conflicts within this system architecture are incredible. The DHS as part of its election governance, uses the HSIN (Homeland Security Information Network) via fusion center nodes during elections to monitor elections and the transfer of election data, while at the same time, the DHS has now established the exact same apparatus for "sharing information and intelligence

---

[393] https://www.dhs.gov/news/2022/02/07/dhs-issues-national-terrorism-advisory-system-ntas-bulletin
[394] https://www.dhs.gov/news/2021/05/11/dhs-creates-new-center-prevention-programs-and-partnerships-and-additional-efforts

CHAPTER 15

with our partners across every level of government and in the private sector"[395] with regard to "domestic terrorists." Remember that in the 2018 midterm election "DHS embedded a DHS Intelligence & Analysis representative at the EI-ISAC headquarters for more than a month prior to the election..."[396] Armed with this knowledge, a review of chapter twelve of this report yields numerous examples of the politicization of fusion centers, clear incidences of spying perpetrated from within them including specifically domestic spying from inside a CIA fusion center with a set mission and target of building the Trump/Russia collusion narrative, in addition to other significant shortcomings and flaws known to exist within the national fusion center system.

Consider then the ease to which the DHS adds people and groups to the list of domestic terrorists, and the tools the DHS has at its disposal to handle anything considered terrorism, including fusion centers; then consider the tools the DHS uses in elections including fusion centers, ISACs, the HSIN, and other information sharing platforms and organizations which comprise a large portion of the entire discussion of this report. When the DHS puts out any sort of terror notice or bulletin pertaining to awareness of "continued calls for violence directed at U.S. critical infrastructure," the agency is always inherently including the United States election system in that description. As such, if any American stands up, whether in an established voter integrity group, or as part of a grass roots group of people that show up at any capitol building, (i.e. the protests that eventually fueled the Arizona Senate to undertake an audit, or a group like *True The Vote*), the DHS now has given themselves authority to name such activists as domestic terrorists directing violence against critical infrastructure. Certainly, such power and

---

[395] https://www.dhs.gov/news/2022/02/07/dhs-issues-national-terrorism-advisory-system-ntas-bulletin
[396] https://www.cisecurity.org/wp-content/uploads/2019/02/EI-ISAC-2018-YIR.pdf

Countdown to Chaos

authority could be and may already have been easily abused. For example, was U.S. Attorney General Merrick Garland's threat to the State of Arizona in early June of 2021 regarding the audit of the 2020 Presidential Election the Arizona Senate was then undertaking[397] born from the May 11, 2021 announcement of the formation of the Office of Intelligence and Analysis (I&A) by the Biden Administration? Additionally, what would stop the DHS from amalgamating information sharing regarding elections with intelligence collected about people they deem "domestic terrorists"?

To explain the immediate potential conflict such a system creates, on July 1, 2020, the New York Daily News ran an opinion piece bearing the headline "There is No Longer Any Doubt: Trump is a White Supremacist."[398] On September 30, 2020, NPR ran an article titled "From Debate Stage, Trump Declines To Denounce White Supremacy."[399] No news organization had ever been able to prove such an allegation, yet these organizations chose to fuel the topic by including it in the presidential debates on national television.[400] Despite presenting any proof for the allegations whatsoever, the media continued to run such headlines right up to the election. Additionally, it is important to note in the context of this report and this chapter that the FBI clearly had previously labeled white supremacy a grave domestic terror threat on June 4, 2019.[401]

With the media continuing to forward the narrative that a sitting president was basically a terrorist by labelling him a white

---

[397] https://www.washingtonexaminer.com/news/garland-charts-doj-collision-course-with-maricopa-county-election-audit
[398] https://www.nydailynews.com/opinion/ny-oped-trump-white-supremacist-20200701-5zumhjygabhgfckydm7xyhbm6a-story.html
[399] https://www.npr.org/2020/09/30/918483794/from-debate-stage-trump-declines-to-denounce-white-supremacy
[400] https://abcnews.go.com/Politics/trumps-failure-condemn-white-supremacy-debate-part-established/story?id=73340315
[401] https://www.fbi.gov/news/testimony/confronting-white-supremacy

CHAPTER 15

supremacist, and because the Associated Press is a founding member of the Election Infrastructure Subsector Government Coordinating Council (EI-GCC) and part of the DHS governance of elections, voters and legislators need to take note of **the direct influence these organizations tasked with "governing elections" now have over all elections.** The questions that now need to be asked include:

- What if someone that is wrongly or inappropriately added to the list of DHS domestic terrorists, that knew someone on the list, or that even talked about someone on the domestic terrorist list, decides to run for public office? Can the DHS use all tools at its disposal to thwart such a candidate?
- Could or would the DHS potentially oversee or spy on any campaign in the name of "homeland security"?
- Could the subject matter of any of the questions here posed have helped to seed the spying on the Trump campaign and White House as alleged by the Durham/Sussman indictment and motion during the period of time of his 2015-2016 campaign, his inauguration and the 2020 Presidential Election?

Further on this topic, skipping just a couple months ahead in the timeline for the sake of information continuity, in April of 2022, just about a week after former President Barack Obama presented an address about "controlling disinformation" at Stanford University,[402] the Department of Homeland Security announced the establishment of a new Disinformation Governance Board. DHS Secretary Mayorkas announced that the board would be chaired by Nina Jankowicz. *Homeland Security Today.us*, a platform run by the Government Technology & Services Coalition

---

[402] https://news.stanford.edu/2022/04/21/disinformation-weakening-democracy-barack-obama-said/

Countdown to Chaos

and overseen by such individuals as former DHS Secretary Michael Chertoff ran a story dated April 27, 2022, about the appointment titled "DHS Standing Up Disinformation Governance Board Led by Information Warfare Expert."[403] In the article Jankowicz is introduced as a Wilson Center global fellow and former advisor to the Ukrainian government on strategic communications. Highlighted front and center in the article were short, but pointed comments about the 2016 election, 2020 election, and the 2022 midterm elections. As elections seem to be a high priority and focus of the comments in the article, little doubt can be placed on the likelihood that this board represents yet another mechanism to both directly and indirectly control the information surrounding, and governance of elections via the DHS.

With respect to this urgent topic of federal officials' ability to not only manage, but directly influence elections by multiple means to include dissemination of information flow, the background of the inaugural chair of this committee raises enormous red flags, particularly in light of the federal court filings by John Durham to be explained in the next pages. On April 29, 2022, in a letter written immediately in response to the Mayorkas announcement, members of the House of Representatives Committee on Oversight and Reform, quickly denounced both the formation of the board and the newly named chair, Nina Jankowicz. In their letter they remark:

> "DHS is creating the Orwellian-named "Disinformation Governance Board" with a mission of "coordinat[ing] countering misinformation related to homeland security, focused specifically on irregular migration and Russia." Nina Jankowicz, a former Fulbright-Clinton Public Policy Fellow, has been tapped to lead the board

---

[403] https://www.hstoday.us/federal-pages/dhs/dhs-standing-up-disinformation-governance-board-led-by-information-warfare-expert/

CHAPTER 15

as its Executive Director. Ms. Jankowicz recently derided defenders of the First Amendment as "free speech absolutists" engaged in "abuse" against "marginalized communities," **promoted the work of Christopher Steele, the author of the widely discredited Steele dossier** whose main sources were exposed as criminals, and **promoted the false narrative that the Hunter Biden laptop story was Russian disinformation**. Her public comments indicate that she is a partisan; neither a defender of the First Amendment, nor possessing instincts that would make her a credible arbiter of truth. Her many public statements undermining First Amendment freedoms further call into question the purpose of the "Disinformation Governance Board," and signal that it is likely being set up to provide political cover for an unpopular Administration and to launder political attacks against its opponents."[404]

This letter and multiple news outlets reported evidence of Ms. Jankowicz's personal discussion posted on Twitter at critical times prior to the election of President Biden. While there are several statements now in question, one Jankowicz tweet stated:[405]

> **Nina Jankowicz**
> @wiczipedia
>
> Back on the "laptop from hell," apparently- Biden notes 50 former natsec officials and 5 former CIA heads that believe the laptop is a Russian influence op.
>
> Trump says "Russia, Russia, Russia."
>
> 10:18 PM · Oct 22, 2020 · Twitter Web App

---

[404] https://republicans-oversight.house.gov/wp-content/uploads/2022/04/Letter-to-DHS-re-Disinformation-Governance-Board-04292022.pdf
[405] https://twitter.com/wiczipedia/status/1319463138107031553?ref_src=twsrc%5Etfw

Countdown to Chaos

In her own defense after Congress, press, and others pointed out this clear partisan comment in October 2020, Jankowicz tried to assert that this statement was made as a part of live debate commentary and thus needed to be taken as an unofficial statement within context. Regardless, this statement shows that information which every person in positions of authority at the FBI, CIA, and the DHS all knew was false, was wildly disseminated throughout the Washington D.C. information network. These agency leaders had no problem using willing participants and figures such as Jankowicz even up to and including the months of 2021 just prior to the Durham filings. The October 22, 2020 tweet is reasonable evidence that Ms. Jankowicz is not qualified to vet intelligence information and is willing to act as a purveyor of government propaganda. The fact that Ms. Jankowicz is an easy and willing propaganda distributor is exceptionally dangerous when she and the Disinformation Governance Board are installed within the Department of Homeland Security which this report will declare ad nauseum is now responsible for the management of American elections.

Prior to release of this report, Nina Jankowicz resigned from her post chairing the DHS Disinformation Governance Board, however, the author has left the topic in place as the board itself is only "paused" according to the DHS.[406] To that end the serious, long-term implications of the DHS acting as governing authority over elections is something not yet fully known, remains a clear and present danger to free speech, and something Americans shouldn't be forced to find out decades down the road. However, the ample evidence pouring out of the 2020 election presented in next chapter is such that, with the information presented throughout the rest of this report, the American voter should be able to clearly see the immediate danger and conflicts the current DHS election

---

[406] https://news.yahoo.com/disinformation-head-nina-jankowicz-resigns-122618567.html

CHAPTER 15

management structure pose to the Constitution and the individual voter. The governance of U.S. elections Constitutionally belongs specifically in the hands of the individual states. It can be soundly argued that the Founders believed **there should be absolutely no participation in the election system or structure in any way by the federal government as it is perhaps the most dangerous centralization of power the federal government could possess**. Evidence of this is seen in dictatorial and communist countries where elections are perhaps always considered tampered or interfered with by people holding the central power.

On February 11, 2022 U.S. Attorney John Durham filed a motion in U.S. District Court[407] which contained information applicable to the findings within this report and as prefaced beginning with chapter eight. With the exception of the Fox News Channel/Fox Corporation, the corporate mainstream media tried its best to ignore the information when it dropped. However, the contents of the motion rocked social media sites describing it as a "bombshell," an "earthquake," "a million times worse than Watergate," and to many, nothing short of "worthy of charges of treason." The contents of the motion contained allegations of surveillance or spying activities perpetrated on the Trump campaign and later the on Trump White House by the Hillary Clinton for President campaign via government cyber contract holder, Neustar Inc., (an IT-ISAC member) run by "Tech Executive-1" in the motion, now publicly identified as Mr. Rodney Joffe.

The contents of the Durham motion in the Michael Sussman case state:

> "4. The Indictment also alleges that, beginning in approximately July 2016, Tech Executive-1 had worked

---

[407] https://irp.cdn-website.com/5be8a42f/files/uploaded/DurhamSussman0211.pdf

with the defendant, a U.S. investigative firm retained by Law Firm-1 on behalf of the Clinton Campaign, numerous cyber researchers, and employees at multiple Internet companies to assemble the purported data and white papers. In connection with these efforts, **Tech Executive-1 exploited his access to non-public and/or proprietary Internet data. Tech Executive-1 also enlisted the assistance of researchers at a U.S.-based university who were receiving and analyzing large amounts of Internet data in connection with a pending federal government cybersecurity research contract. Tech Executive-1 tasked these researchers to mine Internet data to establish 'an inference' and "narrative" tying then-candidate Trump to Russia.** In doing so, Tech Executive-1 indicated that he was seeking to please certain "VIPs," referring to individuals at Law Firm-1 and the Clinton Campaign.

5. The Government's evidence at trial will also establish that among the Internet data Tech Executive-1 and his associates exploited was domain name system ("DNS") Internet traffic pertaining to (i) a particular healthcare provider, (ii) Trump Tower, (iii) Donald Trump's Central Park West apartment building, and (iv) the Executive Office of the President of the United States ("EOP"). (Tech Executive-1's employer, Internet Company-1, had come to access and maintain dedicated servers for the EOP as part of a sensitive arrangement whereby it provided DNS resolution services to the EOP. Tech Executive-1 and his associates exploited this arrangement by mining the EOP's DNS traffic and other

CHAPTER 15

data for the purpose of gathering derogatory information about Donald Trump.)"[408]

In a *New York Post* article about Joffe, the technology industry executive's position and company are described as follows:

> "Rodney Joffe is the person referred to as "Tech Executive-1" in Sussman's indictment for allegedly lying to the FBI by withholding his connections to Hillary Clinton's losing 2016 election campaign against former President Donald Trump, according to CNN... Joffe's LinkedIn profile says he retired earlier this month as senior vice president and security chief technology officer at Neustar Inc., a Reston, Va.-based company that provides various internet-related services and products to more than 8,000 commercial and government clients around the world." [409]

Further research found additional companies directly connected to Rodney Joffe. Those companies include, Packet Forensics, Vostrom, Vostrom Holdings, ERP Services, Inc., and Ultra DNS. A banner at the top of the Neustar website posted as of February 17, 2022 states: "Effective December 1, 2021, Neustar, Inc. is a TransUnion company and Neustar Security™ Services is a Golden Gate Capital and GIC portfolio company."[410] This investigative work also uncovered a resume Rodney Joffe submitted in 2010 to ICANN for a position as "Volunteer Review Member." Within that resume, Mr. Joffe describes the extent of his government positions and access in his own words:

---

[408] https://irp.cdn-website.com/5be8a42f/files/uploaded/DurhamSussman0211.pdf
[409] https://nypost.com/2021/09/30/who-is-rodney-joffe-tech-executive-1-in-durham-indictment/
[410] https://www.home.neustar/

Countdown to Chaos

> "Rodney is frequently called upon to assist Federal Authorities with regards to investigating and protecting against cyber-crime and cyber-terrorist activities where he is a recognized expert. He regularly briefs the White House and House/Senate groups on the subject, and has testified before congress as an expert. In addition to publishing a number of confidential papers in the field, he participated as a "Designated Trusted Agent" on the planning committee for the DHSs CyberStorm II International Cyber-Terrorism exercise in March 2008. He is participating in CyberStorm III as a lead on the core scenario design team."[411]

The same resume lists Mr. Joffe's areas he deemed himself an expert:

> **"Cybersecurity Expert:**
>
> • White House Advisor, CyberSecurity Issues: April 2010 – present [Summer 2010]
>
> • DHS, FBI - March 2007 - **ongoing advisory relationship**
>
> • Head of the Conficker Working Group - March 2009 – ongoing
>
> • Congressional Testimony May 1, 2009 - House Committee on Communications,
>
> Technology, and the Internet on CyberSecurity issues
>
> • Numerous Conferences and Symposia, Keynotes and technical presentations

---

[411] https://gnso.icann.org/sites/default/files/filefield_13823/application-joffe-cv-14jul10-en.pdf

CHAPTER 15

- Cyberstorm III – Lead on the Core Scenario Design Team 2010

- Cyberstorm II - Planning and Exercise for DNS/Cybersecurity Scenario 2008"[412]

Importantly, the reference in the Joffe resume to an ongoing advisory relationship with the DHS and FBI happens at a point in time during which Shawn Henry (later President of CrowdStrike Services) was the Deputy Director of Cyber Security at the FBI. Additionally, the timeframe in which Joffe cites his "ongoing advisory relationship" with the DHS and the FBI encompasses the time of the deployment of the EINSTEIN 2 program (2007) likely through the deployment of the Albert Monitoring pilot (January 2011). Due to the nature of Neustar, Inc.'s services, Mr. Joffe's reputation in the cyber world, and Shawn Henry's position at the FBI at the time, the crossover of time and positions nearly guarantees Mr. Joffe and Mr. Henry had an ongoing professional working relationship.

Another reference of interest in the Durham motion applicable to this report is "Law Firm-1", now understood to be the law firm Perkins Coie, LLP based in Seattle, Washington was retained by the Hillary Clinton campaign and the Democrat National Committee for legal services during the 2016 presidential campaign. Chapters six and eight of this report discuss and preface the connection of Shawn Henry, former FBI Deputy Director and later President of CrowdStrike Services, to Perkins Coie LLP, as CrowdStrike was retained by the DNC through Perkins Coie for services relating to the alleged 2016 DNC server hack. Importantly, chapter six of this report presented relevant information that CrowdStrike Falcon, the tool deployed to investigate the DNC server hack, was and is the main framework for the election monitoring system known as

---

[412] https://gnso.icann.org/sites/default/files/filefield_13823/application-joffe-cv-14jul10-en.pdf

Countdown to Chaos

Albert Monitoring Services - the backbone service offered by the Department of Homeland Security via the Center for Internet Security to both MS-ISAC and EI-ISAC members, which include every state in the Union.

Finally, the "pending government cybersecurity research contract" referred to in the Durham motion is now known to be DARPA (Defense Advanced Research Projects Agency),[413] a subagency of the Department of Defense which includes Fort Meade, the home of U.S. Cyber Command, and a member of the National Defense ISAC (ND-ISAC) and the National Council of ISACs (NCI) (see page nine of this report for more information on the significance of these associations).

An interesting fact uncovered in the investigation of all information relevant to this chapter is that two of Rodney Joffe's Companies, VOSTROM and Neustar Inc., in addition to the company for whom Shawn Henry serves as President, CrowdStrike Serves, are all members of the federal government's Information Technology Sector Coordinating Council (IT-SCC).[414] The IT-SCC was highlighted in chapter four of this report (pages 14-16). The reader may find it important to review that information again. This fact yields a second circumstance in which Mr. Joffe and Mr. Henry likely worked together in a professional capacity.

The connections of each of these companies, agencies, and individuals (i.e. CrowdStrike, Neustar, Perkins Coie, DHS, FBI, etc.) continued to get more complex as time wore on during the summer of 2016 toward the 2016 election, then later during the period of time covered by "Crossfire Hurricane," and finally during the time prior to the 2020 election. A solid review of the 2016 timeline as

---

[413] https://www.breitbart.com/politics/2022/02/12/john-durham-filing-suggests-clinton-operatives-spied-on-trump-in-2016-and-in-white-house/
[414] https://www.cisa.gov/information-technology-sector-council-charters-and-membership

CHAPTER 15

outlined in chapter eight is recommended either before or after consuming information to follow. To highlight the complexity of these relationships, one report by *New York Post* journalist Paul Sperry titled, "'Clinton tech' Rodney Joffe had a shady past before he targeted Trump," stated:

> "Secret Service entrance logs reveal Joffe visited the White House several times during the Obama administration. And in 2013, Comey gave Joffe an award recognizing his work helping agents investigate a cybersecurity case. Sources said that Joffe has also worked as an FBI informant on various cybersecurity cases opened by the bureau over roughly the past 15 years."[415]

Such an ongoing relationship with the inner workings of the Obama White House and the FBI during this particular period of time leave Mr. Joffe in the proverbial crosshairs with regard to suspicion and culpability surrounding all things cyber influenced or perpetrated throughout this timeframe. For example, the timeline of events during 2016 is full of actions by the FBI, the DHS, and the White House, with nearly all actions pertaining to the 2016 Presidential Election. One key chronology of facts from another review of the 2016 timeline (chapter 8), shines a white-hot light on details surrounding the timing of requests made by the Department of Justice and the FBI for the digital forensic evidence necessary to corroborate allegations being made about Russian hacking of the DNC and the further suspicion that they may try to hack the 2016 election. At that moment in time, neither agency was in receipt of the requested information requested and necessary to validate the allegations, yet the White House authorized the United States

---

[415] https://nypost.com/2022/02/21/the-shady-past-of-clinton-tech-joffe-who-targeted-trump/

Countdown to Chaos

Intelligence Community to publicly blame Russia for the alleged DNC email server hack.

Understanding this and understanding the access Joffe had to the White House and the federal agencies, the source of the flow of information must be investigated and closely scrutinized. Investigators working on the details of this report were unable to obtain a firsthand copy of the Secret Service entrance logs referred to by *New York Post* reporter Paul Sperry. The dates of those visits juxtaposed to all other activities outlined in this report during the summer of 2016 would be a prime piece of evidence to complete a proper picture of Mr. Joffe's part in Executive Branch movements and decision making during this time. Mr. Joffe could potentially be under suspicion for influence of not just the White House, but of the FBI, and the DHS of the Executive Branch, and may have had an influential role in the private tech sector to include CrowdStrike Services at this point in time as well. When one considers both the information sharing and the fusion center structures, the products of Joffe's actions could have become deeply embedded in many aspects of information and activities within the workings of the federal intelligence community which was laser focused on the American election system.

The details further revealed in the February 11, 2022 Durham motion demand each and every one of these relationships be very closely examined by not only U.S. Attorney John Durham, but by every elected official at the federal and state levels, and by every American citizen who wishes to preserve this constitutional republic. At the time this investigation and report were initiated, the Durham indictment had not yet been published. The information in 2021 indictment and the subsequent 2022 motions show how the interconnections of the central powers of the federal government are of critical importance to understand, discern, and importantly to suppress in terms of U.S. elections.

CHAPTER 15

Very key to this report is the following from point four of the Durham motion:

> "**Tech Executive-1 [Joffe] exploited his access** to non-public and/or proprietary Internet data. Tech Executive-1 also enlisted the assistance of researchers at a U.S.-based university who were receiving and analyzing large amounts of Internet data **in connection with a pending federal government cybersecurity research contract**. Tech Executive-1 **tasked these researchers to mine Internet data** to establish "an inference" and "narrative" tying then-candidate Trump to Russia." [416]

In addition, the initial Durham indictment of Michael Sussman states the following about "Tech Executive-1," Rodney Joffe:

> "12. Tech Executive-1 was at all times relevant to this Indictment an executive of a particular Internet company ("Internet Company-1"), which offers various Internet-related services and products, including Domain Name System ("DNS") resolution services, to its customers...
>
> 13. By virtue of his position at Internet Company-l and other companies, **Tech Executive-1 maintained direct or indirect access to, and the ability to provide others access to, large amounts of internet and cybersecurity data, including DNS data.**
>
> 15. In or about November 2016, Tech Executive-1 claimed to have been previously offered a position in the government in the event Hillary Clinton won the Presidency, stating in an email days after the U.S. Presidential election: 'I was tentatively offered the top

---

[416] https://irp.cdn-website.com/5be8a42f/files/uploaded/DurhamSussman0211.pdf

Countdown to Chaos

[cybersecurity] job by the Democrats when it looked like they'd win. I definitely would not take the job under Trump.'

21. As alleged in further detail below, in or around the same time period - and in furtherance of his efforts with SUSSMANN and Campaign Lawyer-I to disseminate allegations regarding Trump - **Tech Executive-1 used his access at multiple organizations to gather and mine public and non-public Internet data** regarding Trump and his associates, with the goal of creating a 'narrative' regarding the candidate's ties to Russia.

22. **Tech Executive-1 later shared certain results of these data searches and analysis with SUSSMANN so that SUSSMANN, in turn, could provide them to the media and the FBI.**"[417]

Did Rodney Joffe's exploitation of his access to the government cyber realm as described in the February 2022 Durham motion in any way touch the Department of Homeland Security's ongoing election monitoring systems provided through the MS-ISAC and EI-ISACs? While information presented in this chapter makes a strong case for the likelihood of minimally a professional relationship between Rodney Joffe and Shawn Henry, did Joffe's associations with the DHS and the FBI which were also highlighted previously in reference to Mr. Joffe' resume, connect him any way to CrowdStrike Services via Shawn Henry, thus the Albert Monitoring System, and ultimately the U.S. elections? Were these among relationships Mr. Joffe exploited? How many visits did Mr. Joffe make to the Obama White House as recorded on Secret Service logs particularly during 2016? When do these visits take place in context with other key dates in 2016? Entries of events into the timeline during the entire year of 2016 that interconnect these

---

[417] https://www.justice.gov/sco/press-release/file/1433511/download

CHAPTER 15

individuals, agencies, and services, give weight to these questions, show urgent need to find answers, and demonstrate a necessity to install constitutional voter-protecting solutions urgently and immediately.

In order to begin to find answers to these questions it is important to have an understanding of the depth of the information contained within the Durham indictment and motion in context with the contractual history of Rodney Joffe's company, Neustar, Inc., with the U.S. federal government. A search of federal contracts on the website USAspending.gov found 86 individual contracts between Neustar Inc. and various federal agencies including the Department of Homeland Security, the Department of Justice, and the Department of Defense, with one subagency being the Federal Bureau of Investigation.[418] The other companies associated with Mr. Joffe were not searched as they were not named in the Durham indictment.

A review of the spectrum of contracts revealed information from Neustar, Inc. itself in response to the government contract process. In its November 2018 587-page statement to the U.S. Department of Commerce titled "usTLD Registration Management: Volume 1- Technical Capability" Neustar describes the nature of its business as follows:

> "Over the past two decades, Neustar has carved out an enviable reputation as a leader in the global Internet community. Not only are we the world's largest Registry provider by volume of TLDs; **our DNS and DDoS security business are among the largest and most well-respected in the industry. Having both a Registry and Security business gives Neustar the operating scale and**

---

[418] https://www.usaspending.gov/search/?hash=3f438aa7f3ca853c9bdb137becb08ac1

> **leverage to make substantial investments in infrastructure, cyber-security**, marketing and innovation that directly benefit the usTLD and the United States Internet community." [419]

Regarding contracts with the federal government, this same publication states:

> "Neustar is proactive in monitoring for abuse and malicious activity. Neustar works with the United States Government, international law-enforcement agencies to take down malicious domain names to help keep the usTLD clean."[420]

About the company, Neustar, within a contract with NIST (National Institute of Standards and Technology), the following is presented as a description of services:

> "The Contractor shall provide centralized management and coordination of registry, registrar (where specified), database, and information services for the usTLD in accordance with the Statement of Work"[421]

In a proposal to NIST by Neustar, Inc. titled "Neustar NIST Authentication Commentary" and dated August 10, 2020, Neustar states:

> "As the leader in responsible identity resolution, we use our expertise in real-time addressing, authentication, and analytics to provide marketing, risk, digital defense

---

[419] https://www.ntia.doc.gov/files/ntia/publications/technical_proposal_volume_1.pdf

[420] https://www.ntia.doc.gov/files/ntia/publications/technical_proposal_volume_1.pdf

[421] https://www.ntia.doc.gov/files/ntia/publications/us_mod_0004_11172015.pdf

CHAPTER 15

and performance, and communications solutions for over 11,000 clients globally, including numerous Fortune 500 companies and 60 of the Fortune 100 companies. **Neustar solutions empower major government agencies and security units**, all leading financial institutions and credit card issuers, and all leading communications service providers. **Delivering actionable identity is at the core of everything we do**, and responsible identity has been at the heart of our business since its inception."[422]

Further investigation into details of Rodney Joffe also found the company he was employed by and represented in government contracts, Neustar Inc., was listed on the "2020 Biden For President Campaign" vendor payroll for services that were paid a sum of $18,819.41. The description of services was "Accounting and Compliance Consulting." The payment date recorded was September 29, 2020.[423]

With this understanding of Neustar, Inc., Rodney Joffe, and an understanding of the federal government's monitoring programs outlined in this report (i.e. EINSTEIN and Albert Monitoring Services), the information in the Durham motion is wildly important and begins to address the questions posed throughout this chapter regarding the interconnection of all individuals facing allegations in the Durham filings:

> "4. The Indictment also alleges that, beginning in approximately July 2016, Tech Executive-1 had worked with the defendant, a U.S. investigative firm retained by Law Firm-1 on behalf of the Clinton Campaign, numerous cyber researchers, and employees at multiple Internet

---

[422] https://www.nist.gov/system/files/documents/2020/09/08/Comments-800-63-020.pdf

[423] https://docquery.fec.gov/cgi-bin/fecimg/?202010219326734372

companies to assemble the purported data and white papers. In connection with these efforts, **Tech Executive-1 exploited his access to non-public and/or proprietary Internet data.** Tech Executive-1 also enlisted the assistance of researchers at a U.S.-based university who were receiving and analyzing large amounts of Internet data in connection with a pending federal government cybersecurity research contract. Tech Executive-1 tasked these researchers to mine Internet data to establish "an inference" and "narrative" tying then-candidate Trump to Russia. In doing so, Tech Executive-1 indicated that he was seeking to please certain "VIPs," referring to individuals at Law Firm-1 and the Clinton Campaign.

5. The Government's evidence at trial will also establish that **among the Internet data Tech Executive-1 and his associates exploited was domain name system ("DNS")** Internet traffic pertaining to (i) a particular healthcare provider, (ii) Trump Tower, (iii) Donald Trump's Central Park West apartment building, and (iv) **the Executive Office of the President of the United States ("EOP").** (Tech Executive-1's employer, Internet Company-1, had come to access and maintain dedicated servers for the EOP as part of **a sensitive arrangement** whereby it provided DNS resolution services to the EOP. **Tech Executive-1 and his associates exploited this arrangement by mining the EOP's DNS traffic and other data for the purpose of gathering derogatory information about Donald Trump**.)"[424]

---

[424] https://irp.cdn-website.com/5be8a42f/files/uploaded/DurhamSussman0211.pdf

CHAPTER 15

When Durham alleged that Joffe "exploited his access to non-public and/or proprietary Internet data…tasked researchers to mine Internet data….to please certain 'VIPs,' referring to individuals at Law Firm-1 (Perkins Coie) and the Clinton Campaign" the following issues become critical:

- Considering the timing of the 2016 United States Intelligence Community's statement publicly blaming alleged, and at that point, unproven hacking perpetrated by Russia, was Joffe's access to the White House as recorded by the Secret Service entrance logs evidence that Joffe was directly providing the White House with information personally? Did Joffe share information he had "collected" through both Sussman anonymously and with the White House directly? If so, was Joffe trying to elevate and validate information later shown by the agencies to be both fake and/or "user created" to effect executive decisions? Did the executive branch initiate and mobilize Joffe in this action?
- Knowing the extent of Neustar's access within the cyber sectors of the government (i.e. the White House, Department of Homeland Security, the Department of Justice, the Department of Defense, and the Federal Bureau of Investigation), the simple fact that Joffe is stated to have "exploited" this access opens the door to accessing nearly limitless information, potentially including access to information and information transfer for the elections of 2016, 2018, 2020, and potentially any other state contests in 2017 and 2019. If Rodney Joffe was brazened enough to use his influence to allegedly spy on the Executive Office of President Trump, was Neustar's access to government agencies and officials exploited in any way referenced in the motion to access and surveil election data and data transfer

Countdown to Chaos

that was part of the federal monitoring network via Albert Monitoring Systems, the HSIN, and other fusion centers?

- Did Joffe's desire to "please certain 'VIPs'" allow for any influence by Joffe in the construction of the joint statement created by the intelligence community, and published by the DHS, ODNI, and FBI regarding Russian influence in the 2016 election, and presented directly to President Barack Obama?[425] Did any of the information exploited by Joffe influence President Obama and DHS Secretary Jeh Johnson to establish American elections as critical infrastructure?

- CrowdStrike's Shawn Henry's associations, including his previous positions at the FBI that culminated with the position of Deputy Director of FBI Cybersecurity, CrowdStrike's government contracts, CrowdStrike's position on the IT-SCC, CrowdStrike's contract with CIS for Albert Monitoring Services, Henry's personal friendship with Michael Sussman, CrowdStrike having been retained through Perkins Coie in the summer of 2016 to work on Democratic National Committee Servers, and Henry's likely professional association with Rodney Joffe, all **leave Henry and CrowdStrike prime targets for further <u>intense scrutiny with regard to every server they monitored, to include all elections, including the 2020 Presidential Election.</u>**

- As all election data from voting machine companies is considered fully proprietary, it is not outside the realm of possibility that federal agencies may have targeted that vein of information when considering what is stated within the language and charges in the February 2022 Durham motion.

---

[425] https://www.dni.gov/index.php/newsroom/press-releases/press-releases-2016/item/1616-joint-dhs-odni-fbi-statement-on-russian-malicious-cyber-activity

CHAPTER 15

An additional question that also needs to be asked in light of the everything this report has revealed about the DHS is: Did the Department of Defense, DARPA, and the FBI, all indirectly referenced in Durham's indictment of Michael Sussman[426] give themselves any sort of "license" to thwart then candidate Trump in his campaign for reelection to the Presidency of the United States based upon allegations that he was a white supremacist, which is considered domestic terrorism by the Department of Homeland Security and the FBI? Clearly that is a question that is nearly impossible to find an answer to in the channels of normal research. However, there is a trail of very important breadcrumbs to follow and examine considering the concept.

The February 2022 Durham motion mentions "a U.S.-based university who were receiving and analyzing large amounts of Internet data in connection with a pending federal government cybersecurity research contract." Public reporting has identified the U.S.-based university as Georgia Tech, Researcher-1 as Manos Antonakakis, and the government contractual agency as DARPA as previously discussed.

Within an email thread between Researcher-1, (Manos Antonakakis), and Fabrian Monrose at the University of North Carolina, the group discusses the DARPA Statement of Work (SOW) and other details. Importantly, the name of the DARPA-Georgia Tech program is revealed and referred to as the "EA program" throughout the email discussions.[427] Further research to identify what that specific program entailed unearthed a statement by the Deputy Director of DARPA, Dr. Peter Highnam, filed with the U.S. Senate Armed Services Subcommittee on Emerging Threats and Capabilities on April 21, 2021. This report was filed well before the

---

[426] https://www.justice.gov/sco/press-release/file/1433511/download
[427] https://www.judicialwatch.org/wp-content/uploads/2022/02/Georgia-Tech-Sussmann-November-2021-pg-102-105.pdf

Countdown to Chaos

details emerged from U.S. Attorney John Durham regarding the Michael Sussman indictment and lays out a few interesting points about the EA project. It reads:

> "DARPA researchers are identifying and addressing critical cyber vulnerabilities that threaten global stability and security...
>
> To address this problem, **DARPA launched the Enhanced Attribution (EA) program. EA is making currently opaque malicious cyber adversary actions and individual cyber operator attribution transparent by providing high-fidelity visibility into all aspects of malicious cyber operator actions**. Furthermore, if successful, EA will increase the government's ability to publicly reveal the actions of individual malicious cyber operators without damaging sources and methods. Over the last three years the program has developed techniques and tools for generating operationally and tactically relevant information about multiple concurrent independent malicious cyber campaigns, each involving several operators, and the means to share such information with US. law enforcement, intelligence, and Allied partners.
>
> **Late last year, DARPA EA researchers used their data analytics to develop timely, accurate threat information regarding Russian-attributed malicious cyber infrastructure and associated actor personas. EA shared this information with close partners at the FBI Atlanta and Pittsburgh field offices**, contributing to the October 2020 indictment of six GRU personnel associated with a worldwide destructive malware

CHAPTER 15

campaign and the remediation of that malware campaign in **U.S. and Allied critical infrastructure**."[428]

A cybersecurity expert speaking on the terms of anonymity explained the work DARPA and Georgia Tech was likely undertaking was work to decrypt internet packet payloads. While cybersecurity teams normally monitor traffic using meta data, ping addresses, and other unencrypted information, most "payloads" are sent encrypted.[429] The information provided in the DARPA report lends itself to the understanding that DARPA was working on a method of decrypting intercepted internet traffic and according to the Durham motion, through the Georgia Tech contract, was "analyzing large amounts of [it]." [430]

The DARPA report also mentions that the agency project included the activities of both "opaque malicious cyber adversary actions **and individual cyber operator**[s]." The removal of the term "malicious" in context with "individual cyber operator[s]" in this statement could be incredibly significant considering information alleged in the Durham motion which indicated:

> "Tech Executive-1 [Rodney Joffe, Neustar], tasked these researchers to mine Internet data to establish "an inference" and "narrative" tying then-candidate Trump to Russia. In doing so, Tech Executive-1 indicated that he was seeking to please certain "VIPs," referring to

---

[428] https://www.armed-services.senate.gov/imo/media/doc/Highnam%20Testimony%2004.21.21.pdf
[429] https://www.cisco.com/c/en/us/td/docs/ios/security/configuration/guide/sec_cfg_encrypt_tech.pdf
[430] https://irp.cdn-website.com/5be8a42f/files/uploaded/DurhamSussman0211.pdf

individuals at Law Firm-1 [Perkins Coie] and the Clinton Campaign." [431]

The DARPA report further states **EA shared this information with close partners at the FBI Atlanta and Pittsburgh field offices.** Once again, a review of the information regarding fusion centers in chapter twelve is immensely important in context with this admission by DARPA Deputy Director Dr. Peter Highnam. While details surrounding the operations within the FBI field office in Pennsylvania are unclear, the Georgia FBI field office works very closely with the Georgia ISAC. The GISAC fusion center's mission statement reads in part:

> "GISAC facilitates connectivity between local, state, and federal agencies in Georgia. The purpose is to share resources and information in a way that enhances the capacity to identify, detect, mitigate, prevent and respond to criminal activity. GISAC does not replace or duplicate the counter-terrorism functions of the Federal Bureau of Investigation (FBI); rather, GISAC's efforts to collect information from state and local sources **ensures greater availability and integration of information from those sources**. GISAC enhances lead development and improves the analysis of existing information by identifying state-wide trends and intelligence gaps. GISAC also **ensures other state and local agencies receive bulletins and assessments produced by federal agencies that are relevant to their areas of responsibility.**" [432]

---

[431] https://irp.cdn-website.com/5be8a42f/files/uploaded/DurhamSussman0211.pdf
[432] https://investigative-gbi.georgia.gov/investigative-offices-and-services/specialized-units/ga-information-sharing-analysis-center

CHAPTER 15

Regarding the current status of the EA program, the DARPA report in which it is referenced was dated April 21, 2021 and says:

> "Over the last three years [2018-2021] **the program has developed techniques and tools for generating operationally and tactically relevant information** about multiple concurrent independent malicious cyber campaigns, each involving several operators, and the means **to share** such information **with US. law enforcement, intelligence,** and Allied partners." [433]

Clearly as of April 2021, the DARPA EA program was spoken of in the present tense in Dr. Highnam's report. In addition, he made it evident that the emerging technology was information that was actively shared with law enforcement and intelligence.

Finally, the DARPA statement ends with the acknowledgment that part of the "remediation campaign" of the Enhanced Attribution (EA) project was sent to "U.S. and Allied critical infrastructure." Again, this report allows this to be seen through the clear prism of critical infrastructure to immediately include the American national election infrastructure. Using the example of the Georgia ISAC's relationship with the FBI field office described in the DARPA EA program, a comment made by Fulton County, Georgia's Chief Operating Officer, Anna Roach, raises further questions. In her comments during the January 6th Fulton County Board of Commissioners regular meeting, Ms. Roach made the following remark recorded in the minutes:

> "Another effort that I'm significantly proud of is, under the leadership of then Chief Halbert and now Chief Gates, **we established an election security task force that, in partnership with the FBI,** GBI, and local law

---

[433] https://www.armed-services.senate.gov/imo/media/doc/Highnam%20Testimony%2004.21.21.pdf

Countdown to Chaos

> enforcement, we put in place security protocols for all of our elections, **both early voting as well as Election Day**, and was **able to establish an information sharing protocol that was very useful in helping us track and continued communication throughout those very critical periods during our elections**."[434]

The statement by Fulton County COO, Anna Roach, directly connected the FBI with information tracking and sharing with Fulton County during early voting and on election day. With the information uncovered within the DARPA report by Dr. HIghnam, and in light of the information just reviewed, these questions must be asked:

- ➢ Based upon the knowledge that cyber evidence handled by the federal Intelligence Community was later demonstrated to be false and potentially fabricated, did DARPA use any evidence from within that vein of intelligence in the EA project?
- ➢ Did DARPA's EA project ever yield information pertaining to any election to the FBI field office that was shared with the Fulton County Board of Registration and Elections through the GISAC structure?
- ➢ If the same evidence proven fabricated in 2022 by U.S. Attorney John Durham in the federal case The United States v. Michael Sussman was the basis of the EA project, was the use of this evidence in this manner placed in the project with an intent to have it available in the information sharing ISAC structure in places like the GI-ISAC?
- ➢ Did DARPA's EA project yield a product or service still in use by any branch of the federal government?

---

[434] https://fulton.legistar.com/View.ashx?M=M&ID=867027&GUID=9988AEB8-3608-44B8-A1CA-B2A466BDAF9E

CHAPTER 15

- ➢ Was information collected and analyzed by DARPA's EA project shared with individuals in or associated with the 2016 Clinton campaign that were actively monitoring the election within the ISAC infrastructure?
- ➢ At any time after the initial incident described in 2016 in the Durham indictment, was an internet packet transparency tool potentially developed by the DARPA EA project utilized by any person in any capacity within the HSIN, ISACs or fusion centers during the period of any other election throughout the United States?
- ➢ Was any of the information described in the Durham report intended to "please certain VIPs" relevant information also referenced by the comment made by Fulton County, Georgia Chief Operating Officer, Anna Roach, recorded in the January 6, 2021 minutes from the Fulton County Board of Commissioners? [435]

All of these questions urgently need valid answers. However, continuing to move forward in time, and as referenced in select earlier places within this report, on April 15, 2022, United States Attorney John Durham filed another brief in the Michael Sussman case in federal court. In addition to the information outlined here from the previous filings, the April 15th filing yet again yielded further highly important facts pertinent to this report. The document states:

- "Tech Executive-1 [Rodney Joffe] was a "subject" of the investigation prior to the defendant's indictment; he remained a "subject" following the return of the indictment; and he still remains a "subject" one month short of trial."

---

[435] https://fulton.legistar.com/View.ashx?M=M&ID=867027&GUID=9988AEB8-3608-44B8-A1CA-B2A466BDAF9E

Countdown to Chaos

- "Tech Executive-1 [Rodney Joffe] played a critical leadership role in assembling and submitting the allegations at issue, and therefore would likely carry greater criminal exposure and potential culpability in the event the Government's investigation were to reveal or confirm the commission of crimes other than the offense currently charged.
- "...the fact still remains that the defendant conducted that meeting on behalf of (i) Tech Executive-1 (who assembled the allegations and requested that the defendant disseminate them) and (ii) the Clinton Campaign (which the defendant billed for some or all of his work)."
- "...facts concerning when, why, and how Tech Executive-1 came to possess and/or convey the purported data and analysis are all relevant to the jury's understanding of the critical meeting that the defendant had with the FBI General Counsel on September 19, 2016. In particular, such facts will shed important light on the (i) background and substance of the Russian Bank-1 allegations that the defendant provided to the FBI; (ii) the nature of the defendant's work and relationships with his alleged clients; (iii) the authorship of the various white papers and other materials; (iv) the factual context for the defendant's alleged false statement; and (v) specific reasons why the defendant and/or his clients would have wanted to conceal the origins and provenance of this data and their work. Facts concerning the origins of such purported data and related allegations therefore constitute direct evidence of the charged offense because they are part of the story of the alleged crime and tend to prove the existence of the defendant's attorney-client relationships with both Tech Executive-1 and the Clinton Campaign."
- "The foregoing facts support the inference that the defendant was partially or fully aware of the origins and

CHAPTER 15

provenance of the relevant data, and that he participated meaningfully in the analysis of such data. To the extent such data was obtained in a manner that was illegal or unethical, a jury reasonably could infer that the defendant and his clients shared a potential motive to conceal material facts—particularly since the defendant assured one of the relevant researchers (Researcher-2) that the collection and use of the data was lawful."

- "At a minimum, however, the Government does expect to adduce evidence at trial reflecting (i) the fact **that the FBI and Agency-2 concluded that the Russian Bank-1 allegations were untrue and unsupported** and (ii) the primary bases for these conclusions, including the particular investigative and analytical steps taken by these agencies. (For example, while the FBI did not reach an ultimate conclusion regarding the data's accuracy or whether it might have been in whole or in part genuine, spoofed, altered, or fabricated, Agency-2 concluded in early 2017 that the Russian Bank-1 data and Russian Phone Provider-1 data was not 'technically plausible,' did not 'withstand technical scrutiny,' 'contained gaps,' 'conflicted with [itself],' and was 'user created and not machine/tool generated.'"

- "Separate and apart from whether the data was actually unreliable or provided a motive for the defendant to lie, evidence concerning the steps the FBI and Agency-2 took to investigate these matters is critical to establishing materiality because it will enable the jury to evaluate those steps which, in turn, will inform their conclusions about whether the defendant's alleged false statement was material and could tend to influence or impair government functions."

- "And regardless, such opinions by the Government's expert would also be relevant to explain why Tech Executive-1 and the defendant would have had a motive to instruct his counsel to conceal Tech Executive-1's involvement in these matters."[436]

With no regard to how the cases John Durham has filed on behalf of the United States Government will become adjudicated, the importance of the revelations within the April 15, 2022 filing by John Durham to this report are multiple. The information shows that the potentially criminal acts revealed by John Durham purported to have been committed by Rodney Joffe in the above allegations and statements very likely effected the entire United States election system. The evidence provided in the filings could be incredibly consequential to the country as:

1) The act(s) committed by Tech Executive-1, Rodney Joffe, from the beginning of the investigation according to the Durham filing, rose to the level of potentially "criminal" in nature, and he was referred to as carrying greater criminal exposure and culpability than Michael Sussman.
2) The information collected by Mr. Joffe was eventually provided by Michael Sussman to FBI general counsel, James Baker. The same information was alleged to have been reviewed by Agency-2, widely accepted to be the Central Intelligence Agency.
3) By late 2016 to very early 2017, the CIA determined the data provided to them by Mr. Joffe and Mr. Sussman "was not 'technically plausible,' did not 'withstand technical scrutiny,' 'contained gaps,' 'conflicted with [itself],' and was 'user created and not machine/tool generated,'"[437] and again, collected in a nature considered potentially criminal by the United States Attorney's Office.

---

[436] https://www.scribd.com/document/570091923/70-Memorandum-in-Opposition-Re-Sussmann-Motion-in-Limine-by-USA
[437] https://www.scribd.com/document/570091923/70-Memorandum-in-Opposition-Re-Sussmann-Motion-in-Limine-by-USA

CHAPTER 15

4) The substance of the data collected, created, and shared, by Mr. Joffe and Mr. Sussman was later widely known to be false by the CIA, and likely other agencies to include the FBI.
5) The substance of the data and further use of it rose to the highest level within the agencies to include John Brennan in the CIA and James Comey in the FBI.
6) Already in the summer of 2016, state officials were being pressured by DHS Secretary Jeh Johnson to mitigate risks of Russian interference in the upcoming election through adoption and use of the federal EI-ISAC Albert Monitoring System. It is reasonable to believe the risk that agency referenced came from within the intelligence community, potentially stemming from the information collected and/or created by Mr. Joffe. Conversely, in sworn testimony on August 22, 2018 to the Senate Committee on Intelligence on Russian interference in the 2016 election, Chris Krebs stated "there were no known threats to election infrastructure,"[438] potentially painting a favorable picture of the DHS/CISA cybersecurity program that was being pushed out to the states.
7) **The Intelligence Community Assessment (ICA) ordered by President Obama in late 2016 and completed before the end of his term in 2017 that included an assessment on securing future elections was potentially based to an extensive degree on the information created and/or shared by Mr. Joffe and Mr. Sussman. The ICA would include known false information known as "the Steele Dossier" attached as "Annex A."**
8) According to former member of the National Security Council, and former Senior Dept. of Defense representative

---

[438] https://www.intelligence.senate.gov/sites/default/files/documents/Report_Volume1.pdf

for the Comprehensive National Cybersecurity Initiative (CNCI) Col. John Mills (Ret.), the ICA in point seven above was personally penned by John Brennan and James Comey.[439]

9) On January 5, 2017 a meeting took place in the White House Oval Office with President Barack Obama, Joe Biden, John Brennan, James Clapper, James Comey, Michael Rogers, Sally Yates, and Susan Rice. Immediately thereafter the Obama Administration released the classified ICA report titled "Assessing Russian Activities and Intentions in Recent US Elections."

10) **The resulting ICA was the basis for Executive Order 13757 signed by President Obama which moved the American election system under the Presidential declaration of emergency.**

11) **On January 6, 2017 DHS Secretary Jeh Johnson declared the United States election system to be part of Critical Infrastructure (CI).**

12) **Once United States elections were named part of critical infrastructure, American elections were immediately managed by the Department of Homeland Security under the Executive Branch of the United States Federal Government and were monitored by the agency or agencies under the perpetual state of emergency declared by President Obama.**

13) The evidence brought forth by U.S. Attorney John Durham in oral arguments in federal Criminal Case No. 21-582, The United States v. Michael A. Sussman, further validated previously made allegations brought forth by Attorney Larry Klayman in the federal civil complaint 1:17-cv-01074-RJL filed June 6, 2017 naming James Comey, the FBI, Mike

---

[439] https://www.theepochtimes.com/dod-green-lighted-fake-trump-russia-doc-in-2015-ret-colonel-john-mills_4693981.html

CHAPTER 15

Rogers, the NSA, John Brennan, Mike Pompeo, the CIA, James Clapper, Dan Coats, and Barack Obama as defendants. Specifically, the complaint brought forth by the plaintiffs alleged that the defendants via federal agencies and agency contractors, including one plaintiff, were spying upon and collecting domestic intelligence on not only normal American citizens, but also upon then candidate and later President Donald J. Trump.[440] This civil case was defended on technicalities of the case such as standing and qualified immunity rather than the specific physical data/hard drives brought forth by the plaintiffs.

An additional point of interest when considering the information presented in point thirteen above, as the evidence in the federal case brought by John Durham against Michael Sussman validates claims made in late 2015 by the former CIA contractor and self-identified CIA whistleblower (described in detail in chapter nine of this report), is a letter to California representative Devin Nunes dated March 21, 2017 written by Attorney Larry Klayman and included with his federal court filing - civil complaint 1:17-cv-01074-RJL filed June 6, 2017. The letter specifically states to representative Nunes that the whistleblower "laid out how persons like then businessman Donald Trump were illegally spied upon by Clapper, Brennan, and the spy agencies of the Obama administration. He [whistleblower] even claimed that these spy agencies had manipulated voting in Florida during the 2008 presidential election, where illegal tampering resulted in helping Obama to win the White House."[441] While this is a wild allegation, unprovable with the information available, the simple validation of a portion of the allegations made and filed in federal court by this self-identified whistleblower certainly make this claim regarding

---

[440] https://regmedia.co.uk/2017/06/08/01-main.pdf
[441] https://www.yumpu.com/en/document/read/62646908/2017-03-21-letter-to-nunes

Countdown to Chaos

elections loom large when considering all other information uncovered by this report. Whether true or not, this claim of election tampering puts an emphatic exclamation point on the simple fact that **the federal government should not in any way participate in the administration, management, or simple monitoring of American elections.**

May 17, 2022 was day one of the trial The United States v. Michael A. Sussman. On May 25, 2022, important testimony was given that involved actions by Neustar executive Rodney Joffe. A review of some of the events that were intertwined in this testimony are outlined in this report on pages 46-62. A thorough review of those events is highly recommended after reading the facts divulged in federal court testimony here, after which the reader might perhaps reread the testimony yet again to understand its importance. On May 25, 2022, a retired FBI agent by the name of Tom Grasso testified about his knowledge of the working relationship Rodney Joffe had with FBI cybercrimes.

Mr. Grasso stated that the FBI worked in partnership with Rodney Joffe on a "regular basis." The testimony included the term "Confidential Human Source" (CHS) with regard to Rodney Joffe's role with the agency. The role of an FBI CHS is to be a point of information collection for the agency. Confidential Human Sources require FBI appointed "handlers." According to testimony in the case, Rodney Joffe was such a source for several years, even spanning over a decade. Certainly this fact would validate the evidence already presented in this report that Rodney Joffe of Neustar, Inc. would have had an ongoing long term relationship with former FBI Executive Assistant Director, and current President of CrowdStrike Services, Shawn Henry.

This report clearly outlines the role Shawn Henry played in the forensic examination of the DNC servers in wake of the purported Russian hack by the FBI from mid-2015 through late 2016.

CHAPTER 15

Testimony of importance to review from the United States v. Michael Sussman trial includes:

> "Q. And so Mr. Joffe worked on a number of investigations involving foreign cyber threats; is that right?
>
> Grasso: I would say all a matter of cyber threats, yes.
>
> Q. Okay. So does that include nation state threats? Would he be, you know, working with the Bureau on nation state threats?
>
> Grasso: I believe so, yes.
>
> Q. And so that includes some of the big cyber threat countries, like Russia?
>
> Grasso: Yes. At the time Russia was one of our top threats in the FBI for cyber crime.
>
> ...
>
> Q: And so Mr. Joffe would work on Russian-related cyber matters?
>
> Grasso: I believe so. He — I don't think he was specifically tasked with doing that, but I'm sure the work that he did touched on matters having to do with Russia due to the prevalence of cyber crime activity that comes out of Russia."[442]

Curiously, within the analysis of the testimony, notation was made that as an FBI CHS, Joffe did not go through his assigned FBI handler

---

[442] https://technofog.substack.com/p/was-rodney-joffe-involved-in-the

Countdown to Chaos

with any of the Russian data he was turning over to the FBI. Nothing in the testimony explained why that pathway was forsaken in this matter, but it mentioned here as it was considered a notable factoid.

While this testimony doesn't definitively connect Joffe to the stream of data surrounding the DNC server hack, it certainly raises the suspicion to a very high level. This testimony also raises the likelihood that Shawn Henry and Rodney Joffe could have been working in concert on the DNC server hack case.

When any normal citizen understands the timeline of and nature of activities perpetrated by a very small group of powerful partisan political players during the summer of 2016 through the present time, to include the creation of the DHS Disinformation Governance Board, it is shocking to see how the potentially criminal acts alleged to have been committed by Mr. Joffe and Mr. Sussman may have had a very real reach into multiple areas of not just the 2016 election as proposed by the Durham indictment, but also may have reached into multiple layers of the entire election system, including the incredibly important and foundationally basic area of speech and political discourse. These effects may prove to be irreversible and permanently damaging to the system and ultimately to each individual American voter.

The FBI

On May 11, 2022, this report failed to allow itself to be put to bed, and as time would prove week by week and news cycle to news cycle, the research that encompasses it would continue to be a gift that proverbially keeps giving. On this date the world-renowned whistleblowing deposit outlet, *Project Veritas*, released a report and video featuring whom James O'Keefe identified as an FBI whistleblower. O'Keefe's report enumerated a number of allegations by this self-proclaimed current member and Special

CHAPTER 15

Agent of the FBI who was disturbed by the nature of the agency's environment of targeting investigations toward people and organization for political purposes. Areas of this interview contain pieces of information relevant to this report and give a firsthand inside look into the inner workings of one of the federal agencies now directly connected to the management of American elections. In the interview the unnamed Special Agent states:

> "There's a number of very troubling things that are happening within the FBI. And I would say that the direction that the agency is headed, troubles the vast majority of the agents. *Project Veritas* appears to the victim **of political undertakings, which is where this agency has gone...there appears to be a political vendetta.**"[443]

Within the whistleblower's interview with O'Keefe, the agent pointed out an alpha numeric classification of "56D" which was assigned to the *Project Veritas* investigation. The code denoted that the FBI had opened a special investigation in the case and further the classification of 56D "specifically refers to election crimes." Later within the document one of the tags posted within the investigation includes the FBI's interest in *Project Veritas'* "Liberty Activity." When asked further what the agent's hopes were in bringing this information to light the agent stated:

> "I would hope that we could end up with a non-partisan law enforcement agency in this country that's not doing things that seem inappropriate for the power that it wields. It's an awesome responsibility...it's truly and incredible amount of power if used wrong, the country cannot sustain their largest law enforcement agency. **We cannot have partisan investigations and using the**

---

[443] https://www.projectveritas.com/news/breaking-fbi-whistleblower-leaks-document-showing-bureau-targeting-news/

executive branch as a weapon. It always strived to be an apolitical organization. That's the pitch that I got when I came in. You don't get paid by the cases. You don't get paid by the prosecutions…it doesn't matter. The pursuit should be for truth." [444]

O'Keefe moved forward in the interview to inquire of the special agent about knowledge of surveillance of Americans and abuses of power. With regard to what the FBI labels "intelligence investigations," the special agent further revealed:

"The intelligence investigation is meant for information in the same way the CIA doesn't have to prove a case against anybody overseas. **An intelligence investigation is meant for intelligence,** which is to say knowledge about things, and they continue **to propagate for the sake of knowledge itself.** And the knowledge doesn't have to be actionable. It doesn't have to be operational in what we'd call tactical information. **It could be knowledge that we just have now forever logged in a computer system. And so that doesn't require that you've done anything wrong…** When you open up an intelligence investigation, you have an entire suite of tools. You can write secret subpoenas called NSLs [National Security Letter] that you'll never know about…**the predication of the national security letter is a classified secret.** It's hidden for 25 years. It's not going anywhere. No one's gonna read it outside." [445]

When O'Keefe asked to what end the FBI undertakes such investigations, the answer of the special agent was:

---

[444] https://www.projectveritas.com/news/breaking-fbi-whistleblower-leaks-document-showing-bureau-targeting-news/
[445] https://www.projectveritas.com/news/breaking-fbi-whistleblower-leaks-document-showing-bureau-targeting-news/

CHAPTER 15

"For the purpose of information, the end is ... itself...They could do this to anybody." He further stated, "**I think there have been crimes that have been committed every decade by this organization**. Some of them have been openly acknowledged...tyranny happens incrementally. And it happens by a bunch of people agreeing to small injustices over and over simply to keep their paycheck and their pension...If you're willing to accept incremental tyranny and small abuses of your authority you take your pension and the paycheck and you'll walk it to whatever that darkest end is...I have a problem with people who are doing the wrong thing, and they know it." [446]

The important takeaways from this interview in light of this report are first, of paramount importance, this agent states as many others have speculated, that the FBI has become politically activated. Secondly, the agent further reported that intelligence investigations encompass tools that can be utilized and maintained as classified secrets. When considering the firsthand confession of this FBI whistleblower in light of the information here reported about fusion centers, the Homeland Security Information Network (HSIN), and other career officials from the FBI participating in the election process, to include CrowdStrike's Shawn Henry, the whistleblower's admission is an important datapoint that adds an exclamation point to each of the facts surrounding elections involving the FBI and those close to it presented within this report.

The third important takeaway is the FBI immediately, in this case, assigned the code "56D", an election crime, to a news organization. This is a chilling fact being uncovered for public consumption. The FBI was in essence influencing an election using the simple act of

---

[446] https://www.projectveritas.com/news/breaking-fbi-whistleblower-leaks-document-showing-bureau-targeting-news/

Countdown to Chaos

opening this case and assigning this particular code to it. This is evidence that a federal agency with intrinsic connections to elections through the Department of Homeland Security, was itself, willing and able to interfere in a presidential election using information suppression. The use of a classification tag in the FBI case file report including the words "liberty activities" in connection to the FBI's investigation of *Project Veritas* is also alarming as opponents in elections (and all Americans) must have freedom of speech and expression at all times. Just the use the of words "liberty activities" by the FBI attached to actions they are investigating as potentially criminal is curious on its face and might be simple evidence that the agency is truly deeply politically biased as the unnamed agent alleged. Clearly the FBI was willing to wield its power in this area without proof of the commitment of any crime by James O'Keefe and *Project Veritas*. This action by the FBI adds to the gravity to the point made earlier in this chapter regarding the media's use of the term "white supremacist" to label then President Donald Trump just prior to the 2020 election. This effort by many media outlets was made just less than one year after the FBI declared white supremacy to be a grave domestic threat. Considering the governance of elections via the EI-SCC under the DHS, an unholy alliance has been created between federal agencies, media, and others who are **all not just managing elections, but are now able to directly affect the election process.**

To further place this information provided by the unnamed FBI whistleblower into context regarding the weaponization of the FBI for political purposes, the author of this report found an astonishing connection in yet another case that adds further validity to the argument in this paper. In 2011 and into 2012, investigative reporter Sheryl Attkisson discovered that the FBI and the Department of Justice had infiltrated her personal computer and devices, and the agency was spying and monitoring all of her

CHAPTER 15

activity.[447] In a federal suit filed by Attkisson against the Department of Justice and the FBI, Attkisson presented evidence to include emails from within the Obama White House and Attorney General Eric Holder's office sent to the CBS chief Washington correspondent. Those emails stated that work by Attkisson was "out of control" and that her work was "really bad for AG [Holder]."[448] Two highly significant parts of this incident in light of this report were **that one of the defendants in the Attkisson case was Shawn Henry**, who was at the time the head of the Washington FBI Field office. Of further importance was an email produced by Attkisson in her investigation and reporting that was found in a WikiLeaks Dump. In that email titled "Obama Leak Investigations (internal use only – pls do not forward) the body held the following communication from the global intelligence company Stratfor: **"Brennan is behind the witch hunts of investigative journalists learning information from inside the beltway sources."**[449] The entire email is reproduced below:

---

[447] https://sharylattkisson.com/2021/03/new-decision-in-attkisson-government-computer-intrusion-case/
[448] https://sharylattkisson.com/wp-content/uploads/2020/02/COMPLAINT-Baltimore-File-marked-complaint-Attkisson-MD-Complaint-File-Marked.pdf
[449] https://wikileaks.org/gifiles/docs/12/1210665_obama-leak-investigations-internal-use-only-pls-do-not.html

> **Obama Leak Investigations (internal use only - pls do not forward)**
> Released on 2012-09-10 00:00 GMT
>
> | Email-ID | 1210665 |
> |---|---|
> | Date | 2010-09-21 21:38:37 |
> | From | burton@stratfor.com |
> | To | secure@stratfor.com |
>
> Obama Leak Investigations (internal use only - pls do not forward)
>
> Brennan is behind the witch hunts of investigative journalists learning information from inside the beltway sources.
>
> Note -- There is specific tasker from the WH to go after anyone printing materials negative to the Obama agenda (oh my.) Even the FBI is shocked. The Wonder Boys must be in meltdown mode...

These three cases, in addition to the 2015 Klayman/CIA whistleblower case, display just how such power could be and potentially has been used to not only suppress critical information, but to disseminate equally influential information at will even though it may be false, and that information can be isolated and managed at the highest points of these agencies. Moreover, when the same names continued to repeatedly become part of the discovery of evidence for this report, one can begin to ascertain that these individuals were potentially working in concert for some time with potentially coordinated high stakes goals.

When pulled back into the direct scope of this report and the discussion of the United States system of elections, no American running for office or involved in any campaign should fear the power of the federal government during the election process — ever — especially when no laws have been broken. Furthermore, no reporter or investigator should fear the same. This power of the federal government again moves beyond the usurping of basic state and local management of elections and more importantly shows that the federal structure now associated with elections is easily able to influence or to potentially spy upon elections using

CHAPTER 15

the government superstructure built by the federal executive branch to manage it. The information revealed in the statement by this whistleblowing FBI agent is of key significance in understanding the peril American voters now face regarding the Constitutional protection of their vote.

Returning to the FBI/*Project Veritas* case, a fourth critical takeaway from the whistleblower's interview is the acknowledgment by the whistleblower that the FBI is capable of being logged into a computer system in perpetuity and while within a system the agency propagates information at will. Once again, the Attkisson case was a clear example of such a circumstance. When consideration is given to the breadth, depth, administration, and management of the election monitoring system via the EI-ISAC's Albert Monitoring System managed by the Department of Homeland Security, the American voter must understand that the FBI has been made part of this system at various points within it, and as such, certainly has the ability to be inside any part of the election system at any time. Understanding this, the FBI's potentially unfettered access to America's election system gives grave concern that the chain of custody of data and information surrounding U.S. elections has been broken, the trust violated, and the results able to be drawn into question from any angle in literally any election.

The fifth important takeaway is the following statement made by the agent, "We cannot have partisan investigations and using the executive branch as a weapon." This report has shown alarming circumstances under which such a scenario may have already taken place in the 2020 Presidential Election. History will complete the tale on this allegation, but the investigation being undertaken by U.S. Attorney John Durham has already yielded shocking revelations enumerated in this report, which have been asserted in U.S. Federal Court where they will be adjudicated and remain as part of the permanent judicial record.

Countdown to Chaos

The final takeaway is the unnamed FBI agent was willing to admit that the Federal Bureau of Investigation has certainly committed crimes in the past decades. Chapter twelve of this report about the use of fusion centers has also laid out a good amount of evidence to support this statement. When the framers of the Constitution put elections in the hands of the states, the purpose was not only to secure the vote and preserve the wishes and consent of each individual voter, but it was also **to curb the influence of any centralized power in the process.** Understanding the facts of this report, that elections are now managed by a number of federal bureaus and quasi-governmental agencies, this whistleblowing FBI agent has asserted that a part of this structure, the FBI, an incredible power in a potent centralized system, is riddled with alleged criminal behavior. To that end, why and how would Americans relinquish the management of their vote from the state and local managers to these obese federal agencies with poor track records of trust and function?

As a reminder, the individuals who are mentioned within the scope of this report who were formerly or are currently agents of the FBI include James Comey, Robert Mueller, Shawn Henry (now President of CrowdStrike Services), William Barnett, Andrew McCabe, Peter Strzok, and Lisa Page. As such, the statements made by the whistleblower presented by James O'Keefe create not only an additional layer of suspicion around each and every one of them in their roles within the FBI, both present and past, but also an additional layer of potential criminality in context with the 2020 Presidential Election. The statements by the FBI whistleblower to *Project Veritas* raise loud alarms that the FBI appears to be far too politically charged to be associated with ANY type of election integrity or election intelligence operations.

Moving ahead, time is a gift to this report and as it was being polished, the case of the United States v. Michael Sussman began on May 17, 2022. In context with the discussion of this chapter as

CHAPTER 15

well as the information dropped by *Project Veritas* by the aforementioned FBI whistleblower, opening statements from special counsel Britain Shaw were of unique interest to the topic herein. Within her opening statement Ms. Shaw stated for the record the following allegation about Michael Sussman and his purported delivery to the FBI of fabricated data presented to Mr. Sussman by Mr. Rodney Joffe:

> "[Attorney Michael Sussman] went straight to the FBI general counsel's office, the FBI's top lawyer. He then sat across from that lawyer and lied to him. **He told a lie that was designed to achieve a political end, a lie that was designed to inject the FBI into a presidential election.**"[450]

In context with information presented in this report including information about former FBI Executive Assistant Director of Cyber Security, Shawn Henry, and others in the FBI, DHS and other federal agencies, this allegation adds concrete intensity to the disturbing nature of everything herein presented.

As luck would have it, 2022 continued to be a banner year for the FBI with regard to the substance of this report. On March 24, 2022, Former President Donald Trump filed a federal lawsuit in the Southern District of Florida against Hillary Clinton and many other federal officials. The case alleges RICO offenses (Racketeer Influenced and Corrupt Organizations)[451] against Clinton in addition to significant individuals that appear in this report including: Michael Sussman, Mark Elias, Neustar Inc., Rodney Joffe, James Comey, Peter Strzok, and Lisa Page.[452] The suit alleges that

---

[450] https://technofog.substack.com/p/day-1-of-the-michael-sussmann-trial?s=r

[451] https://www.ussc.gov/sites/default/files/pdf/training/primers/2022_Primer_RICO.pdf

[452] https://s3.documentcloud.org/documents/21506628/trump-v-clinton.pdf

Countdown to Chaos

"Acting in concert, the Defendants maliciously conspired... their far-reaching conspiracy was designed to cripple Trump's bid for presidency by fabricating a scandal that would be used to trigger an unfounded federal investigation and ignite a media frenzy."[453]

Of federally contracted IT company Neustar, the suit alleges:

> "This ill-gotten **data was then manipulated** to create a misleading "inference" and submitted to law enforcement in an effort to falsely implicate Donald J. Trump and his campaign." [454]

Of Rodney Joffe the suite alleges:

> "In doing so, Joffe and Neustar **intentionally accessed, without authorization or in excess of any authorization**, the computers, servers, and/or other sensitive data sources at the above-stated facilities... Furthermore, Joffe and Neustar stole trade secrets, in the form of proprietary, sensitive and confidential data, information, and knowledge, from the above-stated facilities." [455]

Of the FBI the suit maintains:

> "The Federal Bureau of Investigation (FBI)—relying on the Defendants' fraudulent evidence —commenced a large-scale investigation and expended precious time, resources and taxpayer dollars looking into the spurious allegation that the Trump Campaign had colluded with the Russian Government to interfere in the 2016 presidential election... These government officials [James Comey, Andrew McCabe, Peter Strzok, Lisa Page,

---

[453] https://s3.documentcloud.org/documents/21506628/trump-v-clinton.pdf
[454] https://s3.documentcloud.org/documents/21506628/trump-v-clinton.pdf
[455] https://s3.documentcloud.org/documents/21506628/trump-v-clinton.pdf

CHAPTER 15

Kevin Clinesmith, and Bruce Ohr] were willing to abuse their positions of public trust to advance the baseless probe to new levels, including obtaining an extrajudicial FISA warrant and instigating the commencement of an oversight investigation headed by Special Counsel Robert Mueller. As a result, Donald J. Trump and his campaign were forced to expend tens of millions of dollars in legal fees to defend against these contrived and unwarranted proceedings... **In short, the Defendants, blinded by political ambition, orchestrated a malicious conspiracy to disseminate patently false and injurious information about Donald J. Trump and his campaign, all in the hopes of destroying his life, his political career and rigging the 2016 Presidential Election** in favor of Hillary Clinton... Text messages between Strzok and FBI Special Counsel Lisa Page, who were engaged in an illicit affair during that time, reveal that both of them had an utter disdain for the subject of their investigation, Donald J. Trump, and **were determined to ensure that Hillary Clinton won the 2016 presidential election... James Comey was the Director of the FBI and his actions in this capacity allowed the false Trump-Russia collusion narrative to continue to thrive.**" [456]

While there was so much more information in the Trump v. Clinton case that could be cited here, the only point that needs to be made by presenting it at this point in the report is each of these allegations are being made against people explained in the fabric of this report to have, since the series of executive orders made by former President Barack Obama to label elections "critical infrastructure", significant connections to the American election system. Whether it is the FBI's role in the Homeland Security

---

[456] https://s3.documentcloud.org/documents/21506628/trump-v-clinton.pdf

Countdown to Chaos

Information Network (HSIN), the HSIN fusion centers, and election fraud investigations, or the roles of each of those named who have personal and professional connections to people, organizations, or companies now built into the election system such as Shawn Henry, CrowdStrike, CIS, and ultimately the Albert Monitoring System, all those mentioned are either material participants or very directly connected to material participants in U.S. elections. Each and every allegation made within the case of Trump v. Clinton et al, in addition to allegations made in other cases described in this report presents a significant argument as to why the essentially federalized American election structure as it was derived by the Obama executive orders in 2017 must not and cannot stand. These and ANY other individuals within the system that can influence an election in any way cannot be a part of the system at ANY POINT and in ANY MANNER to include the physical election systems or the transfer of election data. Involvement of these individuals in the election system, with the information presented in this report, will (and should) destroy any trust in the federal government's role in any portion of the American election system. What the facts of these cases involving federal individuals demonstrate is the insidious dangers the power of a centralized election system poses to free, fair, transparent, and honestly auditable elections. In fact, the election system that has controlled U.S. elections since 2018 is the antithesis of the intention of the Founders regarding how American elections should be conducted. **As clearly stated in *The Federalist Papers*, elections should be decentralized to avoid the consolidation of power, and immediately managed by states divided into small precincts.**

However, the trail of events involving the federal government and effecting American elections does not end with former President Trump's RICO case. Exactly two weeks after former President Trump filed the RICO case in Florida, on April 7, 2022, the Department of Justice made a public announcement that it was

CHAPTER 15

investigating Trump for mishandling government secrets.[457] In retrospect, on January 19, 2021, former President Trump officially declassified all documents relating to Operation Crossfire Hurricane, undertaken by the FBI.[458] As this report, and a plethora of others in the public domain, have demonstrated, the **FBI intended to use Crossfire Hurricane as a mode of keeping Donald Trump out of the Oval Office.** With regard to the document investigation, on June 3, 2022, upon the invitation of former President Donald Trump, the FBI visited his home, Mar-a-lago, to inspect the location and the security of the documents in question. Of importance to note is that the documents at Mar-a-lago were likely in the SCIF (Sensitive Compartmented Information Facility) built by the Secret Service.[459] Less than a week later, on June 8, 2022, the federal government issued a letter to former President Trump that the inspectors recommended the documents in question simply be secured with an additional lock. The Trump team complied. Further, on June 22, 2022, federal officials requested security video from the document storage facility. Once again, the Trump aides complied. [460]

While the Department of Justice was in a veritable back-and-forth with former President Donald Trump and the National Archives over the location and storage of documents, issues with the FBI festered in Washington D.C. On July 25, 2022, Senator Charles Grassley sent a letter to FBI Director Christopher Wray, and Attorney General Merrick Garland at the Department of Justice

---

[457] https://www.npr.org/2022/04/07/1091431136/justice-department-investigating-trumps-possible-mishandling-of-government-secre

[458] https://trumpwhitehouse.archives.gov/presidential-actions/memorandum-declassification-certain-materials-related-fbis-crossfire-hurricane-investigation/

[459] https://www.realclearpolitics.com/video/2022/08/23/paul_sperry_fbi_trump_raid_scif.html#!

[460] https://abc7ny.com/donald-trump-maralago-fbi-search-classified-documents/12175658/

Countdown to Chaos

informing them that his office was in receipt of numerous FBI whistleblower complaints. The complaints surrounded the weaponization of the FBI by agents, naming specifically Assistant Special Agent in Charge (ASAC) Timothy Thibault and FBI Supervisory Intelligence Analyst Brian Auten. The letter stated:

> "The information provided to my office involves concerns about the FBI's receipt and use of derogatory information relating to Hunter Biden, and the FBI's false portrayal of acquired evidence as disinformation. The volume and consistency of these allegations substantiate their credibility and necessitate this letter... in October 2020, an avenue of additional derogatory Hunter Biden reporting was ordered closed at the direction of ASAC Thibault."[461]

This and further contents of the letter from Senator Grassley to Christopher Wray and Merrick Garland enumerating what whistleblowers reported to Senator Grassley's office outline how the Federal Bureau of Investigation materially interfered in the 2020 election by suppressing the Hunter Biden laptop, labeling it "disinformation" at the direction of FBI ASAC Tim Thibault. This was another of many examples of how the FBI was able to interfere with the American election cycle and infrastructure.

On August 8, 2022, just *ninety days prior to the 2022 midterm election*, in a shocking and unprecedented action, the Federal Bureau of Investigation at the direction of Attorney General Merrick Garland raided former President Trump's Florida home, Mar-a-lago. Among the items removed from the location were documents the FBI and DoJ had inspected and further secured

---

[461] https://www.grassley.senate.gov/imo/media/doc/grassley_to_justice_deptfbipoliticalbiasfollowup.pdf

CHAPTER 15

during the month of June. The raid was based upon an affidavit[462] by an individual, the name of which was redacted from the unsealed court filing. While unconfirmed, multiple independent outlets reported that the source of the affidavit to raid Mar-a-lago likely was either FBI ASAC Timothy Thibault and/or FBI Supervisory Intelligence Analyst Brian Auten. Among documents reported to have been confiscated from the premises were documents declassified by former President Trump on January 19, 2017 and surrounding Crossfire Hurricane.[463] Also confiscated were personal documents protected by attorney-client privilege, and revealed by investigators in court only days later. [464] Those documents protected by attorney-client privilege have been theorized to have been connected to the RICO case filed in federal court in the Southern District of Florida just weeks before the document retrieval case was opened by the Department of Justice.

The next day, on August 9, 2022, investigative reporter from Real Clear Investigations, Paul Sperry, who was front-and-center in reporting details surrounding the Durham investigation during the spring of 2022, was permanently banned from Twitter for tweeting details about the FBI Mar-a-lago raid. About one week later, Sperry would publish an article titled "FBI Unit Leading Mar-a-Lago Probe Earlier Ran Discredited Trump-Russia Investigation" which named FBI agents, Brian Auten and Timothy Thibault, as part of the division overseeing the Trump/Mara-lago raid.[465] This FBI unit was the same unit that was and remains under investigation by Special Counsel John Durham. Of note to report is that during the summer

---

[462] https://www.flsd.uscourts.gov/sites/flsd/files/DE-102.pdf

[463] https://www.breitbart.com/radio/2022/08/29/exclusive-lee-smith-people-i-trust-say-fbi-raid-was-search-for-russiagate-documents-at-mar-a-lago/

[464] https://s3.documentcloud.org/documents/22268848/doj-filing-in-request-for-special-master.pdf

[465] https://www.realclearinvestigations.com/articles/2022/08/18/fbi_unit_leading_mar-a-lago_probe_previously_led_russiagate_hoax_848582.html

of 2020, the FBI attorney embroiled in the Russia-gate investigation by John Durham, and who testified in federal court in John Durham's case against Michael Sussman, Attorney James Baker "landed a role as deputy general counsel at Twitter Inc."[466]

On another front, on August 25, 2022, Facebook/META CEO, Mark Zuckerberg, revealed in an interview with Joe Rogan on the podcast "The Joe Rogan Experience," that prior to the 2020 election, the FBI approached Facebook regarding the Hunter Biden laptop. At this point in time, according to the letter previously cited by Senator Grassley, the FBI was disseminating information at the direction of FBI ASAC, Tim Thibault, that the Hunter Biden laptop was to be considered disinformation. After podcast host, Joe Rogan, asked specifically about censoring the story surrounding the Hunter Biden laptop immediately prior to the 2020 Presidential Election, Mark Zuckerberg answered:

> "The FBI I think basically came to us, some folks on our team, and was like, "Hey, just so you know, you should be on high alert, there was…we thought there was a lot of Russian propaganda in the 2016 election. We have it on notice that basically there's about to be some kind of dump of…that' similar to that, so just be vigilant."[467]

A poll conducted of 1,335 adults in early August 2022 by New Jersey based Technometrica Institute of Policy and Politics, showed clearly that the suppression of the factual evidence surrounding the Hunter Biden laptop had a significant impact on voters, and quite potentially, ultimately, the outcome of the 2020 Presidential Election. A story by investigative reporter, Paul Sperry, about the poll summarized the findings of the poll:

---

[466] https://www.law.com/corpcounsel/2020/06/17/twitter-adds-former-fbi-general-counsel-to-legal-department/?slreturn=20220804144819
[467] https://youtu.be/Mg8PaSYCP5E

CHAPTER 15

"'Terming the laptop 'disinformation' by the FBI, Intelligence Community, Congress, and the Biden campaign, along with Big Tech, impacted voters,' said Technometrica President Raghavan Mayur, who's been recognized as the most accurate pollster in recent presidential elections. 'A significant majority—78 percent—believe that access to the correct information could have been critical to their decision at the polls.'

In fact, 47 percent said that knowing before the election that the laptop contents were real and not 'disinformation' would have changed their voting decision—including more than two-thirds (71 percent) of Democrats.

Almost 8 of 10 respondents said that a truthful interpretation of the laptop would have likely changed the election's outcome more in favor of Trump."[468]

The direct handling of the evidence contained on the Hunter Biden laptop was the sole responsibility of the United States Federal Bureau of Investigation. Whistleblowers have now come forward to the office of Senator Charles Grassley to confirm the mishandling of that evidence by the FB wasI primarily based upon political bias. The late August statement by Mark Zuckerberg about the Hunter Biden laptop validated further allegations made about the politically charged nature inside the FBI and the further suppression operation conducted by the agency. The poll just cited is now evidence directly from voters that **the actions perpetrated by the FBI, an agency intrinsically involved in American election system since 2017, did, in fact, affect the way a large portion of**

---

[468] https://tippinsights.com/shock-poll-8-in-10-think-biden-laptop-cover-up-changed-election/

Countdown to Chaos

people voted in the 2020 Presidential Election and had the potential to have changed its outcome.

On August 26, 2022, the unsealed affidavit[469] leading to the raid of Mar-a-lago was released to the public. Although heavily redacted, many analysts surmised the source of the testimony, as described above, was either FBI ASAC Tim Thibault or Analyst Brian Auten, both specified by Senator Grassley's letter to Garland and Wray and reported by investigative reporter Paul Sperry as cited above. On the same day, later in the afternoon, multiple news outlets reported that Agent Thibault was seen being escorted out of FBI Bureau flanked by "two or three 'headquarters-looking types.'"[470]

Then in another shocking information dump, investigative reporter Paul Sperry posted on September 2, 2022, on the Twitter-alternative social media platform, GETTR, that "A major discrepancy has surfaced between the "detailed property inventory" DOJ filed with the court and the inventory receipt the FBI gave Trump's attorney the day of the search."[471] In another post on September 3, 2022 on the social media site, GETTR, Sperry reported, "the 'SCI' docs photographed in the 'Attachment F' DOJ filed with the court Aug. 30," did not match the Detailed Property Inventory filed with the court.[472] Later on September 3, 2022, *The Gateway Pundit* published a story titled, "CONFIRMED: As Gateway Pundit Reported — FBI Doctored Mar-a-Lago Photo, Added Their Own Docs that DON'T MATCH INVENTORY REPORTS," citing Paul Sperry's investigative posts on GETTR. *The Gateway Pundit* story alleged that a photograph widely disseminated by the DoJ and FBI showing what the agencies reported were highly classified

---

[469] https://www.flsd.uscourts.gov/sites/flsd/files/DE-102.pdf
[470] https://justthenews.com/government/federal-agencies/fbi-special-agent-who-opened-trump-investigation-reportedly-escorted#article
[471] https://gettr.com/post/p1ph1jm9ad6
[472] https://gettr.com/post/p1pkng6f46f

CHAPTER 15

documents in the possession of former President Trump at Ma-a-lago, was manufactured, or "photoshopped." The article states "the FBI inserted their own documents into the photo, then they created a false crime scene. They inserted docs. They tampered with evidence. And the FBI broke the law..."[473] *The publication of the photo by the FBI took place seventy days prior to the November 2022 mid-term election.*

To gain a better understanding of FBI ASAC Tim Thibault, Agent Brian Auten, and the topic of interest to this report, consider the contents of yet another letter from Iowa Senator Charles Grassley to both Attorney General Merrick Garland and FBI Director Christopher Wray. This communication from Senator Grassley exposed grave concerns over conduct Agent Thibault was found to have participated in that was grossly partisan in nature. Grassley's letter of May 31, 2022 stated:

> "It has come to my attention that while serving in a highly sensitive role that includes threshold decision-making over which Federal public corruption matters are opened for investigation, Assistant Special Agent in Charge ("ASAC") at the Washington Field Office, Timothy Thibault, likely violated several federal regulations and Department guidelines designed to prevent political bias from infecting FBI matters, including the Attorney General Guidelines for Domestic FBI Operations and FBI social media policies. Specifically, as illustrated below, based on a review of open-source content, ASAC Thibault has demonstrated a pattern of active public partisanship, such as using his official title for public partisan posts relating to his superiors and matters

---

[473] https://www.thegatewaypundit.com/2022/09/confirmed-gateway-pundit-reported-fbi-doctored-mar-lago-photo-added-docs-alleged-crime-scene-dont-match-inventory-reports/

under the FBI's purview, that is likely a violation of his ethical obligations as an FBI employee. Accordingly, his actions present a grave risk of political infection and bias in his official decision-making process, creating serious questions with respect to oversight of investigative matters under his purview. For example, ASAC Thibault's social media postings, comments, and "likes" (i.e. public expressions of appreciation, validation and approval) demonstrate a pattern of improper commentary related to, for example, ongoing FBI investigations including those under his purview. It is noteworthy that ASAC Thibault's LinkedIn network includes current and former FBI personnel..."[474]

This and the further contents of Grassley's letter to Director Wray and Attorney General Merrick Garland raise not just red flags and sound alarm bells, but this activity is piled highly upon the actions of many others. However, of even more confounding concern are the details surrounding Agent Thibault's post. Agent Thibault was the Assistant Special Agent in Charge (ASAC) at the Washington D.C. Field Office (WFO), as Senator Grassley makes clear in each of his letters to Thibault's leadership. **Thibault's appointment at the WFO included work encompassing election integrity and investigations surrounding election fraud.** On September 21, 2020, just prior to the 2020 Presidential Election, the FBI published a public notification titled, "FBI Washington Field Office Educates Citizens About Election Security and Foreign Malign Influence in Advance of the November Election." The notification states:

---

[474] https://www.grassley.senate.gov/imo/media/doc/CEG%20to%20DOJ%20FBI%20(WFO).pdf

CHAPTER 15

"Protecting our electoral process from interference by criminals and nefarious actors is a top priority of the FBI's Washington Field Office," said James A. Dawson, acting assistant director in charge of the FBI's Washington Field Office. "The FBI will continue to engage with law enforcement partners and election security officials in preparation for our upcoming national elections. The FBI is committed to ensuring safe and secure elections, and to preventing the activities of any foreign actors who may attempt to influence our elections for their own political or national interests. The FBI will swiftly investigate election crimes… The FBI is the primary investigative agency responsible for engaging with local and state election security counterparts to safeguard election integrity."[475]

In a Twitter post authored by the Portland FBI, dated October 8, 2020, FBI ASAC Tim Thibault appears in a video included in the post. The video asks the question, "What is the FBI doing to combat election fraud?"[476] It is Thibault who then appears in the video to represent the FBI and answering the question as the representative for the FBI Washington Field Office

---

[475] https://www.fbi.gov/contact-us/field-offices/washingtondc/news/press-releases/fbi-washington-field-office-educates-citizens-about-election-security-and-foreign-malign-influence-in-advance-of-the-november-election

[476] https://twitter.com/FBIPortland/status/1314268069506629633?s=20&t=P6Gkxw5mMqKrvwA4bz9Ycg

Countdown to Chaos

(WFO). With these facts in place, the questions now in need of answering are: 1) What did the FBI leadership know about the personal political behavior of FBI ASAC Thibault? 2) When was leadership aware of any such bias being applied to cases within the agency? 3) Was James Comey aware of the actions of Thibault and any other agents with similar political biases? 4) Were such political biases overlooked with intent? 5) Were agents with political biases that were active within the agency during operation Crossfire Hurricane collateral operators? 6) Were agents such as Thibault kept in place after the exposure of Operation Crossfire Hurricane for continuity of other political operations? 7) Were cases of election fraud presented by multiple officials and states left unopened, suppressed, or inappropriately closed at the direction of FBI ASAC Thibault or others in the WFO? 8) Was the declaration that "The November 3rd election was the most secure in American history,"[477] by Chris Krebs at CISA in any way influenced by the suppression of evidence reported to the FBI WFO?

Regardless of the outcome of the case for former President Donald Trump, Hunter Biden, the son of President Joe Biden, Hillary Clinton, James Comey and others that face legal jeopardy due to the actions taken by the Federal Bureau of Investigation, the fact remains that too many events reported within these pages did, in fact, have a direct effect on past American elections and are likely to have further impact on impending future elections. Clearly the actions of the FBI over the past several years have created far more questions than answers surrounding the American election process. The summer of 2022 may be a critical point in history for the FBI and for other agencies in the federal government if the actions of these agencies prove to cost them the importance of the

---

[477] https://www.cisa.gov/news/2020/11/12/joint-statement-elections-infrastructure-government-coordinating-council-election

CHAPTER 15

trust of the American people. America must trust its leaders and America MUST trust its election process.

This report has laid bare a history in multiple agencies within the federal government, with one of the most egregious being the FBI, of politically motivated actions used as weapons. These actions include potential spying, lying, potential purjurous testimony, and the likelihood of the fabrication of data and other evidence. What is of utmost importance, is that these same agencies, to include the FBI, and other individuals such as former FBI executive Shawn Henry, now President of CrowdStrike Services, are an intrinsic part of the election process under the Department of Homeland Security – the governing authority over elections. Certainly the history of spying by agencies and individuals presented within the earlier chapters of this report to include, specifically, the spying alleged in the Crossfire Hurricane case involving the FBI should disqualify each and every one of the agencies involved, and the agencies they report to, including the Department of Homeland Security from having any involvement in the American election process whatsoever.

As the summer of 2022 came to and end, the issues unveiled in this report were on a collision course with the November 2022 midterm elections. On August 26, 2022, the National Security Agency (NSA) and U.S. Cybercommand once again publicly announced that they have been activated for the 2022 November elections. In an article published by *Homeland Security Today* titled "How NSA and U.S. Cyber Command Are Defending Midterm Elections: One Team, One Fight" the agency revealed the following:

- "The joint USCYBERCOM-NSA Election Security Group, stood up again in early 2022, aligns both organizations' efforts to disrupt, deter, and degrade foreign adversaries' ability to interfere with and influence how U.S. citizens vote and how those votes are counted.

Countdown to Chaos

- The ESG's [Election Security Group] primary objectives are to generate insights on foreign adversaries who may interfere with or influence elections, **bolster domestic defense by sharing information with interagency, industry, and allied partners**, and impose costs on foreign actors who seek to undermine democratic processes.
- The group directly supports partners like **the Department of Homeland Security and the Federal Bureau of Investigation collecting, declassifying, and sharing vital information** about foreign adversaries to enable domestic efforts in election security."[478]

This declaration by the NSA gave these agencies, in the wake of the series of Executive Orders surrounding elections issued by former President Barack Obama, then culminating with EO 13848 signed by former President Donald Trump, the authority under a declaration of emergency, to monitor elections as they occur. Notable is the assertion that elections are under attack by foreign adversaries which gives agencies the clearance to monitor all components and systems in U.S. elections in real time. **To date, no allegation of foreign interference in any election creating the basis for the Obama executive orders, has ever been proven, and conversely, has been strongly demonstrated to be falsified.**

Also of note is the announcement of information sharing throughout domestic agencies. This system of monitoring and information sharing is well documented in the pages of this report. The federal system devised by the Department of Homeland Security includes the Albert Monitoring System, run by CrowdStrike Falcon software which has been shown to reach all components of an election environment and is now part of a national network superstructure. Election data and traffic are run through the

---

[478] https://www.hstoday.us/subject-matter-areas/cybersecurity/how-nsa-and-u-s-cyber-command-are-defending-midterm-elections-one-team-one-fight/

CHAPTER 15

Homeland Security Information Network (HSIN) which is comprised of numerous fusion centers staffed by officials of several federal intelligence agencies, including, if not primarily, the FBI. The evidence contained in this report supplies sufficient evidence that this system is a federalization of the American election system that is un-auditable, protected from FOIA by multiple layers of counsel and agency charters, and in light of the history of federal agencies, particularly recent history, not trustworthy.

Due to the length of this report, information from page sixty-four is being reprinted here to add an exclamation point to what happened to the American election system in January 2017, and how it happened:

> On December 6, 2016, outgoing President, Barack Obama, in a meeting of the National Security Council instructed Director of National Intelligence James Clapper "...to have the Intelligence Community prepare a comprehensive report on Russian interference in the 2016 presidential election..."[479] The President requested this product be completed by the end of his Administration, January 20, 2017. **"The presidential tasking also requested recommendations on how to prevent interference in the future and how to strengthen electoral systems."** [480]

This report has presented ample evidence from government sources citing the ICA (Intel Community Assessment) ordered by the former President Barack Obama was based on completely fabricated information and in fact, according to Col. John Mills,

---

[479] https://www.intelligence.senate.gov/sites/default/files/documents/Report_Volume4.pdf

[480] https://www.intelligence.senate.gov/sites/default/files/documents/Report_Volume4.pdf

Countdown to Chaos

(Ret), a falsified government document in violation of 18 U.S. Code (see page 65 of this report). Furthermore this report shows with exact detail how, as a result, the federal government networked the American election system, took over as the governing authority of elections via the Department of Homeland Security, and now, under ongoing declarations of emergency, continually monitors all components in the election system throughout the country. Everything the Founders warned about concerning concentrating power in a centralized system has been put on display from 2017 until the present by federal agencies throughout the United States government, particularly with regard to the governance and control, both overly and covertly, of American elections.

Once again, at the very minimum, this information displays the abject, immediate, clear and present danger of yielding any portion of the election system to federal authorities. When state and local personnel within the election system were first convinced to join the MS-ISAC and later join the EI-ISACs for reasons of cybersecurity, these election systems became governed by the DHS and overseen by so many different individuals, systems, algorithms, and monitoring tools, not a single person involved in certifying any election since 2017 could be fully assured of the validity of ANY election without a complete forensic audit of all ballots, machines, network systems and routers. To date, the federal government has expressed vehement objections to the concept of full forensic audits of U.S. elections. The most important simple question of this report here and now might be, "WHY?" As recently as July 28, 2021, the Department of Justice went so far as to publish a whitepaper titled "Federal Law Constraints on Post-Election 'Audits'"[481] enumerating restrictions to audits that the federal agency expressed aligned with federal laws regarding elections.

---

[481] https://www.justice.gov/opa/press-release/file/1417796/download

CHAPTER 15

With the information presented in just this chapter alone, the facts surrounding people and agencies both indirectly connected to and directly implicated in U.S. Attorney John Durham's investigation of Crossfire Hurricane, are beginning to expose very significant and distressing allegations about people and agencies that were and are close to the Department of Homeland Security, and other agencies directly connected to the American election system. Considering the ability of the DHS to share "information and intelligence with our partners across every level of government and in the private sector" [482] through the ISAC, HSIN, and fusion center systems, any information collected by one portion of any one agency, whether it be reliable and proven or not, can be shared freely among any and all of the participating members of all other ISACS, fusion centers, and all federal agencies, and with very little transparency.

Even a hint that federal agencies have an ability to tamper, influence, surveil within, or otherwise maladminister an election in anyway, gives birth to an even greater, more serious problem. In a Constitutional republic where individual states run federal elections, a portion of the police agency and arbiter of election issues becomes federal institutions such as the FBI, the DOJ, and the federal court system. With even the semblance of impropriety by the federal government concerning elections as demonstrated with evidence in this report to include the improper, political use of bureaucratic machinery to influence, censor, and control political discourse, and as demonstrated by the court filings mentioned in this chapter and throughout this report of hands-on direct surveillance and spying upon political campaigns and politicians by federal agencies, contractors, and agents, there can no longer be an impartial arbiter for the American voter in matters of potential election crimes. Evidence of this issue may have

---

[482] https://www.dhs.gov/news/2022/02/07/dhs-issues-national-terrorism-advisory-system-ntas-bulletin

Countdown to Chaos

already appeared after the 2020 Presidential Election where many cases by states and other organizations were never heard, often again dismissed on technicalities. The idea of this problem becomes so large, its genesis and substantial potential reality has the capacity to completely destroy the entire system of free and fair elections in America.

The answers to many of the questions brought to light by this report are being investigated at the very moment in time in which this report is being compiled. Many will not be known until after the release of this document. To tie of up the web of people, their positions, and agencies connected to the topic of this report, the following information consolidates a number of the individuals, **all federal employees, or federal contractors**, either quoted directly in their own words, or via whistleblowing receivers. The sum of the information of the following people quoted is alarming when read with the 2020 Presidential Election in the proverbial rearview mirror:

Election related Quotes from Key Individuals Pertaining to Information Presented in This Chapter & Report:

Shawn Henry

Former FBI Executive Assistant Director of Cyber Security
President CrowdStrike Services
Creator/Administrator of Falcon Software Used by Albert Monitoring Services

October 6, 2016, London, England, to dignitaries at a dinner: **"We are going to show and prove Trump is a Russian asset."**[483]

---

[483] https://frankspeech.com/video/ret-col-john-mills-recaps-how-false-narrative-linking-president-trump-russia-was-created-and

CHAPTER 15

Rodney Joffe

Sr. Vice President and Security Chief Technology Officer
Neustar, Inc. (IT-ISAC Member & Contract Holder with the U.S. Government)
Vostrom, Vostrom Holdings, Packet Forensics, Ultra DNS, ERP Services, Inc.

August 20, 2016 in an email to Researcher-1 and Researcher-2: "Being able to provide evidence of *anything* that shows an attempt to behave badly in relation to this, **the VIPs [Clinton Campaign, etc.] would be happy.** They're looking for a true story that could be used as the basis for closer examination."[484]

November 2016 according to the Durham indictment: "I was tentatively offered the top [cybersecurity] job by the Democrats when it looked like they'd win. **I definitely would not take the job under Trump.**"[485]

Manos Antonakakis aka Researcher-1

Georgia Tech
Employee/Researcher Under Pending Federal Contract with DARPA
Presented in Durham's Indictment of Michael Sussman

August 22, 2016, in an email to include Rodney Joffe: "Let's for a moment think of the best case scenario, where we are able to show (somehow) that DNS communication exists between Trump and Russia. How do we plan to defend against the criticism that this is not spoofed traffic we are observing? There is no answer to that. Let's assume again that they are not smart enough to refute our

---

[484] https://www.justice.gov/sco/press-release/file/1433511/download
[485] https://www.justice.gov/sco/press-release/file/1433511/download

Countdown to Chaos

"best case" scenario. [Tech Executive-I], **you do realize that we will have to expose every trick we have in our bag** to even make a very weak association? Let's all reflect upon that for a moment. Sorry folks, but unless we get combine netflow and DNS traffic collected at critical points between suspect organizations, we cannot technically make any claims that would fly public scrutiny. **The only thing that drive[s] us at this point is that we just do not like [Trump].** This will not fly in eyes of public scrutiny. Folks, I am afraid we have tunnel vision. Time to regroup?"[486]

John Brennan

CIA Director during Obama Administration
Key Architect and Planner of National Network of Fusion Centers

May 2017 in Testimony at the House of Representatives: "I encountered and am aware of information and intelligence that revealed contacts and interactions between Russian officials and US persons involved in the Trump campaign that I was concerned about because of known Russian efforts to suborn such individuals. It raised questions in my mind about whether Russia was able to gain the cooperation of those individuals."[487]

August 17, 2018 from an interview with Rachel Maddow (MSNBC): "...we were picking things up that was of great relevance to the FBI. We wanted to make sure that they were there so they could piece it together with whatever they were collecting domestically here." Maddow: "So it was an intelligence sharing operation." Brennan: "Absolutely. Right. **We put together a fusion center at CIA with the NSA and FBI officers together with CIA to make sure that those proverbial dots would be connected.**" [488]

---

[486] https://www.justice.gov/sco/press-release/file/1433511/download
[487] https://edition.cnn.com/2017/05/23/politics/john-brennan-trump-russia/
[488] https://youtu.be/UV7-ZdDGijY?t=1170

CHAPTER 15

October 7, 2020 in a Twitter post: "In debate, @Mike_Pence lied **about handwritten notes of mine from 2016 that referenced unsubstantiated Russian allegation about Secretary Clinton**. Follows DNI Ratcliffe's politicized release of misleading snippets of documents. **Russia helped Trump, and continues to.** Full stop."[489]

William Barnett
FBI Special Agent

September 17, 2020 in an interview with the FBI about the Trump/Crossfire Hurricane investigation: "The appointment of the SCO [Special Counsel Office] changed everything," stating there was a **"GET TRUMP" attitude** in the office.[490]

Lisa Page
FBI Lawyer

August 8, 2016: Lisa Page texts Strzok, "**[Trump's] not ever going to become president, right? Right?!**"[491]

Peter Strzok
Deputy Assistant Director - FBI Counterintelligence Division

---

[489] https://twitter.com/JohnBrennan/status/1314034940321898498?ref_src=twsrc%5Etfw

[490] https://storage.courtlistener.com/recap/gov.uscourts.dcd.191592/gov.uscourts.dcd.191592.249.0.pdf

[491] https://www.hsgac.senate.gov/imo/media/doc/CFH%20Timeline%20w%20Updates%2020201203%20%28FINAL%29.pdf

Countdown to Chaos

August 8, 2016 in reply to Lisa Page text above "No. No he's [Trump's] not. **We'll stop it**." [492]

August 15, 2016 in a text to Lisa Page: "**I want to believe the path you threw out for consideration in Andy [McCabe]'s office—that there's no way he gets elected**—but I'm afraid **we can't take that risk**. It's like an insurance policy in the unlikely event you die before you're 40 . . . ." [493]

Unnamed FBI Whistleblower via Project Veritas
FBI Special Agent

May 11, 2022: "...political undertakings, which is where this agency has gone...there appears to be a political vendetta...We cannot have partisan investigations and **using the executive branch as a weapon...**An intelligence investigation is meant for intelligence... And the knowledge doesn't have to be actionable. And so that doesn't require that you've done anything wrong...**I think there have been crimes that have been committed every decade by this organization...** I have a problem with people who are doing the wrong thing, and they know it." [494]

Unnamed FBI Whistleblower via Senator Chuck Grassley
FBI Special Agent

July 25, 2022, revealed in a letter from Senator Chuck Grassley to Attorney General Merrick Garland, and FBI Director Christopher

---

[492] https://www.hsgac.senate.gov/imo/media/doc/CFH%20Timeline%20w%20Updates%2020201203%20%28FINAL%29.pdf

[493] https://www.hsgac.senate.gov/imo/media/doc/CFH%20Timeline%20w%20Updates%2020201203%20%28FINAL%29.pdf

[494] https://www.projectveritas.com/news/breaking-fbi-whistleblower-leaks-document-showing-bureau-targeting-news/

CHAPTER 15

Wray: "the FBI developed information in 2020 about Hunter Biden's criminal financial and related activity. It is further alleged that in August 2020, FBI Supervisory Intelligence Analyst Brian Auten opened an assessment which was used by a FBI Headquarters ("FBI HQ") team to improperly discredit negative Hunter Biden information as disinformation and caused investigative activity to cease. Based on allegations, verified and verifiable derogatory information on Hunter Biden was falsely labeled as disinformation."[495]

Chris Krebs
Director CISA

November 2020: "The November 3rd election was the most secure in American history."[496]

In light of all the information presented in the pages of this report, this closing salvo of quotes from members of different key federal agencies and others holding contracts with the federal government gives ample proof that interference from the federal government into any matters regarding elections is extremely dangerous and arguably may have already happened. These quotes demonstrate the abject contempt for a not just a presidential candidate but a sitting president, and perhaps even an entire party. These individuals in their own words also demonstrate a desire to preserve personal positions within the government, a desire to manipulate process, and a sample of the tools those individuals

---
[495] https://www.grassley.senate.gov/imo/media/doc/grassley_to_justice_deptfbipoliticalbiasfollowup.pdf

[496] https://www.cisa.gov/news/2020/11/12/joint-statement-elections-infrastructure-government-coordinating-council-election

Countdown to Chaos

quoted had available to them in their respective positions in the federal government to potentially introduce different methods of meddling and interference.

In terms of the evidence presented by John Durham in his indictment of Michael Sussman and his February 2022 motion, the individuals connected to his investigation, both named in the indictment and unnamed individuals connected to those in the indictment that are materially connected to American elections must be reviewed in their context with the indictment. **These individuals and events named and described are either the most incredible accumulation of coincidences perhaps ever compiled, or they represent evidence of potentially the largest criminal conspiracy ever uncovered in American history** barring perhaps the multiple assassination conspiracies that eventually took President Abraham Lincoln from the American people. Whichever of those two possibilities the facts reveal to be true, this report clearly demonstrates why both Alexander Hamilton and James Madison were beyond correct in their warning in *The Federalist Papers* of the dangers of centralized power and the reason elections must remain under the control and jurisdiction of the individual states. Their belief was affirmed by the United States Constitution which remains the law of a yet free land.

Chapter 16
Discussion

While the subject matter of this report was discovered through the proverbial thread pull surrounding the mysterious stories and the "now-you-see-him now-you-don't" games concerning Dominion Voting Systems executive, Eric Coomer, the real interest in the topic began years ago with the simple activity of hand counting ballots to verify machine totals. The author and researcher of this project undertook the simple task after completing public open records requests to access copies of ballots from an election to verify the vote count of a statewide election. The result of the hand count exposed the stark realization that the physical ballots did NOT match the machine tallies, did not match at an alarming rate, and displayed very strange, patterned anomalies.

When the errors found in the election ballot counting and reporting were of no consequence to the county clerk, the state board of elections, the local news stations, national news outlets, and most egregiously to the Secretary of State overseeing elections, the hunt began in earnest for answers. The findings of the ballot counting exercise matter and always remained a constant driver for fact-finding and truth about our election system.

Other discoveries in the hand recount included obvious errors by voters that caused their vote to be uncounted as these votes were legally overvotes due to the nature of the errors. These and other issues discovered also mattered then and they still matter now. Every single legally cast vote from every single American citizen is not to be overlooked. The findings uncovered in this report make the original issues and now all other voting issues, matter even more so at this pivotal point in time than at any other time perhaps since the Revolutionary War. The freedom of the individual and the integrity of his or her vote is obviously at stake due to the

Countdown to Chaos

flagrant willingness of our government, under the auspices of security, to covertly take over an election system that was to be handled and managed by the people, independently within their states, counties, and local precincts.

A system made up of the people, by the people, and for the people, has been converted into a federally managed system of artificial intelligence, digital information, and invisible technology overseen by individuals and agencies at the federal level able to use classified intelligence, labelling, and surveillance inside the election system. Freedom, particularly freedom manifested in the individual's legal vote, must remain in the physical hands of people who value it, not in the cyber realm of machines that run as digital slaves to algorithms that determine every nanosecond of their existence. Benjamin Franklin famously said, "Those who would give up essential Liberty, to purchase a little temporary Safety, deserve neither Liberty nor Safety." That certainly has quintessential meaning to the topic of this report. Each and every Secretary of State, County Clerk, and member of every Board of Elections should be held to answer for their involvement in or knowledge of the handing over the individual rights and freedoms of voters in exchange for security as peddled by federal officials and agencies. Each and every one of them who know of or has participated in this federalized system should have their positions heavily scrutinized by the people that elected or appointed them, and if necessary, these individuals should be removed and replaced.

The issues presented in this report are true, genuine, and must be dealt with promptly and in a way to yield a permanent, material solution. America has entered into an unwelcome, emerging era of ESG scores (Environment, Social, and Governance scores) and overreach by other public-private partnerships coming to light in the unveiling of *The Great Reset*. The federal takeover of American elections through the similar use of public-private partnerships described within this report cannot and must not be allowed to

CHAPTER 16

stand. Every election that took place since 2017 and that takes place after the exposure of the information contained herein could legitimately be held in question, as control of each of these elections is nebulous, invisible, and largely federal.

In addition, the exposure of facts surrounding spying and surveillance by key people and players responsible for or directly involved in the election system opens the door to the possibility that such data surveillance and information "espionage" facilitated through information sharing channels could potentially be happening within the system as it is now constructed. The facts that bear weight on this topic include that John O. Brennan, former head of the CIA and part architect of the fusion center and information sharing structure, admitted to charges of spying on Senator Diane Feinstein through official monitoring systems, and it was John Brennan that was pegged by the previously cited STRATFOR email as the White House official that gave the order to spy on American reporter Sharyl Attkisson. Further, multiple members of fusion centers were found to have spied on political rivals, employees managed under John Brennan's private intelligence company were found to have illegally accessed information for Barack Obama, Hillary Clinton, and John McCain potentially inside the fusion center environment, and most recently, tech executive Rodney Joffe of Neustar, Inc., has been alleged to have spied upon candidate Donald Trump and later President Donald Trump. Most recently and in his own words, John Brennan publicly admitted using the fusion center structure inside the CIA to share information about Trump/Russia surveillance with the CIA, FBI, and NSA. With the knowledge of these historical facts and allegations, the integrity of American elections from 2016 and forward will be able to be legitimately called into question as the way the current election system is constructed, the chain of custody of election data is unknown, insecure, and as the Arizona audit is beginning to uncover, difficult if not impossible to access

Countdown to Chaos

for verification. Furthermore, the individuals within each part of that chain of custody are also not fully known, and because of limits to open records accessibility within the architecture of the system, may not be accessible for inspection or audit. This is unacceptable.

The review to follow arranges "What We Know," "Questions Presented That Need Answers," and "2020 State Election Problems Ignored by the DHS and DoJ" to compare and contrast directly alongside the information presented in this report. Finally, after the sunlight shines completely on our election system with the information herein presented, this report does offer a logical solution. It is a solution already being brought to the floor by thousands of concerned American citizens, and it is a solution that can be embraced by every person that believes in a Constitutional system of free, fair, and transparent elections supporting the American value of one person having one free, legal, unencumbered, and fully transparent vote. However, the proposed solution would very likely not be well received by individuals, agencies, and organizations who already now are vehemently opposed to full forensic audit processes and have stated as much in the public forum.

WHAT WE KNOW
(References for each of the facts presented here are included in the body of the report)

System Structure Information:

- ➤ The cyber capabilities created by the CNCI (Comprehensive National Cyber Initiative) within the Executive Branch of the federal government around 2002-2003 were described as "magical" and "intoxicating". The remote access capabilities "allowed users to have access and do anything they wanted to." (p. 40-41)
- ➤ The EINSTEIN system failed two federal oversight audits. (p. 70-73, 82-85); The later system, Albert, also fared poorly in

CHAPTER 16

- another GAO audit regarding CISA's oversight and management. (p. 182-184)
- A portion of EINSTEIN 3A known as The Nest was deemed "Top Secret/Sensitive" and yet housed offsite at ISP Compartmented Information facilities. (p. 71)
- EINSTEIN 3A was capable of remotely and modifying configuration settings in real-time. (p. 72)
- Information flows both into and out of the "Top Secret Mission Operating Environment" of monitoring systems. (p. 72)
- MS-ISAC requires participating entity system ports be shared. (p. 31)
- Vulnerabilities in Cisco NetFlow Analysis 4.1 utilized by Albert Monitoring systems exposed connected systems in the 2016 election to hacking attacks. (p. 50-51, 61, 75)
- The Albert System is installed on all components within an election environment and the traffic from the system allows for remote, two-way transfer of information in real time. (p. 56-60)
- The 2019 directive by the Ohio Secretary of State identified the reach of the Albert IDS which included "the voting system, epollbook, voter registration system, and remote marking ballot device vendors that are operational" within the state. (p. 52-53)
- The Albert System software is CrowdStrike Falcon. (p. 56)
- Many of the components of the open-source software of the CrowdStrike Falcon platform are listed as having unresolved vulnerabilities classified as "critical" according to the Vulnerability Database (https://vuldb.com/). (p.56-57)
- Parts of the systems monitoring elections are deemed "classified" by the federal government. (p. 57, 95-97, 147)
- Automated Indicator Sharing (AIS), a Cybersecurity and Infrastructure Security Agency (CISA) capability, enables the

Countdown to Chaos

real-time exchange of machine-readable cyber threat indicators. (p. 77, 85)
- The CISA AIS program set up remote access capabilities to allow providers to access and CHANGE the participant's network environment on demand. (p. 77-79)
- The 2020 EI-ISAC CrowdStrike EDR system used Machine Learning and/or Artificial Intelligence learned algometric models ... required systems to have Capability to send captured EPP log data to a CIS specified log collection platform in a standard log format such as syslog, CSV, or JSON. (p. 178)
- The 2020 EI-ISAC CrowdStrike EDR/EPP system "Mandatory EPP Requirements" included "Capability to uninstall all vendor EPP related components rapidly from SLTT organization endpoints..." (p. 179)
- The 2020 EI-ISAC CrowdStrike EDR/EPP antivirus system required systems to have a "Capability to automatically uninstall the proposed Antivirus capability from specified endpoints..." and the "Capability to disable the existing Antivirus capability on the endpoint..." (p. 180)
- "... all Data provided by Members may be shared with EI-ISAC's federal partners (including, without limitation, the U.S. Department of Homeland Security), and may be shared with other EI-ISAC members." (p. 30-31, 157, 171)
- The information the Intelligence Community Assessment was based upon and delivered to Barack Obama in the White House was known to be false. (p. 122)
- Results from the Maricopa County, Arizona audit reported 37,000 anonymous administrative queries in the Maricopa County EMS system. CyFIR's cyber expert Ben Cotton reported this was "not normal Windows behavior." (p. 261)
- The SolarWinds hack infiltrated the DHS and its agencies. (p. 187-188, 243-245)

CHAPTER 16

- ➤ The SolarWinds hack was believed to have affected the DHS/Albert Systems. (p. 50, 75, 244-245)
- ➤ Despite being sold the opposite concept, the Terms and Conditions of monitoring services expressly state that agencies monitoring and accessing client devices are not responsible for the security of those systems. The monitored agencies and clients are responsible for the security of their own systems. (p. 55, 84)
- ➤ "Some US government cyber-defense systems are so dated, they are merely at "kindergarten level..." - Nicolas Chaillan, former Pentagon Chief of Software (p. 266)

Election Day:

- ➤ Federal agents were present during the 2018 and 2020 elections in the situation room of the HSIN (NCSAR). (p. 160-161)
- ➤ "...the EI-ISAC [set out] to prove its ability to achieve something the election infrastructure community had repeatedly identified as a key goal: *Effective collaboration and communication across agencies and organizations on Election Day.*" (p. 160)
- ➤ "DHS embedded a DHS Intelligence & Analysis representative at the EI-ISAC headquarters for more than a month prior to the election..." (p. 161, 271)
- ➤ "At the end of October, an elections focused Intelligence Analyst from the EI-ISAC was detailed at NCCIC in Washington, D.C., to assist with federal communication with EI-ISAC headquarters." (p. 161)
- ➤ "The elections-focused Intelligence Analyst remained at the NCCIC, joining the ISAC liaison. This facilitated intelligence-sharing with the federal and private sector partners seated at the NCCIC, including DHS I&A and the FBI." (p. 161)

Countdown to Chaos

- "...two ISAC staff were positioned at the National Fusion Center Association (NFCA)... EI-ISAC representatives were able to get a pulse on what fusion center partners were reporting..." (p. 161)
- HSIN Situation rooms included multiple hundreds federal agents and intelligence officers: "On Election Day 2018, an additional HSIN situation room was opened and managed by the ETF. While the EI-ISAC NCSAR remained active, 225 federal employees were kept informed through this additional channel." (p. 161)

General Findings:

- When DHS Sec. Jeh Johnson declared elections "critical infrastructure" their management was placed directly under the Department of Homeland Security and as the SSA, the DHS became the "governing authority" over United States elections. (p. 127, 152-154)
- The MS-ISAC is currently made up of members from all fifty states and over 4,000 entities. (p. 29)
- MS-ISAC services were provided for free in exchange for specific information provided by the entity receiving services. (p. 29-31)
- Terms and Conditions of MS-ISAC states that all Data provided by Members may be shared with MS-ISAC's federal partners (including, without limitation, the U.S. Department of Homeland Security), and may be shared with other MS-ISAC members... (p. 30-31, 157, 171)
- CrowdStrike was materially involved in events that are currently under investigation by John Durham regarding Crossfire Hurricane. (p. 57, 90-115, 281-292)
- CrowdStrike was contracted by the Democrat National Committee for services. (p. 57, 90-115)

CHAPTER 16

- "Information about security and vulnerabilities that is shared under the restrictions of the Critical Infrastructure Information Act is considered Protected Critical Infrastructure Information (PCII). PCII is not subject to the many disclosure regulations, such as those found in the Freedom of Information Act and its state-level counterpart." (p. 129)
- The initial membership of the EI-SCC was comprised of the Associated Press, voting machine manufacturers, ballot printing companies, and voting organizations funded by entities such as the Rockefeller Brothers Fund. (p. 155)
- The EISCC council acts as A REPRESENTATIVE for those entities in the election subsector. (p. 152-153)
- SLTT participation in the CISA AIS program was reciprocated with exemption from anti-trust laws; exemption from federal, state, tribal, and local disclosure laws; exemption from certain state and federal regulatory uses; not subject to any executive branch rules or judicial doctrine regarding ex parte communications with a decision-making official, among other waivers and exemptions. (p. 79)
- Sector Coordinating Councils (SCCs) are "self-organized, self-run, and self-governed private sector councils." (p. 128)
- The concept of information sharing and fusion centers was a core ideology of former CIA Director John Brennan. (p. 37-40, 135-139, 235-238)
- Former CIA Director John Brennan had a history of illegally spying on government employees with federal monitoring systems as well as spying on private citizens in other capacities in which he functioned. (p. 37, 73-74, 138, 222, 236)
- May 11, 2021, the DHS organized the Department's Office of Intelligence & Analysis to "continue leveraging the National Network of Fusion Centers and our deployed

Countdown to Chaos

intelligence professionals who collect and analyze threat information alongside our state, local, tribal, territorial, and private sector partners to increase timely and actionable information sharing in a dynamic threat environment." (p. 270)

- ➤ After 2017, when the DHS puts out any sort of terror notice or bulletin pertaining to awareness of "continued calls for violence directed at U.S. critical infrastructure," the agency is inherently including the United States election system in that description. (p. 269)
- ➤ The Department of Homeland Security as part of its election governance, uses the HSIN (Homeland Security Information Network) via fusion center nodes during elections to monitor elections and the transfer of election data, while at the same time, the DHS has now established the exact same apparatus for "sharing information and intelligence with our partners across every level of government and in the private sector." (p. 269-271)
- ➤ Upon leaving his position as CIA Director in January 2017, John Brennan admitted he directed the agency to form a fusion center inside the CIA as an intelligence sharing operation with the FBI and the NSA tasked with a mission of gathering and analyzing Trump/Russia surveillance data. (p. 138, 236)

QUESTIONS THAT NEED TO BE ASKED AND ANSWERED

- ➤ Do states lose their jurisdiction over their local elections at some point in modern day federal elections when digital information is transferred?

CHAPTER 16

- Are Presidential Executive orders with regard to election monitoring and management an infringement of Articles I & II of the Constitution and the 10th Amendment?
- Did CrowdStrike employ the same Falcon monitoring technology used and networked throughout all government systems "as ALBERT or EINSTEIN" within the DNC network environment? If so, was the organization part of any information sharing platforms?
- Why would the Albert Sensors originally be systems that were to remain hidden from the public?
- Why would the Department of Homeland Security move forward with the implementation of the NetFlow Analysis capability in the Albert Monitoring Systems just months after a very serious vulnerability involving SQL injections was discovered and just months prior to the 2016 election?
- Who was responsible for the deployment architecture of the Albert Monitoring System?
- Was the placement of the Albert Sensors in the election environment in previous elections gross malfeasance or intentional? (Placed in a position to not monitor open ports). (p. 58-60)
- Is it oversight, ignorance, or intent that platform upgrades contained key vulnerabilities in a system as widely used as the Cisco NetFlow platform is, and as widely as it is deployed to include most government systems, would emerge only months prior to key elections (both 2016 and 2020)?
- Who is responsible for the data and network information on either side of the federal cyber structure?
- Who can see SLTT data and when is it shared? How secure is that data? How true and accurate is the data? When and for how long is the non-federal data available to other information sharing entities?

Countdown to Chaos

- Why does any portion of the election network system need to be deemed as "classified" by the federal government? Is this isolation of the system by "classification" in violation of the Constitution?
- Why do American voting system companies need a special interest group under the cover of an ISAC?
- On what platform(s) is EI-SIG information shared?
- What type of information is specifically shared by EI-SIG members and what is the limit of that sharing within the ISAC(s), if any?
- Do the members of the EI-SIG have access to election night National Cyber Situational Awareness Rooms (NCSAR)?
- Do the member of the EI-SIG also have the same limits to liability as other EI-ISAC, MS-ISAC, and IT-ISAC members?
- Do members of the EI-SIG also have the same protections as other ISAC members from Freedom Of Information Act (FOIA) requests?
- As members of the EI-SIG are also members if the EI-SCC, and are responsible for industry wide "representation" in connection with the Department of Homeland Security and all agencies to which they are connected, including the EAC, how can any audits of any elections in which any of these companies participate be valid if they are NOT performed by independent companies who do NOT share information with other ISAC members, are not present in NSCAR election night situation rooms, or other ISAC SOCs?
- How is the organization of each of these public-private partnerships, ISACs, SIGs, and other governance of elections under the Department of Homeland Security not a clear violation of the plenary power delegated to the state legislatures by the Constitution of the United States to determine the time and manner of elections, and how is it not a federal takeover of the American election process?

CHAPTER 16

- Was part subject matter of the January 5, 2017, meeting in the White House Oval office between Barack Obama, Joe Biden, John Brennan, James Clapper, James Comey, Linda Rice, et al, the declaration to be made by DHS Secretary Jeh Johnson, the next day, January 6, 2017, declaring elections "critical infrastructure"?
- When systems within an election environment can be interacted with remotely and in real time by both humans and artificial intelligence, how can any system's certification have any validity or legality?
- As revealed by declassified intelligence, knowing all Russian information reported now by the ODNI and the DHS in the Intelligence Community Assessment was based upon information known to be false, was CrowdStrike Services president, Shawn Henry, part of a wide domestic misinformation campaign? Did his position at CrowdStrike expose the national election infrastructure to bias at a very high technical level?
- If the FBI was truly watching the nation-state of Russia, specifically who the agency believed was the Russian government hacking the DNC servers, why didn't they take immediate action to block those IP addresses? Why, when trying to lead the DNC IT security team to the purported evidence of a foreign hack, did the FBI redact very important key information to find the access and the damage, such as infiltrating IP addresses? Furthermore, considering the information known about the alleged phishing email, how was the FBI able to intercept such an email sent to a private company? If the FBI's intercept of this email was legitimate, why wasn't the email isolated and remediated immediately if it was truly being sent from a threatening nation state hacker? Why didn't the FBI present the phishing email in an isolated environment, not allowing it to actually reach its destination? If the FBI

Countdown to Chaos

believed the phishing email was the back door into the DNC server, how does one explain the evidence presented by the DNC IT security team team led by Yared Tamene that all but one email was isolated in a spam filter, and the last one reaching its destination was confirmed unopened?

- What was the script the FBI asked the DNC to run on their system and why did they ask for the DNC to run such a script/program? Did the DNC know specifically what the script did versus just trusting what someone told them it would do? Was the script fully vetted before installation? Did the script in any way pervert the forensic integrity of the system being monitored?
- Why did the FBI have forensic evidence that CrowdStrike did not initially possess according to the testimony of Shawn Henry, when CrowdStrike was the firm hired to assess and confirm the forensic footprints of an alleged hack?
- As the FBI was the first to notify the DNC of the alleged hack of its server, and to assign responsibility to the Russian government, was the recommendation to retain CrowdStrike Services made by the FBI to the DNC? Was the choice to retain CrowdStrike Services at all based upon the CrowdStrike Services President Shawn Henry's previous position at the FBI as Executive Assistant Director of Cyber Security? Was the choice to retain CrowdStrike Services at all based upon the number of former federal agents and contractors employed by their cyber forensics division?
- What type of information that was being collected by a government agency by a monitoring system would have been of interest to the Clinton campaign? Was the management of the government contract using the integrated system for purposes beyond its assigned scope? What role, if any, did CrowdStrike Falcon technology play in the monitoring and collection of the data within the

CHAPTER 16

government operation described in the Durham case? Who or what was the mode of sharing the information?

➢ Was the government agency work revealed in the Sussman indictment to "protect U.S. networks from cyberattacks" in any way connected to government work rooted in EINSTEIN 1, 2, 3, 3A, or ALBERT?

➢ Was Shawn Henry part of a wide domestic misinformation campaign, and did his position at CrowdStrike expose the national election infrastructure to bias at a very high technical level?

➢ As the CIA/NSA/FBI fusion center personally divulged by former CIA Director John Brennan was later proven to collect Trump, Russia, and election related intelligence, what information was collected, and was it shared anywhere else in the vast information sharing network related to elections? Was this CIA/FBI/NSA fusion center running within the walls of the CIA active, operational, and live within the HSIN network on Election Day 2020?

➢ Considering the admission from Eric Coomer in his official court deposition, was his admission of an intense visceral hate of President Trump a direct threat to the election operations?

➢ How can any government organization, particularly the Department of Homeland Security that implements politically charged policies such as border protection and immigration, and which touches issues relating to the second amendment, etc., logically and constitutionally also be in control of the elections as the "governing authority"?

➢ How is the Executive Branch of the United States government constitutionally able to hold control over the nation's election system, exposing it to instant change by Executive Orders?

➢ How can the executive branch of government that appears highest on the ballot every four years, and is not only the

Countdown to Chaos

national domestic policy driver, but the main global policy driver, be singularly trusted to remain bipartisan and fair while in control of a majority portion of the management and maintenance of the country's election infrastructure?
- Why were those most opposed to fully forensically auditing the election, the federal government, the intelligence agencies, quasigovernmental agencies, and those within the states with the closest ties to these organizations?
- Is the American voter ready and willing to let federal government agencies and intelligence officials covertly move about in a classified election system in the name of security?
- Why were former high level federal employees, Shawn Henry (FBI) and Chris Krebs (CISA), able to find immediate positions in private companies playing significant roles in the federal cybersecurity infrastructure, i.e. CrowdStrike and SolarWinds respectively?
- Who had access to the Arizona Election Management System to be able to be anonymously logged into the administrative interface?
- What caused 37,000 anonymous administrative queries within the Maricopa County EMS system which was described as "not normal Windows behavior"?
- How and why were all the IT findings in the Arizona audit not detected or explained by CISA, CIS, or DHS?
- In addition to the general management of elections by DHS, was one of the primary goals of declaring elections as Critical Infrastructure to get elections monitored specifically by the diverse, multi-state fusion center system?
- Was the push to keep the narrative of Russian interference in the 2016 election one of the necessities needed to allow the use of fusion centers in the election system?

CHAPTER 16

- Was Obama's request for an Intelligence Community Assessment (ICA) with a focus on securing elections not just an executive order but also an invitation for the Intelligence Community to have an active and permanent roll in American elections? Was this action part of a long-planned strategy to federalize management of U.S. elections?
- Was U.S. Attorney General Merrick Garland's threat to the State of Arizona in early June of 2021 regarding the audit of the 2020 Presidential Election the state was then undertaking[497] born from the May 11, 2021 announcement of the formation of the Office of Intelligence and Analysis (I&A) by the Biden Administration?
- What would stop the DHS from amalgamating information sharing regarding elections with intelligence collected about people they deem "domestic terrorists"?
- What if someone that is wrongly added to the list of DHS domestic terrorists knew someone on the list, or even talked about someone on the domestic terrorist list, decides to run for public office? Can the DHS use all tools at its disposal to thwart such a candidate?
- Could the DHS potentially oversee or spy on any campaign in the name of "homeland security?"
- Did Rodney Joffe's exploitation of his access to the government cyber realm as described in the February 2022 Durham motion in any way touch the Department of Homeland Security's ongoing election monitoring systems provided through the MS-ISAC and EI-ISACs?
- Did Joffe's associations with the DHS and the FBI connect him any way to the Albert Monitoring System and ultimately the U.S. elections?

---

[497] https://www.washingtonexaminer.com/news/garland-charts-doj-collision-course-with-maricopa-county-election-audit

Countdown to Chaos

- Did Joffe's desire to "please certain 'VIPs'" allow for any influence by Joffe in the construction of the joint statement created by the intelligence community, and published by the DHS, ODNI, and FBI regarding Russian influence in the 2016 election, and presented directly to President Barack Obama?
- How many visits did Mr. Joffe make to the Obama White House as recorded on Secret Service logs particularly during 2016? When do these visits take place in context with other key dates in 2016?
- According to the February 2022 Durham motion, if Rodney Joffe was brazened enough to use his influence to allegedly spy on the Executive Office of President Trump, was Neustar's access to government agencies and officials exploited in any way referenced in the motion to access and surveil election data that was part of the federal monitoring network via Albert Monitoring Systems, the HSIN, and other fusion centers?
- Considering the timing of the 2016 United States Intelligence Community's statement publicly blaming alleged, and at that point, unproven hacking on Russia, was Joffe's access to the White House as recorded by the Secret Service entrance logs evidence that Joffe was directly providing the White House with information personally? Did Joffe share information he had "collected" through both Sussman anonymously and with the White House directly? If so, was Joffe trying to elevate and validate information later shown by the agencies to be both fake and/or "user created" to effect executive decisions? Did the executive branch mobilize Joffe in this action?
- Did the Department of Defense, DARPA, and the FBI, all indirectly referenced in Durham's indictment of Michael

CHAPTER 16

Sussman[498] give themselves any sort of 'license' to thwart then candidate Trump in campaign for reelection to the Presidency of the United States based upon allegations that he was a white supremacist which is considered domestic terrorism by the Department of Homeland Security and the FBI?
- Based upon the knowledge that cyber evidence handled by the federal Intelligence Community was later demonstrated to be false and potentially fabricated, did DARPA use any evidence from within that vein of intelligence in the EA project?
- Did DARPA's EA project ever yield information pertaining to any election to the FBI field office that was shared with the Fulton County Board of Registration and Elections through the GISAC structure?
- If the same evidence proven fabricated in 2022 by U.S. Attorney John Durham in the federal case The United States v. Michael Sussman was the basis of the EA project, was the use of this evidence in this manner placed in the project with an intent to have it available in the information sharing ISAC structure in places like the GI-ISAC?
- Did DARPA's EA project yield a product or service still in use by any branch of the federal government?
- Was any of the information described in the Durham report intended to "please certain VIPs" relevant information also referenced by the comment made by Fulton County, Georgia Chief Operating Officer, Anna Roach, recorded in the January 6, 2021 minutes from the Fulton County Board of Commissioners?
- At any time after the initial incident described in 2016 in the Durham indictment, was an internet packet transparency tool potentially developed by the DARPA EA project utilized

---

[498] https://www.justice.gov/sco/press-release/file/1433511/download

by any person in any capacity within the HSIN, ISACs or fusion centers during the period of any other election throughout the United States?
- What did the FBI leadership know about the personal political behavior of FBI ASAC Thibault? When was leadership aware of any such bias being applied to cases within the agency? Was James Comey aware of the actions of Thibault and any other agents with similar political biases? Were such political biases overlooked with intent? Were agents with political biases that were active within the agency during operation Crossfire Hurricane collateral operators? Were agents such as Thibault kept in place after the exposure of Operation Crossfire Hurricane for continuity of other political operations? Were cases of election fraud presented by multiple officials and states unopened, suppressed, or inappropriately closed at the direction of FBI ASAC Thibault or others in the WFO? Was the declaration that "The November 3rd election was the most secure in American history," by Chris Krebs at CISA in any way influenced by the suppression of evidence reported to the FBI WFO?

2020 STATE ELECTION PROBLEMS IGNORED BY THE DHS, EISCC, AND FEDERAL AGENCIES
(Evidence of the danger of federalizing elections)

Following is a sample of problems uncovered involving the November 2020 Presidential Election presented by state. While there are numerous outstanding claims of fraud and other problems surrounding the election at the state level, the issues presented here are those best documented and most current.

ARIZONA

CHAPTER 16

- Following the audit report of the 2020 election commissioned by the Arizona State Senate, the state is still seeking the following[499]:
    - Routers
    - Splunk logs
    - A response from the Maricopa Board of Supervisors
    - A response regarding voter registration records from the Secretary of State

GEORGIA

- An initial hand review by voter integrity group, VoterGA, "found at least 36 batches of mail-in ballots with 4,255 total extra votes were redundantly added to Fulton November audit results."[500]
- Voter integrity group, True The Vote, has uncovered evidence that is admissible in court, of a mass ballot trafficking operation that took place in Georgia and other key swing states during the November 2020 election.[501]
- "Over 4,700 of Georgia's Absentee Votes in November 2020 Election Tied to Non-Residential Addresses"[502]
- Details still being questioned regarding video from Fulton County showing a poll worker allegedly scanning stacks of ballots multiple times.[503]

MICHIGAN

---

[499] https://www.azag.gov/criminal/eiu
[500] https://voterga.org/wp-content/uploads/2021/11/Press-Release-Georgia-Audit-Riddled-by-Massive-Errors-Fraud.pdf
[501] https://www.breitbart.com/politics/2021/08/24/exclusive-true-the-vote-conducting-massive-clandestine-voter-fraud-investigation/
[502] https://www.judicialwatch.org/press-releases/ga-non-residential/
[503] https://nationalfile.com/video-georgia-poll-worker-ruby-freeman-runs-same-ballots-through-tabulation-machine-multiple-times/

Countdown to Chaos

- Michigan Attorney Matthew DePerno continues to present findings regarding the 2020 Presidential Election. Mr. DePerno assisted in an audit of Antrim County, Michigan.[504]

WISCONSIN

- Voter turnout and ballot return statistic questioned[505]
- Subpoenas issued statewide for audit of 2020 election[506]
- Allegations by postal workers that mail-in ballots were ordered to be back dated[507]
- Recent audit result caused the Racine County sheriff to announce the election violations were actionable as a Class I felony.[508]
- The Wisconsin State Senate has requested a full investigation of the 2020 election.[509]
- Racine County Sheriff Christopher Schmaling announced the Wisconsin Elections Commission broke the law and committed election fraud in connection to ballot collection from nursing home residents.[510]

PENNSYLVANIA

- Truck driver, Jesse Morgan, testified he drove his semitruck from New York to Pennsylvania carrying a load of printed

---

[504] https://www.depernolaw.com/press-june24-2021.html
[505] https://county.milwaukee.gov/EN/County-Clerk/Off-Nav/Election-Results/Election-Results-Fall-2020
[506] https://www.dailycardinal.com/article/2021/10/election-audit-advances-in-wisconsin-as-election-officials-across-the-state-receive-subpoenas
[507] https://www.theepochtimes.com/wisconsin-usps-subcontractor-alleges-backdating-of-tens-of-thousands-of-mail-in-ballots_3601580.html
[508] https://www.fox6now.com/news/wisconsin-election-law-violations-racine-county-sheriff-reveals-findings
[509] https://www.thegatewaypundit.com/2021/10/breaking-wisconsin-senate-finally-decides-request-investigation-2020-election-will-finally-look-milwaukee/
[510] https://www.msn.com/en-us/news/us/racine-county-sheriff-alleges-elections-commission-broke-the-law/ar-AAQ7dXU

CHAPTER 16

ballots and that the truck was stolen at his first drop location. Former US Attorney General Bill Barr ordered the investigation into the incident to end.[511]

- Multiple reports of ballot descrepancies[512]
- The PA Secretary of State overrode the statutory signature matching requirement for mail-in ballots.[513]
- Statistical impossibility reported in batch of ballots with winning margin 99.4% to 0.6%[514]

NEVADA

- Allegations made by attorneys that evidence showed over 42,000 voters voted multiple times, and 1,500 voters were dead.[515]
- An entire local election was thrown out in Clark County after numerous discrepancies were found.[516]

With a new year came new information. To add to the findings from the Arizona audit, on February 1, 2022, election integrity group *True The Vote* in coordination with documentary director Dinesh D'Souza released information regarding an alleged massive coordinated ballot harvesting effort that took place during the 2020 Presidential Election. The information, presented in the form of a pair of movie trailers for the documentary film *2000 Mules*,

---

[511] https://djhjmedia.com/steven/ag-bill-barr-ordered-lt-col-tony-shaffer-to-stop-looking-into-truck-driver-jesse-morgans-testimony-that-he-moved-more-than-200000-fraudulent-ballots/
[512] https://www.msn.com/en-us/news/politics/pennsylvania-republicans-find-alarming-discrepancy-twice-the-margin-of-biden-s-victory/ar-BB1ckmZm
[513] https://apnews.com/article/pennsylvania-election-2020-pittsburgh-elections-presidential-elections-fc464c287c18823ff57fedc13facf7e5
[514] https://www.realclearpolitics.com/2020/12/01/pennsylvania_bombshell_biden_994_vs_trump_06_530297.html#!
[515] https://www.washingtonexaminer.com/washington-secrets/nevada-fraud-1-500-dead-voters-42-248-voted-multiple-times-rv-camps-as-homes
[516] https://pjmedia.com/news-and-politics/carminesabia/2020/11/17/entire-local-election-in-nevada-thrown-out-after-discrepancies-found-n1153458

Countdown to Chaos

claims video and cellphone geo tracking data evidence connects thousands of individuals to mass ballot trafficking by way of remote ballot drop boxes set up all over the country for the 2020 election.[517] The evidence said to be included in the upcoming documentary includes:

- One "mule" made 53 trips to 20 drop boxes.
- Geo tracking allowed for the tracking of 2000 "mules" making multiple ballot drops.
- "Mules" are seen on video wearing and removing gloves to protect from leaving fingerprints.
- "Mules" are seen on video taking photos of themselves alleging this is the mode necessary for them to get paid.
- Evidence was found in all the key states needed to decide the election.

The evidence presented by the film *2000 Mules* is alarming in light of what was found in the Arizona audit, the numerous issues found in other states just mentioned, and the fact that the federal government took over governance of the 2018 and 2020 elections. As of May 19, 2022, since the release of the D'Souza documentary, Americans have taken keen interest in the substance of the film, making it the most successful political documentary in a decade, grossing over $10,000,000 in a period of just a few weeks,[518] causing demand for facilitating an initially unscheduled second weekend of nationwide in-theater screening.

The *True The Vote* movie *2000 Mules* and the preceding lists of complaints by individual states are presented as a sample of problems that state and local election officials, voter integrity groups, and individual voters presented regarding allegations of impropriety in the 2020 Presidential Election. Many of these

---

[517] https://www.truethevote.org/coming-this-spring/
[518] https://investor.salemmedia.com/news-events/press-releases/detail/753/2000-mules-becomes-the-most-successful-political

CHAPTER 16

groups continue to pursue answers to the issues they presented to their state representatives, courts, and local boards of elections with few issues having been addressed by any of these officials to date.

The Department of Homeland Security, CISA, the EI-ISAC, the MS-ISAC, the EI-SCC, the CIS, and all other organizations discussed in this report have not participated in any of these investigations. The only statement made by the "governing authority" of the 2020 election, the Department of Homeland Security, was the statement drafted and endorsed by these groups directly overseen by the DHS. Their statement was released on November 18, 2020, which stated, "The November 3rd election was the most secure in American history."[519] This statement juxtaposed against the list of election problems listed above by individual states is all the evidence needed to understand why centralized federalized elections should be wildly opposed as Alexander Hamilton and James Madison both argued before drafting the Constitution.

---

[519] https://www.cisa.gov/news/2020/11/12/joint-statement-elections-infrastructure-government-coordinating-council-election

Countdown to Chaos

Chapter 17
Solution and Conclusion

The entirety of evidence presented within this report demonstrates clearly why the federal government cannot have any part of the administration of elections whatsoever, as the founders established in the United States Constitution. Every moment of research undertaken to uncover each piece of information presented within this report was the result of a single American voter asking simple investigative questions and performing independent work and research to get them answered. The information uncovered and the story it tells were never expected, but it was and continues to be truly a phenomenal discovery. While America thought it was returning the power of governance back into the hands of the people to whom it belongs when Donald Trump was elected in 2016, and while America bought into the streak of "wins" tallied by that administration, little did America realize that while the country celebrated what it thought was a rebirth of liberty and freedom, behind the scenes the massive bureaucratic government machine was in fact putting finishing touches on the federalization of the American election system it had apparently begun a decade earlier.

Beginning as early as 2004, when the MS-ISAC was formed, the federal government seized upon those in local governments, not only strapped for cash, but also lacking knowledge about cyber security and sold them systems and services the local governments could not manage, audit, or simply understand themselves. To those employed in local government offices, certainly the officials must have felt these systems were a good solution to a problem they knew existed, but otherwise likely mostly knew nothing about. Little could most of these state and local government officials have known that their actions would become part of a federalized election system. But when it comes to elections, and protecting an individual's right to vote, "good enough for government work" was and is not only NOT good enough, but it also literally jeopardizes our individual freedoms, and it jeopardizes freedom throughout the world, for as America goes, so will go the rest of the nations on earth. America was, is, and must remain, as Ronald Reagan so beautifully described it – "the shining city upon the hill."[520]

Independence and freedom live within and emanate from the individual souls of humanity. Freedom, however, is fragile and must be protected as the millennia of history has proven. Freedoms are protected by the individual soldier carrying a rifle in defense of his country and the Constitution that holds it together. However, freedom and independence are also fiercely protected by the individual through his or her right to vote. Because the source of the entire concept of freedom comes from deep within the individual - every individual, no matter who they are or where they reside, must have this right protected to the greatest degree possible. Hamilton, Madison, and many others since the writing of *The Federalist Papers* and the U.S. Constitution understood, agreed, and defended the individual's right to vote and its equal protection under law as having jurisdiction as close to the individual as possible. For this reason, elections are held, managed, audited, and adjudicated according to laws provided the states by Articles I & II of the U.S. Constitution and the Tenth Amendment.

The evidence presented within these chapters must serve as an intense wake up call to the citizens of the United States of America and to freedom lovers all over the world. Freedom has come under attack by an American bureaucracy, drunk with and angry for power, in the name of "security". Additionally, the threats to freedom cloaked in the form of public-private partnerships have been shown in this report to be widely endorsed by globalist

---

[520] https://youtu.be/UKVsq2daR8Q?t=1112

CHAPTER 17

organizations including the World Economic Forum,[521] as well as individuals espousing globalism such as John Brennan and James Clapper (INSA).[522] The ideologies of globalists are published to include, in their own words, "compelled participation, and blended governance" in systems using public-private partnerships comprised of the top levels of government in and with powerful private corporations and carefully constructed quasigovernmental agencies. Globalism does not equal freedom.

The system the federal government built over the decades following the September 11, 2001 terrorist attack on the United States, and that was cemented into place by Department of Homeland Security Secretary, Jeh Johnson, in 2017, is far worse than any stolen election. This federal apparatus amounts to an entirely stolen election system.

A federalized election system is the ultimate centralized power and the implicit reason it was set forth in the United States Constitution as being assigned to the individual states. When such a system hides in cyberspace run by people employed by federal agencies including intelligence agencies, the power is ultimate and complete. If abused, such a power could amount to closet tyranny where people think they are free, but in the dark realm of a deep IT network infrastructure sheltered from the Freedom of Information Act, the centralized power is able to be preserved with the ability to monitor, surveil, spy, and manipulate information at will, out of the site of the states and the individual voters, by people hand chosen by those in positions of incredible power within the federal government superstructure.

Prior to 2017, citizens could have argued that the sheer amount of money poured into the states election systems through

---

[521] https://www3.weforum.org/docs/GAC16_Cybersecurity_WhitePaper_.pdf
[522] https://www.insaonline.org/wp-content/uploads/2017/04/INSA_CritialIssuesCyber_WP-1.pdf

Countdown to Chaos

government programs was already essentially the federalization of elections. However, money did not set forth governance. The action by the Department of Homeland Security in 2017 did. With this federal structure in place on top of billions of dollars already invested into state elections by the federal government, the only tool of justice remaining to affirm the consent of the governed for the poorest of the common man is the simple right to count the vote in a clear, visible, transparent, concise way. Then furthermore, it is the right of the American citizen voter to know the vote was lawfully counted by way of an audit of any portion of any state, county, or precinct to once again, as stated in the Declaration of Independence, confirm the consent of the governed.

Freedom came under even greater attack in 2020 when, in addition to a multi-billion dollar cyber network infrastructure overseeing and monitoring state elections, tech titans from many different Silicon Valley companies to include Facebook's CEO Mark Zuckerberg, poured additional hundreds of millions of dollars into carefully selected states and precincts throughout the country.[523] As story after story was brought forward by individuals and organizations the country over regarding allegations of maladministration of the election and election fraud, a groundswell of citizens began demanding not just recounts of ballots cast and counted by machines effectuated by the federal government, but millions of American citizens demanded forensic audits, giving the individuals in the furthest reaches of states, counties, and precincts, a fully transparent verification that their individual vote not only counted, but was not interfered with. Interestingly, the federal government stepped in with conjoined federal governmental agency statements, departmental threats, and the

---

[523] https://nypost.com/2021/10/14/zuckerberg-election-spending-was-orchestrated-to-influence-2020-vote/

CHAPTER 17

media machine to try to extinguish the rights of the individuals to simply know and verify their vote was cast and counted legally.

Evidence of dangers lurking within the waters of freedom regarding states' rights versus the power of the federal government was recorded and can be seen in the words and publications of the federal government after the 2018 and 2020 elections. Upon review of the EI-ISAC Year In Review for 2018[524], and the EI-ISAC Year In Review for 2020[525], the tone of the organization changed. The 2018 Year In Review displayed federal chest thumping over the structure the CIS, DHS, CISA, FBI, and other agencies had built and utilized during the 2018 election. From a fifty-state cyber infrastructure and multiple national situation rooms and fusion centers to federal agents and intelligence officers deployed throughout the HSIN management system, the EI-ISAC and its partners flaunted a system they touted tight control over. The EI-ISAC 2020 Year In Review, while mentioning the monitoring system and national situation room, was a report that was very careful to introduce the presentation with a statement concerning local control of elections. This statement and publication, in light of the November 18th, 2020 statement by Chris Krebs, CISA, the DHS, and other federal agencies, has a tone of asking for forgiveness rather than for permission for the deep federal system that now appears to tightly govern the American election system.

America is at a crossroads as we face the consequences of the actions of the Department of Homeland Security, especially since 2017. This federal takeover of the election system might be the most serious situation the United States of America has faced since the Revolutionary War. Interfering with the right to vote is interfering with freedom itself. When the American election

---

[524] https://www.cisecurity.org/wp-content/uploads/2019/02/EI-ISAC-2018-YIR.pdf
[525] https://www.cisecurity.org/white-papers/the-2020-elections-year-in-review/

Countdown to Chaos

system is currently governed and managed with a structure that is invisible, accessible in real-time by federal agents of all kinds hidden within national fusion centers, equipped by artificial intelligence and other cyber tools that are able to access and change the election system while it is being utilized, transparency is no longer any part of the system.

Since the 2020 election, individuals across all of America have expressed serious concerns with its maladministration. Calls for forensic audits are now commonplace, and many are underway. These reactions are evidence that freedom is still alive in the hearts of Americans. However, while audits are a potent solution to expose the problem America now faces with the election system, that tool can only be utilized after the fact and does not remedy the greatest underlying violation. Time has never been on the side of the American voter or candidate when it comes to post-election election verification. Voters need to demand a solution that can either subvert or disable the mammoth cyber network put into place by the federal government. When one considers the vastness of the federal system put into place by the Department of Homeland Security and the Obama Administration, it is foolish to think the federal government will ever yield the control it built over such a behemoth of an election system. The best and easiest solution in light of the breadth of the issue at hand (besides find an army of constitutional attorneys to fight it from state to state in what could prove to be a decades-long battle) is for Americans to vote on verifiable, currency-like paper, for the votes to be counted either by hand, or by the most rudimentary scanning machines possible, and for ballots to be available for audit by the public at any point after any election. In short, our vote must be unplugged from the federal cyber network and able to be verified via audit by people at every level within state and local government.

If ingenuity can send people to the depths of the ocean and to the farthest reaches of space, if freedom can dream and create systems

CHAPTER 17

that are fully run by artificial intelligence, then an election system can be created through low tech hi-tech with an ability to restore the validity of the election process and protect every individual's right to know their vote was legally cast and transparently counted. There are minds and inventors busy at work in America today that certainly already have the blueprints needed to create and build a system that can scan a vote on verifiable, currency-type paper, scan and count it in a secure, unhackable, LOCAL manner, and audit the results quickly, if not instantly, with one hundred percent accuracy. Any system put into place post 2020 Presidential Election that is not executed on fully verifiable, auditable paper, and able to be fully audited and/or counted by hand, should have the leaders running such a deficient process immediately scrutinized as to where their allegiance lies. Those resisting such systems should be removed from offices of trust.

If companies and systems that run the lottery know instantly if a lottery number held by a player matches the winning combination, how many different winning combinations were sold, and immediately know where the winning tickets were sold, then a properly devised election system can take a ballot voted by an individual in person, scan it on a simple scanner, record and count it immediately with no need for later tabulation, and verify results immediately. The mere fact that the American election system doesn't already do this is also evidence of a government that lives and breathes on an election system that is not easily verifiable and potentially deeply corrupt. Members of both parties have complained of a broken system, and now it is time to finally burn the current system to the ground and build it back from the ground up.

In lieu of new, perfectly secure, unhackable, fully auditable, and unnetworked election system, the minimal solution may be for individual states, counties, and precincts to do what those in the state of Washington did during the spring and summer of 2022.

Countdown to Chaos

Dismantling the massive federal cyber network would be as simple as unplugging and removing the states' election environments from the Albert Monitoring System. Furthermore, states might consider retracting their membership from the EI-ISAC and the MS-ISAC, removing the Department of Homeland Security as the governing authority over the state-run elections. States would then need to consider replacing their cybersecurity with private firms. The benefit of this would be that states would then have an entity outside of themselves responsible for all cybersecurity, for as it stands under the current EI-ISAC terms and conditions, each state is individually fully responsible for any and all intrusions into their system.

The United States of America is made up of a citizenship that loves a competition and can lose with dignity if it is clear who the winner is. The lottery pulls the numbers for their prize live on television, the coin flip for the Super Bowl takes place live on television not just for the players and fans to see, but for the books in Las Vegas that pay out on the winners. The winner of the Kentucky Derby can't interfere in the stretch, must prove an undeniable winner in an immediate photo taken at the wire, and must pass a drug test. When the game is played on a level playing field, the rules are clear, the judges are impartial, and the scoring is transparent, to the victor go the spoils and the loser lives to play another day. In America, fans can watch their NCAA, NFL, NBA teams, or favorite baseball organizations win and lose and live with the final outcome as long as the game was fairly played, refereed, and scored. So it can be in elections, provided the process is free, fair, and transparent.

In 2017, when the Department of Homeland Security became the governing authority over American elections, the playing field was no longer level, the judges were no longer unbiased, the rules were no longer clear, the score was not tallied in the open, and there was no instant replay. In an election the playing field is the small

CHAPTER 17

precinct with workers representing both sides of the race assigned in one place to be sure the proceedings are carried out fairly. The judges are the county sheriffs, the precinct judges as well as the state and local boards of elections that are composed of a bipartisan commission who hold no other elected seat or work within another public capacity in positions effected by agendas. The rules are the state and local election laws with a jurisdiction in the state and locality in which the vote is cast and counted. The score is the process of vote tabulation that has now become hidden in cyberspace, and the instant replay is the forensic audit.

This report has laid out unequivocal proof that the election system, once managed by state legislatures and local boards of elections has had its state constitutional powers severely reduced if not removed by the Executive Branch of the U.S. Government by utilizing a combination of federal government agencies, quasigovernmental agencies, and public-private partnerships loaded with biased leadership and union infringement. Any election system that has components that are classified, run with artificial intelligence, can change the digital election environment, and execute functions invisibly in cyberspace all while these components and those running them can reach directly into the election environment, is a clear and present danger to the Constitution and the American election system which had once been held up in the world as a beacon of freedom.

Perhaps one of the greatest dangers with the election system being networked in a federal election superstructure run in the cloud is that such a system, monitored by federal government agencies, fusion centers, and intelligence officers, leaves far too much room for individual voters to question what goes on in the cyber matrix of ones and zeros in the virtual cloud that has been declared to be securely tallying votes. When it is widely known and self-admitted by American intelligence agencies that in that past these very intelligence agencies within the United States have on several

Countdown to Chaos

occasions meddled in foreign elections[526], that staff of fusion centers responsible for monitoring election data have in the past spied on political opponents, that an FBI whistleblower admitted the agency is both politicized and weaponized, that a CIA self-identified whistleblower confessed to participating in domestic spying on behalf of the CIA on the Trump campaign, and that an individual from a federally contracted corporation has been alleged to have given access to sensitive data from the White House itself to the political campaign of the opposition, how can any election system that is built and run by these agencies be trusted in any way by its own citizens? Additionally, when the facts surrounding high tech vulnerabilities within the deployed federal cyber structure are revealed, high level hacks are perpetrated, executives of tech companies are shown to be severely politically biased, and directors of federal agencies are proven to lie openly to the entire American population, why would any individual feel any confidence in any portion of such a structure?

In a retrospective of what the country went through in the 2020 Presidential Election, and the allegations of literally hundreds of thousands, if not millions, across the country of widespread problems with the 2020 election process, a serious question posed in the list of questions in the previous chapter is: Why is it that the federal agencies and agents that this report has shown ran both the 2018 and 2020 elections are the most averse to close inspections or full forensic audits of the ballots and the system? The people who vote and want to know whether they won or lost, just as they want to know after a buzzer-beater play in an NCAA March Madness game, need to know in a very transparent manner that the game was fair, and need to have the ability to review the game winning play at the buzzer by a complete review from multiple angles. Voters simply want to know and trust their vote was legally

---

[526] https://www.foreignaffairs.com/articles/united-states/2020-06-21/cia-interferes-foreign-elections

cast, all other votes were legally cast, and the votes were counted properly. Knowing this, the result stands securely.

With the information here exposed, and knowing how many different agencies, public-private partnerships, and quasigovernmental agencies now control and manage the American election process at the federal level, how is any American to rest assured that there has not been, nor would there be any material foreign interference in elections going forward through money being siphoned into the country's coffers from foreign countries? How are Americans to know whether the election system could ever be safe from deals being made in places like Davos, Switzerland, or in other foreign places by it is by diplomats, legislators, or presidents behind the scenes? When the election process is federalized, none of these scenarios is far-fetched conspiracy theory. When the election process is federalized, the individual voter has lost his or her access to their ballot, the process, and the ability to secure their right to equal protection under the law. When the election process is federalized, the common individual citizen becomes nothing more than the color conferred to a county or a precinct, or merely a portion of a winning margin percentage and nothing more to the massive entity that is the governing authority over the process. When the election process is federalized and is governed under the Executive Branch, it is enslaved to the authority of the power of executive orders.

This brings the discussion back again to *The Federalist Papers* that point out that the individual in the most remote places in farmlands, such as those in Pennsylvania, upstate New York, Kansas, Nebraska, Montana, or anywhere else in this fine country, must be protected equally and to the fullest extent by every Constitutional power written for this purpose. Hamilton and Madison's warning in *Federalist 61* regarding the incredible dangers of a centralized power particularly in connection to election are just as valid today as they were in 1788. Turning the

Countdown to Chaos

American voting process into a mammoth invisible cyber security network is not a system that focuses on the independence of the individual but only addresses the fears of the collective. The intent of the writers of both *The Federalist Papers* and the Constitution was to ensure the rights of the individual and preserve the power of governance to the governed. The intent of the executive orders written by Barack Obama over his presidency was to circumvent the powers of the governed and place them firmly into the hands of not only the federal government, but into the hands of policy makers and those wielding the power which they so incredibly desire. Such an intent was not, nor will it ever be what the United States of America was founded upon.

The contents of this report need to be taken up by free and freedom-loving individuals throughout this country and a new revolution needs to happen to replace our voting system with a structure similar to that which this country was founded upon. And while there is still room for technology to play a part in the process at only the local level, America's voting system must be comprised of the most rudimentary and simple technology needed to achieve its purpose, and there must be rigid and logical limits to its use under protected, local control.

Certainly, with the release of the information presented in this report, some will allege and accuse it to be conspiracy theory, however, no firm conclusions are being asserted here outside the fact that the Department of Homeland Security became the governing authority over American elections in 2017 and built an obese, complex cyber network, riddled with vulnerabilities to oversee and interact with elections. Those who interact within the system are individuals with documented bias and other malfeasance, while the structure is governed by councils populated by corporations shown to have the power to interfere with the process versus governed by or closest to individual voters. This is not conspiracy theory; these are simple facts. However, we live in

CHAPTER 17

a country of dreamers who understand the mantra "if you can dream it, you can do it." With this in mind, Americans know that intelligence and IT officials at high and hidden levels within the government and military infrastructure dream and do big things that are unseen, unknown, and outside most average people's wildest ambitions. The information presented within this report is simply public evidence that is currently known and verifiable. Certainly, there are people behind the classified curtain of this technological system continuing to be built, that dream and wish to do so much more with it than it is already capable of doing.

Information technology through artificial intelligence is believed to be limitless. Voters deeply desiring to protect their freedom should know that the circumstance under which the American election system is now governed by the Department of Homeland Security is a limitless realm that includes both the IT community and the intelligence community. With that said, yes, in America, if we dream it, not only can we do it, but "they" can do it too. Within the context of the American voting system being covertly and invisibly run and managed, we must believe and know that with regard to that system – if we, the common American citizen can dream it, that is, imagine the out-of-control federal machinery of an election system hiding behind technology in cyberspace, able to do practically anything its creators and facilitators can dream, we can be nearly certain it can be done. But, we can also dream of STOPPING such a scenario. In the name of freedom and for the rights of every dreamer in this beautiful free country, we MUST stop this scenario, and arrest the system currently in place.

Finally, after American voters are fully educated about the federalization of the American election system over the past decades and understand who of their own elected officials knew about the structure, participated in building it, encouraged its use, or potentially hid its capabilities, the voters need to understand that any of these elected officials who took an oath of office to

Countdown to Chaos

protect and defend the Constitution of the United States have all severely violated that oath. As a citizen of the United States of America governed under its Constitution, it is very important to consider that elected and appointed officials do not swear their oath to protect the Constitution of the United States to the person giving the oath, to the open air, or to television or media - they are swearing that oath to each and every American living in this country and to the very document as it is written. They are promising each individual American citizen, from the writer of this report, the writer of the code that kick starts artificial intelligence, to both the writer and reader of a children's book, or the reader of a verdict, that our rights and freedoms lie in their hands within the scope of the position they were elected to. These very officials have sworn to each individual American that they WILL DEFEND each of our Constitutional rights they are immediately responsible for within the scope of their job. Anything less should be a reason for such an official to be recalled or removed from office during the next election and replaced with someone who knows and understands the fragility of freedom and the responsibility foisted upon those willing to undertake such positions to defend it.

The United States of America is a gift from God to be cherished, preserved, and defended. This country was built upon the notion that the free individual could and should govern himself and oversee his own pursuit of happiness. Ronald Reagan once said, "Freedom is never more than one generation from extinction."[527] While to again quote Benjamin Franklin, "Those who would give up essential Liberty, to purchase a little temporary Safety, deserve neither Liberty nor Safety." We are the generation that now faces this realization as much as the "Greatest Generation" of World War II, or the generation that fought the Revolutionary War. If Americans do not understand the clear and present danger posed by the federalization of the election system in the United States,

---

[527] https://www.reagan.com/ronald-reagan-freedom-speech

CHAPTER 17

we will no longer be the lighthouse on the rampart in the storm. The United States of America is now calling upon the free citizens of this great country to stand up and protect freedom and liberty, protect our Constitutional rights, protect the right to vote, protect the integrity of each individual's vote, and protect this last greatest beacon of freedom on earth. We are the United States of America, and we must remain free, and we must always be "the shining city upon the hill."

Countdown to Chaos

CONSOLIDATED TIMELINE

CONSOLIDATED TIMELINE

References for timeline entries are provided within the text of the report.

May 22, 1998: **Presidential Decision Directive-63 signed** and enacted by Bill Clinton

1996 – 1999: John O. Brennan serves as the CIA's "Chief of Station" in Saudi Arabia.

August 22, 2000: **CIS (Center for Internet Security) is founded** by tech company executives, beginning the era of cyber information sharing. Frank Reeder & Allen Paller are co-founders; Tony Sager is Sr. VP; Clint Creightner key builder.

1999 – 2001: John Brennan serves as Chief of Staff to CIA Director George Tenet.

September 11, 2001: **Terrorist attack on World Trade Center, NY, the Pentagon, Washington D.C.,** and failed flight that crashes in Shanksville, PA

March 2001 – March 2003: John Brennan serves as CIA Deputy Executive Director.

November 19, 2002: Congress passes the Homeland Security Act of 2002, **establishing the Department of Homeland Security.**

June 1, 2003: **The National Council of ISACs (NCI) is formed.**

September 2003: **The DHS cyber security division created the United States Computer Emergency Readiness Team (US-CERT)** which is responsible for analyzing and reducing cyber threats and vulnerabilities.

December 17, 2003: **The EINSTEIN program, developed by US-CERT is mandated** by Homeland Security Presidential Directive-7

Countdown to Chaos

September 2004: The DHS provides funding for development of the MS-ISAC.

October 2004: **The MS-ISAC is started** and designated by the DHS as its key cybersecurity resource for state, local, tribal, and territorial governments (SLTTs).

March 2005: The National Protection and Programs Directorate begins deployment of network sensors – **EINSTEIN 1**.

November 2005: John Brennan leaves the CIA for a private position as President and CEO of The Analysis Corp.

January 27, 2006: **The IT-SCC (IT-Sector Coordinating Council) is formed** and recognizes IT-ISAC as the sector's official information sharing mechanism.

Throughout 2006: **SolarWinds,** formed in 1999, begins acquiring **contracts with Federal government for Orion network Management products**. Agencies contracted include the DHS, FBI, and State Department.

During 2006: **Shawn Henry (later CrowdStrike Services President) becomes Deputy Assistant Director of the FBI Cyber Division.**

July 12, 2006: **US-CERT identified by regulation as the federal incident response center** to which all federal agencies are required to report cybersecurity incidents.

April 2007: John Brennan is appointed Chairman of the Board of The Injtelligence and National Security Alliance (INSA). INSA is a not-for-profit professional association of public and private sector leaders of the intelligence and national security communities.

July 15, 2007: John Brennan pens his "Draft of Intelligence" outlining need for "a "national" security architecture that knits together the capabilities and requirements of all levels of government as well as those of the private sector."

CONSOLIDATED TIMELINE

August 3, 2007: **US Code 6 U.S. Code § 485 - Information sharing codified:** "Federal agency standards in effect on August 3, 2007, for the collection, sharing, and access to information within the scope of the information sharing environment, including homeland security information..."

November 20, 2007: **EINSTEIN 2 is deployed** across all federal agencies except the DoD and Intelligence Community.

January 8, 2008: Comprehensive National Cybersecurity Initiative directs the **DHS to deploy intrusion detection and prevention sensors across federal civilian agencies.**

March 22, 2008: CNN Reports The Analysis Corp. (John Brennan, President) is being investigated after multiple alleged security breaches by the company into passports of presidential candidates Barack Obama, Hillary Clinton, and John McCain.

During 2008: **Shawn Henry** (later CrowdStrike Services President) **becomes head of FBI Cyber Division**.

January 20, 2009 – March 2013: John Brennan becomes Asst. to President Barack Obama for Homeland Security and Counterterrorism, in addition to Deputy National Security Advisor for Homeland Security.

January 20, 2009: DHS, IT-ISAC and the Communications ISAC collaborate to **form the National Cybersecurity and Communications Integration Center (NCCIC)** - a single combined operations center.

June 1, 2009: The Obama White House publishes a Cybersecurity Policy Review that concludes the United States needs to create **a nationwide cyber network of information and infrastructure capable are sharing information among federal government, SLTTs and private entities through more public-private partnerships.**

Countdown to Chaos

September 2009: MS-ISAC Charter is updated.

January 2010: MS-ISAC is "absorbed" into CIS in order to provide SLTTs services at "no charge".

March 18, 2010: **EINSTEIN 3 is presented by DHS** for a pilot program.

October 2010: Shawn Henry (later of CrowdStrike) becomes the Executive Assistant Director (EAD) of the FBI Cyber Division under FBI Director Robert Mueller.

January 2011: **The Albert Monitoring System Pilot is launched.** Albert runs CrowdStrike Falcon software.

March 2012: Shawn Henry retires as FBI Executive Assistant Director of Criminal Cyber Response and Services Branch to immediately join CrowdStrike Services as President.

December 2012: IT-ISAC becomes first organization to sign a CRADA Agreement with the DHS.

January 16, 2013: The **DHS files a Privacy Impact Assessment (PIA) to add Enhanced Cybersecurity Services (ECS) to EINSTEIN systems** and participating Federal civilian Executive Branch agencies.

February 12, 2013: **President Barack Obama signs executive order 13636** titled "Improving Critical Infrastructure Cybersecurity" which calls for goals to be reached through "cybersecurity information sharing."

March 8, 2013: **John Brennan is sworn in as CIA Director.**

June 9, 2013: Edward Snowden reveals he is the source of intelligence leaks about NSA surveillance of private citizens.

July 24, 2013: **EINSTEIN E3A (aka EINSTEIN Accelerated) is deployed.**

CONSOLIDATED TIMELINE

March 11, 2014: **Senator Feinstein claims CIA was monitoring computers of congressional staffers.** Brennan denies.

July 31, 2014: **John Brennan** apologizes to the Senate Intelligence Committee and **acknowledges that the CIA did in fact use system monitoring capabilities to spy on congressional staffers.**

February 12, 2015: **President Obama signs an Executive Order Promoting Private Sector Cybersecurity Information Sharing** which "encourages the development of information sharing and analysis organizations (ISAOs) to serve as focal points for cybersecurity information sharing and collaboration within the private sector and between the private sector and government..."

March 2, 2015: **A vulnerability/exploit of SolarWinds Orion platform discovered that reported SQL Injection vulnerabilities including to NetFlow Traffic Analyzer 4.1.**

June 16, 2015: **Donald Trump announces his candidacy for President of the United States.**

September 2015: **IT-ISAC deploys AUTOMATIC information sharing capability.**

September 16, 2015: **The Global Cyber Alliance is formed.** The GCA designs and supports the Cybersecurity Toolkit for Elections for CIS. CrowdStrike President, Shawn Henry, joins the Board of Directors.

November 30, 2015: **The Dept. of Homeland Security** files Privacy Impact Assessment (PIA) **to expand ECS to add CISCO Netflow Analysis** citing EO 13636 for its implementation.

December 1, 2015: **Congress enacts the Cybersecurity Act of 2015.** CISA 2015 is codified at 6 U.S.C. §§ 1501–1510 and provides increased authority for cybersecurity information sharing between and among the private sector; state, local, tribal, and territorial governments; and the Federal Government.

Countdown to Chaos

December 21, 2015: Self-described CIA whistleblower meets with FBI agents Walter Gairdina and William Bennett for a three hour interview regarding alleged spying by the agency on Presidential candidate Donald J. Trump.

January 2016: **EINSTEIN 3 fails GAO Audit** only detecting 6% of tested intrusions.

January 26, 2016: **DHS publicly announces the addition of CISCO Netflow Analysis to the DHS monitoring programs** (i.e. EINSTEIN, Albert montors, etc.)

March 2016: **IT-ISAC joins the DHS Automated Indicator Sharing Program (AIS)**

April 2016: **The World Economic Forum** publishes a white paper outlining and **endorsing public/private partnerships, information sharing, and CIS best practices in line with the DHS.**

April 2016: Neustar Inc. executive, **Rodney Joffe, via Perkins Coie Attorney Michael Sussman, turns over digital data in his possession he claims to have been collected from a phone and servers alleged to be owned/operated by presidential candidate Donald Trump.**

April 2016: **CrowdStrike/Shawn Henry is paid by the DNC to investigate a DNC server hack.**

May 2, 2016: **CrowdStrike was retained by Perkins Coie (Michael Sussman) as vendor for the DNC/ CrowdStrike deployed 200 sensor devices on the DNC network** specifically utilizing the CrowdStrike Falcon software.

May 4, 2016: **Donald Trump becomes the presumptive GOP nominee for President.**

CONSOLIDATED TIMELINE

June 1, 2016: On this date, per testimony by CrowdStrike President Shawn Henry, CrowdStrike may have provided the FBI information regarding DNC server.

July 31, 2016: **FBI opens the Crossfire Hurricane investigation.**

August 2016: "**John O. Brennan**, then the C.I.A. director, was so concerned about increasing evidence of **Russia's election meddling** that he began a series of urgent, individual briefings for eight top members of Congress, some of them on secure phone lines while they were on their summer break."

September 8, 2016: Comey, Jeh Johnson, and Lisa Monaco brief members of Congress about the Russian Government's attempts to interfere in the 2016 election.

September 19, 2016: **Clinton lawyer Michael Sussman allegedly lies to the FBI general counsel James Baker** during a meeting on this date where he provided to Baker materials and information purported to link the Trump Organization with Russian entity Alfa Bank.

September 27, 2016: The Department of Justice emails Attorney Michael Sussman to try to obtain data and files in the possession of CrowdStrike Services needed to verify claims of Russian hacking.

September 30, 2016: The FBI emails Attorney Michael Sussman to try to obtain and unredacted report regarding the DNC case from CrowdStrike Services, in addition to firewall and system logs, and disk images to verify allegations of Russian hacking.

October 6, 2016: CrowdStrike executive, Shawn Henry, appears at a dinner in London and publicly declares Trump to be a Russian asset.

October 7, 2016: President Barack Obama authorized a public statement made by the United States Intelligence Community (USIC) blaming Russia for the hack of the Democrat National

Countdown to Chaos

Committee server. The statement included a petition to state election officials to secure their election platforms through services offered by the Department of Homeland Security.

October 13, 2016: Michael Sussman contacted Ryan McCombs and Justin Weissert of CrowdStrike Services to inquire again about CrowdStrike fulfilling FBI requests for forensic imaging data which the bureau was not yet in possession of.

October 2016: "DHS briefed DNC and RNC staff on DHS's Election Day activities, making both organizations aware that DHS was working with the states to secure voting infrastructure."

October 2016: From information declassified by acting Director of National Intelligence, Ric Grenell, in a letter to Senators Grassley and Johnson in April 2020, by October **2016 the FBI knew the Fusion GPS Steele Dossier was false information** the agency was unable to corroborate.

November 2016: Contract Signed between Government agency (possibly DHS) and a university to enable researchers who worked under the Agency-I Contract to "protect U.S. networks from cyberattacks." Information provided in this indictment considered CLASSIFIED. (From Durham indictment USA vs. Sussmann) Researchers working on the classified project also provided data to Clinton campaign.

November 8, 2016: **United States Presidential Election Trump v. Clinton**; 14 DHS/CIS Albert sensors deployed

December 6, 2016: **President Barack Obama instructs James Clapper to prepare an Intel Community Assessment (ICA) and prepare a comprehensive report on Russian interference in the 2016 presidential election to include recommendations regarding strengthening electoral systems.**

CONSOLIDATED TIMELINE

Dec. 14, 2016: Samantha Power, John Brennan, Treasury Secretary Jacob Lew, and five other Treasury Department officials ask to unmask a U.S. person in intelligence reporting that turns out to be Gen. Michael Flynn.

Dec. 15, 2016: James Comey, John Brennan, and several other U.S. officials ask to unmask a U.S. person in intelligence reporting who turns out to be Gen. Michael Flynn.

Dec. 28, 2016: James Clapper asks to unmask a U.S. person in intelligence reporting that turns out to be Gen. Michael Flynn Flynn.

December 28, 2016: **Obama Signs Executive Order 13757 amending EO 13694 specifying elections to be included within the scope of the original declaration** of a national emergency with respect to cybersecurity.

December 29, 2016: **ODNI and DHS release a public statement about Russian cyber attacks including attacks on critical infrastructure.**

December 30, 2016: **The Intelligence Community Assessment (ICA)**, directed by President Obama on December 6, 2016, **was completed and delivered as "Memorandum for the President"**. The report reflected false intelligence collected regarding Russian interference in the 2016 election.

January 5, 2017: **Meeting in the White House Oval Office** with President Barack Obama, Joe Biden, John Brennan, James Clapper, James Comey, Michael Rogers, Sally Yates, and Susan Rice.

January 5, 2017: **The Obama Admin. Releases classified ICA report** titled "Assessing Russian
Activities and Intentions in Recent US Elections."

Countdown to Chaos

January 6, 2017: Department of Homeland Security Secretary Jeh Johnson **DECLARES THE NATION'S ELECTION SYSTEM WILL BECOME PART OF DHS "CRITICAL INFRASTRUCTURE."**

January 6, 2017: **James Clapper, John Brennan, and James Comey brief incoming President Trump** on FBI intelligence that they attribute to the Russians that compromises the Steele Dossier.

January 10, 2017: **The Senate Committee on Intelligence holds two hearings to take testimony on the ICA** from Director Clapper, FBI Director James Comey, Director Brennan, and Admiral Rogers.

January 15, 2017: John Brennan tells Fox News' Chris Wallace that he doesn't believe President-elect Donald Trump has "a full appreciation of Russian capabilities, Russia's intentions." Brennan publicly states his anger regarding Donald Trumps views regarding the Intelligence Community.

January 20, 2017: **John Brennan leaves his position at the CIA.**

April 2017: **SolarWinds security adviser Ian Thornton-Trump warns** company executives of cybersecurity risks he found in their platforms.

May 2017: Bloomberg news reports on the SolarWinds software engineer, Thornton-Trump's, warning to the company about a "major breach" being inevitable.

May 18, 2017: **Former FBI Director Robert Mueller is appointed Special Counsel** to investigate any Russian collusion in the case dubbed "Crossfire Hurricane".

May 23, 2017: John Brennan tells House investigators that "Russia brazenly interfered" in the 2016 U.S. election. He tells the House that members of the Trump campaign were involved.

June 21, 2017: Acting Deputy Undersecretary of the DHS National Protection & Programs Directorate, Jeannette Manfra, testifies to

CONSOLIDATED TIMELINE

a Congressional Committee hearing that the DHS did not conduct any forensic analysis of voting machine. In a prepared statement, the **DHS declared that is "likely that cyber manipulation of U.S. election systems intended to change the outcome of a national election would be detected."**

October 17, 2017: The Government Coordinating Council (GCC) is formed in conjunction with elections being deemed "critical infrastructure" by the DHS.

December 5, 2017: CrowdStrike President, Shawn Henry, testifies to the Executive Session of the Permanent Selection Committee on Intelligence in the House of Representatives. His testimony yields information that government monitoring systems using the CrowdStrike Falcon platform is "CLASSIFIED."

February 15, 2018: **The EI-SCC is formed** (Election Infrastructure Sector Coordinating Council) to serve as the principal asset owner infterface with the DHS, EAC, and GCC.

March 1, 2018: **The EI-ISAC is formed.** (Election Infrastructure Information Sharing Analysis Center).

March 23, 2018: **President Donald Trump signs the Consolidated Appropriations Act of 2018 into law.** Funds would be encouraged to be spent by states on upgrading election network systems through the DHS.

May 18, 2018: **The Senate publishes findings of the Russian interference probe**. Within the findings the Senate **recommends further expansion of the DHS Albert monitoring network.**

August 8, 2018: **The IT-ISAC forms the EI-SIG (Election Integrity Special Interest Group).** Its members are Dominion Voting Systems, ES&S, Hart Intercivic, and Unisyn Voting Systems.

August 22, 2018: Daniel Coats (DNI), Christopher Wray (FBI), Kirstjen Nielsen (DHS), and Christopher Krebs (then DHS) testify to

Countdown to Chaos

Senators that **"there were no known threats to election infrastructure."**

September 12, 2018: **President Trump signs Executive Order 13848 laying the framework for the federal government to monitor state and local elections** under a declaration of a state of emergency.

October 2, 2018: **DHS HOLDS CLASSIFIED BRIEFING FOR PRIVATE SECTOR ELECTION COMPANIES**: "Senior officials from the U.S. Department of Homeland Security (DHS) met today with members of the Sector Coordinating Council (SCC) for the Election Infrastructure Subsector and conducted a classified briefing on the current cyber threat landscape for the election community."

November 6, 2018: **The United States midterm elections are held.** Democrats gain 41 House seats to regain control of the House of Representatives. 135 Albert Monitors were deployed in addition to a HSIN Situation Room, and hundreds of federal employees and intelligence officers.

February 2019: **The EI-ISAC Charter is adopted.** (Elections Infrastructure Information Sharing Analysis Center)

September 12, 2019: **The first strip of code that becomes the SolarWinds Orion hack is placed within systems, including inside the DHS, FBI, and other federal government systems.**

September 19, 2019: **CISA hosts the 2nd Annual Cybersecurity Summit** in National Harbor, Maryland. The Summit **features EI-SIG members** addressing a breakout session of the summit.

December 20, 2019: **The Consolidated Appropriations Act of 2020 passes** designating $425M to states for expenditures including upgrades to election related computer systems in order to address vulnerabilities outlined by the DHS.

CONSOLIDATED TIMELINE

February 6, 2020: **GAO Releases findings** in response to Conference Report (H. Rep. No.116-9) accompanying the 2019 Consolidated Appropriations Act showing **"CISA is not well-positioned** to execute a nationwide strategy **for securing election infrastructure** prior to the start of the 2020 election cycle." Open action items from audit fail to be resolved.

February 12, 2020: CIS deploys monitoring beyond Albert. "EDR agents from a single vendor (CrowdStrike) were deployed to thousands of endpoints, which span across several hundred election entities."

March 2020: **Updated versions of SolarWinds Orion are infiltrated by "and outside nation state."**

June 3, 2020: **CISCO Systems announces a vulnerability in its NetFlow Version 9 packet processor** used by DHS monitoring systems.

August 4, 2020: In Congressional Testimony **John Gilligan, CIS President and CEO Reports the new pilot programs deployed for the election:** Endpoint Detection and Response (EDR) Pilot for Elections Infrastructure, Malicious Domain Blocking and Reporting (MDBR) Pilot, and (ongoing) RABET-V pilot system.

August 31, 2020: In an op-ed for The Washington Post, **Brennan says Trump intends to do whatever necessary to stay in office and "there should be no doubt in anyone's mind that he will attempt to suffocate the flow of any intelligence** to Congress that could upend his ruthless ambition."

September 17, 2020: FBI Special Agent, William Barnett, investigating the Crossfire Hurricane case testifies that immediately upon former Director Robert Mueller's appointment as Special Counsel, the entire focus of the Special Counsel's Office was one of "Get Trump," and to get to Michael Flynn to get Trump.

Countdown to Chaos

September 28, 2020: **EI-SCC Executive Committee publishes an open letter to voters urging patience on Election Day in light of expected delays.**

October 1, 2020: 51 Former Intelligence officials including John Brennan and James Clapper, sign a letter claiming the Hunter Biden laptop is a part of a Russian Counter Intelligence campaign.

October 6, 2020: Dominion employee, Eric Coomer, is reported to have personally updated all 34,000 voting machines in Georgia just days prior to the beginning of early voting.

November 3, 2020: **The United States Presidential Election – Trump v. Biden.** 751 Albert Sensors and a HSIN Situation Room are deployed in addition to the EI-ISAC CIS SOC.

November 12, 2020: **DHS issues a statement from EI-GCC, CISA, EI-SCC, and NASED stating the 2020 election was "the most secure in history."**

November 17, 2020: **President Donald Trump fires CISA Director Chris Krebs after** agencies' declaration regarding the security of the 2020 Presidential Election.

November 18 & 19, 2020: **SolarWinds CEO sells a combine $15,000,000 worth of company stock.**

December 7, 2020: **Leading SolarWinds investors Silver Lake and Thoma Bravo sell $280,000,000 worth of SolarWinds stock.**

December 8, 2020: **FireEye reports the largest cyber attack in U.S. history via SolarWinds Orion platform.**

December 9, 2020: **SolarWinds announces new CEO Sudhakar Ramakrishna.**

December 13, 2020: **FireEye reports details about initial forensic review of situation surrounding the SolarWinds hack** but makes

CONSOLIDATED TIMELINE

no mention of source of attack outside of initial statement claiming it was an "outside nation-state".

December 14, 2020: **SolarWinds files official SEC report about ORION attack** which states: "SolarWinds has been advised that this incident was likely the result of a highly sophisticated, targeted and manual supply chain attack by an outside nation state, but SolarWinds has not independently verified the identity of the attacker."

December 22, 2020: **CIS Publishes information about the SolarWinds Orion hack as it affected the Albert Monitoring sytems.** "The SolarWinds Cyber-Attack: What SLTTs Need to Know" (Webpage has been removed Sept. 2021)

December 31, 2020: **CIS Reports in 2020 Year In Review that the EI-ISAC employed 751 Albert Sensors and an HSIN Situation Room for the 2020 Presidential Election.**

January 5, 2021: **In a joint statement from intelligence agencies, the combined Intelligence Community states the SolarWinds Orion attack was "likely Russian in origin."**

January 8, 2021: **SolarWinds hires Chris Krebs and Facebook exec Alex Stamos** as consultants 30 days after the announcement of Sudhakar Ramakrishna as CEO

January 19, 2021: President Donald Trump declassifies all documents pertaining to Operation Crossfire Hurricane.

February 23, 2021: **SolarWinds CEO Sudhakar Ramakrishna files a written statement with eh Senate Select Committee on Intelligence.** Mr. Ramakrishna never identifies a single nation state as the origin of the SolarWinds hack.

March 11, 2021: **Release of "Key Findings & Recommendations From the Joint Report from the DoJ and DHS"** which states: "Since 2018, federal, state, local, and private sector partners nationwide

Countdown to Chaos

worked together in unprecedented ways ... to support state and local officials in safeguarding election infrastructure..." (EO 13848 § 8(d)).

April 23, 2021: **The Arizona State Senate has a full forensic audit undertaken** by the company The Cyber Ninjas. 73 Democrat lawyers travel to Phoenix to file cases to stop the audit.

June 11, 2021: United States Attorney General Merrick Garland attempted to assert the power of the federal government by applying "new scrutiny" to post election audits by individual states.

September 7, 2021: **The Biden White House extends Executive Order 13848 to allow for federal monitoring of midterm elections in 2022.**

September 21, 2021: **CIS announces new MS-ISAC elections leadership team**: Kathy Bookvar, former PA SoS (D), Jared Dearing, KY State Board of Elections Director (D), and Marci Andino (I) South Carolina Elections Director

September 23, 2021: **Dominion executive, Eric Coomer, is deposed in a suit related to the 2020 Presidential Election.**

September 24, 2021: **Judge Marie Avery Moses seals Eric Coomer's deposition testimony "sua sponte" and issues a protective order.**

September 24, 2021: **The Arizona State Senate holds a public hearing detailing the results of the forensic audit.** The findings of the inspection of the cyber network infrastructure and environment directly contract the CISA statement of November 12, 2020.

October 11, 2021: **The full deposition of Dominion Voting Systems employee, Eric Coomer, is released to the public.** In it Coomer admits all social media posts previously in question were in fact made by him.

CONSOLIDATED TIMELINE

October 11, 2021: **Nicolas Chaillan, the Pentagon's first software officer resigns** claiming China has already won the tech war, and "Some US government cyber-defense systems are so dated, they are merely at "kindergarten level…"

February 1, 2022: *True The Vote* via Director Dinesh D'Souza, released a brief of information regarding a national ballot trafficking operation. The information was teased in a trailer for D'Souza's documentary *2000 Mules*.

February 7, 2022: **The Department of Homeland Security issued a National Terrorism Advisory** System Bulletin (NTAS) highlighting domestic terror threats including threats to critical infrastructure.

February 11, 2022: **U.S. Attorney John Durham filed a motion in the Sussman indictment** in U.S. District Court **describing alleged surveillance of the office of the President of the United States** by a top U.S. cyber contractor Neustar, Inc.

February 14, 2022: Ferry County, Washington removed the Albert Monitoring System from its election environment.

March 24, 2022: Former President Donald Trump filed a RICO case against Hillary Clinton and many federal officials involved in Operation Crossfire Hurricane.

April 15, 2022: **U.S. Attorney John Durham filed Memorandum in Opposition Re Sussmann Motion in Limine by USA** detailing specific allegations surrounding Michael Sussman and Rodney Joffe.

April 21, 2022: Former President Barack Obama presents a keynote address at Standford University calling for regulation of disinformation in digital media.

April 27, 2022: Department of Homeland Security Secretary Mayorkas announced the establishment of a new Disinformation Governance Board.

Countdown to Chaos

May 2, 2022: Dinesh D'Souza in cooperation with True the Vote releases a documentary film *2000 Mules* exposing hard evidence of election fraud in the 2020 election.

June 3, 2022: With an invitation by former President Donald Trump, the FBI visited Trump's Florida home, Mar-a-lago, to conduct a search of presidential documents retained by Trump, after a months-long paper trail between Trump and the National Archives to discern which documents were in Trump's possession.

June 8, 2022: Former President Trump received a letter from federal investigators stating the room in Mar-a-lago that housed the presidential documents be further secured with a padlock. Officials at Mar-a-lago comply.

June 22, 2022: Federal investigators demand surveillance video from the room that secured federal presidential documents at Mar-a-lago. Trump officials comply.

July 25, 2022: Senator Chuck Grassley sends a letter to FBI Director Christopher Wray citing information from numerous whistleblowers that the FBI was intentionally covering up the validity of Hunter Biden's laptop in the lead-up to the 2020 Presidential Election.

August 8, 2022: The FBI executed an armed search of Mar-a-lago to confiscate documents and records sought by the National Archives.

August 25, 2022: Facebook/META CEO, Mark Zuckerberg, admits in an interview on the Joe Rogan Show that the FBI approached Facebook about the Hunter Biden laptop story prior to the 2020 Presidential Election and told the company to be on high alert for such "Russian disinformation."

August 26, 2022: The affidavit supporting the raid of former President Trump's home, Mar-a-lago, was released. FBI Assistant

CONSOLIDATED TIMELINE

Special Agent in Charge, Tim Thibault was escorted out of FBI Headquarters for suppressing details about the Hunter Biden laptop prior to the 2020 Election.

August 29, 2022: The Department of Justice admits in an official court filing, that among documents seized by the FBI in the Mar-a-lago raid were documents understood to be attorney-client privileged.

Countdown to Chaos

EPILOGUE

Very late on the night of October 3, 2022, a headline showed up via a push notification on the phone of the author. The massive topic that encompasses this report had not only become a heavy burden to bear while waiting for its release, but each and every headline involving named individuals and federal agencies stood out like a beacon when considered in context with the facts laid out in these seventeen chapters. Headlines catching attention involved the Department of Homeland Security's inability to control the border[528], the revelation that former Attorney General heading up the Department of Justice during the 2020 Presidential Election, Bill Barr, did not open a single election related investigation after states in a dozen federal districts had filed formal complaints with the Justice Department[529], in addition to the headline revealing the arrest of Konnech CEO, Eugene Yu, for stealing election worker data from multiple precincts across the United States, and storing the data on a server in Wuhan, China.[530] As serious and important as each of those headlines and intermingling events were to the topic of this report, it was the headline of late October 3, 2022, that demanded to be included within these pages.

Finding a home on the website of John O. Solomon's *Just The News* website was a story by reporter Greg Piper headlined, "Federally

---

[528] https://abcnews.go.com/Politics/border-apprehensions-exceed-million-year-enforcement-increases-gop/story?id=90167749

[529] https://www.thegatewaypundit.com/2022/09/bill-barr-lied-foia-requests-reveal-no-doj-investigations-election-fraud-2020-election-bill-barr-claimed-video/

[530] https://www.foxnews.com/us/ceo-software-company-targeted-election-deniers-arrested-suspicion-stealing-data

Countdown to Chaos

backed censorship machine raises separation of powers, election meddling questions."[531] Further investigation uncovered a headline just days before on September 30, 2022 by Greg Piper and John Solomon that read, "Outsourced censorship: Feds used private entity to target millions of social posts in 2020."[532] The depth of what was disclosed in these stories makes the urgency of America's election crisis, in the light of revelations in this report, one of absolute immediacy.

The first article opens with this statement, "A federal agency-backed censorship machine that affected thousands of web URLs and millions of social posts during the 2020 campaign put a focus on some members of Congress and candidates for federal office, raising concerns about the separation of powers and election meddling." [533] This first statement ushers the warnings laid out in chapter fifteen of this report into fact-based reality, and now historical record. While the DHS tried to create a Disinformation Governance Board in 2022 within the confines of its own walls, with its own handpicked people, and its own controllable information trail, the revelations in the Piper article as well as its predecessor unveil the DHS had, in fact, been conducting censorship actions with the use of a well-hidden public-private partnership in the time leading up to the 2020 Presidential Election. The opening salvo in the preceding September 30th article by both Greg Piper and John Solomon read:

> "A consortium of four private groups worked with the departments of Homeland Security (DHS) and State to censor massive numbers of social media posts they

---

[531] https://justthenews.com/government/congress/federally-backed-censorship-machine-raises-separation-powers-election-meddling#digital-diary
[532] https://justthenews.com/government/federal-agencies/biden-administration-rewarded-private-entities-got-2020-election
[533] https://justthenews.com/government/congress/federally-backed-censorship-machine-raises-separation-powers-election-meddling#digital-diary

EPILOGUE

considered misinformation during the 2020 election, and its members then got **rewarded with millions of federal dollars from the Biden administration** afterwards, according to interviews and documents obtained by Just the News.

The Election Integrity Partnership is back in action again for the 2022 midterm elections, raising concerns among civil libertarians that a chilling new form of public-private partnership to evade the First Amendment's prohibition of government censorship may be expanding."[534]

Let this all sink in for a moment, then, let's unpack what was just quietly dropped on the American voting public. Decades prior to the 2020 Presidential Election, the federal government began using public-private partnerships in the form of ISACs for a number of purposes. The drivers of the emergence of this protocol were the terror attacks of September 11, 2001. The Patriot Act was the result of investigations that determined that administrative walls between federal agencies needed to be torn down to make the government far more efficient and agile, and to create transparency between agencies. These public-private partnerships have evolved and are now used in nearly every aspect of governance.

This report explained in chapter two that many Constitutional analysts have both sharply criticized and warned that public-private partnerships create "end-arounds" to the Constitution. Truly public-private partnerships allow for government bodies and agencies to conduct operations not allowed them under the restrictions of the constitutions of both the United States and their individual states. These partnerships allow governments and government agencies to undertake otherwise unconstitutional

---

[534] https://justthenews.com/government/federal-agencies/biden-administration-rewarded-private-entities-got-2020-election

Countdown to Chaos

actions via private entities not constitutionally constrained under the general freedom of "free and private enterprise." These public-partnerships are not only federal, but they have reached to the state and local level. This report has shown fusion centers, now an integral part of the election system, are also a public-private partnership entity involving private IT companies, local government officials, federal agents, intelligence officials, and others. The MS-ISAC and further, the EI-ISAC are both public-private partnerships directly involved in U.S. elections. Further reading into the Piper/Solomon article revealed that the EI-ISAC was and remains the chosen node or point of participation for its members to liaison with the Election Integrity Partnership.[535]

The next point in the deconstruction of the quote above from the *Just The News* report, is that the Department of Homeland Security (DHS), the governing authority over all elections after the formation of the EI-ISAC and more specifically the EI-SCC, was one of the federal agencies directing the Election Integrity Partnership with a protocol of opening service or complaint tickets, to censor "massive numbers of social media posts."

First, an understanding of the construction of the Election Integrity Project and its ticket protocol is worth review. From a report published in 2021 by the Election Integrity Partnership itself titled "The Long Fuse: Misinformation and the 2020 Election," the EIP described itself in these terms:

> "The Election Integrity Partnership was formed to enable **real-time information exchange between election officials, government agencies, civil society organizations, social media platforms, the media, and the research community**. It aimed to identify and

---

[535] https://www.eac.gov/sites/default/files/partners/EI_ISAC_Reporting_Misinformation_Sheet102820.pdf

EPILOGUE

analyze online mis- and disinformation, and to communicate important findings across stakeholders. It represented a novel collaboration between four of the nation's leading institutions focused on researching mis- and disinformation in the social media landscape:

- The Stanford Internet Observatory (SIO)

- The University of Washington's Center for an Informed Public (CIP)

- Graphika

- The Atlantic Council's Digital Forensic Research Lab (DFRLab)"[536]

Under a header titled, "What We Did," the following concise confession of their information control protocol was enumerated:

"The EIP's primary goals were to: (1) identify mis- and disinformation before it went viral and during viral outbreaks, (2) share clear and accurate counter messaging, and (3) document the specific misinformation actors, transmission pathways, narrative evolutions, and information infrastructures that enabled these narratives to propagate.

...The EIP used an innovative internal research structure that leveraged the capabilities of the partner organizations through a tiered analysis model based on "tickets" collected internally and from our external stakeholders. Of the tickets we processed, **72% were related to delegitimization of the election.**"[537]

---

[536] https://stacks.stanford.edu/file/druid:tr171zs0069/EIP-Final-Report.pdf
[537] https://stacks.stanford.edu/file/druid:tr171zs0069/EIP-Final-Report.pdf

Countdown to Chaos

Once again, take a moment to let this fact sink in. The governing authority over all elections in the United States, the DHS, was materially participating in the suppression of speech that dealt directly with the 2020 election, through a public-private partnership with the Election Integrity Project (EIP). In its own post-election publication, the EIP specified that they not only actively and routinely engaged in censoring speech, but they also participated in what the consortium described as "clear and accurate counter messaging." The DHS and the EIP were, in effect, in complete control of political discourse in the digital realm which is now "the public square" prior to the 2020 Presidential Election.

An additional point of interest in this arrangement also appeared within the pages of the EIP publication "The Long Fuse." On page fourteen of the report, the EIP states, "Civil society collaborators submitted tips through the trusted partner tip line and interacted with the EIP research team through briefings, partner meetings, and shared findings." [538] The report then listed a select list of partners in this "tip line" partnership. Included in the group is the Defending Digital Democracy Project. The significance of this particular participant is that a co-founder of the Defending Digital Democracy Project is Robby Mook. Not mentioned by name yet within the pages of the extensive report in hand, Robby Mook was Hillary Clinton's campaign manager during the 2016 Presidential Election. He is also a senior fellow at the Belfer Center. The Belfer Center describes Mr. Mook's history in this way:

> "Mook is co-founder and former senior fellow with Defending Digital Democracy (D3P), a Belfer Center project launched in 2017 to identify and recommend strategies, tools, and technology to protect democratic processes and systems from cyber and information

---

[538] https://stacks.stanford.edu/file/druid:tr171zs0069/EIP-Final-Report.pdf

EPILOGUE

attacks - particularly around the 2020 presidential election."[539]

The reader should recall and perhaps reread each event that unfolded during the spring and summer of 2016, through the 2016 Presidential Election, and beyond – the period of time the FBI was engaged in the "Crossfire Hurricane" investigation. During that period, Mr. Robby Mook not only materially participated in events surrounding the illegal spying and collection of information about candidate for president, Donald J. Trump by Neustar executive Rodney Joffe, but Mr. Mook later appeared as a witness to the events in federal court during the John Durham trial of Attorney Michael Sussman.[540]

According to the Belfer Center description of Mr. Mook, it was after the 2016 election and during the period referred to "Crossfire Hurricane" that Robby Mook launched the Defending Digital Democracy Project (D3P), and according to Belfer Center website, did so to specifically "identify and recommend strategies, tools, and technology to protect democratic processes and systems from cyber and information attacks - particularly around the 2020 presidential election." [541] This brief timeline would suggest that Mr. Mook left the campaign of Hillary Clinton after her defeat in 2016, and immediately undertook the development of a wide ranging censorship strategy via D3P, that would specifically take aim at the 2020 Presidential Election. The body of evidence presented by the EIP publication "The Long Fuse" suggests that the prime target of the activity propagated by D3P from the point of inception in 2017 (as well as activity from other private civil society

---

[539] https://www.belfercenter.org/person/robby-mook
[540] https://justthenews.com/politics-policy/elections/clinton-campaign-manager-who-spread-trump-alfa-bank-hoax-involved-dhs
[541] https://www.belfercenter.org/person/robby-mook

Countdown to Chaos

organizations), was one party and the sitting President of the United States.

The legal definition of "election interference" by a federal employee or official is explained in a publication by the United States Justice Department titled, "Federal Prosecution of Election Offenses - Eighth Edition." The legal explanation of 18 U.S.C. § 595 reads:

> **"(c) Interference in election by employees of federal, state, or territorial governments: 18 U.S.C. § 595**
>
> Section 595 was enacted as part of the original 1939 Hatch Act. The statute prohibits any public officer or employee, in connection with an activity financed wholly or in part by the United States, from using his or her official authority to interfere with or affect the nomination or election of a candidate for federal office. This statute is aimed at the misuse of official authority. It does not prohibit normal campaign activities by federal, state, or local employees. Violations are one-year misdemeanors.
>
> Section 595 applies to all public officials, whether elected or appointed, federal or non-federal. For example, an appointed policymaking government official who bases a specific governmental decision on an intent to influence the vote for or against an identified federal candidate violates Section 595. The nexus between the official action and an intent to influence must be clear to establish a violation of this statute."[542]

This definition and explanation appear to fit the actions of the DHS and CISA. However these agencies used a public-private partnership to undertake the specifics of their operation. Herein is

---

[542] https://www.justice.gov/criminal/file/1029066/download

EPILOGUE

both a current and directly applicable example of the constitutional dangers of public-private partnerships. Beyond election interference, those in the crosshairs of the actions by the DHS have attributed the activity to an election contribution in-kind. As a result, did the DHS, the governing authority of the 2020 election, materially interfere with the election, or did the DHS illegally contribute to one candidate's campaign with in-kind contributions with federal money in the form of federal grants after the election? Both of these questions again point straight back to all the problems this report has divulged with the current federal construct of the American election system.

The next point of the statement made in the *Just The News* story may be the most serious and addresses the question just posed. The Piper/Solomon story states that after the 2020 election, the private agencies involved with the censorship of social media posts that clearly benefitted one candidate over another, were "rewarded with millions of federal dollars from the Biden administration." One of the targets of the censorship campaign was Robby Starbuck, a first generation Cuban American and candidate for the U.S. House of Representatives for Tennessee's 5th Congressional District. Mr. Starbuck now has a team of attorneys working on his behalf in a case against the DHS and the State Department. In a social media thread, Starbuck shared details from evidence and discovery being collected for the pending legal case. Mr. Starbuck made reference to an "enemies list" as well as to a list of federal payments made to named recipients, all members of the EIP.

The "enemies list" information Robby Starbuck referred to was sourced from the same report earlier cited and published by the Election Integrity Partnership. Once again, the title is "The Long Fuse: Misinformation and the 2020 Election."[543] Found on pages

---

[543] https://stacks.stanford.edu/file/druid:tr171zs0069/EIP-Final-Report.pdf

Countdown to Chaos

188-192 of the EIP report, in a number of graphics in a chapter the report titled "Actors and Networks: Repeat Spreaders of Misinformation" the EIP shared lists of individuals, websites, and organizations it actively turned over to social media platforms ultimately for censorship on the basis of the violation of platform "community standards." In this chapter, the EIP states in its own words:

> "Perhaps a reflection on both the nature of information threats to election integrity and our process for identifying them ... all 21 of the repeat spreaders were associated with conservative or right-wing political views and support of President Trump..."

True to this assertion, the EIP report is nearly entirely framed with one political ideology being targeted, tracked and censored. Understanding that one source turning information over to the EIP and contained in its post-election report was Robby Mook's Defending Digital Democracy Project, the concentration of targets is logical. As Hillary Clinton's former campaign manager, Mook and all others in that defeated campaign for president certainly must have held animosity for those that defeated them, and it is not unrealistic to ascertain this list included those the Clinton campaign likely regarded as "enemies" and "high value targets" after 2016. Here are the "enemies lists" highlighted by former candidate for the U.S. House of Representatives, Robby Starbuck, as presented in the pages of the EIP report:

EPILOGUE

5. Actors and Networks: Repeat Spreaders of Election Misinformation

Rank	Account	Verified	Incidents	Tweets w/ >1000 Retweets	Followers	Retweets in Incidents	Left or Right
1	RealJamesWoods	True	27	36	2,738,431	403,950	Right
2	gatewaypundit	True	25	45	424,431	200,782	Right
3	DonaldJTrumpJr	True	24	27	6,392,929	460,044	Right
4	realDonaldTrump	True	21	43	88,965,710	1,939,362	Right
4	TomFitton	True	21	29	1,328,746	193,794	Right
6	JackPosobiec	True	20	41	1,211,549	188,244	Right
7	catturd2	False	17	20	436,601	66,039	Right
8	EricTrump	True	16	25	4,580,170	484,425	Right
9	ChuckCallesto	True	15	17	311,517	117,281	Right
10	charliekirk11	True	13	18	1,915,729	232,967	Right
11	marklevinshow	True	12	10	2,790,699	90,157	Right
11	cjtruth	False	12	27	256,201	66,698	Right
11	JamesOKeefeIII	False	12	64	1,021,505	625,272	Right
11	prayingmedic	False	12	26	437,976	57,165	Right
15	RichardGrenell	True	11	12	691,441	143,363	Right
15	pnjaban	True	11	14	208,484	58,417	Right
17	BreitbartNews	True	10	11	1,647,070	38,405	Right
17	TheRightMelissa	False	10	31	497,635	73,932	Right
17	mikeroman	False	10	10	29,610	128,726	Right
17	robbystarbuck	True	10	15	204,355	65,651	Right
17	seanhannity	True	10	22	5,599,939	96,641	Right

Table 5.2: Repeat Spreaders: Twitter accounts that were highly retweeted across multiple incidents. Twitter has since suspended the accounts of realDonaldTrump (January 6), The Gateway Pundit (February 6), cjtruth, and prayingmedic (January 8).[16] Account verification status as of 11/10/2020.

Rank	Channel	Incidents	Total Tweets	Videos	YouTube Views
1	Project Veritas	7	128,734	26	9,613,437
1	CDMedia	7	258,314	1	691,395
3	Donald J Trump	6	4,338	10	10,849,373
3	One America News Network	6	207,544	15	4,034,274
3	GOP War Room	6	186,106	8	1,732,847
3	Dr. Shiva Ayyadurai	6	196,292	1	1,052,429
7	Gateway Pundit	5	10,015	13	4,085,657
8	NewsNOW from FOX	4	406	7	9,450,514
8	StevenCrowder	4	15,490	3	8,159,462
8	BlazeTV	4	314	6	3,900,083
8	Judicial Watch	4	1,333	7	511,568
8	MR. OBVIOUS	4	283	5	401,481

Table 5.4: Repeat Spreaders: YouTube channels that were highly tweeted (>=10 times/incident) across multiple (>=4) incidents.

Countdown to Chaos

Rank	Account Name	Facebook Page/Group	# of Incidents	# of Posts	Total Engagement
1	Breitbart	Page	8	20	831,452
1	The Silent Majority	Page	8	7	69,763
3	Heather Cox Richardson	Page	6	8	816,755
3	David J Harris Jr.	Page	6	11	282,652
3	James O'Keefe	Page	6	20	194,596
3	Project Veritas	Page	6	20	165,377
7	NowThis Politics	Page	5	11	244,023
7	Team Trump	Page	5	5	153,118
7	Ryan Fournier	Page	5	6	67,885
7	Wendy Bell Radio	Page	5	6	62,020
7	#WalkAway Campaign	Group	5	12	51,854
7	StandwithMueller	Page	5	7	19,345

Table 5.5: Repeat Spreaders: Facebook Pages and public Groups that were highly engaged with (>=1000 engagements) across multiple (>=5) incidents.

Rank	Domain	Incidents	# Original Tweets	Total Retweets	≈% Left Spread	≈% Right Spread
1	www.thegatewaypundit.com	46	29,207	840,740	0.08%	99.92%
2	www.breitbart.com	26	8,569	394,689	0.94%	99.06%
3	www.youtube.com	21	14,040	269,996	2.51%	97.49%
4	www.washingtonpost.com	18	1,986	74,360	84.76%	15.23%
5	www.foxnews.com	14	1,330	34,143	0.91%	99.09%
6	www.theepochtimes.com	12	2,167	86,325	0.00%	100.00%
7	nypost.com	11	4,513	178,176	2.27%	97.73%
8	www.zerohedge.com	10	1,043	27,687	0.52%	99.48%
8	www.cnn.com	10	1,269	100,642	89.28%	10.71%
10	apnews.com	9	432	13,067	33.84%	66.14%
10	justthenews.com	9	1,035	61,305	0.00%	100.00%
10	www.nytimes.com	9	776	50,021	63.88%	36.11%
10	thedcpatriot.com	9	572	26,417	0.00%	99.99%
14	gellerreport.com	8	516	15,075	0.00%	99.99%
14	thenationalpulse.com	8	770	39,160	0.00%	99.99%
14	nationalfile.com	8	4,443	195,489	0.51%	99.48%
17	www.washingtontimes.com	7	280	11,445	1.45%	98.54%
17	www.pscp.tv	7	2,067	83,269	0.47%	99.53%
17	saraacarter.com	7	531	81,172	1.39%	98.60%
17	www.washingtonexaminer.com	7	1,518	75,939	0.98%	99.02%

Table 5.3: Domains, extracted from tweets, that were highly tweeted (>500) across multiple incidents. Shortened URLs were followed when possible to extract original domains. The incident count includes the number of incidents for which the domain was linked to in over 500 tweets or retweets in our incident-related Twitter data. The original tweets are the count of non-retweets (including quote tweets and replies) that mentioned the domain within those incidents, while the total retweets column is a count of the retweets, both from within our incident-linked Twitter data. Finally, the estimated right/left spread is the proportion of original tweets made by influential users classified on the ideological spectrum based on our network analysis, above. Users not included in that network analysis are excluded from the estimate.

EPILOGUE

Rank	Account Name	Verified	# of Incidents	# of Posts	Total Engagement
1	KAGBABE 2.0	Not verified	12	33	80,484
2	Breitbart	Verified	10	14	670,577
2	The Gateway Pundit	Not verified	10	20	132,440
4	James O'Keefe	Verified	6	20	410,335
4	Baller Alert	Verified	6	7	102,837
6	Michael Hennessey	Not verified	5	82	169,623
6	Occupy Democrats	Not verified	5	5	51,289
6	Latinos With Trump	Not verified	5	14	47,167
6	Ben & Hannah	Not verified	5	11	19,529
6	#HisNameWasSethRich	Not verified	5	7	18,814

Table 5.6: Repeat Spreaders: Facebook Pages and public Groups that were highly engaged with (>=1000 engagements) across multiple (>=5) incidents.

The list of targets presented in the EIP report, with the exception of perhaps only four entities, were as the EIP report stated in its own words, "associated with conservative or right-wing political views and support of President Trump..." Of interest in a quick review of the 292-page EIP report published in 2021, is that of a large number of examples cited in the EIP report from social media posts labeled as "dis- or misinformation," many if not a large majority have since been proven factual. For example, one section targeted concerns posted on social media about the mishandling of mail-in ballots by postal workers. The evidence presented in the censored posts has since been proven factual with the arrest of postal workers,[544,545] the delivery of 2020 Presidential Election ballots two years later, in August of 2022,[546] among other factual examples available from many news outlets throughout the country.

Other instances cited by the EIP report as dis- or misinformation and censored via their ticketing process between the EI-ISAC and their big tech partners included what their report deemed "ballot

---

[544] https://www.washingtontimes.com/news/2020/oct/30/mailman-arrested-delaying-mail-during-election-sea/
[545] https://nypost.com/2020/11/06/usps-worker-arrested-at-canadian-border-with-undelivered-ballots/
[546] https://www.wmar2news.com/matterformallory/mail-in-ballots-from-2020-discovered-in-baltimore-usps-facility

Countdown to Chaos

harvesting conspiracies." Since then, the independent integrity group, True The Vote, made its findings of ballot harvesting and ballot box stuffing public. Through a nationwide effort by way of FOIA requests, True The Vote obtained and carefully analyzed isolated video camera footage from cameras installed to monitor election ballot drop boxes used in the 2020 election. The evidence they retrieved was made public with the widely distributed movie *2000 Mules*. Within just months of its release, while the media was actively trying to claim the video and GPS tracking evidence had been "debunked", video-based data presented in the film helped to secure a guilty plea in federal court on charges of ballot harvesting levied upon one of the individuals featured in the film.[547] Other cases remain open and are being actively investigated around the country.

Yet another favorite topic heavily censored by the EIP consortium had to do with the security of Dominion Voting Systems which were widely used by precincts throughout the United States in the 2020 Presidential Election. Since the censorship actions on this specific topic undertaken by the EIP in concert with and at the direction of CISA, on June 3, 2022, CISA itself was forced to admit in a press release published on its own website that Dominion Voting Systems were and are in fact, vulnerable to hacking and attack.[548]

Finally, the EIP report also included Hunter Biden's connections to China in its dis-, mis-, and mal-information campaign. Since that time, multiple reporters from a number of different agencies and outlets now report that all the information reported during the election cycle that had originated from the abandoned Hunter Biden laptop, including information about his Chinese connections and business dealings, are one hundred percent factual. Clearly the

---

[547] https://thewashingtonstandard.com/2000-mules-vindication-first-person-to-plead-guilty-to-voter-fraud-conspiracy-in-2020-election/
[548] https://www.cisa.gov/uscert/ics/advisories/icsa-22-154-01

EPILOGUE

DHS via the EI-ISAC, CISA, and the EIP, undertook not only a censorship campaign that interfered with the 2020 Presidential Election, they also undertook a misinformation campaign of their own, that directly affected its outcome. This declaration is soundly presented, as previously cited in chapter fifteen, a poll conducted of 1,335 adults in early August 2022 by New Jersey based Technometrica Institute of Policy and Politics, clearly demonstrated that the suppression of the factual evidence surrounding the Hunter Biden laptop had a significant impact on voters, and quite potentially, ultimately, the outcome of the 2020 Presidential Election. [549]

Beyond the blatant targeting and actions taken against one political ideology over another by the DHS, the governing authority over elections, was the shocking revelation that the EIP's participants in this public-private pre- and post-election operation "then got **rewarded with millions of federal dollars from the Biden administration** afterwards..."[550] In the September 30, 2022 *Just The News* article from which this statement was quoted, authors Greg Piper and John Solomon specified the amount of money that made up these payments of federal funds and to whom they were directed:

> "The partners all received federal grants from the Biden administration in the next two years.
>
> The National Science Foundation awarded the Stanford and UW projects $3 million in August 2021 'to study ways to apply collaborative, rapid-response research to mitigate online disinformation.'

---

[549] https://tippinsights.com/shock-poll-8-in-10-think-biden-laptop-cover-up-changed-election/

[550] https://justthenews.com/government/federal-agencies/biden-administration-rewarded-private-entities-got-2020-election

Countdown to Chaos

UW's press release about the award noted their earlier work on the partnership and praise for the report from ex-CISA director Krebs, who called it 'the seminal report on what happened in 2020, not just the election but also through January 6.'

Graphika, also known as Octant Data, received its first listed federal grant several weeks after the 2020 election: nearly $3 million from the Department of Defense for unspecified 'research on cross-platform detection to counter malign influence.' Nearly $2 million more followed in fall 2021 for 'research on co-citation network mapping,' which tracks sources that are cited together.

The Atlantic Council, which hosted then-Vice President Joe Biden for a keynote address at its 2011 awards dinner, has received $4.7 million in grants since 2021, all but one from the State Department. That far exceeds the think tank's federal haul in previous years, which hadn't approached $1 million in a single year since 2011.

Those figures don't include the federal contracts for each partnership member. Graphika/Octant, for example, received nearly $100,000 in 2021 for its 'Contagion Monitor' surveillance and services that use 'advanced network science to analyze PRC [Chinese] influence.'" [551]

The information reported upon by Piper and Solomon enumerated $12.7 million in federal funds handed by the Biden administration to the participants of the EIP/DHS partnership to undertake what the DHS later tried to build as the Misinformation Governance Board. The evidence presented by Piper and Solomon supported

---

[551] https://justthenews.com/government/federal-agencies/biden-administration-rewarded-private-entities-got-2020-election

EPILOGUE

that the payments of federal funds were made to entities as a direct "reward" for their participation in the quiet suppression of political speech. Their story pointed out that the University of Washington issued a press release[552] directly referring to their $2.25 million portion of the award received as a result of their EIP election work. The UW press release then also directly referenced the EIP report titled "The Long Fuse: Misinformation and the 2020 Election," highlighted in the preceding pages. Clearly the facts reported by Piper and Solomon strongly support that the $12.7 million dollars paid to the EIP consortium was, as some of those named in its reports are alleging, a political payment in-kind for the influence of the 2020 Presidential Election at minimum, and at worst a payment for "services rendered" that affected the outcome of the 2020 Presidential Election. Either of these conclusions deduced concerning the use of the federal funds is not only illegal, but also incredibly alarming. According to evidence here presented, federal taxpayer dollars were used by the administration that *benefited directly* from the actions of the Election Integrity Partnership as a type of reward for their success. The article by Piper and Solomon notes that the EIP structure is galvanized, ready, and in place for the 2022 midterm elections.

In light of the direct responsibility the EI-ISAC had in the EIP operation, the reader might recall how ISACS are organized. Each ISAC is governed independently by a self-appointed council. One word that keeps haunting the author of this report after the year-long research into the contents herein presented is the term "soviet." The reader might remember a quick reference to the word in chapter ten about the EI-SCC (The Election Integrity Sector Coordinating Council), the governing authority of the EI-ISAC. A literal English translation of the term "soviet" is "council." Over the past two decades, the DHS has created a vast network of ISACs,

---

[552] https://ischool.uw.edu/news/2021/08/225-million-nsf-funding-will-support-center-informed-public-research

Countdown to Chaos

each governed by its own sector coordinating council. Former President Barack Obama created this structure via Executive Order 13636:

> "The cyber threat to critical infrastructure continues to grow and represents one of the most serious national security challenges we must confront. The national and economic security of the United States depends on the reliable functioning of the Nation's critical infrastructure in the face of such threats. It is the policy of the United States to enhance the security and resilience of the Nation's critical infrastructure and to maintain a cyber environment that encourages efficiency, innovation, and economic prosperity while promoting safety, security, business confidentiality, privacy, and civil liberties. **We can achieve these goals through a partnership with the owners and operators of critical infrastructure to improve cybersecurity information sharing** and collaboratively develop and implement risk-based standards."[553]

With the facts and definitions here reported, a sound argument can be made that the only soviet union, alive and functioning on earth in the years since the fall of the Russian Soviet Union resides, in all places, but within the United States of America through the countless councils that now govern all sectors of "critical infrastructure," to include American elections. If the United States of America is now the only home of a soviet union, then Barack Obama was its architect. Certainly, this is an issue of semantics and open for debate, but due to one side of the political divide being obsessed with definitions, this argument is definitely interesting when considering the architectural source of the

---

[553] https://www.federalregister.gov/documents/2013/02/19/2013-03915/improving-critical-infrastructure-cybersecurity

EPILOGUE

structure, and how it has now permeated the American election system.

In the end, the author climbed in bed late on the night of October 3, 2022 with this realization: The Department of Homeland Security, the governing authority over American elections, engaged in a public-private partnership using the EI-ISAC, CISA, and the EIP, both ahead of and following the 2020 Presidential Election. The actions of the DHS were isolated nearly entirely on one party and party's candidate. The target of the DHS actions was the loser of the 2020 Presidential Election. The beneficiary of the actions of the DHS, the governing authority over American elections, was the candidate that prevailed in the race. The administration of the prevailing candidate, the next President of the United States, awarded the operatives of the actions via the DHS with millions and millions of dollars sourced from the federal government and taxpayer money.

The party affiliations in the above statements were removed intentionally to let the reader understand that it doesn't matter which party one aligns with, the actions outlined in the summary above by the author are not only wrong, but they are also likely incredibly illegal, and finally, in terms of election management, grossly unconstitutional.

The events didn't end the evening of October 3 for the author, or for the United States of America. On October 7, 2022, the federal government continued to move forward with the galvanization of yet another piece of the massive federal cybernetwork which included the election system. On this Friday, **one month before the 2022 midterm election**, the White House had the President sign and publicize yet another executive order. This order, too new to have been assigned its Federal Register number (but likely to bear the number 14086), was named "Executive Order On Enhancing Safeguards For United States Signals Intelligence

Countdown to Chaos

Activities."[554] The National Security Agency (NSA) defines signals intelligence (SIGINT) as "intelligence derived from electronic signals and systems used by foreign targets, such as communications systems, radars, and weapons systems that provides a vital window for our nation into foreign adversaries' capabilities, actions, and intentions."[555] The executive order signed by President Biden on October 7, 2022 was written with a general directive of establishing "safeguards for such signals intelligence activities." However, a few key components were nestled within the many lines of the order. What this order did, in essence, was give the President of the United States and the Executive Branch the ability to authorize instant changes to United States Signal Intelligence Activities, otherwise referred to or known as electronic spying.

While the EO states "Signals intelligence activities shall be subjected to rigorous oversight in order to ensure that they comport with the principles identified..." and, that "Signals intelligence collection activities shall be conducted in pursuit of legitimate objectives," the document also prominently declares:

> "The President may authorize updates to the list of objectives in light of new national security imperatives, such as new or heightened threats to the national security of the United States, for which the President determines that signals intelligence collection activities may be used. The Director of National Intelligence (Director) shall publicly release any updates to the list of objectives authorized by the President, unless the

---

[554] https://www.whitehouse.gov/briefing-room/presidential-actions/2022/10/07/executive-order-on-enhancing-safeguards-for-united-states-signals-intelligence-activities/
[555] https://www.nsa.gov/Signals-Intelligence/Overview/

EPILOGUE

President determines that doing so would pose a risk to the national security of the United States." [556]

At the very end of a long list of authorized and arguably highly noble objectives that included assessment of foreign militaries, international terrorist organizations, the taking and holding of hostages, espionage, sabotage, and assassination, appeared the following:

> "(11) protecting the integrity of elections and political processes, government property, and United States infrastructure (both physical and electronic) from activities conducted by, on behalf of, or with the assistance of a foreign government, foreign organization, or foreign person; and
>
> (12) advancing collection or operational capabilities or activities in order to further a legitimate objective identified in subsection (b)(i) of this section." [557]

The reader should review the historical trail of executive orders presented throughout this report but concentrated in chapter nine. The Obama era executive orders and one Trump executive order (the only Trump era executive order kept in place by the Biden administration), laid the platform for the intelligence community to "monitor" elections as part of critical infrastructure with a declaration of a state of emergency regarding the threat of foreign interference in an election. The Biden executive order signed on October 7, 2022, in the perspective of elections, appeared to shift the directive of the intelligence community from one of

---

[556] https://www.whitehouse.gov/briefing-room/presidential-actions/2022/10/07/executive-order-on-enhancing-safeguards-for-united-states-signals-intelligence-activities/

[557] https://www.whitehouse.gov/briefing-room/presidential-actions/2022/10/07/executive-order-on-enhancing-safeguards-for-united-states-signals-intelligence-activities/

Countdown to Chaos

"monitoring" elections to one of signal intelligence (SIGINT) collection, including bulk collection of signals intelligence.

The significance of this executive order within the framework of the others highlighted in this report created a better understanding as to why the federal government needed to continually push a Russian collusion narrative in context with both candidate and President Donald Trump. The federal government and the intelligence community appeared to have wanted and needed a foreign adversary target somewhere near the election system to install an election system controlled and monitored at the federal level by select federal entities including the intelligence community.

This conclusion resurrects the story alluded to at the beginning of this epilogue about Konnech, Inc. Executive Eugene Yu. Just three days prior to Biden's executive order regarding signal intelligence collection, on October 4, 2022, Eugene Yu was arrested in Michigan for extradition to Los Angeles County, California on charges of "Embezzlement of Public Funds."[558] The company Konnech, Inc. owns and runs software named Poll Chief® that is widely used in the administration of elections in multiple states throughout the United States.[559] The greatest curiosity about this arrest included that the details of the case were discovered by *True The Vote* investigators Catherine Englebrecht and Gregg Phillips who attempted to involve the FBI in their findings in the months preceding Yu's arrest.[560] Both news stories as well as Phillips and Englebrecht contend the FBI was neither interested or involved in apprehension and arrest of Yu. Evidence shows the case is being

---

[558] https://www.documentcloud.org/documents/23119267-skm_454e22100511220
[559] https://www.konnech.com/Election-Worker-Management.html
[560] https://www.truethevote.org/statement-regarding-arrest-konnech-ceo-eugene-yu/

EPILOGUE

handled by Los Angeles District Attorney George Gascon,[561] while the initial arrest, arraignment and extradition were handled by Michigan's 55th Judicial District Court.[562] Whether this case is state or federal, the arrest in Michigan and the jurisdiction having landed in Los Angeles County are both very interesting. The facts of the case have not been completely divulged, but what is known is that Konnech, Inc. has been accused of storing American election workers' data on servers in China. Whether this is proven or not, the question that arises from this incident is this: Did the Chinese ownership of Konnech, Inc. in addition to its wide use within the American election infrastructure create a necessary opportunity for the federal government and intelligence community to roll out President Biden's October 7th executive order one month prior to the 2022 midterm election? Certainly, only a congressional level investigation would ever uncover the information necessary to answer that question. However, timelines unlocked everything presented in this report, and the timing and details surrounding both the arrest of Konnech, Inc. CEO Eugene Yu and the contents and release date of the executive order titled "Executive Order on Enhancing Safeguards For United States Signals Intelligence Activities" are very oddly intertwined, and quite frankly deeply troubling in context with the evidence that the American election system is now governed and run by the Department of Homeland Security, and the Executive Branch of the federal government.

This report will neither say nor conclude that the Biden executive order of October 7, 2022 allows federal agents or agencies to spy directly on election data. However, the historical facts cannot be ignored in consideration of the contents of the order. These are the facts this report stands behind:

---

[561] https://www.npr.org/2022/10/05/1126881222/a-software-ceo-was-arrested-on-suspicion-of-storing-poll-worker-data-in-china
[562] https://www.documentcloud.org/documents/23119267-skm_454e22100511220

Countdown to Chaos

- In 2017 outgoing President Barack Obama via his Department of Homeland Security Secretary, Jeh Johnson, declared American elections part of the United States critical infrastructure.
- As critical infrastructure, the EI-SCC named the Executive Branch Department of Homeland Security the "governing authority" over U.S. elections.
- Executive Orders 13636, 13694, and 13757 created the environment to and made American Elections critical infrastructure. Executive Order 13878 further gave the intelligence community the ability to monitor elections.
- Federal officials from the DHS, FBI, NSA, and other agencies have actively participated in the monitoring of U.S. elections since 2018.
- The October 7, 2022 Executive Order signed by President Biden gave the intelligence community the ability to conduct signals intelligence activities, including bulk SIGINT, as the federal executive branch determines is necessary with respect to the American election system.
- Fusion centers are an activated node of the Homeland Security Information Network (HSIN) utilized to monitor elections and election data transfer.
- Fusion centers are staffed with state officials, state law enforcement, federal agency officials, federal intelligence officials, and others.
- Fusion centers have a history of domestic spying and abuse of data collection.
- Fusion centers have had circumstances in which data was illegally collected and used against political opponents.
- The CIA, NSA, and FBI set up a fusion center inside the CIA prior to the 2020 election to collect information about the Russian collusion narrative/theory. History has shown the Russia collusion narrative to be deeply false and intentionally fabricated.

EPILOGUE

- Fusion centers are an active point of collection of general SIGINT – signals intelligence (cyber data intelligence or spying.
- Neustar executive, Rodney Joffe, is under investigation for potentially having fabricated large amounts of data collected through SIGINT (signals intelligence bulk data collection).
- Rodney Joffe was an FBI Confidential Human Source (CHS) for a number of years, including during the time he has been accused of collecting and fabricating bulk data falsely attributed to and used against former President Donald Trump.
- Several FBI whistleblowers have come forward since the 2020 Presidential Election with alarming evidence of the politicization of the agency and abuse of its power for political purposes.
- The FBI has a recent history of spying upon U.S. citizens to intimidate their targets, and for political purposes.
- Past audits oversight of fusion centers and the federal digital security/monitoring system have shown both to have significant problems to include their ineffectiveness, their poor management, and their capabilities abused.
- The Department of Homeland Security, the governing authority over elections in the United States, set up the Election Integrity Partnership ahead of the 2020 Presidential Election to censor political speech and to control public messaging.
- The Election Integrity Partnership published a report that demonstrated a vast majority of its targets of monitoring and censorship comprised one political party and ideology.
- The FBI actively worked with social media and others to hide and all information about the Hunter Biden laptop they had in their possession, while peddling a narrative that the stories about it were Russian disinformation.

Countdown to Chaos

The distilled version of these facts is: the majority of the American election system is federalized, the powers in control of the election system are centralized, these powers lie exclusively in the Executive Branch of the federal government to include the Department of Homeland Security and the intelligence community, and the powers that control and govern the U.S. election system have demonstrated extreme abuses of power throughout their histories. The American Founders who drafted the Constitution warned of such an abject danger that could descend upon a constitutional republic.

With all these other facts that are known and have been presented about the federal government, the clear and present danger of what was authorized by the October 7, 2022 Biden executive order needs no further explanation. The American election system as orchestrated by Barack Obama's declaration of it as critical infrastructure has enslaved the entire system to the power of the executive order. It was overtaken by executive order, it was weaponized by executive order, and it is now forever able to be manipulated by the power of the executive branch of the federal government. Clearly, the centralization of power is dangerous and deadly to freedom and independence. The further use of centralized power for the administration of American elections could prove to be the beginning of the end for constitutional, free, fair, and completely transparent, fully auditable elections.

Is America now a "little soviet union"? Is our Constitutionally based system of free, transparent, and fair elections to determine the consent of the governed now gone? Has the federal government stolen not just AN election from us, but has it stolen the entire election system from us? Is it too late to return the election system to We The People? Can there literally be any question that with the involvement of the DHS, FBI, CIA, CISA, and the DOJ in the current construct of the American election system demonstrated by this report, that the federal government, the literary feared "big

EPILOGUE

brother", has hijacked not only political speech but the entire election process? Will we continue the fight for our right to vote in the face of Alinsky-style name calling as we, the warriors on this front, are continually labeled "election deniers" and "conspiracy theorists" by media, government, and academia? Will we find a Constitutional legal warrior or army to fight for our Constitutionally guaranteed voting rights? Will we all educate ourselves and begin to fix the situation from the precinct level upward as was demonstrated and started by the three precincts in Washington state in 2022?

The author has sacrificed much in terms of job security and reputation during the past year with the work required to undertake the encompassing research and writing of this report. The time was uncompensated but done relentlessly as a personal investment for fellow Americans to do what little can be done by one person to not only return elections to the people for whom they were created to serve, but also to reinforce and rejuvenate the heart and soul of freedom that burns within Americans as we all face perhaps one of the most tumultuous presidential administrations in the history of this once free nation. It is the desire of the author that each American, regardless of race, creed, sex, or sexual orientation have their sacred legal vote count, for it to count without interference, and without cancellation by illegally cast, trafficked, or manipulated ballots. This is the time. We are the generation, many of us being the Reagan generation that grew up understanding that America is indeed The Shining City Upon the Hill. We are now charged to preserve it. God help us all, and God bless America.

Countdown to Chaos

BIBLIOGRAPHY

(In order of appearance within the report.)

INTRODUCTION

Loucks, Don. (January 30, 2019) "The Greatest News Media Fail Of All Time - The Nick Sandmann Case." *Austin American-Statesman*. (https://www.statesman.com/story/news/local/bastrop/2019/01/31/commentary-greatest-news-media-fail-of-all-time-nick-sandmann-case/6152565007/)

The White House. (May 22, 1998) "Presidential Decision Directive/NSC-63." President Bill Clinton. Public Domain. (https://irp.fas.org/offdocs/pdd/pdd-63.pdf)

The National Council of ISACs. (©2020) "Member ISACs." *National Council of ISACs*. (https://www.nationalisacs.org/member-isacs-3)

Chapter 1 - DECENTRALIZED ELECTION HISTORY AND SECURITY

Hamilton, Alexander. (February 26, 1788). Federalist No. 61: The Same Subject Continued: Concerning the Power of Congress to Regulate the Election of Members. *The New York Packet*. (https://guides.loc.gov/federalist-papers/text-61-70)

Morley, Michael T. and Tolson, Franita. (©2022) Common Interpretation Elections Clause. *Constitutioncenter.org*.

Countdown to Chaos
(https://constitutioncenter.org/interactive-constitution/interpretation/article-i/clauses/750)

U.S. Election Assistance Commission. (March 20, 2007). U.S. Constitutional Provisions on Elections. *EAC.gov*.(https://www.eac.gov/sites/default/files/eac_assets/1/1/U.S.%20Constitutional%20Provisions%20on%20Elections.pdf)

Constitution of the United States – Tenth Amendment. *Constitution.congress.gov*. (https://constitution.congress.gov/constitution/amendment-10/)

Olson, Walter. (December 3, 2020). "The Framers Wisely Left Election Practice Decentralized." *Cato Institute*. (https://www.cato.org/blog/framers-wisely-left-election-practice-decentralized)

Landsburg, Steve. (November 11, 2020). "Want a Coup? Abolish The Electoral College." *The Wall Street Journal*. (https://www.wsj.com/articles/want-a-coup-abolish-the-electoral-college-11605134162)

BIBLIOGRAPHY
Chapter 2 – A BRIEF HISTORY OF ISACs

Information Technology Information Sharing and Analysis Center. (©2021). 20th Anniversary of the IT-ISAC. *IT-ISAC.org*. (https://www.it-isac.org/20th-anniversary)

Information Technology Information Sharing and Analysis Center. (©2021). About Us. *IT-ISAC.org*. (https://www.it-isac.org/about)

Information Technology Information Sharing and Analysis Center. (2021). 2021 Membership Brochure. *IT-ISAC.org*. (https://130760d6-684a-52ca-5172-0ea1f4aeebc3.filesusr.com/ugd/b8fa6c_181a8bf980554d6aad98607495f3448b.pdf)

Perl, Raphael, Congressional Research Service. (©2004). "The Department of Homeland Security: Background and Challenges." Terrorism: Reducing Vulnerabilities and Improving Responses. *The National Academies Press*. (https://www.nap.edu/read/10968/chapter/24)

107th Congress. (November 19, 2002). Homeland Security Act of 2002 (H.R. 5005). *Congress.gov*. (https://www.congress.gov/bill/107th-congress/house-bill/5005)

National Council of ISACs. (©2020). About NCI. *National Council of ISACs*. (https://www.nationalisacs.org/about-nci)

National Defense ISAC. (©2020). Partners. *National Defense ISAC*. (https://ndisac.org/partners/)

Magnotti, Ernie. (2021). Professional Resume. *Linkedin.com*. (https://www.linkedin.com/in/erniemagnotti/)

Countdown to Chaos

Chapter 3 – THE EVOLUTION OF THE DHS CYBER PROGRAMS (EINSTEIN) (2000-2004)

U.S. Department of Homeland Security, Hugo Teufel, III, Reviewing Official. (May 19, 2008). "Privacy Impact Assessment for EINSTEIN 2." *DHS.gov* (https://www.dhs.gov/sites/default/files/publications/privacy-pia-nppd-einstein2-june2013-3-year-review_0.pdf)

Oree, William L. (March, 2013). "Analysis of the United States Computer Emergency Readiness Team's (U.S. CERT) Einstein III Intrusion Detection System, and its Impact on Privacy." *NPS Archive: Calhoun*. Dudley Knox Library/Naval Post Graduate School. (https://calhoun.nps.edu/bitstream/handle/10945/32877/13Mar_Oree_William.pdf?sequence=1)

Cybersecurity & Infrastructure Security Agency. (December 17, 2003). "Homeland Security Presidential Directive 7: Full text" *CISA.gov*. (https://www.cisa.gov/homeland-security-presidential-directive-7)

Chapter 4 - MS-ISAC, IT-SCC, AND US-CERT (2004 – 2006)

Subcommittee on Cybersecurity, Infrastructure Protection, & Innovation Committee on Homeland Security. (August 4, 2020). Testimony of John M. Gilligan - Center For Internet Security. *Homeland.house.gov*. (https://homeland.house.gov/imo/media/doc/Testimony%20-%20Gilligan.pdf)

Center For Internet Security. (2020). 20 Years of Creating Confidence in the Connected World. *Cisecurity.org*.

BIBLIOGRAPHY

(https://www.cisecurity.org/blog/20-years-of-creating-confidence-in-the-connected-world/)

Center For Internet Security. (August, 17, 2021). MS-ISAC® Charter. *Cisecurity.org.* (https://www.cisecurity.org/ms-isac/ms-isac-charter/)

MS-ISAC® Multi-State Information Sharing & Analysis Center®. (August 16, 2021). Services Guide. *Marc.org.* (https://www.marc.org/Government/Cybersecurity/assets/MS-ISAC_ServicesGuide_8-5x11_Print_v2.aspx)

Nolan, Andrew. (March 16, 2015). "Cybersecurity and Information Sharing: Legal Challenges and Solutions." *Congressional Research Service.* (https://sgp.fas.org/crs/intel/R43941.pdf)

Information Technology Sector Coordinating Council. (January 27, 2006). "Bylaws of Information Technology Sector Coordinating Council." *IT-SCC.org.* (https://www.it-scc.org/uploads/4/7/2/3/47232717/it_scc_bylaws_update_final_030817.pdf)

Information Technology Sector Coordinating Council. (Accessed January 26, 2022) Current Members. *IT-SCC.org.* (https://www.it-scc.org/current-members.html)

Chapter 5 - US-CERT, EINSTEIN 2, AND EINSTEIN 3 PILOT (2006 – 2010)

Department of Homeland Security. (September 2004). Privacy Impact Assessment – EINSTEIN Program. "Collecting, Analyzing, and Sharing Computer Security Information Across the Federal Civilian Government." Department of Homeland Security National Cyber Security Division,

Countdown to Chaos

United States Computer Emergency Readiness Team (US-CERT). *DHS.gov*. (https://www.dhs.gov/xlibrary/assets/privacy/privacy_pia_eisntein.pdf)

U.S. Code. (2004). 6 U.S. Code § 485 - Information Sharing. (From Intelligence Reform and Terrorism Prevention Act of 2004 & National Security Intelligence Reform Act of 2004). *Cornell Law School*. (https://www.law.cornell.edu/uscode/text/6/485)

Department of Homeland Security. (April 19, 2013). "Privacy Impact Assessment for EINSTEIN 3 – Accelerated (E^3A)." *CISA.gov*. (https://www.cisa.gov/sites/default/files/publications/PIA%20NPPD%20E3A%2020130419%20FINAL%20signed-%20508%20compliant.pdf)

Department of Homeland Security. (May 19, 2008). "Privacy Impact Assessment for EINSTEIN 2." *DHS.gov*. (https://www.dhs.gov/sites/default/files/publications/privacy-pia-nppd-einstein2-june2013-3-year-review_0.pdf)

Bolduan, Kate. (March 22, 2008). "Chief of Firm Involved in Breach is Obama Adviser." *CNN Politics*. (https://www.cnn.com/2008/POLITICS/03/22/passport.files/index.html)

INSA. (Accessed 2021). "Who We Are – The Intelligence and National Security Alliance." *INSA*. (https://www.insaonline.org/about/)

Brennan, John. (July 15, 2007). "Intelligence to Meet the Challenges of the 21st Century." *Wikileaks.org*. (https://wikileaks.org/cia-emails/Draft-Intel-Position-Paper/Draft-Intel-Position-Paper.pdf).

BIBLIOGRAPHY

INSA. (2017). "Critical Issues for Cyber Assurance Policy Reform – An Industry Assessment." *INSA*. (https://www.insaonline.org/wp-content/uploads/2017/04/INSA_CritialIssuesCyber_WP-1.pdf)

Algeier, Scott. (July 8, 2019). "ISACs: Beyond Information Sharing and Analysis." *IT-ISAC.org*. (https://www.it-isac.org/post/isacs-beyond-information-sharing)

The White House. (2009). "Cyberspace Policy Review – Assuring a Trusted and Resilient Information and Communications Infrastructure." *Webarchive.org*. (https://web.archive.org/web/20110424173823/http:/www.whitehouse.gov/assets/documents/Cyberspace_Policy_Review_final.pdf)

Mills, Col. John. (2021). John Mills Senior Fellow. Center For Security Policy. (https://centerforsecuritypolicy.org/author/john-mills/)

Center For Internet Security. (2020). 20 Years of Creating Confidence in the Connected World. *Cisecurity.org*. (https://www.cisecurity.org/blog/20-years-of-creating-confidence-in-the-connected-world/)

Department of Homeland Security. (March 18, 2010). "Privacy Impact Assessment for the Initiative Three Exercise." *DHS.gov*. (https://www.dhs.gov/sites/default/files/publications/privacy_pia_nppd_initiative3.pdf)

Chapter 6 - THE ALBERT SENSOR
Albert Monitoring Services

Countdown to Chaos

Slagg, Alexander. (November 4, 2019). "States Can Get an Election Security Assist from Albert Sensors." *StateTechMagazine.com* (https://statetechmagazine.com/article/2019/11/states-can-get-election-security-assist-albert-sensors)

Center For Internet Security. (©2022, Accessed 2021). "About Us." *Cisecurity.org* (https://www.cisecurity.org/about-us/)

Center For Internet Security. (February 2018). "A Handbook For Elections Infrastructure Security." *Center For Internet Security*. (https://www.cisecurity.org/wp-content/uploads/2018/02/CIS-Elections-eBook-15-Feb.pdf)

Center For Internet Security. (November 29, 2021). "Standard Terms And Conditions For Albert Monitoring & Management Services." *Center For Internet Security*. (https://www.cisecurity.org/terms-and-conditions-table-of-contents/cis-albert-network-monitoring-services/)

City of Jersey City. (June 10, 2020). "Resolution of the City of Jersey City, N.J. Res. 20-388" *Cityofjerseycity.civicweb.net* (https://cityofjerseycity.civicweb.net/document/27088)

Center For Internet Security. (©2022, Accessed 2021). "Albert Network Monitoring and Management." *Center For Internet Security*. (https://www.cisecurity.org/services/albert-network-monitoring/)

Bandura Cyber. (2020). "A Holistic Intelligence-Driven Approach to Protecting Election Systems and Government Networks." *Nass.org*. (https://www.nass.org/sites/default/files/2020-01/white-paper-bandura-cyber-nass-winter20.pdf)

BIBLIOGRAPHY

Oree, William L. (March, 2013). "Analysis of the United States Computer Emergency Readiness Team's (U.S. CERT) Einstein III Intrusion Detection System, and its Impact on Privacy." *NPS Archive: Calhoun*. Dudley Knox Library/Naval Post Graduate School. (https://calhoun.nps.edu/bitstream/handle/10945/32877/13Mar_Oree_William.pdf?sequence=1)

US-CERT. (June 13, 2004). "About Us." *Web.archive.org*. (https://web.archive.org/web/20080525134358/http:/www.us-cert.gov/aboutus.html#events)

Kagan, Mark (July 27, 2010). "Top Ten Government IT Security Vendors – Picking Security Companies to Stop Malicious Network Intruders." *Government Technology*. (https://www.govtech.com/pcio/top-ten-government-it-security-vendors.html)

Department of Homeland Security. (January 16, 2013). "Privacy Impact Assessment for the Enhanced Cybersecurity Services (ECS)." *Web.archive.org*. (https://web.archive.org/web/20161018125245/https:/www.dhs.gov/sites/default/files/publications/privacy_pia_28_nppd_ecs_jan2013.pdf)

The White House. (February 12, 2013). Executive Order 13636: "Improving Critical infrastructure Cybersecurity." *National Archives Federal Register*. (https://www.federalregister.gov/documents/2013/02/19/2013-03915/improving-critical-infrastructure-cybersecurity)

Department of Homeland Security. (November 30, 2015). "Privacy Impact Assessment for the Enhanced Cybersecurity Services (ECS)." *Web.archive.org*. (https://web.archive.org/web/20161018125255/https://w

ww.dhs.gov/sites/default/files/publications/privacy-pia-28-a-nppd-ecs-november2015.pdf)

Perry, Brandon. (March 4, 2015). "SolarWinds Orion Service – SQL Injection." *Exploit Database*. (https://www.exploit-db.com/exploits/36262)

Greenberg, Andy. (August 29, 2016). "Hack Brief: As FBI Warns Election Sites Got Hacked, All Eyes Are on Russia." *Wired*. (https://www.wired.com/2016/08/hack-brief-fbi-warns-election-sites-got-hacked-eyes-russia/)

Bing, Christopher. (August 16, 2018). "More U.S. States Deploy Technology to Track Election Hacking Attempts." *Reuters*. (https://www.reuters.com/article/us-usa-election-cyber/more-u-s-states-deploy-technology-to-track-election-hacking-attempts-idUSKBN1L11VD)

U.S. Election Assistance Commission. (2017). "Starting Point: U.S. Election Systems as Critical Infrastructure. *EAC.gov*. (https://www.eac.gov/sites/default/files/eac_assets/1/6/starting_point_us_election_systems_as_Critical_Infrastructure.pdf)

United States Senate: Permanent Subcommittee on Investigations, Homeland Security & Government Affairs Committee. (March 7, 2019). Testimony of John M. Gilligan – Chief Executive Officer, Center For Internet Security. *Hsgac.sentate.gov*. (https://www.hsgac.senate.gov/imo/media/doc/Gilligan%20Testimony.pdf)

LaRose, Frank. (June 11, 2019). "Directive 2019-08." *Ohiosos.gov*. (https://www.ohiosos.gov/globalassets/elections/directives/2019/dir2019-08.pdf?__cf_chl_jschl_tk__=.EO7cJjGOQOswf7QjcS_fZnY3mo8Eo7t4RknxEsD08Q-1643302430-0-gaNycGzNCD0)

BIBLIOGRAPHY

Center For Internet Security. (2020). "Year In Review." *Center For Internet Security*. (https://learn.cisecurity.org/CIS-YIR-2020)

United States Senate Select Committee on Intelligence. (July 25, 2019). "Russian Active Measures Campaigns and Interference in the 2016 U.S. Election, Volume 1: Russian Efforts Against Election Infrastructure with Additional Views." *Intelligence.senate.gov*. (https://www.intelligence.senate.gov/sites/default/files/documents/Report_Volume1.pdf)

Election Systems & Software. (August 23, 2018). "ES&S Establishes Top-Level Partnerships, Albert Installation To Further Security. *Cision PR Newswire*. (https://www.prnewswire.com/news-releases/ess-establishes-top-level-partnerships-albert-installation-to-further-security-300701631.html)

Hall, Susan. (January 23, 2017). "Phantom Coordinates Security Software for Playbook Automation." *Thenewstack*. (https://thenewstack.io/phantom-coordinates-security-software-playbook-operations/)

Center For Internet Security. (©2022, Accessed 2021). "CIS Critical Security Controls v7.1." *Center For Internet Security*. (https://www.cisecurity.org/controls/v7/)

Center For Internet Security. (©2022, Accessed 2021). "Four States Join SOAR Cybersecurity Automation Pilot." *Center For Internet Security*. (https://www.cisecurity.org/media-mention/four-states-join-soar-cybersecurity-automation-pilot/)

IACD. (October, 2, 2018). "IACD Perspectives." *IACD* via *YouTube*. (https://www.youtube.com/watch?v=gQ29k-lq_l0&t=243s&ab_channel=IACD)

Countdown to Chaos

Center For Internet Security. (©2022, Accessed 2021). "Terms of Use for Non-Member CIS Products." *Center For Internet Security*. (https://www.cisecurity.org/terms-of-use-for-non-member-cis-products/)

Travers, Karen. (October 2019). "Collaborating at the Pace of Innovation: Securing 5G, Supply Chains, and the 2020 Elections." Palo Alto Networks Ignite. (https://youtu.be/e-DhumE2gaI)

CrowdStrike. (July 14, 2021). "Open Source Attribution for CrowdStrike Falcon as of July 14, 2021." *CrowdStrike*. (https://falcon.crowdstrike.com/login/open-source)

U.S. House of Representatives, Permanent Select Committee on Intelligence. (December 5, 2017). "Interview of: Shawn Henry." *Intelligence.house.gov*. (https://intelligence.house.gov/uploadedfiles/sh21.pdf)

Mills, Col. John. (2021). John Mills Senior Fellow. Center For Security Policy. https://spectrumgrp.com/john-mills/

Boyce, Paul. (July 2, 2008). "Army Activates Network Warfare Unit." U.S. Army. *Army.mil*. (https://www.army.mil/article/10569/army_activates_network_warfare_unit)

New America. (Accessed 2021). "Jen Easterly." *Newamerica.org*. (https://www.newamerica.org/our-people/jen-easterly/)

Harbinger, Jordan. (October 18, 2020). "Harri Hursti – The Cyber War on America's Elections." *The Jordan Harbinger Show*. (https://www.jordanharbinger.com/harri-hursti-the-cyber-war-on-americas-elections/)

Government Accountability Office. (January 2016) "INFORMATION SECURITY - DHS Needs to Enhance Capabilities, Improve Planning, and Support Greater Adoption of Its National

BIBLIOGRAPHY

Cybersecurity Protection System." *Gao.gov.* (https://www.gao.gov/assets/gao-16-294.pdf)

Parks, Miles. (August 28, 2022). "Some Republicans in Washington state cast a wary eye on an election security device." *NPR.org.* (https://www.npr.org/2022/08/28/1119692541/washington-state-albert-sensor-cybersecurity-election-security)

Chapter 7 - EINSTEIN 3A, The CIA, IT-ISAC, CROWDSTRIKE, THE BIRTH OF ELECTION RELATED EXECUTIVE ORDERS, AND THE CYBERSECURITY ACT OF 2015 (2013-2015)

Department of Homeland Security. (January 16, 2013). "Privacy Impact Assessment for the Enhanced Cybersecurity Services (ECS)." *Web.archive.org.* (https://web.archive.org/web/20161018125245/https://www.dhs.gov/sites/default/files/publications/privacy_pia_28_nppd_ecs_jan2013.pdf)

The White House. (February 12, 2013). "Improving Critical infrastructure Cybersecurity." *National Archives Federal Register.* (https://www.federalregister.gov/documents/2013/02/19/2013-03915/improving-critical-infrastructure-cybersecurity)

Madison, Lucy. (March 7, 2013). "Brennan Confirmed as CIA Director – But Not Without Drama." *CBS News.* (https://www.cbsnews.com/news/brennan-confirmed-as-cia-director-but-not-without-drama/)

Countdown to Chaos

Ray, Michael. (July 8, 2013). "Edward Snowden – American Intelligence Contractor." *Britannica*. (https://www.britannica.com/biography/Edward-Snowden)

Department of Homeland Security – Office of Inspector General. (March 2014) "Implementation Status of EINSTEIN 3 Accelerated. *OIG.dhs.gov*. (https://www.oig.dhs.gov/assets/Mgmt/2014/OIG_14-52_Mar14.pdf)

Lengell, Sean. (March 11, 2014). "Dianne Feinstein: CIA Spied on Senate Intelligence Committee." *Washington Examiner*. (https://www.washingtonexaminer.com/dianne-feinstein-cia-spied-on-senate-intelligence-committee)

O'Donnell, Kelly and The Associated Press. (July 31, 2014). "CIA Director Brennan Apologizes to Senate Leaders for Computer Hack." *NBC News*. (https://www.nbcnews.com/news/us-news/cia-director-brennan-apologizes-senate-leaders-computer-hack-n169706).

The White House. (February 12, 2015). "FACT SHEET: Executive Order Promoting Private Sector Cybersecurity Information Sharing." *Obamawhitehouse.archives.gov*. (https://obamawhitehouse.archives.gov/the-press-office/2015/02/12/fact-sheet-executive-order-promoting-private-sector-cybersecurity-inform)

The White House. (2009). "Cyberspace Policy Review – Assuring a Trusted and Resilient Information and Communications Infrastructure." *Webarchive.org*. (https://web.archive.org/web/20110424173823/http://www.whitehouse.gov/assets/documents/Cyberspace_Policy_Review_final.pdf)

BIBLIOGRAPHY

Perry, Brandon. (March 4, 2015). "SolarWinds Orion Service – SQL Injection." *Exploit Database*. (https://www.exploit-db.com/exploits/36262)

Lyngaas, Sean. (January 27, 2017). "DHS Adds Traffic Tool to Intrusion – Prevention Program." *FCW.com*. (https://fcw.com/security/2016/01/dhs-adds-traffic-tool-to-intrusion-prevention-program/221206/)

Ozment, Andy. (January 26, 2016). "DHS's Enhanced Cybersecurity Services Program Unveils New "Netflow" Service Offering." *Web.archive.org*. (https://web.archive.org/web/20160812172519/https://www.dhs.gov/blog/2016/01/26/dhs%E2%80%99s-enhanced-cybersecurity-services-program-unveils-new-%E2%80%9Cnetflow%E2%80%9D-service-offering)

Greenberg, Andy. (August 29, 2016). "Hack Brief: As FBI Warns Election Sites Got Hacked, All Eyes Are on Russia." *Wired*. (https://www.wired.com/2016/08/hack-brief-fbi-warns-election-sites-got-hacked-eyes-russia/)

Information Technology Information Sharing and Analysis Center. (©2021). 20th Anniversary of the IT-ISAC. *IT-ISAC.org*. (https://www.it-isac.org/20th-anniversary)

Global Cyber Alliance. (©2022). "Our History." *Globalcyberalliance.org*. (https://www.globalcyberalliance.org/our-history/)

The Department of Homeland Security and The Department of Justice. (October 2020). "Guidance to Assist Non-Federal Entities to Share Cyber Threat Indicators and Defensive Measures with Federal Entities Under the Cybersecurity Information Sharing Act of 2015). *CISA.gov*. (https://www.cisa.gov/sites/default/files/publications/Non-

Countdown to Chaos

Federal%20Entity%20Sharing%20Guidance%20under%20the%20Cybersecurity%20Information%20Sharing%20Act%20of%202015_1.pdf)

Cyber & Infrastructure Security Agency. (2015). "Automated Indicator Sharing." *CISA.gov*. (https://www.cisa.gov/ais)

Kaylman, Larry, Esq. (Klayman Law Group, P.A.). (June 5, 2017). "In The United States District Court For The District of Columbia: Compliant. Case 1:17-cv-01074-RJL" *Regmedia.co.uk*. (https://regmedia.co.uk/2017/06/08/01-main.pdf)

Chapter 8 - EINSTEIN 3, ALBERT MONITORING, AIS, CROWDSTRIKE, AND THE PRESIDENTIAL ELECTION (2016)

Stockman, Rachel. (February 2, 2016). "What Actually Happened in Iowa Caucus Alleged 'Voter Fraud' Video." *Law & Crime*. (https://lawandcrime.com/high-profile/what-actually-happened-in-iowa-caucus-alleged-voter-fraud-video/)

Sainato, Michael. (July 14, 2016). "California Calls Fraud: Demands DNC Investigation." *Observer*. (https://observer.com/2016/07/california-calls-fraud-demands-dnc-investigation/)

Government Accountability Office. (January 2016) "INFORMATION SECURITY - DHS Needs to Enhance Capabilities, Improve Planning, and Support Greater Adoption of Its National Cybersecurity Protection System." *Gao.gov*. (https://www.gao.gov/assets/gao-16-294.pdf)

BIBLIOGRAPHY

Ms. Smith (Pen name). (February 4, 2016). "DHS EINSTEIN Firewall Fails to Detect 94% of Threats, Doesn't Monitor Web Traffic." *CSOonline.com* (https://www.csoonline.com/article/3030028/dhs-einstein-firewall-fails-to-detect-94-of-threats-doesnt-monitor-web-traffic.html)

Information Technology Information Sharing and Analysis Center. (©2021). 20th Anniversary of the IT-ISAC. *IT-ISAC.org.* (https://www.it-isac.org/20th-anniversary)

World Economic Forum. (April 2016). "Global Agenda Council on Cybersecurity." *Weforum.org.* (https://www3.weforum.org/docs/GAC16_Cybersecurity_WhitePaper_.pdf)

Durham, John H. (April 15, 2022). "Memorandum in Opposition Re Sussmann Motion in Limine by USA." Scribd.com. (https://www.scribd.com/document/570091923/70-Memorandum-in-Opposition-Re-Sussmann-Motion-in-Limine-by-USA)

U.S. House of Representatives, Permanent Select Committee on Intelligence. (December 5, 2017). "Interview of: Shawn Henry." *Intelligence.house.gov.* (https://intelligence.house.gov/uploadedfiles/sh21.pdf)

Trend Micro Incorporated. (2022). "Hash Values." *Trendmicro.com.* (https://www.trendmicro.com/vinfo/us/security/definition/hash-values). Accessed July 7, 2022.

United Stated House of Representatives Permanent Select Committee on Intelligence. (August 30, 2017). "Interview of Yared Tamene Wolde-Yohannes." *DNI.gov* (https://www.dni.gov/files/HPSCI_Transcripts/Yareda_Tamene-MTR_Redacted.pdf)

Countdown to Chaos

Newell, Sean. (September 27, 2016). "Follow Up." Email to Michael Sussman from Sean Newell. *Documentcloud.org* (https://www.documentcloud.org/documents/22046130-dx-147_redacted)

Hawkins, Adrian. (September 30, 2016). "Re: Follow Up" Email to Michael Sussman, Sean Newell from Adrian Hawkins. *Documentcloud.org* (https://www.documentcloud.org/documents/22046130-dx-147_redacted)

United States Senate Select Committee on Intelligence. (July 25, 2019). "Russian Active Measures Campaigns and Interference in the 2016 U.S. Election, Volume 1: Russian Efforts Against Election Infrastructure with Additional Views." *Intelligence.senate.gov.* (https://www.intelligence.senate.gov/sites/default/files/documents/Report_Volume1.pdf)

Mills, Col. John. (April 8, 2022). "Ret Col John Mills Recaps How The False Narrative Linking President Trump To Russia Was Created and being Pressured to Sign Off On It." Worldviewradio.com. (https://frankspeech.com/video/ret-col-john-mills-recaps-how-false-narrative-linking-president-trump-russia-was-created-and)

DHS Press Office. (October 7, 2016). "Joint Statement from the Department of Homeland Security and Office of the Director of National Intelligence on Election Security." DHS.gov (https://www.dhs.gov/news/2016/10/07/joint-statement-department-homeland-security-and-office-director-national)

Weissert, Justin. (October 13, 2016). "Re: DNC/DCCC data." Email to Michael Sussman, Ryan McCombs from Justin Weissert. *Documentcloud.org*

BIBLIOGRAPHY

(https://www.documentcloud.org/documents/22046125-dx-152_redacted)

Carter, Adam. (October 2020). "Guccifer 2.0: Evidence Versus GRU Attribution." (http://g-2.space/guccifer2-evidence-versus-gru-attribution/) Accessed August 2022.

Johnson, Ron and Grassley, Charles E. (April 16, 2020). Senate Committee on Homeland Security and Government Affairs Letter to FBI Director Christopher Wray. *Hsgac.senate.gov*. (https://www.hsgac.senate.gov/imo/media/doc/2020-04-16%20RHJ-CEG%20to%20FBI%20(Crossfire%20Hurricane%20Intel%20Memos).pdf)

Durham, John H. September 16, 2021. "United States of America v. Michael A. Sussmann, Defendant." Criminal Case No. 21-cr-00582-CRC. United States District Court for the District of Columbia. *Justice.gov*. (https://www.justice.gov/sco/press-release/file/1433511/download)

Bing, Christopher. (August 16, 2018). "More U.S. States Deploy Technology to Track Election Hacking Attempts." *Reuters*. (https://www.reuters.com/article/us-usa-election-cyber/more-u-s-states-deploy-technology-to-track-election-hacking-attempts-idUSKBN1L11VD)

Chapter 9 – CROSSFIRE HURRICANE, CRITICAL INFRASTRUCTURE, SOLARWINDS, AND THE GCC (2016 – 2017)

Friedman, George. (March 16, 2017). "The Deep State Is A Very Real Thing." *Huffpost.com*.

Countdown to Chaos

(https://www.huffpost.com/entry/the-deep-state_b_58c94a64e4b01d0d473bcfa3)

The Associated Press. (December 7, 2016). "Why Donald Trump's NSA Pick Is Scaring Some National Security Experts." *Fortune.com* (https://fortune.com/2016/12/07/donal-trump-michael-flynn-national-security-advisor/)

Homeland Security and Governmental Affairs Committee. (December 3, 2020). "Timeline of Key Events Related to Crossfire Hurricane Investigation." *Hsgac.senate.gov*. (https://www.hsgac.senate.gov/imo/media/doc/CFH%20Timeline%20w%20Updates%2020201203%20%28FINAL%29.pdf)

United States Senate Select Committee on Intelligence. (2019). "Russian Active Measures Campaigns and Interference in the 2016 U.S. Election, Volume 4: Review Of The Intelligence Community Assessment." *Intelligence.senate.gov*. (https://www.intelligence.senate.gov/sites/default/files/documents/Report_Volume4.pdf)

Greaney, Paul. (April 8, 2022). "DOD Green-Lighted Fake Trump-Russia Doc in 2016: Ret. Colonel John Mills." *Fresh Look America. The Epoch Times*. (https://www.theepochtimes.com/dod-green-lighted-fake-trump-russia-doc-in-2015-ret-colonel-john-mills_4693981.html)

The White House. (December 28, 2016). Executive Order 13757: "Taking Additional Steps to Address the National Emergency With Respect to Significant Malicious Cyber-Enabled Activities." *National Archives Federal Register*. (https://www.federalregister.gov/documents/2017/01/03

BIBLIOGRAPHY

/2016-31922/taking-additional-steps-to-address-the-national-emergency-with-respect-to-significant-malicious)

Johnson, Ron and Grassley, Charles E. (April 16, 2020). Senate Committee on Homeland Security and Government Affairs Letter to FBI Director Christopher Wray. *Hsgac.senate.gov.* (https://www.hsgac.senate.gov/imo/media/doc/2020-04-16%20RHJ-CEG%20to%20FBI%20(Crossfire%20Hurricane%20Intel%20Memos).pdf)

Director of National Intelligence. (December 29, 2016). "Joint DHS, ODNI, FBI Statement on Russian Malicious Cyber Activity." *DNI.gov.* (https://www.dni.gov/index.php/newsroom/press-releases/press-releases-2016/item/1616-joint-dhs-odni-fbi-statement-on-russian-malicious-cyber-activity)

U.S. House of Representatives, Permanent Select Committee on Intelligence. (December 5, 2017). "Interview of: Shawn Henry." *Intelligence.house.gov.* (https://intelligence.house.gov/uploadedfiles/sh21.pdf)

Pentchoukov, Ivan. (June 29, 2020). "Attorney General Says New Strzok Notes Described Obama White House Meeting." *The Epoch Times.* (https://www.theepochtimes.com/attorney-general-says-new-strzok-notes-described-obama-white-house-meeting_3404650.html)

Schleifer, Theodore; Walsh, Deirdre; Barrett, Ted. (January 6, 2017). "Trump Electoral College Win Certified Despite Democratic Objections." *CNN.com.* (https://www.cnn.com/2017/01/06/politics/electoral-college-vote-objections/index.html)

Countdown to Chaos

Johnson, Jeh Charles. (2017). Memorandum For Suzanne Spaulding, Under Secretary for National Protection and Programs Directorate. "Designation of Election Infrastructure as a Subsector of the Government Facilities Critical Infrastructure." *Epic.org*. (https://epic.org/wp-content/uploads/foia/dhs/cybersecurity/russian-interference/EPIC-17-03-31-DHS-FOIA-20191113-CISA-Production-Reprocessed.pdf)

U.S. Election Assistance Commission. (2017). "Starting Point: U.S. Election Systems as Critical Infrastructure. *EAC.gov*. (https://www.eac.gov/sites/default/files/eac_assets/1/6/starting_point_us_election_systems_as_Critical_Infrastructure.pdf)

United States Senate Select Committee on Intelligence. (July 25, 2019). "Russian Active Measures Campaigns and Interference in the 2016 U.S. Election, Volume 1: Russian Efforts Against Election Infrastructure with Additional Views." *Intelligence.senate.gov*. (https://www.intelligence.senate.gov/sites/default/files/documents/Report_Volume1.pdf)

Hanson, Victor Davis. (October 1, 2013). "Obama: Transforming America." *Real Clear Politics*. (https://www.realclearpolitics.com/articles/2013/10/01/obama_transforming_america_120170.html)

Reid, Paula. (May 7, 2017). "Robert Mueller Appointed Special Counsel." *CBS News*. (https://www.cbsnews.com/news/doj-appoints-special-counsel-in-wake-of-comey-developments/)

Sherwin, Michael R., Atty. (September 24, 2020). "United States of America v. Michael T. Flynn, Defendant." Criminal Case No. 17-232 (EGS). United States District Court for the District

BIBLIOGRAPHY

of Columbia. *Storage.courtlistener.com.* (https://storage.courtlistener.com/recap/gov.uscourts.dcd.191592/gov.uscourts.dcd.191592.249.0.pdf)

Department of Homeland Security. (January 18, 2018). "EIS Communique – Sharing Election Infrastructure News and Resources." *CISA.gov.* (https://www.cisa.gov/sites/default/files/publications/Issue%201%20Communique_0.PDF)

Homeland Security Intelligence Council, Intelligence and National Security Alliance. (November 2016). "Protecting The Homeland: Intelligence Integration 15 Year after 9/11." *INSA.* (https://www.insaonline.org/wp-content/uploads/2017/04/INSA_WP_ProtectHomeland.pdf)

Perez, Evan; Sciutto, Jim; Tapper, Jake. (January 12, 2017). "Intel Chiefs Presented Trump With Claims of Russian Efforts To Compromise Him." *CNN Politics.* (https://edition.cnn.com/2017/01/10/politics/donald-trump-intelligence-report-russia/index.html)

MSNBC. (August 17, 2018). "John O. Brennan: I Gave Trump A Year To Live Up To The Office. Hid Didn't." *Youtube.com* (https://www.youtube.com/watch?v=UV7-ZdDGijY&t=1170s)

Kaylman, Larry, Esq. (Klayman Law Group, P.A.). (June 5, 2017). "In The United States District Court For The District of Columbia: Compliant. Case 1:17-cv-01074-RJL" *Regmedia.co.uk.* (https://regmedia.co.uk/2017/06/08/01-main.pdf)

Office of the Inspector General U.S. Department of Justice. (December 2019). "Review of Four FISA Applications and Other Aspectes of the FBI's Crossfire Hurricane

Countdown to Chaos

Investigation." *Justice.gov* (https://www.justice.gov/storage/120919-examination.pdf)

Readler, Chad A.; D'Alessio Jr., C. Salvatore; Whitman, James R. (September 13, 2017). "In The United States District Court for the District of Columbia. Civil Action No. 1:17-cv-1074-RJL. Memorandum in Support of Individual-Capacity Defendants' Motion to Dismiss." *Us.archive.org*. (https://ia800807.us.archive.org/34/items/gov.uscourts.dcd.187032/gov.uscourts.dcd.187032.36.1.pdf)

Gallagher, Ryan. (December 22, 2020). "SolarWinds Adviser Warned of Lax Security Years Before Hack." Bloombergquint.com. (https://www.bloombergquint.com/business/solarwinds-adviser-warned-of-lax-security-years-before-hack)

National Association of State Election Directors. (March 16, 2018). "An Open Letter to American Voters From the Executive Committee of the Government Coordinating Council." *NASED.org*. (https://www.nased.org/news/2018/4/16/an-open-letter-to-american-voters-from-the-executive-committee-of-the-government-coordinating-council)

U.S. Election Assistance Commission. (©2022. Accessed 2021). "Elections Government Sector Coordinating Council Established, Charter Adopted. *EAC.gov*. (https://www.eac.gov/news/2017/10/14/elections-government-sector-coordinating-council-established-charter-adopted)

Cybersecurity & Infrastructure Security Agency. (October 2, 2018). "DHS Holds Classified Briefing For Private Sector Election Companies." *Fbcoverup.com*. (https://www.fbcoverup.com/docs/library/2018-10-02-

BIBLIOGRAPHY

DHS-HOLDS-CLASSIFIED-BRIEFING-FOR-PRIVATE-SECTOR-ELECTION-COMPANIES-incl-Dominion-ESS-Scytl-Smartmatic-Press-Release-Natnl-Protectn-and-Progs-Directorate-CISA-Oct-02-2021.pdf)

Chapter 10 EI-SCC, EI-ISAC, IT-ISAC, EXECUTIVE ORDER 13848, HELP AMERICA VOTE ACT, CISA CYBERSECURITY SUMMIT, SOLARWINDS (2018-2019)

U.S. Election Assistance Commission. (©2022. Accessed 2021). "Elections Government Sector Coordinating Council Established, Charter Adopted. *EAC.gov*. (https://www.eac.gov/news/2017/10/14/elections-government-sector-coordinating-council-established-charter-adopted)

The Free Dictionary [Internet]. (2003-2022). "soviet". The Columbia Electronic Encyclopedia®, *Columbia University Press*, 2013 [cited 30 Jan. 2022]. (https://encyclopedia2.thefreedictionary.com/soviet)

Election Infrastructure Subsector Coordinating Council. (February 15, 2018). "Election Infrastructure Subsector Coordinating Council Charter Version 1.0." *CISA.gov*. (https://www.cisa.gov/sites/default/files/publications/govt-facilities%20-EIS-scc-charter-2018-508.pdf)

Center For Internet Security. (February 2019. Updated January 2020). "EI-ISAC Charter." *Cisecurity.org*. (https://www.cisecurity.org/ei-isac/ei-isac-charter/)

Countdown to Chaos

U.S. Code. (2004). 6 U.S. Code § 485 - Information Sharing. (From Intelligence Reform and Terrorism Prevention Act of 2004 & National Security Intelligence Reform Act of 2004). *Cornell Law School*. (https://www.law.cornell.edu/uscode/text/6/485)

Department of Homeland Security. (June 21, 2021). "HSIN 2020 Annual Report: Delivering Mission Success." *DHS.gov* (https://www.dhs.gov/hsin-annual-report).

Center For Internet Security. (2018). "Elections Infrastructure ISAC – 2018 Year in Review." *Cisecurity.org*. (https://www.cisecurity.org/wp-content/uploads/2019/02/EI-ISAC-2018-YIR.pdf)

Homeland Security Intelligence Council, Intelligence and National Security Alliance. (November 2016). "Protecting The Homeland: Intelligence Integration 15 Year after 9/11." *INSA*. (https://www.insaonline.org/wp-content/uploads/2017/04/INSA_WP_ProtectHomeland.pdf)

International Association of Government Officials. (©2022. Accessed 2021). "Who We Are." *Iaogo.org* (https://iaogo.org/content.aspx?page_id=0&club_id=610929)

U.S. Election Assistance Commission. (March 30, 2018). "2018 HAVA Funds FAQS." *EAC.gov*. (https://www.eac.gov/payments-and-grants/2018-hava-funds-faqs)

United States Senate Select Committee on Intelligence. (July 25, 2019). "Russian Active Measures Campaigns and Interference in the 2016 U.S. Election, Volume 1: Russian Efforts Against Election Infrastructure with Additional Views." *Intelligence.senate.gov*.

BIBLIOGRAPHY

(https://www.intelligence.senate.gov/sites/default/files/documents/Report_Volume1.pdf)

IT-ISAC. (August 8, 2018) "IT-ISAC Partners with Elections Infrastructure Sector Coordinating Council to Launch Threat Information-Sharing Group." *IT-ISAC.org*. (https://130760d6-684a-52ca-5172-0ea1f4aeebc3.filesusr.com/ugd/b8fa6c_765f03ef0e584e7ca6819b41b7d16847.pdf)

The White House. (September 14, 2018). Executive Order 13848: "Imposing Certain Sanctions in the Event of Foreign Interference in a United States Election." *National Archives Federal Register*. (https://www.federalregister.gov/documents/2018/09/14/2018-20203/imposing-certain-sanctions-in-the-event-of-foreign-interference-in-a-united-states-election)

The Last Refuge. (September 8, 2021). "White House Extends National Election Emergency Granting Authority for Federal Intelligence Agencies to Enter State Election Databases for Mid-Term Election." *Theconservativetreehouse.com*. (https://theconservativetreehouse.com/blog/2021/09/08/white-house-extends-national-election-emergency-granting-authority-for-federal-intelligence-agencies-to-enter-state-election-databases-for-mid-term-election/)

Grayer, Annie. (April 19, 2018). "These Former Intel Professionals Are Running For Office to Check Trump." *CNN.com*. (https://www.cnn.com/2018/04/18/politics/intel-officers-running-against-trump-2018/index.html)

Cybersecurity & Infrastructure Security Agency. (2019). "2019 CISA Cybersecurity Summit." *CISA.gov*.

Countdown to Chaos

(https://www.cisa.gov/uscert/event/2019-cisa-cybersecurity-summit)

CISA. (September 18, 2019). "2nd Annual Cybersecurity Summit." *CISA.gov*. (https://www.cisa.gov/uscert/sites/default/files/2019-09/2019_Cybersecurity_Summit_Agenda_S508C_13.pdf)

MacGuill, Dan. (December 29, 2020). "Did A Dominion Voting Systems Employee Brag About Rigging the Election Against Trump?" *Snopes.com*. (https://www.snopes.com/fact-check/eric-coomer-dominion-trump/)

Weinberger, Sharon; Winter, Jana; De Bourmont, Martin. (March 30, 2020). "Suspected SARS Virus and Flue Samples Found in Luggage: FBI Report Describes China's 'Biosecurity Risk.'" *News.yahoo.com*. (https://news.yahoo.com/suspected-sars-virus-and-flu-found-in-luggage-fbi-report-describes-chinas-biosecurity-risk-144526820.html?guccounter=1)

National Public Radio. (April 16, 2021). "A 'Worst Nightmare' Cyberattack: The Untold Story Of The SolarWinds Hack." *NPR.org*. (https://www.npr.org/2021/04/16/985439655/a-worst-nightmare-cyberattack-the-untold-story-of-the-solarwinds-hack)

116th Congress. (December 20, 2019). "H.R. 1158 – Consolidated Appropriations Act, 2020." *Congress.gov*. (https://www.congress.gov/bill/116th-congress/house-bill/1158/text)

BIBLIOGRAPHY
Chapter 11 - EDR MONITORING BEYOND ALBERT, RABET-V PILOT SYSTEM, THE 2020 PRESIDENTIAL ELECTION, SOLARWINDS (2020)

Center For Internet Security. (February 22, 2021). "SLTT Endpoint Protection Platform (EPP) Program." *Cisecurity.org.* (https://www.cisecurity.org/wp-content/uploads/2021/02/2021-02-24-EPP-RFI-FINAL.pdf)

LaRose, Frank. (June 11, 2019). "Directive 2019-08." *Ohiosos.gov.* (https://www.ohiosos.gov/globalassets/elections/directives/2019/dir2019-08.pdf?_cf_chl_jschl_tk_=.EO7cJjGOQOswf7QjcS_fZnY3mo8Eo7t4RknxEsD08Q-1643302430-0-gaNycGzNCD0)

Government Accountability Office. (February 2020) "ELECTION SECURITY - DHS Plans Are Urgently Needed to Address Identified Challenges Before the 2020 Elections." *GAO.gov.* (https://www.gao.gov/assets/gao-20-267.pdf)

Department of Homeland Security. (February 12, 2020). "Privacy Impact Assessment for the Continuous Monitoring as a Service (CMaaS)." *DHS.gov.* (https://www.dhs.gov/sites/default/files/publications/privacy-pia-dhs082-cmaas-february2020.pdf)

Department of Homeland Security. (November 13, 2021). "Privacy." *DHS.gov.* (https://www.dhs.gov/topics/privacy)

National Public Radio. (April 16, 2021). "A 'Worst Nightmare' Cyberattack: The Untold Story Of The SolarWinds Hack." *NPR.org.* (https://www.npr.org/2021/04/16/985439655/a-worst-nightmare-cyberattack-the-untold-story-of-the-solarwinds-hack)

Countdown to Chaos

Crane, Emily. (December 21, 2020). "SolarWinds Was Warned THREE YEARS Ago That it Was Prone to a Cyberattack- as it's Revealed Russian Hackers Also Breached Major Tech and Accounting Firms, a Hospital System and a University." *DailyMail.com*. (https://www.dailymail.co.uk/news/article-9076045/SolarWinds-adviser-warned-cybersecurity-risks-2017-Russian-hack.html?ito=email_share_article-factbox)

Cisco Security. (June 3, 2020). "Cisco IOS XE Software Flexible NetFlow Version 9 Denial of Service Vulnerability." *CISCO.com*. (https://tools.cisco.com/security/center/content/CiscoSecurityAdvisory/cisco-sa-iosxe-fnfv9-dos-HND6Fc9u)

Center For Internet Security. (©2022, Accessed 2021). "Albert Network Monitoring and Management." *Center For Internet Security*. (https://www.cisecurity.org/services/albert-network-monitoring/)

United States House of Representatives. (August 4, 2020). "Testimony of John M. Gilligan, President and Chief Executive Officer, Center for Internet Security At the hearing entitled 'Secure Safe, and Auditable: Protecting the Integrity of the 2020.'" *Homeland.house.gov*. (https://homeland.house.gov/imo/media/doc/Testimony%20-%20Gilligan.pdf)

Center for Internet Security. (January 2021). "RABET-V Pilot Update and SolarWinds Mitigations." *NASS.org*. (https://www.nass.org/sites/default/files/2021-01/cis-white-paper-nass-winter21.pdf)

Brennan, John. (August 31, 2020). "Opinion: John Brennan: Trump Will Suffocate the Intelligence Community to Get

BIBLIOGRAPHY

Reelected." *The Washington Post.* (https://www.washingtonpost.com/opinions/2020/08/31/john-brennan-trump-national-intelligence-congress/)

Hart Intercivic. (September 28, 2020). "Election Technology Providers Urge Patience on Election Day." *Hartintercivic.com.* (https://www.hartintercivic.com/eisccelectiondaystatement/)

Dunleavy, Jerry. (May 10, 2021). "Ex-intel Officials Silent Over Letter Claiming Russian Involvement in Hunter Biden Laptop Saga." *Washington Examiner.* (https://www.washingtonexaminer.com/news/intel-officials-silent-letter-russian-involvement-hunter-biden-laptop-saga?utm_source=msn&utm_medium=referral&utm_campaign=msn_feed)

Brennan, John O. (October 7, 2020). Untitled. *Twitter.com* (https://twitter.com/JohnBrennan/status/1314034940321898498?ref_src=twsrc%5Etfw)

Niesse, Mark. (September 29, 2020). "State: Fix Coming to Georgia Touchscreens to Restore Missing Senate Candidates." *The Atlanta Journal-Constitution.* Retrieved on *Newspapers.com.* (https://www.newspapers.com/clip/63955060/coomer-pre-election-update-to-software/)

MIT Election Data and Science Lab. (April 28, 2021). "Voter Turnout." *Electionlab.mit.edu.* (https://electionlab.mit.edu/research/voter-turnout)

Center For Internet Security. (2020). "Year In Review." *Center For Internet Security.* (https://learn.cisecurity.org/CIS-YIR-2020)

Countdown to Chaos

Department of Homeland Security and The Department of Justice. (March 2021). "Key Findings and Recommendations From the Joint Report of the Department of Justice and the Department of Homeland Security on Foreign interference Targeting Election Infrastructure or Political Organization, Campaign, or Candidate Infrastructure Related to the 2020 US Federal Elections." *DHS.gov*. (https://www.dhs.gov/sites/default/files/publications/21_0311_key-findings-and-recommendations-related-to-2020-elections_1.pdf)

The Last Refuge. (September 8, 2021). "White House Extends National Election Emergency Granting Authority for Federal Intelligence Agencies to Enter State Election Databases for Mid-Term Election." *Theconservativetreehouse.com*. (https://theconservativetreehouse.com/blog/2021/09/08/white-house-extends-national-election-emergency-granting-authority-for-federal-intelligence-agencies-to-enter-state-election-databases-for-mid-term-election/)

Cybersecurity & Infrastructure Security Agency. (November 12, 2020). "Joint Statement From Elections Infrastructure Government Coordinating Council & The Election Infrastructure Sector Coordinating Executive Committees." *CISA.gov*. (https://www.cisa.gov/news/2020/11/12/joint-statement-elections-infrastructure-government-coordinating-council-election)

Election Infrastructure Subsector Coordinating Council. (February 15, 2018). "Election Infrastructure Subsector Coordinating Council Charter Version 1.0." *CISA.gov*. (https://www.cisa.gov/sites/default/files/publications/govt-facilities%20-EIS-scc-charter-2018-508.pdf)

BIBLIOGRAPHY

Johnson, Ron and Grassley, Charles E. (April 16, 2020). Senate Committee on Homeland Security and Government Affairs Letter to FBI Director Christopher Wray. *Hsgac.senate.gov*. (https://www.hsgac.senate.gov/imo/media/doc/2020-04-16%20RHJ-CEG%20to%20FBI%20(Crossfire%20Hurricane%20Intel%20Memos).pdf)

Stilgherrian. (April 11, 2018). "Blaming Russian for NotPetya was Coordinated Diplomatic Action." *ZDNet.com*. (https://www.zdnet.com/article/blaming-russia-for-notpetya-was-coordinated-diplomatic-action/)

Carlson, Jeff. (November 16, 2020). "Dominion Part of Council That Disputed Election Integrity Concerns in DHS Statement." *The Epoch Times*. (https://www.theepochtimes.com/dominion-part-of-council-that-disputed-election-integrity-concerns-in-dhs-statement_3581659.html?utm_source=newsnoe&utm_medium=email&utm_campaign=breaking-2020-11-16-5)

Chapter 12 - TIME OUT TO FOCUS ON: NATIONAL FUSION CENTERS (2001 - present)

Center For Internet Security. (2018). "Elections Infrastructure ISAC – 2018 Year in Review." *Cisecurity.org*. (https://www.cisecurity.org/wp-content/uploads/2019/02/EI-ISAC-2018-YIR.pdf)

Terrorism Research Center, Inc. (©2012. Accessed 2021). "Historic Projects." *Terrorism Research Center*. (https://www.terrorism.org/historic-projects/)

Countdown to Chaos

110th Congress of the United States. (August 3, 2007). "Public Law 110-53. Implementing Recommendations of the 9/11 Commission Act of 2007." *Congress.gov*. (https://www.congress.gov/110/plaws/publ53/PLAW-110publ53.pdf)

The United States House of Representatives. (July 2013). "Majority Staff Report on the National Network of Fusion Centers." *Archives.gov*. (https://www.archives.gov/files/isoo/oversight-groups/sltps-pac/staff-report-on-fusion-networks-2013.pdf)

Department of Homeland Security and The Department of Justice. (August 2006). "Fusion Center Guidelines – Developing and Sharing Information and Intelligence in a New Era." *Bja.ojp.gov*. (https://bja.ojp.gov/sites/g/files/xyckuh186/files/media/document/fusion_center_guidelines_law_enforcement.pdf)

National Fusion Center Association. (2018-2021). "National Strategy for the National Network of Fusion Centers 2018 - 2021." *National Fusion Center Association*. (https://nfcausa.wpengine.com/wp-content/uploads/2020/10/2018-to-2021-National-Strategy-for-the-NNFC7715.pdf)

Federal Emergency Management Agency. (February 2021). "FEMA Preparedness Grants Manual." *FEMA.gov*. (https://www.fema.gov/sites/default/files/documents/FEMA_2021-Preparedness-Grants-Manual_02-19-2021.pdf)

United States Senate. (October 3, 2012). "Federal Support for and Involvement in State and Local Fusion Centers." *Hsgac.senate.gov*. (https://www.hsgac.senate.gov/imo/media/doc/10-3-

BIBLIOGRAPHY

2012%20PSI%20STAFF%20REPORT%20re%20FUSION%20CENTERS.2.pdf)

Inspectors General of the Department of Homeland Security, Department of Justice. (March 2017). "Review of Domestic Sharing of Counterterrorism Information." *Oversight.gov.* (https://www.oversight.gov/sites/default/files/oig-reports/OIG-17-49-Mar17.pdf)

American Civil Liberties Union. (July 29, 2008). "What's Wrong With Fusion Centers – Executive Summary." *ACLU.org* (https://www.aclu.org/report/whats-wrong-fusion-centers-executive-summary?redirect=cpredirect/32966)

Department of Homeland Security. (December 11, 2008). "Privacy Impact Assessment for the Department of Homeland Security State, Local, and Regional Fusion Center Initiative." *DHS.gov.* (https://www.dhs.gov/xlibrary/assets/privacy/privacy_pia_ia_slrfci.pdf)

Ms. Smith (Pen name). (November 4, 2012). "Microsoft Provides Fusion Center Technology and Funding for Surveillance." *CSOonline.com* (https://www.csoonline.com/article/2223440/microsoft-provides-fusion-center-technology-and-funding-for-surveillance.html)

Novak, Edward F. (August 18, 2021). "Response to Legislator Request for Investigation." *Azag.gov.* (https://www.azag.gov/sites/default/files/docs/complaints/sb1487/21-002/LT_AG_re_Legislative_Subpoena_8-18-21-c.pdf)

Rollins, John. (January 18, 2008). "CRS Report for Congress- Fusion Centers: Issues and Options for Congress."

Countdown to Chaos

    Congressional Research Service. (https://sgp.fas.org/crs/intel/RL34070.pdf)

American Civil Liberties Union. (December 19, 2012). "Spying on First Amendment Activity – State-by-State." *ACLU.org.* (https://www.aclu.org/sites/default/files/field_document/spying_on_first_amendment_activity_12.19.12_update.pdf)

American Civil Liberties Union. (November 4, 2011). "Spying on First Amendment Activity – State-by-State." *ACLU.org.* (https://www.aclu.org/files/assets/policingfreespeech_20111103.pdf)

Rittgers, David. (February 2, 2011). "We're All Terrorists Now." *CATO@Liberty.* (https://web.archive.org/web/20110415064139/http://www.cato-at-liberty.org/we%E2%80%99re-all-terrorists-now/)

The Constitution Project. (2012). "Recommendations for Fusion Centers – Preserving Privacy & Civil Liberties while Protecting Against Crime & Terrorism." *Constitution Project.org.* (https://archive.constitutionproject.org/pdf/fusioncenterreport.pdf)

Monahan, Torin; Palmer, Neal A. (2009). "The Emerging Politics of DHS Fusion Centers." *SAGE Publications.* (https://publicsurveillance.com/papers/FC-SD.pdf)

Monahan, Torin. (2009). "The Murky World of 'Fusion Centres.'" *Centre For Crime and Justice Studies.* (https://publicsurveillance.com/papers/FC-CJM.pdf)

Craven, Krista; Monahan, Torin; Regan, Priscilla. (April 22, 2014). "Compromised Trust: DHS Fusion Centers' Policing of the

BIBLIOGRAPHY

Occupy Wallstreet Movement." *Sociological Research Online*. (https://publicsurveillance.com/papers/FC_Compromised_Trust.pdf)

National Association of Secretaries of State. (October 2019). "Cybersecurity Resource Guide." *NASS.org*. (https://www.nass.org/sites/default/files/Cybersecurity/10.11_NASS_Cyber_Resource_Guide.pdf)

Morley, Michael T. and Tolson, Franita. (©2022) Common Interpretation Elections Clause. *Constitutioncenter.org*. (https://constitutioncenter.org/interactive-constitution/interpretation/article-i/clauses/750)

U.S. Election Assistance Commission. (March 20, 2007). U.S. Constitutional Provisions on Elections. *EAC.gov*.(https://www.eac.gov/sites/default/files/eac_assets/1/1/U.S.%20Constitutional%20Provisions%20on%20Elections.pdf)

Wolverton, Joe. (October 11. 2020). "Colorado Election Security in the Hands of DHS Fusion Center." *The New American*. (https://thenewamerican.com/colorado-election-security-in-the-hands-of-dhs-fusion-center/)

U.S. Election Assistance Commission. (2017). "Starting Point: U.S. Election Systems as Critical Infrastructure. *EAC.gov*. (https://www.eac.gov/sites/default/files/eac_assets/1/6/starting_point_us_election_systems_as_Critical_Infrastructure.pdf)

MSNBC. (August 17, 2018). "John O. Brennan: I Gave Trump A Year To Live Up To The Office. Hid Didn't." *Youtube.com* (https://www.youtube.com/watch?v=UV7-ZdDGijY&t=1170s)

Countdown to Chaos

The United States Senate. (May 24, 2022). "Congressional Record Volume 168, Number 90." Pages S2647-S2648. *The Government Publishing Office* (www.gpo.gov). (https://www.govinfo.gov/content/pkg/CREC-2022-05-24/html/CREC-2022-05-24-pt1-PgS2647.htm)

MS-ISAC®. (Accessed 2021). "MS-ISAC Multi-State Information Sharing & Analysis Center Services Guide." *Marc.org*. (https://www.marc.org/Government/Cybersecurity/assets/MS-ISAC_ServicesGuide_8-5x11_Print_v2.aspx)

Chapter 13 - SOLARWINDS (POST ELECTION 2020 - 2021)

Tikhonova, Polina. (December 14, 2020). "SolarWinds Hack: Outgoing CEO Sold Huge Amount of Stock in Nov." *Insider Paper*. (https://insiderpaper.com/solarwinds-hack-outgoing-ceo-sold-huge-amount-of-stock-in-nov/)

Crane, Emily. (December 21, 2020). "SolarWinds Was Warned THREE YEARS Ago That it Was Prone to a Cyberattack- as it's Revealed Russian Hackers Also Breached Major Tech and Accounting Firms, a Hospital System and a University." *DailyMail.com*. (https://www.dailymail.co.uk/news/article-9076045/SolarWinds-adviser-warned-cybersecurity-risks-2017-Russian-hack.html?ito=email_share_article-factbox)

United States Securities and Exchange Commission. (December 14, 2020). "SolarWinds Corporation. 001-38711." *SEC.gov*. (https://www.sec.gov/Archives/edgar/data/0001739942/000162828020017451/swi-20201214.htm)

BIBLIOGRAPHY

Cimpanu, Catalin. (December 13, 2020). "Microsoft, FireEye Confirm SolarWinds Supply Chain Attack." *ZDNet*. (https://www.zdnet.com/article/microsoft-fireeye-confirm-solarwinds-supply-chain-attack/)

Center For Internet Security. (December 22, 2020). "The SolarWinds Cyber-Attack: What SLTTs Need to Know." *Web.archive.org*. (https://web.archive.org/web/20210116034200/https:/www.cisecurity.org/ms-isac/solarwinds/)

Center For Internet Security. (2020). "Center For Internet Security – Year in Review 2020." *Center For Internet Security*. (https://learn.cisecurity.org/CIS-YIR-2020)

LaRose, Frank. (June 11, 2019). "Directive 2019-08." *Ohiosos.gov*. (https://www.ohiosos.gov/globalassets/elections/directives/2019/dir2019-08.pdf?_cf_chl_jschl_tk_=.EO7cJjGOQOswf7QjcS_fZnY3mo8Eo7t4RknxEsD08Q-1643302430-0-gaNycGzNCD0)

Cybersecurity & Infrastructure Security Agency. (January 5, 2021). "Joint Statement by the Federal Bureau of Investigation (FBI), The Cybersecurity And Infrastructure Security Agency (CISA), The Office of the Director of National Intelligence (ODNI), and the National Security Agency (NSA)." *CISA.gov*. (https://www.cisa.gov/news/2021/01/05/joint-statement-federal-bureau-investigation-fbi-cybersecurity-and-infrastructure)

Cisco Security. (June 3, 2020). "Cisco IOS XE Software Flexible NetFlow Version 9 Denial of Service Vulnerability." *CISCO.com*. (https://tools.cisco.com/security/center/content/CiscoSecurityAdvisory/cisco-sa-iosxe-fnfv9-dos-HND6Fc9u)

Countdown to Chaos

NIST. (September 24, 2020). "CVE-2020-3492 Detail." *National Vulnerability Database*. (https://nvd.nist.gov/vuln/detail/CVE-2020-3492)

Cybersecurity & Infrastructure Security Agency. (November 12, 2020). "Joint Statement From Elections Infrastructure Government Coordinating Council & The Election Infrastructure Sector Coordinating Executive Committees." *CISA.gov* (https://www.cisa.gov/news/2020/11/12/joint-statement-elections-infrastructure-government-coordinating-council-election)

Lin, Herbert; Zegart, Amy. "Bytes, Bombs, and Spies – The Strategic Dimensions of Offensive Cyber Operations." *The Brookings Institute*. (https://www.brookings.edu/wp-content/uploads/2018/10/978081573547_ch1.pdf)

Edwards, Jane. (January 11, 2021). "SolarWinds Hires Consulting Firm Krebs Stamos Group to Assist in Cybersecurity Assessment." *Govcon Wire*. (https://www.govconwire.com/2021/01/solarwinds-hires-consulting-firm-krebs-stamos-group-to-assist-in-cybersecurity-assessment/)

United States Senate Select Committee on Intelligence. (February 23, 2021). "Written Testimony of Sudhakar Ramakrishna, Chief Executive Office, SolarWinds Inc." *Intelligence.senate.gov*. (https://www.intelligence.senate.gov/sites/default/files/documents/os-sramakrishna-022321.pdf)

Stilgherrian & Duckett, Chris. (October 27, 2020). "APT Groups Aren't All From Russia, China, and North Korea." *ZDNet*. (https://www.zdnet.com/article/apt-groups-arent-all-from-russia-china-and-north-korea/) NotP

BIBLIOGRAPHY

Stilgherrian. (April 11, 2018). "Blaming Russian for NotPetya was Coordinated Diplomatic Action." *ZDNet.com*. (https://www.zdnet.com/article/blaming-russia-for-notpetya-was-coordinated-diplomatic-action/)

Lizza, Ryan; Bade, Rachael; Daniels, Eugene. (September 21, 2021). "POLITICO Playbook: Double Trouble for Biden." *Politico.com* (https://www.politico.com/newsletters/playbook/2021/09/21/double-trouble-for-biden-494411)

Johnson, Ron and Grassley, Charles E. (April 16, 2020). Senate Committee on Homeland Security and Government Affairs Letter to FBI Director Christopher Wray. *Hsgac.senate.gov*. (https://www.hsgac.senate.gov/imo/media/doc/2020-04-16%20RHJ-CEG%20to%20FBI%20(Crossfire%20Hurricane%20Intel%20Memos).pdf)

Department of Homeland Security and The Department of Justice. (March 2021). "Key Findings and Recommendations From the Joint Report of the Department of Justice and the Department of Homeland Security on Foreign interference Targeting Election Infrastructure or Political Organization, Campaign, or Candidate Infrastructure Related to the 2020 US Federal Elections." *DHS.gov*. (https://www.dhs.gov/sites/default/files/publications/210311_key-findings-and-recommendations-related-to-2020-elections_1.pdf)

Cybersecurity & Infrastructure Security Agency. (Accessed February 17, 2022). "The President's National Infrastructure Advisory Council." *CISA.gov*. (https://www.cisa.gov/niac)

Countdown to Chaos

The President's National Infrastructure Advisory Council. (January 21, 2021). "Actionable Cyber Intelligence: An Executive-Led Collaborative Model." *CISA.gov*. (https://www.cisa.gov/sites/default/files/publications/NIAC%20Actionable%20Cyber%20Intelligence_FINAL_508_0.pdf)

Chapter 14 – THE ARIZONA AUDIT, EI-ISAC APPOINTMENTS, ERIC COOMER DEPOSITION (2021)

Hoft, Jim. (April 23, 2021). "'Democrats Sent 73 lawyers to AZ – THEY KNOW WHAT THEY DID!' – BREAKING: President Trump Releases Statement on Forensic Audit in Maricopa, County Arizona." *The Gateway Pundit*. (https://www.thegatewaypundit.com/2021/04/democrats-sent-73-lawyers-az-know-breaking-president-trump-releases-statement-forensic-audit-maricopa-county-arizona/)

Parks, Miles. (June 3, 2021). "Experts Call It A 'Clown Show' But Arizona 'Audit Is A Disinformation Blueprint. *NPR*. (https://www.npr.org/2021/06/03/1000954549/experts-call-it-a-clown-show-but-arizona-audit-is-a-disinformation-blueprint).

Cybersecurity & Infrastructure Security Agency. (November 12, 2020). "Joint Statement From Elections Infrastructure Government Coordinating Council & The Election Infrastructure Sector Coordinating Executive Committees." *CISA.gov* (https://www.cisa.gov/news/2020/11/12/joint-statement-elections-infrastructure-government-coordinating-council-election)

BIBLIOGRAPHY

Swenson, Ali; Fichera, Angelo. (September 27, 2021). "FACT FOCUS: AZ Election Review Spurs False Claims Online." *AP News*. (https://apnews.com/article/joe-biden-media-social-media-arizona-presidential-elections-9a68234adab79b0f8a55e189af5a16e4)

Chaitin, Daniel. (June 11, 2021). "Garland Charts DOJ Collision Course With Maricopa County Election Audit." *Washington Examiner*. (https://www.washingtonexaminer.com/news/garland-charts-doj-collision-course-with-maricopa-county-election-audit)

Rogers, Wendy. (Jun 11, 2021). "Wendy Rogers to AG Garland: 'You Will Not Touch Arizona Ballots' or You Will Go To Jail." *Wendyrogers.org*. (https://wendyrogers.org/az-state-senator-wendy-rogers-to-ag-garland-you-will-not-touch-arizona-ballots-or-you-will-go-to-jail/)

Cotton, Ben. (September 24, 2021). "Digital Findings – Arizona State Senate Audit." *CyFir*. (https://c692f527-da75-4c86-b5d1-8b3d5d4d5b43.filesusr.com/ugd/2f3470_2a043c72ca3e4823bdb76aaa944728d1.pptx?dn=Cotton%20Presentation.pptx)

Howley, Partrick. (July 15, 2021). "BREAKING: 37,000 Anonymous Queries To Access 2020 Election In Arizona 'Do Not Follow That Pattern of Normal Windows Behavior.'" *National File*. (https://nationalfile.com/breaking-37000-anonymous-queries-to-access-2020-election-in-arizona-do-not-follow-that-pattern-of-normal-windows-behavior/)

Department of Homeland Security and The Department of Justice. (March 2021). "Key Findings and Recommendations From the Joint Report of the Department of Justice and the

Countdown to Chaos

Department of Homeland Security on Foreign interference Targeting Election Infrastructure or Political Organization, Campaign, or Candidate Infrastructure Related to the 2020 US Federal Elections." *DHS.gov.* (https://www.dhs.gov/sites/default/files/publications/21_0311_key-findings-and-recommendations-related-to-2020-elections_1.pdf)

The White House. (September 12, 2018). Executive Order 13848: "Imposing Certain Sanctions in the Event of Foreign Interference in a United States Election." *National Archives Federal Register.* (https://www.federalregister.gov/documents/2018/09/14/2018-20203/imposing-certain-sanctions-in-the-event-of-foreign-interference-in-a-united-states-election)

Center For Internet Security. (September 21, 2021) "Center for Internet Security Announces New Elections Leadership Team." *Cisecurity.org.* (https://www.cisecurity.org/press-release/center-for-internet-security-announces-new-elections-leadership-team/)

World Tribune Staff. (October 1, 2021). "Judge Puts Protective Order on Eric Coomer Testimony in Deposition by Sidney Powell." *Worldtribune.com.* (https://www.worldtribune.com/judge-puts-protective-order-on-eric-coomer-testimony-in-deposition-by-sidney-powell/)

Wetmore, Ben. (October 12, 2021). "EXCLUSIVE: Coomer Deposition Released! Verifies Antifa Facebook Posts, Extreme Left Bias." *Gateway Pundit.* (https://www.thegatewaypundit.com/2021/10/exclusive-coomer-deposition-released-verifies-antifa-facebook-posts-extreme-left-

BIBLIOGRAPHY

bias/?utm_source=Telegram&utm_medium=PostTopSharingButtons&utm_campaign=websitesharingbuttons)

Brown, Lee. (October 11, 2021). "Pentagon's First Software Chief Quit Because China Has Already Won Global Tech War." *New York Post*. (https://nypost.com/2021/10/11/pentagon-software-chief-nicolas-chaillan-resigns/)

Olson, Walter. (December 3, 2020). "The Framers Wisely Left Election Practice Decentralized." *Cato Institute*. (https://www.cato.org/blog/framers-wisely-left-election-practice-decentralized)

Chapter 15 – DHS TERROR WARNING, JOHN DURHAM FILING, NEUSTAR INC., RODNEY JOFFE, HILLARY CLINTON AND SPYGATE, DHS DISINFORMATION GOVERNANCE BOARD, SUSSMAN TRIAL, THE FBI (2022)

Department of Homeland Security. (February 7, 2022). "DHS Issues National Terrorism Advisory System (NTAS) Bulletin. *DHS.gov*. (https://www.dhs.gov/news/2022/02/07/dhs-issues-national-terrorism-advisory-system-ntas-bulletin)

Department of Homeland Security. (May 11, 2021). "DHS Creates New Center for Prevention Programs and Partnerships and Additional Efforts to Comprehensively Combat Domestic Violent Extremism." *DHS.gov*. (https://www.dhs.gov/news/2021/05/11/dhs-creates-new-center-prevention-programs-and-partnerships-and-additional-efforts)

Countdown to Chaos

Center For Internet Security. (2018). "Elections Infrastructure ISAC – 2018 Year in Review." *Cisecurity.org*. (https://www.cisecurity.org/wp-content/uploads/2019/02/EI-ISAC-2018-YIR.pdf)

Chaitin, Daniel. (September 24, 2021). "Garland Charts DOJ Collision Course With Maricopa County Election Audit." *Washington Examiner*. (https://www.washingtonexaminer.com/news/garland-charts-doj-collision-course-with-maricopa-county-election-audit)

Rosenfeld, Ross. (July 1, 2020). "There's No Longer Any Doubt: Trump is a White Supremacist." *NYdailynews.com*. (https://www.nydailynews.com/opinion/ny-oped-trump-white-supremacist-20200701-5zumhjygabhgfckydm7xyhbm6a-story.html)

McCammon, Sarah. (September 30, 2020). "From Debate Stage, Trump Declines To Denounce White Supremacy." *NPR.org*. (https://www.npr.org/2020/09/30/918483794/from-debate-stage-trump-declines-to-denounce-white-supremacy)

Karl, Jonathan; Phelps, Jordyn. (September 30, 2020). "Trump's Failure to Condemn White Supremacy at Debate Part of Well-Established Pattern." *ABC News*. (https://abcnews.go.com/Politics/trumps-failure-condemn-white-supremacy-debate-part-established/story?id=73340315)

Federal Bureau of Investigation. (June 4, 2019). "Confronting White Supremacy." *FBI.gov*. (https://www.fbi.gov/news/testimony/confronting-white-supremacy)

BIBLIOGRAPHY

De Witte, Melissa; Kubota, Taylor; Than, Ker. (April 21, 2022). "'Regulation Has to be Part of the Answer' to Combating Online Disinformation, Barack Obama Said at Stanford Event." *Stanford News*. (https://news.stanford.edu/2022/04/21/disinformation-weakening-democracy-barack-obama-said/)

Johnson, Bridget. (April 27, 2022). "DHS Standing Up Disinformation Governance Board Led by Information Warfare Expert." Homelandsecuritytoday.us. (https://www.hstoday.us/federal-pages/dhs/dhs-standing-up-disinformation-governance-board-led-by-information-warfare-expert/)

Committee on Oversight and Reform, The United States Congress; Comer, James, Ranking Minority Member. (April 29, 2022). Letter to: The Honorable Alejandro Mayorkas Secretary U.S. Department of Homeland Security. Republicans-oversight.gov. (https://republicans-oversight.house.gov/wp-content/uploads/2022/04/Letter-to-DHS-re-Disinformation-Governance-Board-04292022.pdf)

Jankowicz, Nina. (October 22, 2022). Untitled. *Twitter.com* (https://twitter.com/wiczipedia/status/1319463138107031553?ref_src=twsrc%5Etfw)

Shabad, Rebecca. (May 19, 2022). "Disinformation Head Nina Jankowicz Resigns After DHS Board is Paused." *Yahoo!news*. (https://news.yahoo.com/disinformation-head-nina-jankowicz-resigns-122618567.html)

Durham, John H. (February 11, 2022). "United States of America v. Michael A. Sussmann, Defendant - Government's Motion to Inquire Into Potential Conflicts of Interest." Criminal Case No. 21-cr-00582-CRC. United States District

Countdown to Chaos

Court for the District of Columbia. *Irp.cdn-website.com*. (https://irp.cdn-website.com/5be8a42f/files/uploaded/DurhamSussman0211.pdf)

Golding, Bruce. (September 30, 2021). "Who is Rodney Joffe, aka 'Tech Executive-1' in Durham Indictment?" *New York Post*. (https://nypost.com/2021/09/30/who-is-rodney-joffe-tech-executive-1-in-durham-indictment/)

Neustar, Inc. (Accessed February 17, 2022). "Home." *Neustar, Inc*. (https://www.home.neustar/)

Joffe, Rodney. (July 14, 2010). "Curricula Vitae." *GNSO.ICANN.org*. (https://gnso.icann.org/sites/default/files/filefield_13823/application-joffe-cv-14jul10-en.pdf)

Pollak, Joel B. (February 12, 2022). "John Durham Filing Suggests Clinton Operatives Spied on Trump in 2016 and in White House." *Breitbart.com*. (https://www.breitbart.com/politics/2022/02/12/john-durham-filing-suggests-clinton-operatives-spied-on-trump-in-2016-and-in-white-house/)

Cybersecurity & Infrastructure Security Agency. (Accessed February 2022). "Information Technology Sector: Charters and Membership." CISA.gov. (https://www.cisa.gov/information-technology-sector-council-charters-and-membership)

Sperry, Paul. (February 21, 2022). "'Clinton Tech' Rodney Joffe had a Shady Past Before He Targeted Trump." *New York Post*. (https://nypost.com/2022/02/21/the-shady-past-of-clinton-tech-joffe-who-targeted-trump/)

BIBLIOGRAPHY

Durham, John H. (September 16, 2021). "United States of America v. Michael A. Sussmann, Defendant." Criminal Case No. 21-cr-00582-CRC. United States District Court for the District of Columbia. *Justice.gov*. (https://www.justice.gov/sco/press-release/file/1433511/download)

USASPENDING.gov. (Accessed February 16, 2022). "Spending by Prime Award." USASPENDING.gov. (https://www.usaspending.gov/search/?hash=3f438aa7f3ca853c9bdb137becb08ac1)

Neustar, Inc. (November 21, 2018). "usTLD Registration Management Volume 1 – Technical Capability." *Ntia.doc.gov*. (https://www.ntia.doc.gov/files/ntia/publications/technical_proposal_volume_1.pdf)

National Institute of Standards and Technology (NIST). (November 17, 2015). "Amendment of Solicitation/Modification of Contract." *Ntia.doc.gov*. (https://www.ntia.doc.gov/files/ntia/publications/us_mod_0004_11172015.pdf)

Neustar, Inc. (August 10, 2020). "Neustar NIST Authentication Commentary." NIST.gov. (https://www.nist.gov/system/files/documents/2020/09/08/Comments-800-63-020.pdf)

Biden For President. (September 29, 2020). "Schedule B-P Itemized Disbursements." FEC.gov. (https://docquery.fec.gov/cgi-bin/fecimg/?202010219326734372)

Director of National Intelligence. (December 29, 2016). "Joint DHS, ODNI, FBI Statement on Russian Malicious Cyber

Activity." *DNI.gov.*
(https://www.dni.gov/index.php/newsroom/press-releases/press-releases-2016/item/1616-joint-dhs-odni-fbi-statement-on-russian-malicious-cyber-activity)

Antonakakis, Manos. (January 11, 2017). "Re: Question Regarding Start Date." Georgia Tech Email Thread. *Judicial Watch.* (https://www.judicialwatch.org/wp-content/uploads/2022/02/Georgia-Tech-Sussmann-November-2021-pg-102-105.pdf)

Highnam, Peter. (April 21, 2021). "Statement by Dr. Peter Highnam. Defense Innovation and Research." U.S. Senate Armed Services Committee. (https://www.armed-services.senate.gov/imo/media/doc/Highnam%20Testimony%2004.21.21.pdf)

Cisco Systems, Inc. (2007). "Configuring Cisco Encryption Technology." Cisco Systems, Inc. (https://www.cisco.com/c/en/us/td/docs/ios/security/configuration/guide/sec_cfg_encrypt_tech.pdf)

Georgia Bureau of Investigation. (Accessed February 22, 2022). "GA Information Sharing Analysis Center." *GBI.Georgia.gov.* (https://investigative-gbi.georgia.gov/investigative-offices-and-services/specialized-units/ga-information-sharing-analysis-center)

Fulton County, GA. (January 6. 2021). "Fulton County Board of Commissioners Regular Meeting." *Fulton.legistar.com.* (https://fulton.legistar.com/View.ashx?M=M&ID=867027&GUID=9988AEB8-3608-44B8-A1CA-B2A466BDAF9E)

Durham, John H. (April 15, 2022). "Memorandum in Opposition Re Sussmann Motion in Limine by USA." Scribd.com.

BIBLIOGRAPHY

(https://www.scribd.com/document/570091923/70-Memorandum-in-Opposition-Re-Sussmann-Motion-in-Limine-by-USA)

United States Senate Select Committee on Intelligence. (July 25, 2019). "Russian Active Measures Campaigns and Interference in the 2016 U.S. Election, Volume 1: Russian Efforts Against Election Infrastructure with Additional Views." *Intelligence.senate.gov.* (https://www.intelligence.senate.gov/sites/default/files/documents/Report_Volume1.pdf)

Greaney, Paul. (April 8, 2022). "DOD Green-Lighted Fake Trump-Russia Doc in 2016: Ret. Colonel John Mills." Fresh Look America. The Epoch Times. (https://www.theepochtimes.com/dod-green-lighted-fake-trump-russia-doc-in-2015-ret-colonel-john-mills_4693981.html)

Kaylman, Larry, Esq. (Klayman Law Group, P.A.). (June 5, 2017). "In The United States District Court For The District of Columbia: Compliant. Case 1:17-cv-01074-RJL" *Regmedia.co.uk.* (https://regmedia.co.uk/2017/06/08/01-main.pdf)

Klayman, Larry, Esq. (March 21, 2017). "Re: Unasked Questions About Whistleblower Dennis Montgomery at Committee Hearings on Surveillance, Leaks and Alleged Russian Involvement in 2016 Presidential Elections." Letter to The Honorable Devin Nunes. *Yumpu.com* (https://www.yumpu.com/en/document/read/62646908/2017-03-21-letter-to-nunes)

Techno Fog. (May 25, 2022). "Was Rodney Joffe involved in the Trump/Russia investigation?" The Reactionary.

Countdown to Chaos

Substack.com. (https://technofog.substack.com/p/was-rodney-joffe-involved-in-the)

Project Veritas. (May 11, 2022). "FBI Whistleblower Leaks Documents Showing Bureau Targeting 'News Media.'" *Projectveritas.com*. (https://www.projectveritas.com/news/breaking-fbi-whistleblower-leaks-document-showing-bureau-targeting-news/)

Attkisson, Sharyl. (August 7, 2013). "NEW: Decision in Attkisson Government Computer Intrusion Case." *Sharylattkisson.com* (https://sharylattkisson.com/2021/03/new-decision-in-attkisson-government-computer-intrusion-case/)

Muncy, David. (January 10, 2020). "Plaintiffs' Complaint." United States District Court of Maryland Baltimore Division. *Sharylattkisson.com*. (https://sharylattkisson.com/wp-content/uploads/2020/02/COMPLAINT-Baltimore-File-marked-complaint-Attkisson-MD-Complaint-File-Marked.pdf)

Stratfor. (September 21, 2010). "Obama Leak Investigations (Internal Use Only – Pls Do Not Forward." *The Global Intelligence Files. WikiLeaks.* (https://wikileaks.org/gifiles/docs/12/1210665_obama-leak-investigations-internal-use-only-pls-do-not.html)

Techno Fog. (May 17, 2022). "Day 1 of the Michael Sussmann Trial." *The Reactionary. Techofog.substack.com.* (https://technofog.substack.com/p/day-1-of-the-michael-sussmann-trial?s=r)

United States Sentencing Commission (2022). "RICO Offenses (Racketeer Influenced and Corrupt Organizations).

BIBLIOGRAPHY

Prepared by the Office of the General Counsel. *USSC.gov.* (https://www.ussc.gov/sites/default/files/pdf/training/primers/2022_Primer_RICO.pdf)

Ticktin, Peter, Esq. (March 24, 2022). "Donald J. Trump v. Hillary R. Clinton et al; Complaint For Damages and Demand For Trial By Jury." Documentcloud.org. (https://s3.documentcloud.org/documents/21506628/trump-v-clinton.pdf)

Johnson, Carrie. (April 7, 2022). "Justice Department is investigating Trump's possible mishandling of government secrets." NPR.org (https://www.npr.org/2022/04/07/1091431136/justice-department-investigating-trumps-possible-mishandling-of-government-secre)

Trump, Donald J. (January 19, 2021). "Memorandum on Declassification of Certain Materials Related to the FBI's Crossfire Hurricane Investigation." The White House. (https://trumpwhitehouse.archives.gov/presidential-actions/memorandum-declassification-certain-materials-related-fbis-crossfire-hurricane-investigation/)

Hains, Tim. (August 23, 2022). "RealClearInvestigations Writer Paul Sperry On Twitter Ban After Posting About War Between Former President And FBI." *Real Clear Politics* (https://www.realclearpolitics.com/video/2022/08/23/paul_sperry_fbi_trump_raid_scif.html)

CNN Wire. (Sunday, August 28, 2022). "Timeline: DOJ's criminal inquiry into Trump taking classified documents to Mar-a-Lago." Eyewitness News ABC 7. (https://abc7ny.com/donald-trump-maralago-fbi-search-classified-documents/12175658/)

Countdown to Chaos

Grassley, Senator Charles. (July 25, 2022). Letter to The Honorable Merrick Garland Attorney General and The Honorable Christopher Wray. *Senate.gov.* (https://www.grassley.senate.gov/imo/media/doc/grassley_to_justice_deptfbipoliticalbiasfollowup.pdf)

Gonzalez, Juan Antonio. (August 26, 2022). "Notice of Filing of Redacted Search Warrant Affidavit and Redacted Ex Parte Memorandum of Law Concerning Proposed Redactions." Case No. 22-MJ-8332-BER. United States District Court Southern District of Florida. *FLSD.uscourts.gov.* (https://www.flsd.uscourts.gov/sites/flsd/files/DE-102.pdf)

Kraychik, Robert. (August 29, 2022). "Exclusive — Lee Smith: People I Trust Say FBI Raid Was Search for Russiagate Documents at Mar-a-Lago." *Breitbart.* (https://www.breitbart.com/radio/2022/08/29/exclusive-lee-smith-people-i-trust-say-fbi-raid-was-search-for-russiagate-documents-at-mar-a-lago/)

Gonzalez, Juan Antonio. (August 29, 2022). "Notice of Receipt of Preliminary Order and Attorney Appearance." Case No. 22-CV-81294-AMC. *Documentcloud.org.* (https://s3.documentcloud.org/documents/22268848/doj-filing-in-request-for-special-master.pdf)

Sperry, Paul. (August 18, 2022). "FBI Unit Leading Mar-a-Lago Probe Earlier Ran Discredited Trump-Russia Investigation." Real Clear Investigations. (https://www.realclearinvestigations.com/articles/2022/08/18/fbi_unit_leading_mar-a-lago_probe_previously_led_russiagate_hoax_848582.html)

BIBLIOGRAPHY

Clark, Dan. (June 17, 2020). "Twitter Adds Former FBI General Counsel to Legal Department." ALM Global LLC/Law.com. (https://www.law.com/corpcounsel/2020/06/17/twitter-adds-former-fbi-general-counsel-to-legal-department/?slreturn=20220804144819)

Fox News. (August 26, 2022). "Mark Zuckerberg's shocking revelation to Joe Rogan." *YouTube*. (https://youtu.be/Mg8PaSYCP5E)

Sperry, Paul. (August 24, 2022). "Shock Poll: 8 in 10 Think Biden Laptop Cover-Up Changed Election." *Tippinsights.com*. (https://tippinsights.com/shock-poll-8-in-10-think-biden-laptop-cover-up-changed-election/)

Whedon, Ben. (August 30, 2022). "FBI special agent who opened Trump investigation reportedly escorted out of bureau." *Just The News*. (https://justthenews.com/government/federal-agencies/fbi-special-agent-who-opened-trump-investigation-reportedly-escorted#article)

Sperry, Paul. (September 2, 2022). Untitled Post. *Gettr*. (https://gettr.com/post/p1ph1jm9ad6)

Sperry, Paul. (September 3, 2022). Untitled Post. *Gettr*. (https://gettr.com/post/p1pkng6f46f)

Hoft, Jim. (September 3, 2022). "CONFIRMED: As Gateway Pundit Reported — FBI Doctored Mar-a-Lago Photo, Added Their Own Docs that DON'T MATCH INVENTORY REPORTS." *Gateway Pundit*. (https://www.thegatewaypundit.com/2022/09/confirmed-gateway-pundit-reported-fbi-doctored-mar-lago-photo-added-docs-alleged-crime-scene-dont-match-inventory-reports/)

Countdown to Chaos

Grassley, Senator Charles. (May 31, 2022). Letter to The Honorable Merrick Garland Attorney General and The Honorable Christopher Wray. *Senate.gov.* (https://www.grassley.senate.gov/imo/media/doc/CEG%20to%20DOJ%20FBI%20(WFO).pdf)

Federal Bureau of Investigation. (September 21, 2020). "FBI Washington Field Office Educates Citizens About Election Security and Foreign Malign Influence in Advance of the November Election." *FBI.gov.* (https://www.fbi.gov/contact-us/field-offices/washingtondc/news/press-releases/fbi-washington-field-office-educates-citizens-about-election-security-and-foreign-malign-influence-in-advance-of-the-november-election)

FBI Portland. (October 8, 2020). "What is the FBI doing to combat election fraud." *Twitter.com* (https://twitter.com/FBIPortland/status/1314268069506629633?s=20&t=P6Gkxw5mMqKrvwA4bz9Ycg)

Homeland Security Today. (August 26, 2022). "How NSA and U.S. Cyber Command Are Defending Midterm Elections: One Team, One Fight." *Homeland Security Today.* (https://www.hstoday.us/subject-matter-areas/cybersecurity/how-nsa-and-u-s-cyber-command-are-defending-midterm-elections-one-team-one-fight/)

United States Senate Select Committee on Intelligence. (2019). "Russian Active Measures Campaigns and Interference in the 2016 U.S. Election, Volume 4: Review Of The Intelligence Community Assessment." *Intelligence.senate.gov.* (https://www.intelligence.senate.gov/sites/default/files/documents/Report_Volume4.pdf)

BIBLIOGRAPHY

U.S. Department of Justice. (July 28, 2021). "Federal Law Constraints on Post-Election 'Audits.'" Justice.gov. (https://www.justice.gov/opa/press-release/file/1417796/download)

Cillizza, Chris. (May 23, 2017). "This John Brennan Quote on Russian Just Made Donald Trump's Life Much Harder." *CNN Politics*. (https://edition.cnn.com/2017/05/23/politics/john-brennan-trump-russia/) Timeline of Key Events

MSNBC. (August 17, 2018). "John O. Brennan: I Gave Trump A Year To Live Up To The Office. Hid Didn't." *Youtube.com* (https://www.youtube.com/watch?v=UV7-ZdDGijY&t=1170s)

Brennan, John O. (October 7, 2020). Untitled. *Twitter.com* (https://twitter.com/JohnBrennan/status/1314034940321898498?ref_src=twsrc%5Etfw)

Sherwin, Michael R., Atty. (September 24,2020). "United States of America v. Michael T. Flynn, Defendant." Criminal Case No. 17-232 (EGS). United States District Court for the District of Columbia. *Storage.courtlistener.com*. (https://storage.courtlistener.com/recap/gov.uscourts.dcd.191592/gov.uscourts.dcd.191592.249.0.pdf)

Homeland Security and Governmental Affairs Committee. (December 3, 2020). "Timeline of Key Events Related to Crossfire Hurricane Investigation." *Hsgac.senate.gov*. (https://www.hsgac.senate.gov/imo/media/doc/CFH%20Timeline%20w%20Updates%2020201203%20%28FINAL%29.pdf)

Cybersecurity & Infrastructure Security Agency. (November 12, 2020). "Joint Statement From Elections Infrastructure

Countdown to Chaos

Government Coordinating Council & The Election Infrastructure Sector Coordinating Executive Committees." *CISA.gov*. (https://www.cisa.gov/news/2020/11/12/joint-statement-elections-infrastructure-government-coordinating-council-election)

Chapter 16 – DISCUSSION

Brnovich, Mark. (Accessed 2021). "Election Integrity Unit." *Azag.gov*. (https://www.azag.gov/criminal/eiu)

Voter GA. (July 13, 2021). "New Evidence Reveals GA Audit Fraud and Massive Errors." *Voterga.org*. (https://voterga.org/wp-content/uploads/2021/11/Press-Release-Georgia-Audit-Riddled-by-Massive-Errors-Fraud.pdf)

Boyle, Matthew. (August 24, 2021). "Exclusive – True The Vote Conducting Massive Clandestine Voter Fraud Investigation." *Breitbart.com* (https://www.breitbart.com/politics/2021/08/24/exclusive-true-the-vote-conducting-massive-clandestine-voter-fraud-investigation/)

Judicial Watch. (January 5, 2021). "Judicial Watch: Over 4,700 of Georgia's Absentee XVotes in November 2020 Election Tied to Non-Residential Addresses." *Judicial Watch*. (https://www.judicialwatch.org/ga-non-residential/)

Keane, Gabriel. (December 4, 2020). "VIDEO: Georgia Poll Worker Ruby Freeman Runs SAME BALLOTS Through Tabulation Machine MULTIPLE TIMES." *National File*. (https://nationalfile.com/video-georgia-poll-worker-ruby-

BIBLIOGRAPHY

freeman-runs-same-ballots-through-tabulation-machine-multiple-times/)

DePerno Law Office. (June 24, 2021) "Press Release." *DePernolaw.com*. (https://www.depernolaw.com/press-june24-2021.html)

Milwaukee County Clerk. (November 4, 2020). "Milwaukee County Election Results." *County.milwaukee.gov*. (https://county.milwaukee.gov/EN/County-Clerk/Off-Nav/Election-Results/Election-Results-Fall-2020)

Wilder, Ian. (October 6, 2021). "Election Audit Advances in Wisconsin as Election Officials Across the State Receive Subpoenas." *The Daily Cardinal*. (https://www.dailycardinal.com/article/2021/10/election-audit-advances-in-wisconsin-as-election-officials-across-the-state-receive-subpoenas)

VanBrugen, Isabel. (December 2, 2020). "Wisconsin USPS Subcontractor Alleges Backdating of Tens of Thousands of Mail-In Ballots." *The Epoch Times*. (https://www.theepochtimes.com/wisconsin-usps-subcontractor-alleges-backdating-of-tens-of-thousands-of-mail-in-ballots_3601580.html)

Calvi, Jason. (October 28, 2021). "Wisconsin Election Laws Violations, Racine County Sheriff Alleges." *Fox6 Milwaukee*. (https://www.fox6now.com/news/wisconsin-election-law-violations-racine-county-sheriff-reveals-findings)

Hoft, Joe. (October 26, 2021). "BREAKING: Wisconsin Senate Finally Decides to Request Investigation Into 2020 Election – Will They Finally Look Into Milwaukee?" *Gateway Pundit*. (https://www.thegatewaypundit.com/2021/10/breaking-

Countdown to Chaos

wisconsin-senate-finally-decides-request-investigation-2020-election-will-finally-look-milwaukee/)

Redman, Henry. (October 29, 2021). "Racing County Sheriff Alleges Elections Commission Broke The Law." *MSN.com*. (https://www.msn.com/en-us/news/us/racine-county-sheriff-alleges-elections-commission-broke-the-law/ar-AAQ7dXU)

Ahle, Steven. (August 21, 2021). "AG Bill Barr Ordered Lt. Col. Tony Shaffer to Stop Looking Into Truck Driver Jesse Morgan's Testimony That He Moved More Than 200,000 Fraudulent Ballots." *DJHJ Media*. (https://djhjmedia.com/steven/ag-bill-barr-ordered-lt-col-tony-shaffer-to-stop-looking-into-truck-driver-jesse-morgans-testimony-that-he-moved-more-than-200000-fraudulent-ballots/)

Levy, Marc, (September 15, 2020). "Pennsylvania: Mail Ballots Can't Be Discarded Over Signature." *AP News*. (https://apnews.com/article/pennsylvania-election-2020-pittsburgh-elections-presidential-elections-fc464c287c18823ff57fedc13facf7e5)

Kengor, Paul. (December 1, 2020). "Pennsylvania Bombshell: Biden 99.4% vs. Trump 0.6%." *RealClear Politics*. (https://www.realclearpolitics.com/2020/12/01/pennsylvania_bombshell_biden_994_vs_trump_06_530297.html)

Bedard, Paul. (December 2, 2020). "Nevada 'Fraud': 1,500 'Dead' Voters, 42,248 Voted 'Multiple Times,' RV Camps as 'Homes." *Washington Examiner*. (https://www.washingtonexaminer.com/washington-secrets/nevada-fraud-1-500-dead-voters-42-248-voted-multiple-times-rv-camps-as-homes)

BIBLIOGRAPHY

Sabia, Jr., Carmine. (November 17, 2020). "Entire Local Election in Nevada Thrown Out After 'Discrepancies' Found." *PJmedia.com*. (https://pjmedia.com/news-and-politics/carminesabia/2020/11/17/entire-local-election-in-nevada-thrown-out-after-discrepancies-found-n1153458)

Cybersecurity & Infrastructure Security Agency. (November 12, 2020). "Joint Statement From Elections Infrastructure Government Coordinating Council & The Election Infrastructure Sector Coordinating Executive Committees." *CISA.gov*. (https://www.cisa.gov/news/2020/11/12/joint-statement-elections-infrastructure-government-coordinating-council-election)

D'Souza Media. (February 1, 2022). *"2000 Mules."* Truethevote.org. (https://www.truethevote.org/coming-this-spring/) Accessed February 10, 2022.

Chapter 17 -SOLUTION AND CONCLUSION

Reagan, Ronald. (January 11, 1989). "President Reagan's Farewell Address to the Nation – 1/11/89." *Reagan Foundation*. (https://youtu.be/UKVsq2daR8Q?t=1112)

World Economic Forum. (April 2016). "Global Agenda Council on Cybersecurity." *Weforum.org*. (https://www3.weforum.org/docs/GAC16_Cybersecurity_WhitePaper_.pdf)

INSA. (2017). "Critical Issues for Cyber Assurance Policy Reform – An Industry Assessment." *INSA*. (https://www.insaonline.org/wp-content/uploads/2017/04/INSA_CritialIssuesCyber_WP-1.pdf)

Countdown to Chaos

Nelson, Steven. (October 14, 2021). "Zuckerberg's Election Spending Was 'Carefully Orchestrated' to Influence 2020 Vote: Ex-FEC Member." *New York Post*. (https://nypost.com/2021/10/14/zuckerberg-election-spending-was-orchestrated-to-influence-2020-vote/)

Center For Internet Security. (2018). "Elections Infrastructure ISAC – 2018 Year in Review." *Cisecurity.org*. (https://www.cisecurity.org/wp-content/uploads/2019/02/EI-ISAC-2018-YIR.pdf)

Center For Internet Security. (© 2021). "The 2020 Elections Year In Review." *Cisecurity.org*. (https://www.cisecurity.org/white-papers/the-2020-elections-year-in-review/)

Shimer, David. (June 21, 2020). "When the CIA Interferes in Foreign Elections – A Modern-Day History of American Covert Action." *Foreign Affairs*. (https://www.foreignaffairs.com/articles/united-states/2020-06-21/cia-interferes-foreign-elections)

Reagan, Ronald. (August 21, 2018). "Freedom is Never More Than One Generation From Extinction." *Reagan.com*. (https://www.reagan.com/ronald-reagan-freedom-speech)

EPILOGUE

Owen, Quinn. (September 19, 2022). "Border Apprehensions Exceed 2 million This Year: Enforcement Increases as GOP Buses Migrants Elsewhere." *ABCNews.com*. https://abcnews.go.com/Politics/border-apprehensions-exceed-million-year-enforcement-increases-gop/story?id=90167749

BIBLIOGRAPHY

Hoft, Jim. (September 22, 2022). "BARR LIED! FOIA Requests Reveal There Were No DOJ Investigations on Election Fraud After 2020 Election as Bill Barr Claims (VIDEO)." *The Gateway Pundit*. https://www.thegatewaypundit.com/2022/09/bill-barr-lied-foia-requests-reveal-no-doj-investigations-election-fraud-2020-election-bill-barr-claimed-video/

Associated Press. (October 5, 2022). "CEO of MI tech company Konnech arrested on suspicion of stealing data from hundreds of LA County poll workers." Fox News Inc. https://www.foxnews.com/us/ceo-software-company-targeted-election-deniers-arrested-suspicion-stealing-data

Piper, Greg. (October 3, 2022). "Federally Backed Censorship Machine Raises Separation of Powers, Election Meddling Questions." *Just The News*. https://justthenews.com/government/congress/federally-backed-censorship-machine-raises-separation-powers-election-meddling#digital-diary

Piper, Greg, and Solomon, John. (September 30, 2022). "Outsourced Censorship: Feds Used Private Entity to Target Millions of Social Posts in 2020." *Just The News*. https://justthenews.com/government/federal-agencies/biden-administration-rewarded-private-entities-got-2020-election

Center For Internet Security. (October 28, 2020). "Reporting Misinformation to the EI-ISAC." *EAC.gov*. https://www.eac.gov/sites/default/files/partners/EI_ISAC_Reporting_Misinformation_Sheet102820.pdf

The Election Integrity Partnership. (June 15, 2021). "The Long Fuse: Misinformation and the 2020 Election." *Stanford.edu*.

Countdown to Chaos

https://stacks.stanford.edu/file/druid:tr171zs0069/EIP-Final-Report.pdf

Belfer Center for Science and International Affairs. (August 24, 2021). "Biography. (Senior Fellow Robby Mook). *Belfercenter.org*. https://www.belfercenter.org/person/robby-mook

Pilger, Richard C., Editor. (December 2017). "Federal Prosecution of Election Offenses - Eighth Edition." *Justice.gov*. https://www.justice.gov/criminal/file/1029066/download

Dinan, Stephen. (October 30, 2020). "Postal Worker Arrested for Delaying Mail During Election Season." *The Washington Times*. https://www.washingtontimes.com/news/2020/oct/30/mailman-arrested-delaying-mail-during-election-sea/

Hobbs, Jack. (November 6, 2020). "USPS Worker Arrested at Canadian Border with Bin of Mail, Undelivered Ballots." *New York Post*. https://nypost.com/2020/11/06/usps-worker-arrested-at-canadian-border-with-undelivered-ballots/

Sofastaii, Mallory. (August 23, 2020). "Mail-in Ballots From 2020 Discovered in Baltimore USPS Facility." WMAR 2 News. https://www.wmar2news.com/matterformallory/mail-in-ballots-from-2020-discovered-in-baltimore-usps-facility

Brown, Time. (May 27, 2022). "2000 Mules Vindication: First Person To Plead Guilty To Voter Fraud & CONSPIRACY In 2020 Election (Video)." *The Washington Standard*. https://thewashingtonstandard.com/2000-mules-vindication-first-person-to-plead-guilty-to-voter-fraud-conspiracy-in-2020-election/

BIBLIOGRAPHY

Cybersecurity & Infrastructure Security Agency (CISA). (June 3, 2022). "ICS Advisory (ICSA-22-154-01) Vulnerabilities Affecting Dominion Voting Systems ImageCast X." *CISA.gov*. https://www.cisa.gov/uscert/ics/advisories/icsa-22-154-01

Sperry, Paul. (August 24, 2022). "Shock Poll: 8 in 10 Think Biden Laptop Cover-Up Changed Election." *Tipp Insights*. https://tippinsights.com/shock-poll-8-in-10-think-biden-laptop-cover-up-changed-election/

Grass, Michael. (August 17, 2021). "$2.25 Million in NSF Funding Will Support Center for an Informed Public Research." Information School University of Washington. https://ischool.uw.edu/news/2021/08/225-million-nsf-funding-will-support-center-informed-public-research

The White House. (February 12, 2013). Executive Order 13636: "Improving Critical infrastructure Cybersecurity." *National Archives Federal Register*. (https://www.federalregister.gov/documents/2013/02/19/2013-03915/improving-critical-infrastructure-cybersecurity)

The White House. (October 7, 2022). "Executive Order On Enhancing Safeguards For United States Signals Intelligence Activities." *Whitehouse.gov*. https://www.whitehouse.gov/briefing-room/presidential-actions/2022/10/07/executive-order-on-enhancing-safeguards-for-united-states-signals-intelligence-activities/

National Security Agency. (Accessed October 10, 2022). "Signals Intelligence (SIGINT) Overview." *NSA.gov*. https://www.nsa.gov/Signals-Intelligence/Overview/

The State of Michigan 55th Judicial District. (October 4, 2022). "The State of Michigan v Eugene Yu." *Documentcloud.org*.

Countdown to Chaos

https://www.documentcloud.org/documents/23119267-skm_454e22100511220

Konnech, Inc. (Accessed October 10, 2022). "PollChief® Election Worker Management System." Konnech Inc. https://www.konnech.com/Election-Worker-Management.html

True The Vote. (October 4, 2022). "True The Vote Issues Statement Regarding the Arrest of Eugene Yu." *Truethevote.org*. https://www.truethevote.org/statement-regarding-arrest-konnech-ceo-eugene-yu/

Dreisbach, Tom. (October 5, 2022). "A Software CEO was Arrested on Suspicion of Storing Poll Worker Data in China." *NPR.org*. https://www.npr.org/2022/10/05/1126881222/a-software-ceo-was-arrested-on-suspicion-of-storing-poll-worker-data-in-china

Index

INDEX

A

ACLU 211, 220, 467, 468
Albert Monitoring........2, 45, 48, 49, 50, 53, 54, 55, 56, 59, 61, 62, 63, 75, 78, 81, 85, 97, 115, 148, 157, 161, 164, 165, 177, 188, 195, 208, 226, 231, 238, 239, 243, 244, 246, 258, 263, 281, 282, 286, 289, 292, 303, 315, 320, 332, 336, 347, 353, 359, 360, 376, 388, 399, 401, 439, 440
Albert Sensor... 2, 45, 46, 48, 51, 55, 56, 59, 60, 63
Antonakakis, Manos 293, 337, 482
Arizona...2, 3, 4, 54, 195, 214, 230, 234, 235, 252, 255, 256, 257, 258, 261, 262, 263, 266, 271, 345, 348, 358, 359, 363, 365, 366, 400, 474, 475
Artificial Intelligence 178, 348
Attkisson 312, 313, 315, 345, 484
Auten, Brian......322, 323, 326, 327, 341

B

Baker, James 89, 110, 302, 324, 391
Bennett, William........................ 80, 390
Biden
  also Biden Administration, Biden White House, Biden-Harris. 191, 193, 195, 252, 253, 264, 270, 272, 289, 304, 325, 330, 355, 359, 393, 398, 400, 407, 413, 419, 420, 425, 426, 427, 430, 473, 481, 487, 492, 497
Biden, Hunter...193, 248, 275, 322, 324, 325, 330, 341, 398, 402, 403, 418, 419, 429, 463
Biden, Joseph 241
Biden, Vice President..... 126, 275, 424, 427, 428

Brennan, John 37, 38, 69, 73, 74, 90, 115, 116, 119, 120, 125, 131, 135, 138, 139, 140, 143, 144, 164, 168, 191, 192, 193, 194, 200, 222, 235, 236, 237, 238, 239, 303, 304, 305, 338, 345, 351, 352, 355, 357, 371, 385, 386, 387, 388, 389, 393, 394, 398, 462, 489

C

Carter, Ash 122
Central Intelligence Agency 138, 302
Chertoff, Michael 274
CIA 2, 37, 67, 69, 73, 80, 88, 89, 90, 116, 125, 131, 138, 139, 140, 141, 143, 144, 145, 168, 170, 191, 192, 194, 199, 201, 235, 236, 237, 238, 239, 271, 276, 302, 303, 305, 310, 314, 338, 345, 351, 352, 357, 378, 385, 386, 388, 389, 390, 394, 428, 430, 445, 446, 494
CIS..... .15, 29, 30, 31, 32, 41, 43, 45, 46, 47, 48, 50, 51, 52, 53, 54, 59, 63, 77, 78, 86, 148, 159, 162, 177, 178, 179, 180, 183, 188, 190, 192, 195, 242, 244, 246, 258, 261, 264, 292, 320, 348, 358, 367, 373, 385, 388, 389, 390, 392, 397, 398, 399, 400, 440, 443, 444, 463, 471
CISA........ 2, 6, 31, 56, 59, 60, 62, 77, 78, 79, 127, 132, 134, 147, 148, 151, 166, 171, 172, 173, 182, 183, 189, 193, 195, 196, 198, 199, 200, 202, 217, 243, 245, 247, 250, 251, 252, 255, 256, 262, 263, 265, 303, 330, 341, 347, 348, 351, 358, 362, 367, 373, 389, 396, 397, 398, 400, 412, 418, 419, 420, 423, 430, 436, 438, 447, 448, 454, 455, 457, 459, 460, 464, 471, 472, 473, 474, 480, 490, 493, 497

Countdown to Chaos

Cisco 31, 49, 50, 187, 188, 244, 246, 347, 353, 462, 471, 482

Clapper, James 119, 120, 124, 131, 135, 138, 140, 143, 168, 200, 304, 305, 333, 355, 371, 392, 393, 394, 398

Clinton Campaign 278, 289, 291, 296, 300, 337

Clinton, Hillary 2, 37, 81, 222, 269, 277, 279, 281, 285, 317, 319, 330, 345, 387, 401, 410, 411, 414

CMaaS 184, 185, 186, 461

CNCI 40, 111, 121, 304, 346

Comey, James ...90, 116, 118, 120, 121, 122, 125, 126, 131, 138, 140, 141, 143, 145, 191, 248, 283, 303, 304, 316, 317, 318, 319, 330, 355, 362, 391, 393, 394

Coomer, Eric 2, 173, 174, 194, 255, 265, 266, 343, 357, 398, 400, 476

Critical Infrastructure 8, 15, 19, 24, 25, 32, 50, 51, 67, 68, 69, 124, 127, 128, 129, 130, 132, 134, 136, 148, 151, 152, 153, 154, 158, 169, 171, 172, 182, 192, 197, 198, 201, 206, 207, 210, 222, 225, 234, 235, 249, 250, 252, 253, 267, 269, 270, 271, 292, 295, 297, 304, 319, 350, 352, 355, 393, 395, 401, 422, 425, 428, 430

Crossfire Hurricane 2, 57, 115, 119, 133, 138, 142, 191, 248, 282, 321, 323, 330, 331, 335, 339, 350, 362, 391, 394, 397, 399, 401, 411, 452, 455, 485, 489

CrowdStrike 2, 32, 56, 57, 58, 61, 67, 76, 81, 90, 96, 98, 99, 101, 102, 103, 104, 105, 107, 108, 109, 111, 112, 114, 115, 124, 148, 177, 248, 263, 281, 282, 284, 286, 292, 306, 311, 316, 320, 331, 332, 336, 347, 348, 350, 353, 355, 356, 357, 358, 386, 387, 388, 389,390, 391, 392, 395, 397, 444

D

DARPA 282, 293, 294, 295, 296, 297, 298, 299, 337, 360, 361

Democratic National Committee ..... .57, 99, 292

Department of Defense. 19, 36, 99, 111, 121, 282, 287, 291, 293, 360, 420

Department of Homeland Security.... 2, 16, 17, 18, 19, 23, 24, 26, 29, 31, 32, 33, 36, 41, 45, 49, 50, 51, 53, 54, 55, 63, 67, 70, 75, 77, 78, 82, 85, 90, 102, 116, 124, 127, 132, 134, 135, 139, 146, 147, 151, 152, 153, 154, 156, 157, 166, 167, 169, 171, 172, 175, 182, 184, 185, 187, 190, 195, 196, 198, 201, 202, 206, 207, 208, 211, 213, 215, 219, 224, 227, 231, 242, 250, 251, 256, 261, 263, 267, 269, 273, 276, 282, 286, 287, 291, 293, 304, 312, 315, 331, 332, 334, 335, 348, 350, 352, 353, 354, 357, 359, 361, 367, 371, 372, 373, 374, 376, 380, 381, 385, 392, 394, 396, 401, 405, 408, 423, 427, 428, 429, 430, 435, 436, 437, 438, 439, 441, 445, 446, 447, 450, 455, 458, 461, 464, 466, 467, 473, 475, 477, 479

DHS 2, 18, 19, 23, 24, 30, 31, 35, 36, 39, 41, 42, 43, 49, 50, 51, 53, 54, 56, 59, 67, 71, 72, 76, 81, 82, 83, 84, 85, 109, 110, 113, 115, 124, 125, 127, 128, 129, 130, 134, 137, 145, 147, 148, 151, 152, 153, 156, 158, 160, 161, 162, 168, 169, 175, 177, 182, 183, 184, 185, 186, 187, 189, 195, 197, 199, 200, 201, 206, 207, 209, 210, 211, 213, 216, 217, 223, 224, 225, 227, 228, 229, 231, 233, 234, 239, 242, 244, 249, 250, 255, 256, 258, 261, 262, 263, 266, 269, 270, 271, 273, 274, 275, 276, 280, 281, 282, 283, 284, 286, 292, 293, 303, 304, 308, 312, 317, 334, 335, 346, 348, 349, 350, 351, 352, 355, 358,

Page 500

Index

359, 360, 362, 367, 373, 385, 386, 387, 388, 390, 392, 393, 394, 395, 396, 397, 398, 399, 406, 408, 410, 412, 413, 419, 420, 421, 423, 428, 430, 436, 438, 439, 444, 447, 448, 449, 450, 453, 454, 456, 458, 461, 464, 465, 467, 468, 469, 473, 476, 477, 479, 481

Director of National Intelligence.... 116, 120, 124, 135, 136, 137, 201, 243, 248, 333, 392, 424, 450, 453, 471, 481

Disinformation Governance Board 2, 269, 273, 274, 276, 308, 401, 406, 479

DNC... 57, 88, 89, 90, 91, 92, 93, 94, 96, 97, 98, 99, 100, 102, 103, 104, 105, 106, 107, 108, 109, 110, 112, 114, 124, 237, 248, 281, 283, 306, 308, 353, 355, 356, 390, 391, 392, 448, 450

Dominion 56, 59, 60, 148, 155, 163, 165, 167, 173, 194, 199, 202, 245, 246, 255, 259, 265, 266, 343, 395, 398, 400, 418, 457, 460, 465, 497

Durham, John
 also Durham Investigation, Durham Report, Durham Indictment...89, 2, 88, 89, 90, 96, 97, 108, 109, 116, 122, 126, 141, 144, 145, 201, 236, 237, 248, 253, 269, 273, 274, 276, 277, 281, 282, 284, 285, 286, 287, 289, 291, 292, 293, 294, 295, 298, 299, 302, 304, 305, 308, 315, 323, 324, 335, 337, 342, 350, 357, 359, 360, 361, 392, 401, 411, 449, 451, 479, 480, 481, 482

E

EA program 293, 297
EAC.... 58, 129, 134, 152, 166, 256, 259, 354, 395, 434, 442, 454, 456, 457, 458, 469, 495
Easterly, Jen 60, 61, 262, 444

EI-ISAC....... 2, 18, 51, 60, 151, 152, 156, 157, 158, 159, 160, 161, 162, 163, 164, 166, 170, 171, 177, 188, 189, 192, 199, 205, 207, 210, 213, 218, 229, 231, 234, 238, 239, 246, 255, 261, 263, 265, 271, 282, 303, 315, 348, 349, 350, 354, 367, 373, 376, 395, 396, 398, 399, 408, 417, 419, 421, 423, 457, 458, 465, 474, 478, 494, 495

EINSTEIN ... 2, 23, 26, 29, 35, 36, 41, 42, 43, 49, 50, 67, 68, 70, 71, 72, 73, 79, 81, 82, 85, 117, 158, 163, 255, 266, 281, 289, 346, 347, 353, 357, 385, 386, 387, 388, 390, 436, 437, 438, 445, 446, 448, 449

EI-SCC...2, 151, 152, 153, 154, 155, 166, 192, 193, 198, 199, 200, 201, 245, 250, 256, 262, 312, 351, 354, 367, 395, 398, 408, 421, 428, 457

EI-SIG.. ...... 16, 165, 166, 167, 173, 265, 354, 395, 396

Election Systems & Software........... 155, 163, 167, 199, 443

Elias, Mark 103
EO 13636 .... 131, 133, 389
EO 13694 .... 131, 123, 393
EO 13757 .... 131, 123, 124
EO 13878 .... 131, 428
ES&S........... 53, 163, 167, 192, 395, 443
Executive Order.. ....2, 50, 68, 74, 123, 131, 136, 151, 152, 169, 197, 249, 262, 264, 304, 389, 393, 396, 400, 422, 423, 427, 428, 441, 446, 452, 459, 476, 497

F

FBI... ..... 2, 19, 51, 57, 58, 76, 80, 88, 89, 90, 91, 92, 93, 94, 96, 97, 98, 99, 100, 101, 102, 103, 104, 105, 106, 107, 108, 109, 110, 111, 112, 114, 115, 116, 122, 125, 131, 133, 137, 138, 139, 140, 141, 143, 144, 145, 147, 159, 161, 168, 191, 195, 196, 199, 220, 229, 233, 235, 236, 238,

Countdown to Chaos

239, 242, 243, 245, 248, 251, 255, 269, 272, 276, 279, 280, 281, 282, 283, 284, 286, 292, 293, 294, 296, 297, 298, 300, 301, 302, 303, 304, 306, 307, 308, 309, 310, 311, 312, 315, 316, 317, 318, 319, 321, 322, 323, 324, 325, 326, 327, 328, 329, 330, 331, 333, 335, 336, 338, 339, 340, 345, 349, 352, 355, 356, 357, 358, 359, 360, 361, 362, 373, 378, 386, 387, 388, 390, 391, 392, 394, 395, 396, 397, 402, 403, 411, 426, 428, 429, 430, 442, 447, 451, 453, 455, 460, 465, 471, 473, 477, 478, 481, 484, 485, 486, 487, 488

Federalist Papers 11, 12, 267, 320, 342, 370, 379, 380, 433

Feinstein, Sen. Diane...73, 74, 345, 389, 446

Flynn, Gen. Michael 1, 119, 120, 126, 134, 142, 393, 397, 454, 489

FOIA...26, 117, 127, 166, 229, 234, 333, 354, 418, 454, 495

Fusion Center..........138, 139, 144, 161, 205, 207, 209, 210, 211, 212, 213, 214, 215, 216, 217, 218, 219, 221, 222, 224, 225, 226, 227, 229, 230, 233, 234, 235, 236, 237, 238, 239, 270, 271, 284, 296, 335, 338, 345, 350, 352, 357, 358, 428

G

GAO 81, 83, 85, 146, 182, 183, 255, 266, 347, 390, 397, 461

Garland, Merrick.....257, 272, 321, 322, 326, 327, 328, 340, 359, 400, 475, 478, 486, 488

Gilligan, John.....52, 162, 188, 189, 190, 397, 436, 442, 462

Global Cyber Alliance......... 76, 389, 447

Governing Authority 127, 137, 151, 169, 175, 195, 197, 198, 201, 205, 210, 250, 256, 269, 270, 276, 331, 334, 350, 357, 367, 376, 379, 380,

408, 410, 413, 419, 421, 423, 428, 429

Grassley, Sen. Charles.... 248, 321, 322, 324, 325, 326, 327, 328, 340, 392, 402, 451, 453, 465, 473, 486, 488

Grenell, Ric.......116, 122, 201, 248, 392

GRU......................... 114, 115, 294, 451

Guccifer............112, 113, 114, 115, 451

H

Hamilton, Alexander... 11, 12, 267, 342, 367, 370, 379, 433

Hart Intercivic 56, 167, 192, 395, 463

Henry, Shawn.................................. 389

Highnam, Peter...... 293, 295, 296, 297, 482

House Select Committee 91, 109

HSIN...36, 144, 158, 159, 160, 161, 170, 175, 181, 195, 205, 206, 207, 208, 231, 238, 270, 271, 292, 299, 311, 320, 333, 335, 349, 350, 352, 357, 360, 362, 373, 396, 398, 399, 428, 458

I

IACD 54, 255, 258, 443

ICA ...120, 121, 122, 123, 125, 126, 131, 249, 303, 304, 333, 359, 392, 393, 394

INSA 37, 38, 39, 135, 136, 137, 161, 371, 386, 438, 439, 455, 458, 493

Intelligence Community Assessment... 120, 122, 125, 131, 303, 348, 355, 359, 393, 452, 488

IT-ISAC.......2, 15, 16, 18, 32, 33, 39, 67, 76, 85, 151, 165, 166, 173, 277, 337, 354, 386, 387, 388, 389, 390, 395, 435, 439, 445, 447, 449, 457, 459

IT-SCC........2, 29, 32, 33, 282, 292, 386, 436, 437

Index

J

Jankowicz, Nina. 273, 274, 275, 276, 479
Joffe, Rodney 2, 237, 253, 269, 277, 279, 280, 281, 282, 283, 284, 285, 286, 287, 289, 291, 292, 295, 299, 300, 302, 303, 306, 307, 308, 317, 318, 337, 345, 359, 360, 390, 401, 411, 429, 480, 483
Johnson, Jeh 51, 110, 124, 127, 130, 132, 152, 169, 192, 201, 207, 263, 270, 292, 303, 304, 350, 355, 371, 391, 394, 428

K

Krebs, Chris. 2, 53, 56, 63, 168, 193, 198, 202, 247, 303, 330, 341, 358, 362, 373, 395, 398, 399, 420, 472

L

Laptop.....193, 194, 248, 275, 322, 324, 325, 398, 402, 403, 418, 419, 429, 463, 487, 497

M

Madison, James 267, 342, 367
Maricopa ...3, 4, 54, 214, 220, 230, 234, 235, 255, 256, 258, 259, 261, 262, 263, 348, 358, 363, 474, 475, 478
Mayorkas, Secretary. 273, 274, 401, 479
McCabe, Andrew 316, 318, 340
Mills, Col. John...40, 111, 121, 122, 125, 304, 333, 439, 444, 450, 452, 483
MS-ISAC 2, 18, 29, 30, 31, 41, 52, 85, 151, 159, 162, 166, 229, 234, 239, 264, 282, 286, 334, 347, 350, 354, 359, 367, 369, 376, 386, 388, 400, 408, 436, 437, 470
Mueller, Robert
   also Mueller Report 58, 114, 133, 316, 319, 388, 394, 397, 454

N

NASS
   also National Assoc. of Secretary of States 134, 146, 190, 198, 231, 462, 469
National Security Council... 40, 60, 111, 120, 121, 125, 242, 303, 333
NCCIC 39, 161, 349, 387
NCSAR 160, 161, 166, 181, 261, 349, 350, 354
NetFlow
   also Netflow Analysis.. .... 50, 51, 61, 75, 187, 188, 244, 245, 246, 347, 353, 389, 397, 462, 471
Neustar... ....2, 32, 237, 253, 269, 277, 279, 281, 282, 287, 288, 289, 291, 295, 306, 317, 318, 337, 345, 360, 390, 401, 411, 429, 480, 481
NSA........... 23, 40, 41, 49, 54, 69, 93, 99, 119, 125, 126, 138, 140, 141, 143, 144, 236, 238, 239, 243, 305, 331, 332, 338, 345, 352, 357, 388, 424, 428, 452, 471, 488, 497

O

O'Keefe, James...08, 309, 310, 312, 316
Obama, President Barack
   also, Obama, Obama White House, Obama Administration...0, 9, 24, 37, 39, 40, 50, 60, 67, 68, 69, 74, 90, 94, 112, 114, 118, 120, 121, 122, 123, 125, 126, 127, 132, 133, 135, 140, 143, 144, 151, 164, 168, 169, 191, 192, 201, 206, 207, 222, 231, 235, 246, 248, 263, 270, 273, 283, 286, 292, 303, 304, 305, 313, 319, 332, 333, 338, 345, 348, 355, 359, 360, 374, 380, 387, 388, 389, 391, 392, 393, 401, 422, 425, 428, 430, 438, 453, 454, 479, 484

Countdown to Chaos

P

Page, Lisa 316, 317, 318, 319, 339, 340
Patriot Act................................ 127, 407
Perkins Coie 90, 281, 282, 291, 292, 296, 390
Power, Samantha............ 119, 120, 393
Presidential Directive....15, 23, 24, 385, 436
Project Veritas 308, 309, 312, 315, 316, 317, 340, 484

R

RABET-V.. ....2, 177, 189, 190, 397, 461, 462
Ramakrishna, Sudhakar...247, 398, 399, 472
Ratcliff, John 122
Rice, Susan 126, 304, 393
Rogers, Michael 126, 138, 304, 393
Russian Collusion 131, 133, 394, 426, 428
Russian Interference...... 109, 116, 120, 121, 125, 145, 167, 191, 201, 303, 333, 358, 392, 393, 395

S

Sector Coordinating Council .. 2, 16, 19, 32, 135, 165, 198, 202, 282, 386, 395, 396, 421, 437, 456, 457, 459
Senate Select Committee...53, 109, 120, 125, 130, 131, 164, 247, 399, 443, 450, 452, 454, 458, 472, 483, 488
Snowden, Edward........69, 70, 143, 144, 145, 388, 446
SolarWinds....2, 75, 119, 148, 151, 174, 175, 177, 187, 241, 242, 243, 244, 247, 248, 261, 348, 349, 358, 386, 394, 396, 397, 398, 399, 442, 447, 456, 460, 461, 462, 470, 471, 472
Splunk 33, 186, 214, 234, 262, 363
SQL...50, 51, 61, 75, 353, 389, 442, 447

Steele Dossier...121, 126, 303, 392, 394
Steele, Christopher 275
Strzok, Peter ...316, 317, 318, 319, 339, 453
Sussman, Michael. 2, 88, 89, 90, 96, 105, 107, 108, 109, 110, 114, 115, 117, 118, 124, 141, 144, 201, 237, 269, 273, 277, 279, 285, 291, 292, 293, 294, 298, 299, 302, 303, 304, 305, 306, 307, 308, 316, 317, 324, 337, 342, 357, 360, 361, 390, 391, 392, 401, 411, 450
Swalwell, Eric 91, 94, 95

T

Tamene, Yared...99, 104, 105, 106, 107, 356, 449
The Analysis Corporation 37, 222
The Cato Institute 13, 221, 434, 477
Thibault, Timothy... 322, 323, 324, 326, 327, 328, 329, 330, 362, 403
Thompson, Kevin 241
Trump, Donald 1, 7, 81, 88, 90, 108, 119, 125, 127, 136, 139, 141, 144, 151, 169, 190, 202, 241, 248, 278, 279, 290, 305, 312, 317, 321, 330, 332, 345, 369, 389, 390, 394, 395, 398, 399, 401, 402, 426, 429, 452, 489
Trump, President 1, 2, 4, 121, 138, 169, 177, 191, 249, 291, 320, 321, 322, 323, 327, 357, 360, 394, 396, 402, 414, 417, 450, 474

U

US-CERT 2, 23, 26, 29, 35, 36, 42, 49, 84, 385, 386, 436, 437, 438, 441
USIC 112, 113, 114, 115, 124, 391

W

Whistleblower...80, 139, 140, 141, 143, 144, 145, 305, 308, 309, 310, 311,

Index

312, 314, 315, 316, 317, 322, 340, 378, 390, 484

White House ...39, 41, 69, 74, 111, 121, 125, 126, 135, 242, 252, 253, 264, 273, 277, 280, 283, 284, 286, 291, 304, 305, 313, 345, 348, 355, 360, 378, 387, 393, 400, 423, 433, 439, 441, 445, 446, 452, 453, 459, 464, 476, 480, 485, 497

World Economic Forum 86, 87, 371, 390, 449, 493

Wray, Christopher

also Director Wray 2, 168, 321, 322, 326, 327, 328, 341, 395, 402, 451, 453, 465, 473, 486, 488

Y

Yates, Sally 126, 304, 393

Z

Zuckerberg, Mark... 324, 325, 372, 402, 487, 494

Countdown to Chaos
About The Authors:

Jovan Hutton Pulitzer is widely known for creating the standard by which we can now conduct full forensic audits of our American elections and the election process and its systems. From the time he called out the 2020 election for having serious signs of illegalities and possible nefarious activities, Jovan has been educating American citizens on their rights as Voters.

For almost three decades Americans have been questioning the truthfulness and validity of the American election systems, procedures, and processes. The cry for election integrity has become a running joke. Lawmakers deliver platitudes and the media has trained Americans to look away and truly believe "there is no such thing as election fraud."

The election system and election integrity rhetoric are caught in never ending wash, rinse, and repeat cycle. Voter rolls keep getting dirtier and dirtier and those who seek to undermine American election keep getting bolder and bolder. In the end, the American voters are the ones who suffer and when America suffers the world suffers with it.

Jovan has written over 200 history books and this book is somewhat of a different departure from his normal genre of written works. Although Jovan has written books for over two decades, in the field of election integrity he became a viral sensation calling out the Georgia Senate Members during his presentations for the Subcommittee on Election Integrity. Jovan has consulted Secretaries of State, Governors, and State and Local Election leaders.

Jovan hosts a talk radio program titled "Cut the Crap Show" (Culture, Race and American Politics) and can be found on all social media using the hashtag #JovanHuttonPulitzer. In 2001 Jovan won the Prestigious "Smithsonian Laureate Award" for the Man Most Likely To Change Society As We Know It (in the Arts and Broadcasting Category) and during the Trump Administrations term, Jovan was nominated for the national Medal of Technology and Innovation (NMTI).

This Award is the nation's highest honor for technological achievement, bestowed by the president of the United States on America's leading innovators.

Eve A. Dapita, ED is known for her editorial and deep research skills, particularly when it comes to government documentation. Ironically, her family name Dapita is an ancient Sanskrit - Dravidian word for those awarded for things produced and obtained. This book is a chronological deep dive into the various machinations of the United States government and the Deep State's use of "the system" to disrupt the system. With an eye to meticulous detail, research, and references Eve has edited this book so that the research might be duplicated by all who care to investigate the facts for themselves.

Made in the USA
Monee, IL
22 February 2024

ab317572-43f1-4b0c-93c7-1a9313f31a0eR01